Also by Alvin M. Josephy, Jr.

The Patriot Chiefs

The Nez Perce Indians and the Opening of the Northwest

The Indian Heritage of America

Red Power

The Long and the Short and the Tall

The Artist Was a Young Man

Black Hills—White Sky

On the Hill

NOW THAT THE BUFFALO'S GONE

NOW THAT THE BUFFALO'S GONE

A Study of Today's American Indians

ALVIN M. JOSEPHY, JR.

University of Oklahoma Press: Norman

Owing to limitations of space, all acknowledgments for permission to use illustrations in this book will be found following the index.

Library of Congress Cataloging in Publication Data

Josephy, Alvin M., Jr. Now that the buffalo's gone.

Includes index.
1. Indians of North America.
2. Indians of North America—Government relations. I. Title.
E77.J79   1982   305.8'97'073   82-40283
ISBN: 0-8061-1915-2 (paperback)

Published by arrangement with Alfred A. Knopf, Inc.
Copyright © by Alvin M. Josephy, Jr.
All rights reserved under International and Pan-American Copyright Conventions. Manufactured in the U.S.A. First printing of the University of Oklahoma Press paperback edition, 1984.

The paper in this book meets the guidelines for permanence and durability of the Committee on Production Guidelines for Book Longevity of the Council on Library Resources, Inc.

To Betty

MOST AMERICANS, while they may not know much about Indian cultures or Indian treaty rights, tend to harbor a special sentiment for American Indians that is not held for other minority groups in America. Whether this is a dim recognition of the fact that Indians were here first or whether it is merely a romantic American notion is difficult to determine. The American public has difficulty believing . . . [that] injustice continues to be inflicted upon Indian people because Americans assume that the sympathy or tolerance they feel toward Indians is somehow "felt" or transferred to the government policy that deals with Indians. This is not the case.

—LESLIE MARMON SILKO,
Laguna Pueblo author

CONTENTS

16 pages of photographs follow page 110

ACKNOWLEDGMENTS AND BIBLIOGRAPHICAL NOTE

THIS WORK is the culmination of thirty years of association with Native Americans. The knowledge and experience of so many people—Indians and non-Indians—are reflected in each chapter that it would be impossible to thank them all for what they have taught me. Special appreciation, however, is owed to Suzan Shown Harjo and Robert S. Pelcyger of the Native American Rights Fund, and to John W. Showalter of the U.S. Department of Justice for specific courtesies they rendered me during the preparation of this book. To all others—men, women, and children of scores of tribes, members of organizations in the various fields of Indian affairs, scholars, researchers, and writers, lawyers, government officials, and missionaries—I express my thanks, with the acknowledgment that each and all of them helped in some fashion in instructing me about the subject of this volume.

An explanation must be made concerning the absence of footnotes. A lengthy bibliography of primary and secondary sources, together with a brief bibliographical and acknowledgment note, is included at the end of the book for each chapter. But in many chapters, as indicated, I utilized a mass of contemporary items of documentation drawn from materials in my own files—chiefly typescript and manuscript letters, government memoranda and interoffice communications, legal briefs, handwritten tribal appeals and mimeographed resolutions, scrawled notes and tape recordings of interviews and meetings, drafts of legislation, press releases, and broadsides of Indian organizations—few of which are possessed by any public or private repository. Since this book has been written principally for the general public, I omitted citations to them—and, for the sake of consistency, to any and all sources of documentation—because otherwise, in substantial portions of the book, there would have been so many such citations on almost every page as to overpower and severely hinder the flow of the text. All of these materials, however, organized for ready reference to the individual chapters of this book, will be on deposit in the archives of the Library of the University of Oregon in Eugene and will be available for the inspection and use of accredited scholars and students, who I hope will forgive me understandingly for not having encumbered the book with voluminous footnote citations.

Some of the material in Chapters 4 and 5 appeared more than a decade ago in *American Heritage;* I appreciate the editors' permission to draw upon it again. Finally, I wish to thank Alfred A. Knopf, Angus Cameron, Anthony Schulte, and Ann Close for their faith in this work; Buffy Sainte-Marie for permission to borrow for this book the title of one of her memorable songs; and my dedicated wife, Betty, for her loving help and support, without which the book could not have been written.

A.M.J.

PREFACE

THIS IS A BOOK about the Native Americans of the United States today—about their modern-day feelings and viewpoints, and about what they want and why they want it.

Since the 1950's, Native Americans have experienced great changes. Their population, as recorded by the U.S. Census Bureau, has soared dramatically—almost threefold, from 552,228 in 1960 to 1,418,195 in 1980. Faster than ever before, they have become accustomed to participating in the dominant non-Indian society, even if they live on reservations, as almost 700,000 of them still do. The number of young Indians receiving higher education has swelled from a few hundred in a handful of colleges in the early 1960's to tens of thousands, including many in graduate schools, who are now on university campuses throughout the nation. Thousands also—men and women—have successfully entered fields of industry, science, law, medicine, communications, technology, education, art and literature, and finance, and not a few have acquired national and international reputations in their professions.

At the same time, within the short span of the last two decades, they have regained a pride in their identity as Native Americans and as members of tribal groups. In a burst of resurgent nationalism, they have shed the inhibitions and shame of conquered peoples and, strengthened by their own revitalized cultural heritages, have turned against both governmental paternalism and injustices perpetrated by their fellow Americans. With education and advanced training, they have struggled on the reservations to reassume the management and control of their own affairs and resources—many of which the energy crisis has shown to have great value—and in legislatures and law courts they have fought for their sovereignty as free peoples and for treaty rights that have long been denied them. Occasionally, in the pursuit of their goals, they have engaged in violent and spectacular confrontations, such as at the Bureau of Indian Affairs Building in Washington, D.C., and at Wounded Knee, South Dakota, and some of them have gone to prison or given their lives.

Their new assertiveness has not been understood or accepted easily by most non-Indians. Modern-day Native American claims to more than

12.5 million acres of Maine and to large land areas in other states, to one half of all the fish taken from northwestern rivers, and to precious water rights throughout the West have caused confusion and anger, as have their attempts to gain recognition of various sovereign rights, including those of taxation, police powers, and control of sought-after energy resources, on their reservations. The majority of Americans, it is probable, still show them goodwill and appear to recognize sympathetically, though belatedly, that most of the "bad" Indians of their ancestors' day were, after all, fighting patriotically for the lives and rights of their people. But the conflicts of yesterday, to most non-Indians, are part of the past, a closed chapter of history. What do they have to do, they ask, with the needs and realities of the present-day United States and with the modern generation, which was not to blame for what occurred one or two centuries ago?

This book, about contemporary Native American affairs and their historical underpinnings, attempts to answer such questions and help explain the present status, aims, and thinking of the American Indians. Each chapter discusses a principal theme in the long and continuing relationship between Indians and Whites: the Indians' five centuries' will to endure as Indians; the racial stereotypes that still influence the Whites' treatment of Indians; the Indians' efforts to retain the deep spiritual basis of their life; their fight to hold on to their land base; the reassertion of their rights to water; their claims to fishing and hunting rights; and their modern-day quest to regain self-determination, sovereignty, and control of their affairs and resources. Though these themes do not by any means exhaust all the many facets of Indian-White relations or the various complex problems facing today's Indians, they do encompass the major aspects of contemporary Indian affairs that are least understood by non-Indians, that tend to give rise to most of the continued misunderstandings and conflicts between Whites and Indians, and that are highest on the Indians' own list of contemporary concerns.

The book deals with the different themes by presenting within each chapter a case study of a single tribe or group of Native American peoples, which seemed the best way to make each theme more vivid and understandable, as well as a means to provide the necessary background and roots of modern-day Indian points of view and actions. In each case, the subject of the study exemplifies thematically the experiences of other groups and the feelings and views of most, if not all, modern Native Americans. In addition, the chapters have been divided into three sections, the first one dealing with fundamental concerns that have remained most constant from the past into the present, the second focusing more sharply on the present, and the third recounting more recent events and developments that raise speculations about the future. Finally, by employing the method of historic narration—most heavily in the initial chapters—to link the past and the present, the book tries to illuminate not only contemporary Native Americans but today's non-Indian society also, as the joint inheritors of a part of history that never did get closed, but continues to have urgent meaning for all Americans.

ALVIN M. JOSEPHY, JR.

I

YESTERDAY

THE
INHERITANCE

1

"I WILL DIE AN INDIAN!"

The Native Americans' Five Centuries' Will to Endure

I n the summer of 1978, Fred Coyote, an eloquent Native American writer and speaker, and a traditionalist who carries on the culture and traditions of his ancestors, addressed a conference of non-Indians at Sun Valley, Idaho. After recounting efforts by government agents and public schools to make him assimilate and become a White man, Coyote told the audience proudly, "I will *die* an Indian!"

Coyote is a Wailaki Indian from Round Valley, a small reservation in northwestern California established in 1873 as a home for the dispossessed and scattered remnants of a number of California tribes that had been hunted down and all but wiped out by White miners and settlers in the years following the Gold Rush. By the early 1900's the Wailakis on the reservation, like many other California native groups, were thought by Whites to have died out, and were forgotten. In 1978, the same year that Coyote spoke at Sun Valley, the newly published California volume of the Smithsonian Institution's scholarly *Handbook of North American Indians* announced that while the Round Valley population (approximately 400) "may include some individuals" of the Wailaki and several other tribes, "it will be necessary to speak [of them] as if they have become extinct."

As long as Coyote lives, Wailakis cannot be extinct. Still young and the father of a family, he is, in fact, only one of many Wailaki Indians who are quietly passing on the history and culture of their people to their children. Moreover, as an inspiring writer and teacher, he is a Native

American of influence, not only traveling and awakening pride in traditional Indian beliefs and values among young Indians throughout the country, but bringing to White audiences the lessons of the spiritual ties that still bind the Wailakis to all creation. As an adviser to environmental organizations, including the Sierra Club, and a familiar participant in national and international cultural and environmental meetings, he is an example of the modern-day carrier of an Indian legacy that did not and will not die, and that, despite every annihilating and corrupting force, survives to instruct those who will listen.

The American nation is dotted with communities of Indian peoples who will not die as Whites and whose tribal cultures will not vanish. Perhaps the Wailakis have not had time enough to lose their culture and turn into Whites; it is only a century since non-Indians overran their Eel River homeland in northern California and obliterated their ancestral villages. But in New York State it is almost *two* centuries since the White man and his culture engulfed the Iroquois, yet the League of the Six Nations of Mohawks, Oneidas, Onondagas, Cayugas, Senecas, and Tuscaroras still meets, traditional chiefs still preside, and the laws and spiritual teachings of the Longhouse still flourish. *Three* centuries? Longer ago than that, in the early 1600's, English and Dutch colonists conquered and destroyed the tribes of Connecticut's present-day Fairfield County, the seat of such modern cities as Bridgeport, Stamford, Norwalk, and Greenwich. For many years, schoolchildren were taught that the last Indian in that county had died generations ago. But descendants of original tribes are still there, most notably some one hundred fiercely proud Paugussets, who long before the founding of the American Republic inhabited the Bridgeport-Trumbull-Stratford area. Still possessing a small reservation in Trumbull, they maintain cohesion as an Indian tribe under a hereditary chief whom they call Big Eagle, and participate in national intertribal affairs. There are other Indians, moreover, in almost every urban center in Fairfield County.

One can go even further back in time—indeed, to the very first Native Americans who met and resisted White invaders on territory that is now part of the United States. That was in Florida, less than a decade after Columbus' first voyage. Their history, like that of many other Indian groups, is one of patriotism and heroic struggle, but its long tenaciousness makes it an unusually dramatic example of the Indians' power and will to endure, as well as of native peoples, long thought to have vanished, who now confront the modern-day American nation.

An account of their trials and perseverance begins with a surprising event in our own times. In 1967 the U.S. Court of Claims, turning down a federal government appeal of an Indian Claims Commission decision in favor of the Seminole Indians of Florida, ruled that the government had forced members of that tribe to cede most of the Florida peninsula in 1823 for an unjustly low price—goods, money, and services totaling $152,500 in value. The court's ruling, which directed the government to pay the Indians additional compensation for the land it had taken from them 144 years before, dismayed the Justice Department's lawyers, who had begun the case convinced by history as they knew it that the Seminoles had no legitimate claim to the lands they had lost. Prior to the mid-1700's, there had been no Seminole tribe in Florida—nor, indeed, anywhere else. In the early part of the eighteenth century, in fact, there had been almost no Indians at all in most of the Florida peninsula. The original native inhabitants, numbering perhaps almost 100,000 and organized into powerful, flourishing chiefdoms during the time of Ponce de León, the official "discoverer" of Florida, had all but disappeared. Their names were still on the land—Apalachee, Timucua, Tequesta, Calusa—and so were many of their designations for places—Tampa and Miami among them. But the chiefdoms, the true aboriginal owners of Florida, were gone, obliterated by White men's aggressions and diseases.

After these original people vanished, the vacuum they left had gradually been filled by other Indians. During the mid-1700's, native refugees migrated into Florida from more northerly regions: Oconees, Hitchitis, Guales, Chiahas, and Yamasees—survivors of tribes that had been shattered and driven from their homelands by the expanding White population in Georgia and the Carolinas. Soon afterward, groups of Creek Indians from Georgia and Alabama also began moving south into the empty hunting grounds of northern Florida, establishing permanent villages and gradually severing their connections with the people they had left behind. In addition, a third element, escaped Black slaves from southern plantations, began fleeing to Florida, joining the Indians or establishing their own settlements. The Creeks called the separatists from their own towns *simanoli*, probably a corruption of the Spanish word *cimarrón*, meaning those who had become runaways or wild, but eventually English-speaking Whites corrupted it further to "Seminole" and applied it to all the Indians of Florida. The term, however, masked the true complexion and variety of the new native population of Florida. Some, like many of the Creeks, were agriculturally oriented Muskogee speakers, and others, who were primarily hunters and fishermen, spoke Hitchiti, and called themselves Mikasuki, which it is believed signified "we, the people," distinguishing them from Whites and Blacks, though many Blacks joined the Mikasukis. There was no overall tribal government or political unity. The various peoples were held together by traditional clan relationships, and each settlement and group, guided by a headman, religious leaders, and a council, was free and independent. Their aim was expressed in the motto "Pohaan checkish"—"leave us alone."

But what had happened to the vanished tribes of two hundred years before? To the consternation of the Justice Department's lawyers, the Seminoles in the course of their claims hearing established the fact that those people had never vanished after all, and that descendants of the original tribes were still living in the 1960's among the various Seminole and Mikasuki groups in southern Florida. Evidence of their strong intermixture in the modern native population—previously unsuspected or dismissed by many Whites—was unassailable, and the Seminoles were suddenly seen to have a valid claim of aboriginal title to the lands that had been taken from them. In the eighteenth and nineteenth centuries, it became clear, many of the new migrants into Florida had absorbed, or merged with, pockets and villages of survivors of the original tribes, peoples who had earlier waged a long, desperate struggle on the peninsula to endure as free Indians. Joined with groups of the newcomers, they, too, had eventually become known to the Whites only as Seminoles.

Their troubles had not ended. In the nineteenth century, as part of the Seminole and Mikasuki population, they, along with the Blacks who had joined the Indians, participated in two fiercely defensive wars against the United States. One of them—resulting from an attempt to remove the Indians forcibly from Florida to present-day Oklahoma—was the most expensive and disastrous war the United States ever waged against Indians. Lasting from 1835 to 1842, it took the lives of more than 1,500 soldiers, cost the nation between $40- and $60-million, and only partly achieved its purpose.

When the United States finally abandoned the struggle (which many modern-day writers have likened to the American involvement in Vietnam in the 1960's), the government recognized a large part of southwestern Florida as still belonging to the Seminoles who had frustrated the army and still remained in Florida, and formally created a twenty-mile-wide buffer or neutral zone to protect the Indians in that area from further encroachments by Whites. Adapting themselves to the swampland environment of the Everglades, the various native groups lived in isolation from Florida's growing White population, free to continue their own culture and traditions. Still proudly independent and haunted by memories of American cruelties and treacheries in the 1830's and 1840's (troops had lured one of their bravest leaders, Osceola, to a peace parley and had then seized him under a white flag of truce, imprisoning him until his death), they refused to have anything to do with Whites or the United States government, which had been unable to defeat them and with which they had never made a peace treaty.

Gradually, in the twentieth century, the tight native societies of many of the individual groups were disrupted. Despite the opposition of Indian religious leaders, missionaries converted many of the people to Christianity. With the growth and expansion of the White population in southern Florida and the building of the Tamiami Trail through the Seminoles' lands in the 1920's, contacts between Indians and non-Indians increased, and White aggrandizement forced the natives off large parts of their land. Divided politically, though still maintaining kinship relations, the different groups began to go different ways.

In the 1930's, three small reservations were established as permanent protected homes for the Indians, and people were urged to move onto them. The response was slow, but by the 1950's those who had accepted the reservations, principally Christianized Seminoles who had adopted many White ways, organized themselves formally into a Florida Seminole tribe. A decade later, many of the Mikasukis, who were still mainly traditionalists and had not moved to the reservations, established a second tribe. Spelling their name "Miccosukee," they secured a fifty-year permit from the National Park Service and the Bureau of Indian Affairs for the use of a strip of land 5½ miles long and 500 feet wide along the Tamiami Trail. At the same time, the state of Florida licensed the Seminoles and Miccosukees to use a swampy area of 104,000 acres of state land for hunting, trapping, and frogging, and gave the Miccosukees a use permit to several small tracts along the Tamiami Trail for development. A third group, traditionalists who still wanted little or nothing to do with Whites or the United States government and regarded all of southwestern Florida as still belonging to the Seminole peoples, refused to join either the Seminole or the Miccosukee tribe and continued as independent societies with local, traditional forms of government.

Though many of the groups developed a tourist trade and industries of their own, worked for Whites on truck farms and cattle ranches, and finally permitted their children to go to White-run schools, most of them continued to cherish and safeguard their independence and culture. At the same time, they began the present-day era of negotiation and litigation over payment for the land they had lost—an issue which in the 1970's caused a division between those who would accept money for the land taken from them and the traditionalists who refused to sell land which they claimed still belonged to them even though Whites had overrun it. Today, all the groups—but particularly the Miccosukees and the independent societies—contain determined traditionalists who still say to the Whites, "Pohaan checkish"—just "leave us alone." Among them lives on most fully and uncompromisingly a native heritage not only of the Seminoles who fought together against the United States in the nineteenth century but of the original peoples of Florida who fought Spaniards, Frenchmen, and Englishmen, as well as Americans, and who, before the time of any of the Whites, already had a legacy that was very ancient.

Among Whites, it has been customary to dismiss the pre-Columbian past of a particular Indian group in the United States with the vague acknowledgment that it had lived in a certain place "since time immemorial," or "for hundreds or thousands of years," as if there had been no human history until the coming of the Europeans. This slights the Native Americans, for their traditions tell them of life during that period of "time immemorial" and of people and events in the long intervals of the past. Today, moreover, as a result of archaeological discoveries, the pre-White period need not be a blank to non-Indians. In addition, knowledge of what happened from the very beginning, as far back as man can see, is a tool for the non-Indians' better understanding of Native Americans, which, in turn, is a prerequisite for improved relations between Indians and non-Indians. Indians have stood the insults of ignorance for a long time, and this White lack of knowledge has been harmful to them. White teachers and missionaries, in particular, deriding or ignoring the Indians' past, have robbed Indians of their inheritance, destroying their pride in themselves and undermining their sense of identity. Today, traditionalist Indians like those among the Seminoles and Mikasukis are restoring Indian pride, giving voice to the first and most fundamental assertion that Native Americans can make: "We were here first—long before you. And we had a history."

This chapter will examine the past of Florida's original Native Americans as an example of people with an extraordinary will to endure and with long memories.

In Florida, Indian-White history goes back only 500 years, but Indian history began at least 11,000 years ago. Archaeology tells us that at that remote time bands of big-game hunters, whose ancestors had come across the so-called Bering land bridge from Asia during the Ice Age, were already in the Southeast of what is now the United States, some of them in Florida. As the Ice Age ended and the mastodons and other large animals of the Pleistocene period disappeared, these ancients, some of them using the world's oldest-known hunting boomerangs, became the first permanent inhabitants of the peninsula.

In time, it is known, they settled down within limited areas that included hunting, fishing, and gathering grounds and became efficient in using all manner of locally found foods, including small game, fish and shellfish, reptiles, fruit, berries, nuts, roots, and wild vegetables and grasses. Their population increased and became more concentrated in different sections of the region, and as the environment helped to shape their culture, their societies and ways of life grew more complex. Their tools, utensils, and other material possessions multiplied, becoming more sophisticated, effective, and refined. About 2000 B.C. those who were in northeastern Florida were among the first in the present-day United States to fashion and use pottery; perhaps by that time they were already organized into village groups that traded by seagoing dugout canoes with distant island peoples, for it is thought that the skill of pottery making may have come to them from contacts with Indians who were already using pottery in Mexico or across the Caribbean on the northern coast of South America.

Certainly by 1000 B.C. the Indians of Florida had rich, well-structured societies, whose survival rested on beliefs of their relationship to all creation and the universe as they knew it. Their organizations and day-to-day conduct, as they had been in the past and would be in the future, were bound up intimately with the forces and beings of nature, and the strict rules of their groups were designed to provide well-being by keeping each individual in balance and harmony with the universe. As groups became more specialized, both by continuing to adapt to their localities and by accepting traits that reached them from other southeastern peoples, those who lived in northern Florida developed, in time, into agriculturists, at first cultivating a few local plants and then gourds, squash, beans, and corn, knowledge of which apparently came to them across the Southeast from Mexico. Like other tribes in the East, they began to build earthen mounds, some of them at first for religious purposes and burial of important leaders, and later to raise above the villages the houses and council chambers of their headmen and their "temples," or repositories for religious articles and the remains of certain dead persons. In the water-oriented southern part of Florida, the people did not adopt farming, but continued to rely on the gathering of shellfish and wild foods and on fishing and hunting.

During the first millennium after Christ, the introduction of improved strains of corn and more efficient farming implements and techniques among the peoples of the north provided food surpluses that could be stored for year-round use. With a more secure food base, populations continued to increase and more leisure time was available for the creation of aesthetically satisfying products, including personal ornaments and ritual objects. Late in the millennium, socioeconomic and religious influences of an advanced temple-mound-building culture, known as the Mississippian, which seems to have evolved about A.D. 700 along the middle Mississippi River and been spread across the Southeast by aggressive expanding groups, also reached northern Florida. Characterized by artistic and ritualistic ideas derived from the high civilizations of Mexico, the new customs and beliefs affected the societies of the agricultural towns and further enriched their spiritual and material life. In the south, beyond the range of the Mississippian cultural impact, group political organizations, ceremonies, the building of mounds— often of huge piles of shells that also served as bases for temples, important persons' houses, and whole settlements—and many material and religious traits were all influenced by a distinctive new Gulf culture that spread across the Gulf coast from the lower Mississippi Valley.

In both parts of Florida the abundant food supplies, larger populations, and increasingly complex political and religious systems eventually led to the rise of strong chiefs, who at first simply counseled and guided their people, rather than commanded them. Gradually, however, some of them, acquiring recognition as demigods with supernatural powers, assumed absolute authority. Receiving unquestioned deference from all their people, they headed hierarchies of councillors and political, religious, and military officials who carried out special functions. Creating armies of warriors, they soon established a loose dominion over large areas of towns and villages whose people spoke the same language and possessed the same culture. In these chiefdoms, a few of them already on their way to becoming full-fledged states, the headmen of individual towns filled the role of subchiefs, paying tribute in goods, services, and military allegiance to the head chief. Everywhere, under such leadership, community life flourished, marked by adequate time for the development of highly artistic ritualistic and functional articles (the Indians of southern Florida and the Keys produced some of the finest wood carving in the hemisphere) and more sophisticated social and religious customs.

These were the Florida Indians "discovered" by the Spaniards who followed in the wake of Columbus and who characterized them as savages and barbarians. Although the Christian newcomers, with rare exceptions, felt little need to try to understand, much less respect, the values and beliefs that kept these "heathen" societies in harmony with their universe, some of the Spaniards, and later the French, did leave records of what they observed and what they were told.

The Indian men of Florida, they noted, were usually ranked in importance in their towns according to their age and their talents and accomplishments as councillors, orators, medical and religious figures, tested leaders, and hunters and warriors. They wore painted deerskin breechclouts; used powerful bows as tall as themselves, various types of clubs, lances, atlatls or spear-throwers, and sharp knives made of reed, cane, or bone; trussed their long hair up into topknots in which they often carried their arrows; and tattooed and painted their bodies and faces, frequently with designs of personal symbolic meaning. In the warm climate, the women, who let their hair hang long and were generally admired by the Europeans for their beauty, wore little more than short skirts of tree-hung (Spanish) moss and occasionally a mantle of skins or feathers. Both sexes adorned themselves with ornaments and decorations of feathers, bones, shells, pearls from mussels, fish teeth, beaten lumps of copper, and other materials which they wore in their ears and around their wrists, waists, legs, and ankles. Some of their copper ornaments were fashioned into large round and oval plates that were strung together to make metallic sounds when the wearers walked or danced in a ceremony. Fingernails and toenails were allowed to grow long and were sharpened with shells; the men, said one French observer, used their fingernails as a weapon: "When they take one of the enemy they sink their nails deep in his forehead, and tear down the skin, so as to wound and blind him."

In the north, the villages were composed of small round houses with reed or palmetto roofs, in which the people lived; a large "town house" for the chief and his councillors, which also served as a center for indoor councils, meetings, and ceremonies; storage houses often of stones and earth; and a central open square or plaza for outdoor councils and gatherings, all usually surrounded by a circular palisade of poles, partly spiraled to provide a guarded corridor entranceway. In the south, where the climate was warmer, most buildings were without walls, being simply raised platforms with poles supporting thatched roofs. Many of the principal towns in both sections of Florida contained mounds—of all different heights—surmounted by the chief's house and a "temple."

Near the northern towns, frequently on the bottomlands along streams, were the agricultural fields. The chief would designate the day, usually late in the year, for the planting to begin; the men would do the heavy work of preparing the ground, and the women would make the planting holes and sow the seeds. During the winter the men would hunt in the woods, and late in the spring the crops would be ready for harvest. One of the most important of all the annual rituals would then be observed: the Green Corn ceremony, during which purification rites and the imbibing of the "black drink," a strong caffeine concoction, would occur, and the chief would divide the results of the harvest among the people, placing some in a public granary and withholding some for himself.

A principal concern of the Indians—not so well understood by Whites—was keeping life pure and unpolluted. People were raised in the warmth and security of extended families and matrilineal clans that were associated with particular animals or forces of nature. A child had the protection and care of many family and clan relatives but learned of the need to keep the society in balance with the universe principally from his or her grandparents, through the medium of moralistic tales. A host of rules of behavior, including taboos, existed to maintain the purity and harmony necessary for individual and group survival and well-being. An offense polluted the harmony and endangered the individual or group. It could be punished by ridicule so intense as to cause the offender to commit suicide. Or it might result in illness, a storm, or some setback or disaster that was interpreted by the Indians as the doing of an evil god or force. Ceremonies and rituals, including an occasional or annual human sacrifice to a god, were sometimes considered necessary to set things right and maintain balance and order in a complex world in which everything—man, animals, and plants, the seen and the unseen—was considered to be totally interrelated.

In this highly intricate scheme of existence, all Indian conduct—much of it rarely comprehended by the Europeans—had logical explanations. Society was largely communal, requiring cooperation and sharing. Stinginess was a despicable trait. In the beginning, the Indians gave freely to the Whites of what they owned; when the Whites did not respond similarly and the Indians helped themselves to the Whites' possessions, the Europeans called them thieves and punished them. The astounded Indians quickly labeled such Whites "stingy," one of the worst things they could say about them.

The Europeans' all-out type of war that aimed at total destruction of the enemy was also a shock to the Indians. Certainly, warfare of a sort was common in Florida before the arrival of the Spaniards: there were traditional enmities, which had started over an insult or wrongdoing and had developed into feuds; chiefs could mobilize armies of war leaders and their followers, and they often threatened, or marched against, each other. But hostilities were not over the possession of land, and they were brief and usually ended abruptly. Sometimes, because of an unfavorable omen communicated to the group's religious leader, warfare was aborted before it began. Frequently combat—mostly taunts, threats, and short but deadly skirmishes between individuals—was broken off after a few casualties had been sustained, or when the aim of one side or the other had been achieved. The war aims of the Indians were generally revenge, the acquiring of captives and honors (including the taking of scalps), retaliation for a previous action, or merely the terrorizing of opponents (attained sometimes by the dismemberment of a living prisoner). But after the Europeans watched a chief whip up his people against a native enemy, they were often disgusted by the lack of battlefield action. In turn, when the Spaniards directed against the Florida Indians the full fury of their own brand of warfare, refined in the savage religious wars of

Europe, burning natives at the stake and introducing wholesale slaughter and cruelty, the Indians were horrified.

The peoples of Florida must first have heard of the Whites—of their ships and firearms and other powerful possessions, as well as of their strange and often terrifying conduct—as early as the time of Columbus, for Indians in large canoes, bringing the sensational news, could have crossed to the mainland from the Caribbean islands. When ships of the bearded strangers at length began to appear off the Florida coasts, the tales of the White men's ravages in the islands became real. Most of the big vessels with large sails were on their way back to Spain, simply trying to follow the current and wind northward through the Straits of Florida, and many were wrecked and their crews and passengers cast ashore on the Keys and the southern Florida coast.

This was part of the homeland of a strong maritime-oriented chiefdom, whose people lived in towns on large shell mounds, frequently on sandy islands, and controlled all of southern Florida from present-day Charlotte Harbor on the west coast to Lake Okeechobee (which they called Mayaimi) and the Keys. Their hereditary chief, a revered, aged man who was believed to have supernatural powers which he used for his people's well-being, ruled over the religious and secular life of perhaps more than 4,000 persons in some fifty towns, including one of Arawak Indians who had come earlier from Cuba. In addition, he held dominion over several different tribes on Florida's southeastern coast. Later, he was known to the Spaniards as Carlos, either because it sounded like his own name and that of his territory and principal town, Calos, apparently in San Carlos Bay on the west coast, or because he took for himself the name of the Spaniards' own ruler, Emperor Charles V, about whose greatness he had learned from captured White seamen.

There are no known records to tell whether the first contacts between the Spaniards and Carlos' people, who became known to history as Calusas, were friendly or hostile, but there were soon two developments that foretold a stormy future for all the Florida Indians. Numerous Spanish castaways from the shipwrecks began to be captured by the Calusas and their subjects on the east coast, the Tequestas around present-day Miami, the Jeagas at Jupiter Inlet, and the Ais farther north, and sent to Carlos, who killed or enslaved them, or kept them to sacrifice to Calusa gods on ceremonial occasions. The cargoes of the wrecked vessels, often consisting of large quantities of gold and silver being shipped to Spain, were also sent to Carlos, and the White men's booty, acquired year after year and dispersed by trade to tribes throughout Florida who shaped the precious metals into various ornaments and utensils for themselves (making some later-arriving Europeans think that those Indians possessed rich mines), further enhanced the Calusa chief's power and prestige.

At the same time, other Spanish vessels, beginning to touch here and there along the coasts of the peninsula, were sending armed seamen ashore to try to kidnap Indians for sale as slaves for labor in the Caribbean island mines. As early as 1500, perhaps—a full generation before they knew anything about Mexico or Peru—adventurous Spaniards from Hispaniola and Cuba, unlicensed by royal authority to explore for new lands, were making these secret slave-catching forays along the mainland coast of Florida. Word of the Whites' aggressiveness spread from village to village, and the Florida peoples recognized that something had thrown their world out of balance and a new evil force was threatening them. It is not known which development came first, and whether Carlos' treatment of shipwrecked Spaniards was, partly at least, an attempt to appease his gods and restore harmony. By the time of Ponce de León, however, many of the coastal peoples had come to regard the Spaniards as enemies.

Ponce was only one of the known victims of this hostility. He had accompanied Columbus on his second voyage in 1493 and had remained in the West Indies, becoming a leader in the brutal conquest of the Indians on Hispaniola. Pursuing gold, he had then conquered the Carib population of Puerto Rico, enslaving the Indians, becoming the island's governor, and running a great and profitable plantation for himself. Under his tyrannical rule, the number of natives on Puerto Rico declined quickly from maltreatment and disease.

In 1513, still a decade before Cortez's conquest of Mexico, Ponce, now fifty-two and sailing openly under royal authority, made the "discovery" of Florida official. History relates that he began his voyage in search of a storied spring on an island known as Bimini, which the Puerto Rican Indians had told him would restore a man's youth and vitality. There would have been every reason to believe them. For centuries, Indians in canoes—usually large, shovel-nosed double canoes lashed together like catamarans and equipped with a sail—had navigated long distances across the Caribbean from island to island and to Florida, visiting and trading. The story of a fountain of youth was well known to them. But Ponce was certainly also bent on finding more gold and a new source of slaves.

He failed to discover the fabled fountain, but formally unveiled to the Old World the land he did reach, which he named Pascua Florida for the Eastertime Feast of Flowers of the April season when he first stepped ashore. After touching without trouble on territory of the Timucua Indians of Florida's northeastern coast, he sailed around the Keys and tried to land near Charlotte Harbor on the west coast, apparently, among other things, to seize Indians as slaves. Carlos' tough, canoe-borne warriors were of a different mind and after several armed engagements along the beaches, drove the Spaniards away. More Spaniards returned in 1517, this time as members of a storm-tossed ship that only wished to take on water. Again, Carlos' fighting men attacked and, after inflicting some casualties, forced the Spaniards to sail off. In 1521, Ponce appeared once more, now at the head of 200 would-be Spanish colonists who intended to plant themselves in Carlos' territory. Ponce landed somewhere near Charlotte Harbor and soon after erecting a temporary settlement was attacked by a large force of Calusas. Although the Spaniards' firearms and horses helped the colonists repulse the Indians, the Calusas inflicted grave losses on the Europeans and seriously wounded Ponce. The Spanish leader gave up a second time and with the survivors of his shattered colony sailed back to Havana, where he died of his arrow wound.

The Spaniards, however, kept coming, and with them there soon appeared a new and devastating evil—European diseases, including smallpox, typhus, measles, and influenza, against which the native populations had no resistance. Smallpox was present in the Caribbean at least as early as the winter of 1518–19, and was carried to Florida at that time or soon afterward. In the following years, it and other diseases, transmitted by Spaniards to mainland groups with which they came in contact, wiped out or decimated large numbers of Indians, racing inland from tribe to tribe to infect communities that had not yet even seen a White man. In many places throughout the Southeast, sudden population losses were huge, destroying or undermining entire societies, disrupting the organization and fabric of life in the towns and villages of temple-mound builders, and changing relations of leadership and power among various chiefdoms. Wherever the epidemics hit, the effects were disastrous. It is unlikely that the victims were able to relate their afflictions to the Spaniards, but, instead, viewed them as signs of the displeasure of supernatural forces, recognizing, again, a need to restore harmony, balance, and purity to their world.

In the years after Ponce, diseases were spread even farther by large Spanish expeditions of conquest. In 1528, an expedition under Pánfilo de Narváez, eager to emulate the success of Cortez in Mexico, landed on Florida's west coast near Tampa Bay, north of Carlos' country. This was the territory of one of a group of closely related agricultural chiefdoms that controlled most of the northern part of the peninsula and frequently feuded with each other. Although the Spaniards came to know each of these chiefdoms by a different name—usually a word used identically for their territory, principal town, and ruling chief—all of their people in time were called Timucuas, a word that the Europeans often heard one group employ when referring to a rival and that seems to have signified "enemy."

The Timucuas were very tall, vigorous, and brave and regarded the Spaniards as a loathsome evil. Councillors who recommended driving Narváez's men back into the sea were overruled, however, by the local head chief, Ucita, who knew from the Calusas the ability of the Spaniards to wreak carnage on the towns with their cavalry and flame-belching harquebuses. Supernatural signs told the chief not to fight, and Narváez, a tough, one-eyed bully, plundered Ucita's towns almost at will, imperiously ordering the people to become Christians and give their allegiance to Spain. When the Spaniards at last prepared to set off northward in search of treasure, Narváez ordered Ucita to direct some of his people to accompany the expedition as bearers, interpreters, and guides. The route lay through the lands of Ucita's enemies, and the chief refused to comply. Infuriated, Narváez seized Ucita and brutally sliced off his nose with his sword, then had the chief's aged mother dragged out and thrown to the expedition's mastiffs, which tore her apart and killed her.

From then on, Narváez had trouble, and his march north became a disaster. He floundered in swamps and dense forests and lost men to sickness and constant attacks by Timucuan warriors. The chiefdoms through which he traveled were astounded by the Whites' arrogance and villainy and, regarding them more like wild animals and evil spirits than humans, fought desperately to drive them away. Narváez's expedition finally disintegrated in chaos, and after a long series of hardships only four of its members ultimately survived.

In the meantime, Narváez's wife in Havana became worried about his fate and sent a ship to Florida to search for him. As luck would have it, one of its crew, an eighteen-year-old youth named Juan Ortiz, fell into the hands of Indians, who sent him to Ucita. That aggrieved chief ordered that he be roasted over a fire in revenge for what Narváez had done to himself and his mother. In a forerunner of the John Smith–Pocahontas story, Ortiz was saved at the last minute by the compassionate pleas of Ucita's wife and daughters, one of whom eventually aided his escape to a neighboring Timucuan head chief named Mocoso. Ortiz managed to live with these Timucuas until 1539, when he was found by Hernando De Soto, who had landed at Tampa Bay at the head of another Spanish expedition.

De Soto's ruthless treatment of the Indians eclipsed that of Narváez. His scheme in marching through the Southeast in search of gold was to force each tribe along his route to provide him with food, guides, and bearers by seizing their chiefs and threatening to kill them unless he got what he wanted. Using Ortiz as his interpreter, he headed north through the Timucuas' country, generally following Narváez's route and passing through or skirting the regional chiefdoms of Tocobaga, Ocale, Acuera, Potano, Onatheaque, and Yustaga. Once again, the Indians were horrified by the rudeness and barbarism of the armored conquistadors, and a second time they fought valiantly to drive off the terrible new enemy.

Despite his casualties, De Soto pushed ahead, seizing food, impressing bearers and guides, and ordering chiefs to appear before him to swear allegiance to the Spanish king. Many of the chiefs were uncowed and contemptuously defied the Spaniard. Refusing to come to meet De Soto, the head chief of Acuera sent an angry message to the invader which was interpreted for the Spanish leader: "I am king in my land, and it is unnecessary for me to become the subject of a person who has no more vassals than I. I regard those men as vile and contemptible who subject themselves to the yoke of someone else when they can live as free men. Accordingly, I and all my people have vowed to die a hundred deaths to maintain the freedom of our land. This is our answer, both for the present and forevermore." De Soto failed to find the patriot chief, and throughout his stay in that region, Acueran warriors harassed and ambushed the Spaniards, killing fourteen of them and wounding many more.

Farther on, in the territory of the Timucuan Yustagas, another regional head chief castigated the Spaniards as "sons of the devil" (in the Spanish translation) who "go from land to land killing, robbing and sacking whatever they find, and possessing themselves of the wives and daughters of others . . . without shame of men or fear of any god." Mustering a huge army of warriors, the Yustaga chief fought a fierce all-day battle with the Spaniards. De Soto's cavalry was too much for them, and the Indians were defeated and the chief captured. The Yustaga chief was still not quelled. Lunging at De Soto, he almost killed him with one tremendous blow of his fist. Instantly, Spanish soldiers cut the chief down with their swords and killed him.

At length, De Soto left the Timucuas' country and entered that of the Apalachees, a rich agricultural chiefdom in the northern part of Florida, roughly where the peninsula joins the present state's panhandle. The Spaniards wintered there for six months, seizing Indian stores of food and fighting off repeated Apalachee attacks. Finally, still in quest of treasure, De Soto moved north into present-day Georgia and began a long trek that brought bloodshed and destruction to many southeastern tribes. The Florida Indians never saw him again, and for a generation they were virtually free of White intruders, being aroused only once, in 1549, by the sudden appearance of a few strange unarmed Spaniards at Tampa Bay.

These were Dominican missionaries who had decided to come without soldiers and try peaceably to turn the Indians into Christians. Ucita's people, to whom any Spaniard was still to be feared and hated, killed them before they could explain their mission—which the Indians might have deemed worthy of death anyway, since it is probable that they would have resented attacks on their own spiritual system, the very core of their life.

Up till then, the Timucuan chiefdoms on the northeastern coast of Florida had been relatively untouched by contact with Whites. In 1564 they became suddenly enmeshed in the imperial rivalries of European powers that would eventually lead to the doom of all the Florida Indians. Two years before, at the mouth of the St. Johns River, north of present-day St. Augustine, Timucuas of the Saturiwa chiefdom, one of the largest and most powerful in Florida, numbering perhaps more than 5,000 persons and headed by a strongly built, middle-aged chief also known as Saturiwa, were startled by the arrival of two ships full of White men. The Whites, members of a French Huguenot expedition under Jean Ribault with plans to establish a mainland base from which to raid Spanish sea traffic and threaten Spain's possessions in the West Indies, convinced the Indians that they had no evil designs, and the Timucuas responded with friendship, presenting gifts of corn and other food to the newcomers. The site did not seem satisfactory to Ribault, however, and after erecting a stone column carved with the arms of France to proclaim possession of the region for his country, he sailed farther north and established a colony in the land of the Cusabo Indians on the coast of South Carolina.

The French got on well with the Cusabos and their neighbors, the Guales of the Georgia coast, and word drifted down to the envious Timucuas of the trade goods and other benefits—including increased prestige and power against their Indian enemies—which those tribes acquired as a result of their friendship with the Whites. Starvation and mutiny soon afflicted the French colony in South Carolina, however, and it was abandoned. But in 1564, a new French Huguenot expedition under René Laudonnière landed among Saturiwa's Timucuas at the St. Johns River and this time stayed and built a fort and settlement. Among the group was an artist, Jacques Le Moyne de Morgues, whose paintings—later engraved and published in Europe by a Flemish artist, Théodore de Bry —left a rich pictorial record of Timucuan life at that time.

Saturiwa's people must have had mixed emotions about the Whites in their midst. Pleased at the prospect of acquiring gifts from the White men, as well as at the added strength and prestige derived from having them in their country, they were at the same time suspicious of their motives. While the people gave the French roasted corn, smoked lizards, and other presents, several important men, making themselves understood to a Frenchman who had been there previously with Ribault, told them that Saturiwa, who ruled over thirty lesser chiefs, was so strong that he could raise an army of many thousand fighting men. Soon afterward, a war chief arrived with 120 men, armed with bows and arrows, clubs, and knives, and painted and decorated with feathers, shell necklaces, belts and anklets of fish teeth and mussel pearls, and flat gold and silver disks on their legs. They built a shelter of boughs for the head chief, who with two adult sons finally reached the scene escorted by a large procession of several hundred warriors, a score of musicians blowing on reed pan-pipes, a shaman, or religious adviser, and a "chief councillor."

The bearing of the chief and his sons, one of whom was half a foot taller than the tallest Frenchman, was dignified and reserved. Satisfying Saturiwa that the French wished to become his friends and would give him many strange and wonderful gifts, Laudonnière finally won his permission to remain, receiving, in addition, the help of many of his subjects in building a fort and huts for his men. A gift of a plate of silver from the Indians aroused the Frenchmen's curiosity over its source, and Saturiwa informed Laudonnière that it, as well as gold, came from the country of his enemy, the chiefdom of Utina, the strongest and most numerous of all the Timucuan groups, which extended westward from the St. Johns River. Laudonnière eagerly promised that his men with their powerful firearms would become the enemies of Saturiwa's enemy, which was what the chief wanted to hear. The French leader, however, then deceitfully dispatched members of his expedition up the river to try to find Utina and treat with him privately.

The French eventually met Saturiwa's enemy, an aggressive young head chief still in his twenties, who commanded a large, well-organized army that helped him dominate some thirty or forty towns. The source of the gold and silver was not in Utina's country (actually it had all come in trade from tribe to tribe, beginning with the Calusas and southern Indians who got it from wrecked Spanish ships), and the French were led to believe that their source was farther to the northwest, in certain mountains just beyond the lands of some of Utina's enemies in that direction, the Timucuan Potano, Onatheaque, and Yustaga chiefdoms. Utina, in fact, was not intentionally misleading the French; the Timucuas had one word for all metals, and native copper did come to the Florida Indians from the big Mississippian culture temple-mound centers that still existed in present-day Georgia near the Appalachian Mountains, whereas they acquired the Spanish gold and silver during frequent peaceful trade periods with the northwestern Timucuan chiefdoms.

Anxious to get to the mountains, the French now offered to become the allies of Utina against his enemies who seemed to stand athwart the routes to the gold regions. This disturbed Saturiwa, who was about to launch an attack against Utina. The chief pleaded with Laudonnière to live up to his original promise and aid his warriors, but the Frenchman found a convenient excuse to avoid the entanglement, and Saturiwa and his warriors marched off without him. They won a quick victory, burned a Utina town, and returned with prisoners, two of whom Laudonnière managed to free and return to Utina. A short time later, despite Saturiwa's indignation, the French leader sent twenty-five of his harquebusiers to help Utina in a war of his own against the Potanos, among the Timucuas perhaps second only to the Utinas in numbers and power, and one of the groups that lay across the route to the supposed mines.

Marching along in the center of the massed ranks of his warriors, whose disciplined organization impressed the Europeans, Utina met the Potano chief in a battle marked mostly by brief skirmishes and sudden fierce combat between individuals. The Europeans' firearms finally routed the Potanos, but though the French followed up with probings of the northwestern country, they failed to discover the source of the gold and silver. Soon serious troubles beset their settlement near the mouth of the St. Johns River. Restlessness and lack of results led to mutinies. Their food supplies ran low, and so did those of Saturiwa's people, who stopped trading with them and, abandoning the Whites, moved to inland camps for the winter to hunt. Then Utina also lost patience with the French and was either unwilling or unable to meet their demands for corn. In desperation, the Whites seized him and held him captive until a new harvest permitted his people to ransom him for corn. Soon after the transaction, the angry Utinas ambushed the French, who lost much of the stores they had just received.

The temporary appearance of some English ships and the arrival of new colonists under Ribault brought some relief to the French, who were able to restore good relations with Saturiwa. But a short time later, a large Spanish expedition led by Pedro Menéndez de Avilés, who was determined to drive the French Huguenots out of Florida, erected a fort at present-day St. Augustine just south of the French position (establishing on September 8, 1565, in the main town of the chief of the Timucuan Soloy Indians, who were subjects of Utina, what would become the first permanent White settlement in the United States). In a series of fierce, no-quarter actions, fought out along the coast before the amazed Indians, Whites fell on Whites. It ended with the Spanish seizure of the French fort, ruthless beheadings and massacres of most of the Frenchmen, including Ribault, and the flight of the French survivors. Some managed to get back to Europe; others scattered along the shore or into the interior, where they were killed by Indians whom the Spaniards had won over by feasts and gifts or were loyally sheltered in Indian towns that still considered themselves friends and allies of the Frenchmen who had lived in Saturiwa's country.

The ferocious enmity between the Whites shocked and frightened the people of the chiefdoms. Even the Spaniards' explanation that the French had evil religious beliefs made little sense, for both talked of worshipping the same god. But with all save a few straggling Frenchmen gone, the Indians now had to cope with a seemingly more savage and powerful White man, who quickly showed two faces—a friendship marked by the open-armed offering of feasts and presents, and a sudden ruthlessness characterized by insults, imperious demands and orders, arrogant interference in Indian life, and homicidal assaults on individuals and whole towns.

Menéndez, an aggressive empire-builder intent on planting Spain's power permanently in Florida and in the process creating lucrative land-holdings for himself, was, in addition, fanatically devout. Aided by a continuing stream of military reinforcements, Jesuit priests, and new colonists, he extended his footholds and bases along the Florida and southeastern Atlantic coasts, erecting a thin line of garrisoned posts both for defense against the Indians and occasional French and English marauders and to assist his zealous goal of converting the natives to Christianity and reducing them to submission.

Soon after the massacre of the French, chiefdoms all along the coast were visited by Menéndez, who tried quickly to win their trust by giving them presents. Some, like the Ais on Florida's southeastern coast, permitted him to establish a garrisoned post on their lands, but others, like the Calusas on the southwestern coast, sparred diplomatically with him, exchanging gifts but trying artfully to keep the upper hand. The authoritarian head chief of the Calusas was now a young man of about twenty-five, big and powerfully built, who was known to the Whites as Carlos II, after his father. Although some of the Spanish women who had survived shipwrecks and were living in Calusa towns with Indian mates and their half-blood children refused to return to White society, Menéndez induced Carlos to deliver to him the rest of the Spaniards among his people, as well as some of the silver and gold bullion he had taken from the wrecks.

Eventually, Menéndez was allowed to establish a fort and leave missionaries among the Calusas, but only after much machination and many clashes. Resisting any change that would challenge his authority or bring disharmony to the ordered ways of Calusa life, Carlos nevertheless wished to learn—and, if desirable, to acquire—the secret powers of the

White men's god, and he persuaded Menéndez to "marry" his sister and take her and several other Calusas to Havana to teach them the Spaniards' religion. Baptized and renamed Dona Antonia, the Indian woman, with the other Calusas, was taken to Cuba, where five of the Indians died. When Dona Antonia was returned to her brother, Carlos apparently found nothing useful for himself in the White men's beliefs, and he continued to resist the Spaniards' interference, threatening and harassing Whites after they succeeded finally in winning his permission to build a blockhouse in his principal town and bring in a Jesuit missionary.

The latter, ridiculed by Carlos and threatened by the head chief's religious leader, had no success in making converts, although Carlos' irritation with him was temporarily mollified when Menéndez set off on what appeared to be a military expedition against one of the Calusas' northern enemies, the Timucuan chiefdom of Tocobaga at Tampa Bay. Menéndez, however, only wished to erect a blockhouse there and win agreement to the Christianizing of the Tocobagas. His show of force achieved his aims, but his lack of action against the Calusas' enemies infuriated Carlos, as well as Dona Antonia, who abandoned Christianity, if, indeed, she had ever genuinely accepted it.

Determined now to drive the Spaniards away, Carlos increased his threats and at one point tried to seize a Spanish ship. It was too much for Menéndez, who ordered his execution. The head chief, with twenty of his principal men, was lured into the blockhouse, and all of them were seized and beheaded, stunning and leaving leaderless all the subjects and vassals of the vast Calusa chiefdom. The Spaniards installed a more pliant man whom they called Don Felipe as head chief, but in the Indians' eyes he had no right to the position, and they refused to accept him. Backed by the Spaniards' arms, he became a hated tyrant and caused the deaths of fifteen subchiefs who resisted him. Finally, he was caught in a plot against the Whites, and was killed by his angry Spanish masters, along with fourteen of his followers.

By then, the Calusas had had enough of the Spaniards. They burned their principal town of Calos and fled from the island on which it stood. Without the labor and food which the Indians had been forced to supply them, the Whites in desperation evacuated the chaotic post and left the Calusa country. Angry and frustrated, Menéndez and other Spaniards proposed using fire and steel mercilessly to exterminate the whole Calusa chiefdom or impress all its people into slavery. Practical considerations, as well as the prospect of opposition from the Spanish Crown, made this impossible, however, and the Spaniards simply abandoned the Calusa area, deciding that as a barren, non-agricultural region, unable even to produce corn for their colonies, it had nothing to offer them.

Left to themselves, the Calusas returned to their burned town, installed a proper successor as their head chief, and continued their old ways. A century later, in more benign times, they established amicable relations with the Spanish authorities in Florida, who had never again attempted to subjugate and convert them, and managed to build up a trade with the Spaniards in Cuba, which they could reach in their boats in twenty-four hours. Acquiring some Spanish customs, they became known as "the Spanish Indians" in Florida, but they never accepted Christianity. White men's diseases, which ran wild among all the Florida tribes, eventually reduced their numbers drastically, and in the eighteenth and nineteenth centuries the survivors joined with the Mikasuki and Seminole migrants from the north who had moved into their country, seeking safety from American troops. By then, the strong, independent chiefdom of the Calusas had long since ceased to exist.

Elsewhere in Florida, Spanish pressure, both military and missionary, gradually disturbed and finally subjugated and destroyed the Indian societies. For a long time, the Spanish hold was a tenuous one. Again and again, Spanish high-handedness, interference, and cruelty aroused Indian resentment and led to furious attempts by the chiefdoms to drive the Whites away. Individual Spanish posts were threatened and attacked, and some were abandoned and never reestablished. At first, conflicts erupted when the Spaniards ran out of trade goods with which to pay for corn and other food and took to seizing the Indians' supplies or levied "taxes" on the chiefdoms for so much corn per year. When the Indians objected, they were treated brutally or killed. Inevitably, the Indians retaliated, often laying siege to a post or overrunning it and killing members of the garrison. In turn, Spanish punitive expeditions were sent against them, burning their towns, destroying their fields, and beheading chiefs and their subjects.

From the beginning, the Spaniards threatened Saturiwa because he had befriended the French and was suspected of harboring French stragglers in his towns. The Timucua chief smoldered with resentment and finally sent his warriors against the new Spanish post on the St. Johns River, where the French had once lived. They harassed the garrison and killed some of its members, and when in 1568 an aggressive French expedition, out to avenge the Spanish massacre of Laudonnière's Huguenots, landed among the Timucuan Tacatacuru Indians north of the St. Johns, Saturiwa joined forces with the French and sacked the Spanish fort on the St. Johns. After killing as many Spaniards as they could find, the French, however, sailed away, leaving Saturiwa alone to face retribution.

It was a long time coming, for the Spaniards had continuous troubles elsewhere. The missionaries' dictatorial interference in Indian life and cruel behavior by garrison members resulted in savage slaughters, first of Indians, then of the Spaniards, and various posts were abandoned, some permanently, including, among others, those in the countries of the Ais and Tocobagas. St. Augustine was attacked and set on fire. In 1572, the Jesuits, unable to subvert the strong, religious-based structure of Indian society and persuade individual Indians to turn against their people and the ancient beliefs of their ancestors, quit Florida in disgust. They were soon replaced, however, by eager Franciscan friars.

Punishment, of a sort, was finally directed against the Saturiwas in 1576 and 1577 when warriors and subject towns of that chiefdom struck again at St. Augustine. The Spaniards drove them off, then sent soldiers to support the Utinas against the Saturiwas and their allies, including the Potanos of the interior. The fighting seems to have been inconclusive, save that the aroused Potanos continued their hostility against the Spaniards for another decade.

By then, the steady pressure of the White soldiers and missionaries was beginning at last to erode the foundations of the coastal Indians' societies. The Franciscans were starting to win converts, first among natives who came regularly into the Spanish centers and grew used to the White men's presence, then in towns close to the forts. The friars gradually became bolder and visited towns farther from the White centers, using every means, including bribery, to win important converts. Eventually, they conducted mass baptisms and converted whole towns. Occasionally, their task was eased for them when a local chief or shaman objected, and the Spanish soldiers killed him, rendering the people leaderless and demoralized. New chiefs, often women who could win some acceptance because of the matrilineal clan system, were installed by the Spaniards and would frequently then agree to move all the people to a new town close to the Spanish center, where the friars could work on them at will. At such mission centers, possessing large agricultural fields, the Indians became virtual serfs, enduring strict regulations and punishments and producing food and supplies for the Spaniards.

The disruptions of the chiefdoms inevitably caused desperate revolts, some of them affecting large areas and many different peoples, but these, in turn, led to merciless Spanish punitive expeditions that burned towns, wiped out populations, beheaded stubbornly patriotic chiefs and leaders, and destroyed the traditional structure of Indian society. At the same time, a new series of virulent European diseases swept the peninsula, radiating out from the Spanish centers and missions and claiming thousands of Indian lives. One of them was apparently introduced by English seamen during a raid by Francis Drake against St. Augustine in 1586. Even more devastating epidemics broke out between 1612 and

1617, spreading up the coast as far as New England. During the winter of 1612–13 alone, it is believed, half the remaining Indian population of Florida perished from White men's diseases.

The sicknesses took the heart out of most of the native survivors. Many of them could see that the terrible epidemics had generally spared the Spaniards and, not understanding that the Whites were more resistant to European diseases, accepted the explanation that the powers of the Spaniards' god, being superior to that of the Indians', had saved them. With their own leaders, societies, and values undermined or lost, they bowed to the missionaries and Spanish domination. The last vestiges of the old chiefdoms vanished as the people were regrouped in the regimented mission centers. In 1604 the Ais submitted, though they pleaded that they not be forced to cut their hair short. Four years later, the Apalachees, who had once fought so furiously against De Soto, allowed a mission to be established in their country, and shortly afterward the Utinas agreed to convert. There were still some last courageous revolts of Indians who were determined to be free, but when the final major rebellion—an eight-month war by Saturiwas, Potanos, and other Timucuas, occasioned in 1656 by the harshness of the Spanish officials—was over, the peninsula was finally quiet, the survivors of its original native population disarmed and powerless.

As epidemics continued to reduce their numbers, there was little will left among them to meet a last and almost total disaster. In 1702, the English colonists of South Carolina, joining the mother country in the War of the Spanish Succession, launched a series of devastating raids into Florida designed both to defeat the Spaniards and to capture Indians to use as slaves on the English plantations. Large war parties of Yamasee and Creek Indians, whom the English either led or encouraged, scoured the northern part of Florida, driving the weak Spanish garrisons into their forts and, with their English-supplied guns, killed and captured hundreds of helpless, unarmed Florida Indians gathered around the missions. As the mission system collapsed, those natives who could do so escaped and fled south, but year after year English-inspired raiding parties followed them, wiping whole regions of the peninsula clear of Florida Indians, even overrunning the Keys.

In time, the war and slave-catching parties ceased. The Yamasees and other tribes in the English colonies began to have their own difficulties and wars with their White allies, and soon they were fleeing to the safety of Spanish Florida to find new homes for themselves. By the middle of the seventeenth century, Yamasees, Creeks, and others were spreading over the peninsula, many of them merging with groups and villages of the Florida peoples whom they had previously hunted down. In 1763, when the Spaniards withdrew from Florida (turning it over to the English, who returned it to Spain twenty years later), they took some of the remaining mission Indians with them to Cuba. The rest of the original Florida natives were beyond their reach, living in the interior or in the southern swamps or joined in settlements with the newly arrived Indians. The chiefdoms of the Saturiwas, the Utinas, the Potanos, the Apalachees, the Ais, the Tocobagas, the Yustagas, the Acueras—the people who had fought for their independence against Narváez and Menéndez and had hurled defiance at De Soto—were all extinct. But the survivors were again free people.

Both Great Britain and Spain—the latter after it had reacquired Florida in 1783—made treaties with various individual native groups, confirming their rights to the lands they occupied. But with the birth and growth of the United States, new pressures were brought against the Indians. Southerners invaded their territories, even though they were under Spanish sovereignty, searching for runaway slaves and provoking friction and violence. Murders and skirmishing between the marauding Whites and the Indians, who were now called Seminoles, aroused the neighboring American states, and in 1818 Andrew Jackson invaded the northern part of the Spanish territory, killing Indians, burning their towns, and driving some of the people farther south. The action helped induce Spain to cede Florida to the United States in 1819, and shortly afterward White settlers streamed onto the Seminoles' lands and demanded that the army clear the peninsula of Indians and ship them out West.

The government tried to oblige, first by seeking formal land cessions from the Seminoles. Under pressure from the Americans, leaders and council members of some individual Seminole groups, who had no authority to speak for any but their own people, made such cessions, to which the United States bound all the natives. But when the government tried to round them up and move them west of the Mississippi River, they resisted, and war broke out. Mikasukis, Seminoles, Blacks, and descendants of the original tribes all fought back against the American troops with the same courage, ferocity, and determination to remain free and be left alone that had marked the long struggle of the chiefdoms against the Spaniards years before. The Americans knew nothing of the Acuera head chief who had told De Soto, "I regard those men as vile and contemptible who subject themselves to the yoke of someone else when they can live as free men. Accordingly, I and all my people have vowed to die a hundred deaths to maintain the freedom of our land. This is our answer, both for the present and forevermore." But the words were alive again, and in the spirit, if not the blood, of such new patriot leaders as Osceola,

Holata Mico, Arpeika, Micanopy, Jumper, Alligator, Tiger Tail, Billy Bowlegs, and their council members there surged again the fierce determination to be free that the Spaniards had never fully been able to crush.

When the United States finally abandoned the costly effort to remove the Indians by force, the survivors in Florida were once again free, though now generally compressed in hiding places in the watery lands of the former Calusa chiefdom in the southern part of the peninsula. Seeking an end to friction, the government set apart the area, principally one of swamps and Everglades wilderness not desired by the Whites, "for the use and occupancy of the Seminoles of Florida" (as distinct from the many Seminoles who had been removed to Oklahoma and now formed a new tribe of their own), and designated a buffer zone which was supposed to protect them from further White aggression. Although Whites have since appropriated the buffer zone and much of the Indians' territory, squeezing them into smaller and smaller areas, the Florida natives, in large measure, are still free today, many of them still able to maintain their culture, traditional beliefs, and almost complete independence. Reflecting their continued will to be free Indians, the Miccosukees in 1971 became the only tribe in the United States to take over from the federal government on a permanent basis the full management and control of their own affairs. "Our experience with the United States government has been bitter and we never forget," said the Miccosukee tribal chairman, Buffalo Tiger, a descendant of the Indian leaders of the Seminole War. "We don't hold a grudge against anybody, but we don't want the government to pry into our affairs and to know too much about our ways, because this is how it can exercise control over us." To the knowledgeable, his words were echoes, again, of the great chiefs of the Spanish period.

Despite the Court of Claims decision in 1967, the federal government, at this writing, has not yet paid the tribes compensation for the Florida lands that have been taken from them. Since its inception in the 1940's, the claims case has been controversial among the Florida Indians, being pushed principally by the Christianized Seminoles who were encouraged by the federal and state governments, as well as by White land and water developers, to accept small reservations and sell their claims to other lands in the state. They have been opposed bitterly by traditionalist Indians who feel they have no right to sell their land. At the same time, the Miccosukees instituted (and in 1981 began to settle advantageously) a separate case against the state of Florida for permanent trust possession of the lands the state licensed them to use, as well as an additional portion of southwestern Florida, and for certain rights which they asserted the state violated. Important as they are to the Indians of

Florida, these territorial conflicts are sober reminders to expansive present-day developers and other non-Indians in the state, including rural landowners, the city dwellers and vacationers of Miami, Naples, and other neighboring cities, and the visitors to the Everglades Park, that the heirs of long-vanished tribes are still in their midst—not simply as colorful alligator wrestlers and tourist attractions (which help them survive in the Whites' cash economy), but as the possessors of serious rights that stem from a history which cannot be dismissed as irrelevant and forgotten.

Today, there are some 1,000 Seminoles on their three reservations, perhaps 250 Miccosukees along the Tamiami Trail, and 200 independent traditionalists. Many members of each group, still filled with memories of their people's proud and heroic 500-year struggle for survival, continue to celebrate the Green Corn ceremony with their traditional religious leaders, speak little or no English, observe the ties and customs of their clan relationships, live in *chickees*, the traditional raised-platform buildings without walls and with poles supporting thatched roofs, and maintain many of the beliefs and values of their Indian culture. And away from the traffic and tourists of the Tamiami Trail, close to nature in the privacy of the hammocks and swamps, some of them, it is said, still sing the songs of their Calusa ancestors, the first Native Americans of the present-day United States to resist the White invaders.

"We do not say that we are superior or inferior to the White Man and we do not say that the White Man is superior or inferior to us," said a traditionalist Seminole petition to the President of the United States in 1954. "We do say that we are not White Men but Indians, do not wish to become White Men but wish to remain Indians, and have an outlook on all things different from the outlook of the White Man. We do not wish to own lands because our land is for all of us. We live on our land, which is the land of all of our Tribe, and we live from our land, which is the land of all of our Tribe. We have failed to have your Indian Agent or your Secretary of the Interior or your other government officials understand our outlook."

Throughout Indian America are numerous counterparts to these descendants of the Florida chiefdoms. The best-known premature epitaph for a still-surviving native people was undoubtedly James Fenimore Cooper's *The Last of the Mohicans,* who are today's Mohegans of southeastern Connecticut. But across the United States are Tiguas, Powhatans, Wishrams, Houmas, Mandans, Croatans, Alabamas, Yuchis, Quapaws, Wampanoags, Wailakis, and many others numbering into the tens of thousands who knew themselves as "we, the people" and who all, at one time or another, heard from White men that they were extinct. All of them know that they are still here and that, like the descendants of the

Calusa, Timucua, Apalachee, and other Florida tribes, they will continue to die as Indians.

At the same time, the very first fact that they understand about themselves is what they have been through in order to endure. It is a significant point, for most non-Indians are scarcely aware of what is still locked in their memories. This is what we will look into next.

2

"THE LORD GIVETH AND THE LORD TAKETH AWAY"

The Racial Stereotypes That Still Influence the Whites' Treatment of Native Americans

ONE OF THE MORE enduring characteristics of Indian-White relations has been the susceptibility of non-Indians to thinking about Native Americans in stereotypes. Through the centuries, most Whites have cast all Indians in group images that have changed from time to time to suit new needs and conditions but have always been unreal. They have been regarded successively as innocent children of nature, noble savages, subhuman demons, untrustworthy thieves and murderers, stoic warriors, inferior and vanishing vestiges of the Stone Age, depraved drunkards, shiftless, lazy, humorless incompetents unable to handle their own affairs —almost anything but true-to-life, three-dimensional men, women, and children, as individualistic and human as any other people on earth.

Stemming from the profound differences between the cultures of the Whites and the Native Americans, as well as from the Euro-Americans' self-interest, convictions of superiority, avarice, racism, and a chronic inability or disinclination to view Indian motives and actions from any perspective but their own, these comfortable images defamed and dehumanized Indians, reducing them in the non-Indians' mind to something faceless, akin to the trees and wild animals that the builders of the American nation felt compelled to clear from the land. Not only did the images contribute to endless misunderstandings and friction, but they justified and made more acceptable—as they still do—aggression and injustice.

No false image has been more harmful and lasting than the belief that Indians are so different that they cannot get on with Whites as equals, and that they should be treated as alien, inferior people. The thread of such thinking, nurturing prejudice and belligerence, runs throughout the course of Indian-White history and is still evident wherever Native Americans and Whites live in close proximity. The land claims case of 3,000 Passamaquoddy and Penobscot Indians in Maine who sued for 12.5 million acres, 58 percent of that state, plus $25 billion in damages and money owed to them, startled the American nation when the Indians' suit received wide publicity in the mid-1970's. What was not publicized was the fact that this was the action of ignored and largely forgotten Native Americans in Maine who had been suffering from local discrimination, prejudice, and injustices, including violence and killings that had gone unpunished, and whose efforts to gain fairness and justice had consistently evoked cold indifference from state officials and hostility from White neighbors. The outside world was not informed in the 1970's that for years prior to the claims suit the government and people of Maine had subjected the Indians to every form of inequality—economic, legal, educational, political, and social. The Native Americans had been cheated, humiliated, pauperized, and treated as inferiors, without rights. They were Indians, and to most of the rest of Maine's population they were still the embodiment of stereotyped images of what Indians should be.

But in Maine the tribes held a winning card, and they did everything possible to warn the state that the day might come when they would have to play it. Again and again, during the 1960's and early 1970's, the state and its courts ignored the warnings, thwarting the Indians' repeated efforts to call attention to their grievances. Finally, the dramatic land claims suit was filed, charging that the taking of their lands through the years had violated the Trade and Intercourse Act of 1790, which prohibited the acquisition of Indian-owned land without the approval of the federal government. It was a dark day for the state. The federal courts ruled for the Indians, and Maine was ultimately forced to agree to a compromise settlement with the two tribes. Anti-Indian prejudice and hostility did not die in the state, but a new day dawned for the Indians, who, with court-enforced respect from the Whites, could work more securely for equal treatment, justice, and the improvement of their conditions.

There was irony in the fact that this largest Indian claim to land and money for damages ever brought in the United States occurred in New England, along with Virginia a fountainhead of the most pervasive and deeply rooted stereotypical beliefs that non-Indians have had about Native Americans. The first conflicts between English colonists and Indians took place in those two regions, among them the precedent-setting Puritan assault on the Pequot Indians of Connecticut in 1637. That atrocity-filled war, in particular, hardened many of the Whites' attitudes, fears, and expectations into ones that they have carried with them ever afterward, including the enduring image of the satanic and bloodthirsty savage of the wilderness whom White men had the right to conquer, dispossess, and eliminate. In a sense, the loss of this first major New England war by the Pequots was a loss by all Indians, for in time each tribe felt the impact of the myths created by the Puritan victors.

How did such myths—with which the United States must still reckon —begin? To illuminate their birth, one must look back beyond the Pequot War itself to an appreciation of the pre-White society that had evolved among the Pequots and other native peoples in New England. The English colonists in the region launched their war of extermination against the Pequots only seventeen years after the Pilgrims left the Old World to find new homes among the inhabitants of the New, and only seven years after other Puritans had established themselves among the native population at Massachusetts Bay. The speed with which the newcomers turned from refugees to aggressors was matched only by the abruptness with which they aborted a long period of human development, for by that time Indians had lived in most of New England, including Connecticut, for at least 10,000 years. This chapter deals with those Native Americans, with the Pequot War, and with the hardening of the stereotypes that still injure Indians and their efforts to achieve harmonious relations with the rest of the American people.

The history of the earliest inhabitants in New England was essentially the same as that of Native Americans elsewhere in the East. The first of them, small family groups and bands of nomadic hunters and gatherers, migrated into the area as the Ice Age glaciers melted and the land warmed and became hospitable to animals and men. With the disappearance of the large Ice Age fauna, the people adapted their weapons to hunt smaller game and pursued elk, deer, moose, bear, wild turkeys, and other creatures through newly established forests of spruce and hardwoods. They took fish from streams, gathered nuts, berries, wild fruits and vegetables, and after about 4000 B.C. began to make seasonal visits to coastal areas to collect shellfish.

Gradually, in response to their own northeastern woodland environment, they began to differ from native peoples in other types of terrain and developed specialized traits of their own. Their tools, implements, and artifacts of daily life became varied and more sophisticated; family units coalesced into larger groups and devised more complex social structures to ensure community survival and well-being; and in some areas the people established seasonal hunting, fishing, and gathering camps within defined territories, fashioned semi-permanent shelters and dwellings at some of them, and became only partly nomadic.

From time to time, newcomers entered the region, joining the older inhabitants or finding untenanted territories for themselves. Beginning about 4,000 years ago, population seems to have swelled in certain areas where food resources may have been more abundant than elsewhere. Later, there was more shifting about, or even a decline in population, for some archaeological sites, such as those in the vicinity of Connecticut's Shepaug River, suggest that fewer people inhabited them than had previously. About 3,000 years ago, centuries after it had first been produced by Indians in the Southeast, pottery—though of a different style—appeared in New England. At the same time, many aspects of life, some showing influences from the Ohio Valley and other areas, grew steadily richer and more intricate. Burial mounds were built and cremations of the dead occurred, implying the existence of formalized religious customs and leadership, as well as social stratification. Agriculture, spreading from the south and west, entered the region about 1,000 years ago. Where the soil, climate, number of growing days, and other factors favored the raising of crops, people who still hunted, fished, and gathered wild foods now also began to grow corn, beans, pumpkins, squash, tobacco, and other products. Elsewhere, as in western Connecticut and along some of the coastline, as well as in the north, horticulture was impractical or, for other reasons, was ignored.

Where there was an increased reliance on agriculture and the need to tend gardens, societies became more sedentary. Permanent villages, often at junctures of streams or above riverbanks, grew in number and size, their inhabitants dwelling in bark- or mat-covered circular wigwams or bread-loaf-shaped longhouses that sometimes extended over 100 feet in length and enclosed the fires and living accommodations of a number of families. Most permanent villages were built inland, serving as bases for farming and gathering activities and for fall and winter hunting parties. Settlements along the coast were often little more than camps for inland dwellers who visited the shore for fish and shellfish in the spring and summer and lived on rush mats on the open ground or in light, temporary shelters.

Until the period immediately preceding the arrival of the first Whites, warfare among the New England Indians seems to have been absent or unimportant. How it began and spread is not known. Elsewhere in the area of the present-day United States, militaristic Indian societies were already engaged in conflict, and it is possible that their influence spread to the Northeast. It is also possible, however, that warfare in New England was insignificant until the sixteenth century, when the appearance and trade of the first Whites—many of them still unknown to history —inspired envy and rivalries that set native populations against each other or heightened already existing feuds. By the time that later-arriving Europeans observed and wrote accounts of intertribal wars, the origins of the enmities were obscure and may have either predated the White man's arrival or stemmed from unchronicled events and frictions after European seamen began touching and trading along the coast and up the rivers of the region.

At any rate, the earliest known White reports of warfare speak of it as an established institution and tell of some villages already encircled by defensive palisades of poles. By that time, intertribal hostilities, it was noted, broke out over contested territorial hunting, trapping, and fishing rights, but more often were conducted to seize certain areas from an enemy and drive the enemy away, to force a weaker people into subjection symbolized by the paying of tribute for protection by the victor, or as reprisal for some real or imagined injury. The making of war was not undertaken lightly, but was considered a necessary action to rectify wrongs and injustices and restore respect for established customs. A group about to go to war usually first sent ambassadors to its enemy to announce that it was going to do so and to explain the reasons why. The war bands, which went into battle in massed bodies directed by war leaders, were armed with spears, various types of tomahawks, and bows and arrows, which had first made their appearance in New England about A.D. 500. The conflicts were fierce and noisy, but usually of short duration and with few casualties, ending with the attainment of war aims, accompanied by the seizure of booty, captives, and tribute, or with the repulse of the attackers after they had sustained the loss of one or more of their people.

The onset of militarism—whenever it began—accelerated political and social change. Through the centuries, the material development of the Indians had been accompanied by the combining of family units into strong matrilineal clans that held large bodies of related people together under complex and tightly drawn rules of conduct in matters that ranged from the training of children and the upbringing and marriage of youths to the observance of practices in the providing and apportioning of food supplies. The members of each clan traced themselves back through the female line to a common ancestor, and the different clans, which developed into larger kinship groups composed of a number of closely knit clans, were usually named for living creatures which were conceived to be their supernatural ancestors and spiritual guardians. Gradually—and notably with the spread of warfare—groups of clans drew together for their security and well-being in joint occupancy of villages, each clan assuming responsibility for certain aspects and functions of daily existence.

With the clans enforcing the observance of codes of behavior, there was little need for formal government. Members of village councils and men with special community functions—such as runners or messengers, criers who awoke the village and announced decisions and events, and "owls," who were able speakers with strong memories—were chosen collectively from among the best-qualified clan members. Headmen, who were known as sachems and had little authority save in time of war, were chosen by the councils, usually from among the sons of the preceding headman or those of his sister—a process that had been developed by the individual clans in selecting their own headmen. The headman had the duty of keeping the people's sacred symbols, but the village societies were basically egalitarian and democratic, the sachem and the councillors living like everyone else. When the sachem had to make decisions that affected all the people of the village, he did so with the advice and consent of the council.

In the beginning, villages in New England were autonomous. In time, however, various forces eroded, or ended, the independence of many of them. Intermarriage or conquest sometimes brought two or more villages together under one headman. Some villages banded together in alliance for common defense, retaining their own sachems and councillors but sending delegates to a council of all the federated villages which chose from their number a Great Sachem. Though in honors he stood somewhat above all others in the different villages, he could make no major decisions without the approval of the council of the confederation, and that body could depose him and choose his successor from among his closest male relatives or the sons of his sister. Other villages, defeated in war, were generally permitted to have their own sachems and councils, but were reduced to the status of a protected people who paid tribute for the protection and were bound by the authority and decisions of the Great Sachem and the federation's council.

This political system, which eventually gave rise to a number of sachemdoms of many villages and, in turn, to the alliances or loose confederations of many sachemdoms that the Whites would designate as tribes and nations, had within itself the seeds of personal and group rivalry, politicking, and dissension. From the clan level up, differences that arose over policy decisions, jealousies, relations with other groups, and the selection of successors frequently led to factionalism, the separation of clans and the establishment of new villages, the migrations of some groups to live elsewhere or with different people, and even warfare. At the same time, the system worked well enough to make possible the growth of economically stable and viable communities and the enrichment of the cultural life of a steadily increasing population.

By the end of the 1500's, most of New England was a mosaic of allied groups of various-sized sachemdoms; independent communities; and others that were subject to the authority of one or another of the larger groups, to which they were forced to pay periodic tribute in food or goods in exchange for protection. Some of the confederacies were interrelated by clan ties or marriage, some were allied from time to time, and others intermittently feuded and warred with each other. All of them spoke different dialects of the Algonquian language family and lived somewhat alike, with regional modifications that arose from local environmental differences.

Despite the White man's later overriding image of them as war-oriented, the native peoples were essentially preoccupied with the pursuits of peace. Many of the men were skilled artisans and craftsmen who worked with wood, stone, antler, bone, and other materials and busily produced functional and aesthetically satisfying implements, utensils, and hunting and fishing gear. In addition, the men instructed the youths in the arts, lore, and customs of the people; conducted the annual round of rituals and ceremonies that held together the clans and the village societies; and, most important, as hunters and fishermen provided the people with food and such useful by-products of wild game as hides, sinew, and bone. The men looked up with respect to the community's ablest orators and wisest minds, and by their own conduct, courage, and abilities sought for themselves the approval of the village and the emulation of the young. As warfare increased, the sachems and councillors conducted diplomacy and made decisions of war or peace, but once the tomahawk was raised, symbolizing war, the most valorous men, known as panieses, assumed full authority for the waging of hostilities, relinquishing their authority when warfare ended. Not all the males were warriors, though it became a customary obligation for the able-bodied young men to participate in the defense of the women, children, and older people, and right the wrongs that were done to a community.

Beneath the sachems there arose another group of leading men called sagamores. Sometimes they were men who had attracted followers by their exploits in war; others acquired their status by force of personality, their abilities as spokesmen and village leaders, or their position as head of a large family or group within a village. Honored for their wisdom and talents, they sometimes spoke in behalf of the village to outsiders, but like the sachems, they lived no differently from the rest of the people.

Women had a multitude of responsibilities. Because male leadership derived from relationship to the female line in a clan, women often had considerable behind-the-scenes political influence or power and, indeed, sometimes a woman became a sachem. In daily life, women reared and instructed the younger children, gathered wild foods and tended the gardens, made textiles from fibers, dressed hides, fashioned clothing and decorated it with designs of porcupine quills and shells, and maintained the living quarters. They joined the men in ceremonies, games, and social dances, and sometimes those with supernatural powers or special skills and knowledge of medicinal herbs and plants served—along with male shamans—as soothsayers, curers, or intermediaries with the supernatural. Religion was an everyday affair: everything in creation had spirits to which the people themselves were bound and with which they strove to live in harmony and balance. Over all was one Master of Life or Supreme Being, but through dreams or with the assistance of a shaman, known as a powwow, individuals sought contact with spirits of natural forces or creatures that were familiar to them and that would counsel, cure, or assist them. Male or female, powwows often became powerful personages within a group, employing magic, tricks, medicinal products, hypnosis, or a sense of psychology to help people. In the absence of a formal religion or religious leadership, they personified the link between the people and the spiritual world on which everything in the life of an individual or a group depended.

As early as 1500, if not before, shamans among certain of the peoples must have been anxiously consulted about light-skinned, bearded, and heavily clothed strangers whom some groups living near the coast had seen or heard about, and who appeared suddenly on the sea and came ashore from large sailing vessels bigger than any known canoe or other water craft. The appearance of similar strangers, the Vikings, who presumably met and even lived among various groups in the northeastern part of the continent, had occurred much earlier, but little is yet known about their presence, and they had apparently come and gone without leaving an enduring impact on the native populations. Now, the appearances of the strangers, though still sporadic, were sustained and became increasingly frequent. Indians in coastal fishing and shellfish-gathering camps first saw the big ships, and sped the news inland to the nearest villages and then along trails from one sachemdom to another. Everything about the newcomers was unknown, but the aggressive actions reported about some of them suggested they were an evil force or affliction, sent perhaps by the supernatural as a threat of punishment for errant conduct that had thrown the world out of balance and that needed redressing.

As the contacts increased, the native groups learned better. These were men like themselves, but with strong, previously unknown powers and possessions that caused fear among the villages and at the same time aroused feelings of envy and a desire to acquire the newcomers' knowledge and goods. Little is actually known of the identity of the first White visitors to New England, or of where they came ashore and what they did. In the beginning, perhaps even before the first voyage of Columbus, some of the Portuguese and Basque fishermen who had found the Grand Banks and dried their catch ashore may have come south on the Labrador Current and landed on the coasts of New England and Long Island Sound. John Cabot, in 1497, seems only to have sailed along the coast, but in April and May 1524, when Giovanni da Verrazzano put ashore in Rhode Island's Narragansett Bay, visiting coastal and inland camps and settlements and trading mirrors, bells, knives, pieces of metal, and various trinkets for maize and other food, he reported that the Indians there had "many sheets of worked copper," which may have reached them via intertribal trade from the Great Lakes region or could have been secured from White seamen or from tribes that had traded with them.

Although Verrazzano noted an abundance of hides and fur-bearing animals, he seems not to have traded for them, but the next year Estévan Gomes, a Portuguese navigator in the service of Spain, introduced the idea of trading for furs—if, indeed, it had not already become an established part of meetings between Indians and Whites—and sailed for home with "skins of wild beasts" after possibly having explored high up the Hudson River. Wherever it was that he had been, Gomes also left behind a scar, for in addition to furs, he "filled his ship" with fifty-eight kidnapped Indians to sell as slaves in Spain.

From then on, the White men's visits increased, and the knowledge gradually spread along the coasts and up the rivers, from the St. Lawrence and the upper Hudson River to the villages of New England and farther south, that the coveted metal and other goods of the strangers could be gotten for the furs of beaver, marten, and other creatures of the forest. In 1534, Jacques Cartier saw Indians beckoning to him with furs to trade at the mouth of the St. Lawrence, and there is evidence that soon afterward both French and Spanish traders were dealing for pelts with inland Indians up the Hudson River.

Much of the developing trade was conducted by secretive sea captains and agents who hid their activities and knowledge of geography and fur-trading Indians from competitors and international rivals, and the identities of most of them are still unknown to history. But throughout the rest of the sixteenth and early seventeenth centuries, the increasing presence of these anonymous Whites—principally French, English, and

Dutch—and of the relatively few whose narratives were published brought changes to the native populations and to the relationships between Indians and Whites. In New England, Indians, eager for White men's goods, increased the intensity of their hunting and trapping of fur-bearing animals, changing the habits and routines of community and individual life and making peoples dependent on the Whites. Alcohol was often used to persuade those who felt that the White men's trade goods were not worth the effort, and on occasion Whites would even seize Indian food supplies, withholding them until the harried villagers produced furs.

Trading was generally conducted at coastal sites which Whites periodically visited in their ships or where they established temporary stations. Gradually, some of the Indians' seashore settlements became larger and were occupied for longer periods of time while the people carried on trade. When individual groups began to trap out their own territories and could no longer supply their own furs, rivalries grew, and people nearer the coast set themselves up as middlemen, seizing or buying pelts from interior groups that could still harvest furs and trading them to the Whites on the coast. Some groups even moved their villages to strategic sites along rivers where they could intercept interior Indians who were on their way to the coast with furs.

By the end of the 1500's the fur trade was becoming associated with the use of wampum (a shortened form of a New England Algonquian expression, *wampumpeag,* meaning a string of white shell beads). It is not known for certain whether Indians had produced wampum before the coming of White traders, but as early as 1570 Dutch beads made of glass seem to have won special favor as a trade item. The Indians found many uses for the varicolored beads—as ornaments embroidered on clothing; as necklaces, armlets, and headbands; and as a medium of exchange. In addition, their possession in bulk became evidence of rank and prestige, and, when strung together in straps and belts with various symbolic designs, they acquired new uses as memory aids or as guarantees and reminders of agreements and promises between different peoples. Whether they had previously made shell beads or were inspired to produce their own version of the Dutch beads, various coastal groups which had traditionally gathered shellfish began turning out wampum in quantity, cutting and boring white beads from the columellae of whelks and purple ones from the shells of quahogs. The cylindrical Indian product rapidly became abundant and spread from group to group. It was soon prized by almost every native society in the Northeast, particularly by those in the north and the interior who did not have the required shells in their own territories. The exploiting Whites, too, quickly realized the value of the shell beads: for coarse cloth and other cheap European goods they could buy large amounts of the wampum from the coastal producers and trade the beads to the fur-gathering northern and inland Indians for pelts that would return huge profits in Europe. The three-way commerce, possibly begun by the French, took hold rapidly. The Whites gladly provided metal tools to coastal groups, which facilitated the manufacture of the shell beads, and numerous Indians were soon turning out an enormous supply of wampum for sale to the European traders.

The new industry seems to have become centered on the western edge of Narragansett Bay, which was familiar to traders and where the raw materials were found in quantity. But the proper shells were even more plentiful on the shores of eastern Long Island, and various groups from southern New England crossed Long Island Sound regularly in dugout canoes—some of them large enough to hold forty persons—and camped on offshore islands and beaches in the territories of Long Island Indians to collect whelks and hard-shell clams. The development was a boon to the native peoples of coastal Rhode Island and Connecticut whose lands had quickly become denuded of profitable supplies of fur-bearing animals. Now, as the manufacturers of a commodity increasingly desired by both Indians and Whites, they gained new prestige and power that, in turn, set in motion new jealousies and rivalries. Certain sachems became richer and more powerful and vied with each other for position; stronger groups exacted tribute in wampum from weaker ones and asserted "protective" authority over the inhabitants of shell-gathering areas; and quarrels, factionalism, and feuding intensified over attempts to control or monopolize the trade with the White men.

By 1620, the Whites were no longer strangers to the New England Indians. Trade was still sporadic, and areas of frequent contact were relatively few and distant from each other. But in some places Europeans had come to live among the Indians with whom they traded—the French and English on the Maine coast, giving up after difficult winters, and the Dutch on Manhattan Island and up the Hudson River, remaining permanently—and their influence and impact had spread beyond where they built their huts and palisades. Various Indians had picked up English, French, and Dutch words, including the White men's names for some of their own groups and village sites, and along the shores of Long Island Sound, which Dutch traders frequented after 1614, the Europeans and Indians gradually developed a trade jargon, composed of words and expressions from both their languages.

In general, the Whites, desirous of harmonious relations with the native producers of wampum and furs and the providers of most of their food supplies, conducted themselves peaceably and without deliberately disrupting the Indian societies. But from time to time there were significant White aggressions which disturbed the affronted villages and sachemdoms and made them wary of, or hostile to, the next Whites who appeared in their territories. Occasionally, traders and sea captains became officious and overbearing, and their insults and violations of Indian customs led to resentments and skirmishes with angered villagers. One Dutch trader and fur-post commander, Jacob Eekens, more than once in the early 1600's seized Indian headmen in order to ransom them for wampum. Other Whites, including the English shipmasters and explorer-traders George Waymouth, Edward Harlow, and Thomas Hunt, at different times prior to the settlement of Plymouth caused serious and widespread troubles when they kidnapped Indians, including headmen, on the New England coast to employ as interpreters and guides and to take to Europe to display as curiosities or to sell in the slave markets. News of their hostile conduct spread among the sachemdoms and led to angry attacks on other Europeans and their ships in Massachusetts and Narragansett bays and elsewhere to avenge the injustices and force respect from the Whites. Still other conflicts before the time of the Pilgrims resulted from misunderstandings, and in some places—such as on Cape Cod, where Whites executed a Nauset Indian who, raised in a communally sharing culture, had innocently helped himself to a White man's possession and had then been seized as a thief—fear of the Europeans and attempts to drive them away became chronic.

More disastrous to the Indians were the great epidemics of smallpox and other European sicknesses which periodically swept away large numbers of the native population. In recent years, the studies of Henry F. Dobyns, Sherburne F. Cook, Alfred W. Crosby, and other scholars have dramatically revised upward the estimates of both the original Indian populations along the eastern coast and the calamitous impact of European diseases on those populations even prior to the arrival of the Pilgrim settlers at Plymouth. In certain parts of the Atlantic coast from approximately 1520 to 1584, for instance, diseases introduced by Whites and spread from one native group to another, including peoples whom Europeans had not yet contacted, seem, according to Dobyns, to have reduced the total aboriginal population by 25 to 30 percent. From 1584 to 1620, European diseases apparently reduced the survivors by another 90 percent!

Somewhat the same figures apply to southern New England, whose native population about 1600 is now estimated to have been between 70,000 and 90,000. In the winter of 1616–17, a devastating epidemic, probably of smallpox, killed 50 to 70 percent of the population of many of New England's coastal Indian groups, striking particularly hard from eastern Massachusetts northward. The sickness either originated in Florida, where smallpox was raging among Indians at the Spanish missions, and was carried north from tribe to tribe, or was introduced in New England by seamen and traders, some of whom were wintering among natives on the coast. Two years later, another epidemic struck the New England Indians, this time killing an estimated 60 percent of the survivors of the earlier disaster.

When considered as statistics, it is hard to grasp the immensity of the tragedy, which in the case of one people alone, the Massachuset Indians of present-day northeastern Massachusetts and coastal New Hampshire, so reduced the strength of their villages and sachemdoms that the total number of young men able to sustain their organized societies and, if need be, fight as defenders of their people is estimated to have fallen from 3,000 to 300 between 1616 and 1619. Moreover, entire villages and whole regions, including Patuxet, a populous Wampanoag center which the Pilgrims would later occupy and rename Plymouth, were wiped out or abandoned. The great losses filled the survivors with enduring grief and insecurity and seriously shocked and undermined their societies. Although it is believed that the natives associated the illnesses with the Europeans, the disaster mostly spared the immune Whites—even those who were living among the afflicted Indians—and the powwows interpreted the epidemics as punishment of the native peoples by the supernatural for group or individual misconduct and the breaking of codes of behavior. Gradually, the survivors recovered, but their decreased strength and new doubts and fears made them less self-assured and decisive than they had been before, and more inhibited in their relations with the Whites.

In this psychologically confused and weakened state, they unknowingly entered a new era in their affairs with the Europeans, one in which they would sorely miss the power they had previously possessed. With the landing of the Pilgrims there arrived in New England the first of an endless number of permanent settlers, who would self-righteously flow over the land, threatening the customs, possessions, and lives of every Indian. The new Englishmen, coming with their wives and children, were different from the seamen and traders, although it would take time for the native peoples to become aware of the differences. Discovering the abandoned cornfields and bleached bones of the Wampanoag dead at Patuxet, the Pilgrims gave thanks to their God for having cleared away the Indians and provided a fertile site for His chosen people. This was the way it was going to be thereafter: God was on the side of the Whites, and if it was His intention to exterminate the people of the wilderness so that devout Christians could carry out the divine will and multiply and replenish the earth, so be it. Though the Indians of that day could not have grasped the consequences, it was a license for the beginning of what would become two-and-a-half centuries of continent-wide aggression and dispossession.

Most, if not all, of the native peoples in New England were by that time known to the Dutch and English by name. But during the 1620's and 1630's, the confederacies, sachemdoms, and independent groups assumed, in the minds of the Whites, the form of tribes and nations led by chiefs and subchiefs, or grand and lesser sachems and sagamores. The origins of most of the group and community names that during this period became fixed in history are unknown or uncertain, for they had their beginnings in the days before the arrival of the Pilgrims and came into usage for reasons of which the colonists who would write the histories were often unaware.

Centered on Massachusetts Bay were the epidemic-weakened sachemdoms of the Massachuset Indians. West of them were Nipmucks, and to the south were Wampanoags, a group of interrelated sachemdoms headed by Massasoit, who allied with the English settlers to make his people stronger than their enemies, the Narragansetts of eastern Rhode Island. West of the Narragansetts, along the northern shore of Long Island Sound, were Eastern and Western Nehantics and Pequots. The latter lived between the two Nehantic groups, claiming a large part of eastern Connecticut on both sides of the Thames River.

It is not known for sure how long the Pequots had been there, where they had come from, or even who they were. Uncas, the first historically known chief of the Mohegans, who were once part of the Pequot confederacy but later broke away from it, told the English colonists that about 1590 allied and interrelated Pequot-Mohegan groups had separated from the Mahican Indians, who lived on both sides of the upper Hudson River, and under a succession of head sachems had migrated for about forty years to the Thames River valley and the southeastern coast of Connecticut. On the way, according to the Mohegan's story, they had defeated and established their authority over a number of small tribes in central Connecticut and at the coast had split the Nehantics, driving the easterners out of some of their lands and making the westerners subject to themselves. As late arrivals who had left a trail of conquests behind them and who, in their new home, immediately began subjecting older, established groups on both sides of Long Island Sound, they became known—so this version said—as Pequots, signifying destroyers.

It is true that by 1632 the Pequots had a dreaded reputation among the other native societies for aggressive, domineering conduct and were receiving "protection tribute," symbolizing subject status, from various groups along the Connecticut River, westward along the Connecticut coast, and on eastern Long Island. But the tale of a forty-year migration, commencing in 1590, is erroneous, for the Dutch recorded the presence of Pequots and Mohegans in southeastern Connecticut as early as 1614. Recent archaeological and linguistic studies have supplied strong evidence, moreover, that the Pequots and Mohegans were native to southeastern Connecticut, that they had developed there over many years from ancestral groups, and that they shared a common origin with their coastal neighbors. There seems to be no truth in the assertion that they had been related to the Mahicans and had migrated in recent times from the upper Hudson River valley. The Mohegans and Pequots, it appears, were intermarried and closely integrated, some of them living together, with the Pequots in general occupying the lower country of the Thames and Mystic river valleys and the Mohegans dwelling farther inland along the Thames. When the Whites first wrote about them, the Mohegans seem to have been in the shadow of the Pequots. The relationship was one in which rivalry and factionalism could—and did—take place.

In the years after 1620, the impact of the epidemics, the arrival of the English settlers, the expanding trade activities of the Dutch, who feared competition from the English in Massachusetts, and the intertribal rivalries of the Pequots and others that were motivated or heightened by a jockeying for control of relations with the Whites all combined to set the stage for an explosion in southern New England. At first, the Pequots had no relations with the English at Plymouth, but were aware of the diplomatic help that those Whites gave the Wampanoags against the Narragansetts, as well as of periodic armed conflicts that the newcomers had on their own with members of the Massachuset and Nauset sachemdoms. The groundwork, however, was being laid for future troubles for the Pequots, for during this period their frequent quarrels and hostilities with the Narragansetts, the Nipmucks, various sachemdoms along the Connecticut River and the central Connecticut coast, as well as with Indian groups on Long Island, established them in the minds of White traders as the most belligerent and difficult, or "insolent," of the wampum-producing tribes.

For a time, they got on peaceably with agents of the Dutch West India Company and other traders from the Dutch colony of New Netherlands, who sailed in sloops along the coasts of Long Island Sound and up the Connecticut River, putting in at various points to barter cloth and other goods for wampum and furs. In October 1627, a new development occurred when the secretary of the Dutch West India Company in Manhattan visited Plymouth and sold the English colonists £50 worth of wampum. The Pilgrims were already trading with Indians and were familiar with their desire for wampum. But the Dutch official now apparently told them of its abundant supply in southern New England, and Plymouth traders were soon competing with the Dutch on the Rhode Island and Connecticut coasts, on eastern Long Island, and even up the "Fresh," or Connecticut, River.

Fearing just such competition, the Dutch, by the purchase of Manhattan in 1626, had inaugurated a policy of buying lands from the Indians and acquiring written deeds to them, attested to by the marks of Indians, which by European custom would establish their rights of ownership against any would-be claimant. Now, for the first time, the Dutch began to secure themselves in Connecticut against the English. In 1632, a Dutch West India Company agent purchased land at the mouth of the Connecticut River, intending to erect a fort there, and in June 1633 Jacob van Curler, representing the governor of New Netherlands, bought a tract up the river at the site of present-day Hartford. The area was inhabited by Sicaog Indians, but the Pequots dominated them, and van Curler diplomatically made his purchase from Wopigwooit, the Pequots' grand sachem. Van Curler constructed a small post, which he called the House of Good Hope, and determined to develop a large trade with the inland fur-producing tribes and ensure their safety when they traveled to the post with their pelts, declared the site a neutral territory where warring Indians would have to observe a truce. Wopigwooit, the Pequot headman, agreed to this condition and promised that any of his people or Indians who were subject to him who came to trade would not carry weapons with them.

In the meantime, a large new group of English settlers had arrived in New England in 1630 and established themselves at Massachusetts Bay. The new Puritan colonists appeared almost immediately to be more expansive and aggressive toward Indians than the English at Plymouth. Their attitude may have reflected, in part, expectations acquired as a result of hearing of the ruthless conflict between some Indians and English settlers that had been raging in Virginia. The dispossession of the Indians from their villages, gardens, and hunting grounds in that colony had brought on a violent reaction from the Powhatan Indians in 1622, and many Whites had lost their lives in a sudden uprising. A punitive war against the Powhatan confederacy was still in progress in Virginia, and in England lurid accounts of the conflict and of the "perfidious and inhumane" Indians with "a more unnaturall brutishness than beasts," as works by John Smith and Samuel Purchas described them, heightened fears and hostility toward all Indians among many of those who were planning to go to America.

The newly arrived English who established themselves at Boston seem to have come with such feelings, as well as with some unusual advice given them by their preachers even before they left England and refined for them in their new settlement by leaders like John Winthrop, Sr., a Puritan lawyer who became governor at Massachusetts Bay. The colonists, they were told, had the obligation to purchase land which the Indians cultivated, but any other land over which the Indians merely "roamed" (i.e., hunted) was to be considered "waste" and could be seized from them. The policy was fortified by their religious beliefs: God intended land to be cultivated and not wasted; therefore the Puritans, as God's chosen people, had a divine mission to take the land and "subdue" it. Winthrop made clear the moral and legal justifications: since the Indians had not subdued the land, they had no civil rights, and since they had no governments in the European sense, they had no legal rights of their own but would be bound by the laws and dictates of the Puritans' government, which under their royal charter had the power to rule Indians, as well as Whites, in the name of the Crown, which claimed sovereignty over New England. In practical application, the Massachusetts Bay government used the power to insist that only the government as representative of the sovereign—and not individual colonists, or anyone else—had the right to buy or take land from the Indians. It was of slight benefit to the Indians, being meant primarily to obstruct White dissidents or intruders.

In time, one other belief about Indians became pervasive among the Puritans. By divine design, Satan, they understood from the Bible, ruled the wilderness, and the Indians were the children of Satan, lured to America in the past, before they could know of Christ. Again, as God's elect, the Puritans had the obligation to save the Indians by the example of the Christian society that they would create in the wilderness of New England. If, however, the Indians would not learn voluntarily, the Puritans had the right to instruct the peaceful and exterminate those who resisted. In their natural state, the Indians represented to the Puritans all that was evil, but they were also the personification of God's plan for the Puritans, who would be tested to convert or eliminate them.

The Indians, having no inkling that the people of the large new White settlement held such basically hostile attitudes toward them, regarded the settlers expectantly as another source of trade goods and possibly, like the Wampanoags' friends at Plymouth, as powerful new allies for someone. With just that in mind, an ambassador from a Connecticut River sachemdom had traveled to Boston and Plymouth in 1631, two years before van Curler established his post. The ambassador was a sagamore of the Podunks, a group living near the Sicaogs, and with the help of an English-speaking Massachuset Indian, he invited both colonies to send some of their people to live and trade with the Podunks. Neither colony was able to accept the invitation, and John Winthrop in Boston reacted with anger when he learned that the Podunk's real motive was to involve the English as allies and protectors in his people's war with a powerful shaman named "Pekoath" (Pequot).

It was apparently the first time that the new settlers had heard of the Pequots, but they were soon to hear much more about them. In 1633 the news of van Curler's post on the Connecticut River upset both English colonies, which felt the Dutch were intruding in country claimed by England. This time, Plymouth proposed to the Bay Colony a joint venture on the Connecticut River, but Governor Winthrop again declined, thinking it too dangerous to try to colonize the remote, little-known area where intertribal Indian warfare seemed constant. Instead, Winthrop undertook a reconnaissance voyage, visiting the wampum-producing Montauk Indians on eastern Long Island and learning that they paid a large wampum tribute to the powerful Pequots, who lived across the Sound. On this trip, Winthrop apparently caught the fever of trade himself and, more important, grasped the immensity of the economic wealth produced by the wampum-making Indians. Much of that wealth, he learned, flowed to the Pequots, who controlled many of the wampum-producing tribes, and it is possible that Winthrop's animosity toward the Pequots began with that recognition and with the birth of a desire to take that control away from the Pequots. There was nothing he could do about it then, however, and after negotiating for the gift of a piece of land from some Indians on Long Island, which he may have marked as a likely place for Massachusetts to begin to acquire control over the wampum producers, he returned to Boston.

Meanwhile, Plymouth's leaders had increased their interest in the Connecticut River. A trader named John Oldham, who with three companions had traveled overland and visited one of the sachems on the Connecticut River, had returned with beaver skins and wild hemp and reported that the Indians were hospitable and that the country contained many advantageous sites for a colony. In October of that same year, 1633, Plymouth finally decided to act alone, sending William Holmes and a small company of men up the Connecticut River with a portable house aboard their ship to establish a post. Despite threats from the Dutch, Holmes sailed past van Curler's fort and settled above the House of Good Hope at present-day Windsor, where he could intercept Indians bringing furs downriver to the Dutch. Holmes, however, was risking trouble, for he brought back to the area some sachems whom the Pequots had previously defeated and driven from their homes. Although the Pequots maintained authority over the territory, Holmes, unlike van Curler, avoided them and purchased the site directly from the sachems whom he had brought with him.

The Pequots were aware of the double insult to themselves, but at the time appear to have been distracted by another, more serious matter: Sometime after the establishment of van Curler's post, some Pequots became angered by the appearance of enemies—Narragansetts or Connecticut River Indians—at the Dutch trading house. A quarrel ensued, and the Pequots, violating their grand sachem's pledge, killed their adversaries on the neutral grounds. The Dutch were infuriated, fearing that this would doom future trade. Deciding that drastic action was necessary to teach the Pequots a lasting lesson and reassure the trading Indians, they lured Wopigwooit himself aboard one of their vessels and murdered him, compounding the crime by telling the Pequots that he was still alive and that they would release him for a large payment of wampum. The astounded Pequots paid the ransom for their grand sachem, only to get back his dead body.

The Pequots were filled with grief and rage, but their problems had only begun. When their confederacy council met to name Wopigwooit's successor, it was torn with dissension. Although the chief contender was Wopigwooit's oldest son, Sassacus, factionalism flared, and Sassacus was angrily opposed by his son-in-law, Wonkus ("the one who circles" or "the fox"), an aggressive, domineering Mohegan war leader and sagamore, then about thirty years old, who claimed that by birth he had a better right to the position than Sassacus. Strong, burly, and jealously ambitious, Wonkus—whose name was later corrupted by the English to "Uncas"— was the son of a valorous Mohegan war leader and of the daughter of the man who had preceded Wopigwooit as the grand sachem of the Pequots. Following the custom of succession through the matrilineal line, Uncas —who had also married a daughter of Sassacus—insisted that the position of grand sachem belonged to him through his mother.

When the council finally decided in favor of Sassacus, the irate Mohegan attempted a series of coups, each time being forced to flee with followers to the country of the Narragansetts. Several times, Sassacus, who feared dissension within the Pequot confederacy, permitted Uncas to return on the promise of peaceful behavior, but the Mohegan continued his belligerency and plotting until most of his followers grew weary of his failures and abandoned him. Stripped of their community rights and treated as outcasts, they gradually dispersed, some settling among the Narragansetts and others going to live among the groups along the Connecticut River. Powerless, but still nursing his grievance, Uncas himself was forced to leave the principal Pequot villages near present-day Groton and Mystic, Connecticut. With a handful of relatives and followers, he established a Mohegan center farther north on the west bank of the Pequot (present-day Thames) River, where he continued to plot the overthrow of his rival and woo support against Sassacus from Mohegans, as well as from Connecticut River Indians and even White traders and settlers along that river.

In the meantime, troubles continued to mount for the Pequots. As further punishment for the violence at the House of Good Hope, the Dutch ceased trading with the Pequots, and for a time Sassacus waged a desultory war against the post, sending some halfhearted attacks against it but giving up after both sides had suffered a few casualties. At the same time, the Pequots became enmeshed in another affair that would eventually have even more grievous consequences for them—the murder of an English trader, Captain John Stone, and eight of his companions on the lower Connecticut River. Stone was a freebooting, dissolute troublemaker from Virginia, who had outraged the authorities at both Plymouth and Massachusetts Bay and had been banished from those colonies. Heading back to Virginia, he paused at the Connecticut River and seized two Western Nehantic Indians to force them to guide him up the river. When Stone's guard was down, other Nehantics came aboard, killed Stone and his men, and burned the ship.

The Western Nehantics were neighboring tributaries and allies of the Pequots, and when other traders took the news to Boston and Plymouth, the authorities misunderstood and thought that the Pequots themselves had been the murderers. Much as they had despised Stone—Plymouth had even wished to condemn him to death on a charge of piracy—the colonists were scandalized that Indians had boldly killed Englishmen, a harbinger perhaps of a repeat of the Virginia experience, and fear and hostile feelings were fanned against the Pequots. The murders, however, had been committed far from the settlements and beyond the reach of the colonists' law, and as tempers cooled, the affair was temporarily laid to rest.

The winter of 1633–34, meanwhile, proved calamitous for many of the tribes. The establishment of the Plymouth post above the House of Good Hope on the Connecticut River enabled the English to intercept the fur-trading Indians, and the Dutch were forced to travel to the villages of the interior tribes to buy their furs. During the winter, smallpox broke out in one of the villages and spread rapidly from tribe to tribe. Before it died out in the spring, it had again killed thousands of Indians, ravaging the Connecticut River tribes as well as the Pequots, Narragansetts, Massachusets, and Nipmucks. Once more, villages were silenced, whole regions were depopulated, and the societies of the survivors were demoralized and weakened. Some of the Indians, now aware that the sickness came from the Whites, charged that the Dutch traders had deliberately caused the epidemic by giving the Indians smallpox-infected blankets. Others accused the English. Both denied guilt, and the truth was never known. At Massachusetts Bay, however, the colonists were again able to thank God for clearing more land for their expansion because across all of New England the wholesale deaths of sachems, war leaders, and warriors once more drastically reduced Indian military power.

The epidemic seriously weakened the Pequots. Under the prodding of the Dutch and English traders, sachems on the Connecticut River and elsewhere who had been subject to the Pequots reasserted their own authority by refusing to continue their payments of tribute to the Pequots, and Sassacus now lacked the strength or will to force them to do so. The Narragansetts pushed the Pequots out of lands they had once conquered in Rhode Island, and when Sassacus was unable to retake the lost territory, the two tribes kept up weak and ineffective raids and skirmishes against each other that tired and frustrated both of them. At the same time, Sassacus was helpless to stop the Eastern Nehantics, allies of the Narragansetts, from taking control away from the Pequots on Block Island and in parts of the shell-gathering regions of eastern Long Island.

The rupture with the Dutch traders also affected the Pequots' economy. The stream of trade goods entering their villages dwindled, and the people began to miss the European metal, cloth, and other products on which they had become dependent. In October 1634, the Pequot council, anxious to find a substitute for the Dutch, dispatched a messenger to the English at Massachusetts Bay to ask them to come and trade in the Pequot country. The startled deputy governor of the colony, to whom the messenger presented himself at Boston, was offered about two bushels of wampum and many beaver skins if his people would trade with the Pequots, but the Englishman told the messenger that men of higher rank would have to be sent by the tribe to conduct formal negotiations. Two weeks later, two Pequot sagamores arrived and met with the colony's magistrates, repeating the offer of their messenger and adding, according to John Winthrop, "all their right at Connecticut [River] . . . if we would settle a plantation there."

It was a stroke of good fortune for the Puritans. They still resented the Pequots, who—in their minds—had been implicated in the killing of Englishmen. But they smothered their scorn and pressed their sudden opportunity to exploit—and even win mastery over—the proud and wealthy tribe. Instead of accepting the sagamores' offer, they presented demands: forty beaver skins, thirty otter skins, and four hundred fathoms of wampum (a fathom, often indicated by the distance between a man's widespread arms, was six feet, and a string that long could usually hold about 360 beads). The Puritans' demands represented a total value of about £250, which, as noted by historian Francis Jennings in *The Invasion of America,* was almost half the annual amount of taxes paid by the colonists and in modern-day terms would be the equivalent of approximately $50,000. The demands had a subtle significance, as Jennings also pointed out, for they changed a free-will offer to an equal by an independent Indian group into something smacking of a payment of tribute, which implied acceptance of subordination and loss of sovereignty. Moreover, the Puritans now raised the matter of the Stone killings, and to emphasize their aim of asserting their authority over the Pequots demanded that the Indians also deliver Stone's murderers to the English.

The sagamores had no authority to agree to such demands, and explained patiently that all the men who had participated in the Stone affair were now dead, except two. It is not known whether the Puritans recognized by then that the murderers had been Western Nehantics, who were under the protection of the Pequots; if so, they were being particularly arrogant and humiliating in demanding that the Pequots break the Indian code of conduct by seizing for the English two men whom they should be protecting and who, after all, in Indian eyes had been justly avenging the kidnapping of their own people. The sagamores knew what was being asked of them, but promised only to carry all the demands back to their council. Nevertheless, before the Pequots departed, the Puritans, by some unrecorded means, apparently had them make their marks on a document that contained all the demands, and in the colonists' minds this signified the assent of the tribe to a binding covenant, or a series of promises. To the Indians it would have been an unthinkable usurpation of the authority of their council.

At the sagamores' request, the English agreed to try to effect a truce between the Narragansetts and the Pequots, promising to pay the Narragansetts some of the wampum the Pequots would give the English if the Rhode Island tribe would stop fighting. The Narragansetts were as weary of conflict as the Pequots, and the English managed to bring about a peace between the two tribes even before the Pequot emissaries left Boston. When the sagamores reached home, Sassacus and the Pequot council were pleased with the cessation of hostilities and by the prospect of the arrival of English traders, who they seem to have envisioned would become their strong allies. But they refused the Bay Colony's demands for the four hundred fathoms of wampum, which they viewed as tribute, and for the delivery of Stone's killers, though they promised not to obstruct English efforts to seize the two men if they were, indeed, guilty of a crime. At the same time, they formalized their agreement to abandon all Pequot claims to authority over the sachemdoms on the Connecticut River where the English would establish settlements.

The Puritans, for the moment, overlooked the rebuffs to their demands, and shortly afterward Bay Colony traders, as well as settlers, appeared in the Connecticut country. New colonies were established at Wethersfield and Hartford—the land being purchased from the local sachems without opposition from the Pequots—and the site of the Plymouth trading post at Windsor was belligerently appropriated by a third group of settlers from the Bay Colony. The Pequots welcomed the new traders who appeared in the area, posing no objection late in 1635 when an English group under Lieutenant Lion Gardiner, a professional soldier and military engineer, built Fort Saybrook on the west side of the Connecticut River on the territory of the Hammonasset sachemdom, a group subject to the Pequots. The English post, looking eastward across the mouth of the river to Western Nehantic country, was established to secure the region against the Dutch, to serve as a seat of government for the English settlements on the river, and to provide a base for the wampum and fur trade on the coasts of Long Island Sound.

With the growth of settlements and the expansion of trade to inland Indians, wampum was taking on a new importance to the Whites. The English and Dutch not only used wampum to buy food, furs, and various supplies and services from the Indians, but with a critical shortage of their own national currencies in the colonies, were coming to use the Indian money as a medium of exchange among themselves, setting fixed values for the purple and white shell beads. By 1637, wampum was in use everywhere, and on March 8 of that year the Connecticut settlements made it legal tender, with Massachusetts doing the same in November. By the start of 1636, the increasing significance of wampum to the economic well-being of the colonies had already been giving concern to Puritan authorities, because the "treasury," in effect, was in the hands of Indians, rather than themselves. As manufacturers and sellers of the currency, the tribes controlled its supply and therefore its value. When it was scarce, it hurt the Whites, who had to pay more for it and whose own products brought less in the market. Moreover, the wampum-controlling Indians could offer higher prices for furs to the inland tribes, causing the cost of furs to rise. There was little, at first, that the English could do about the problem, but the Pequots' position as controllers of a large part of the wampum "mint" did nothing to better the Puritans' feelings toward that tribe. Someday there might be an accounting, but meanwhile the colonists had to accommodate to the Indians' control of their money supply.

An opportunity for an accounting came suddenly and, oddly,

through conflict between two of the colonies. Some of the Connecticut River settlers proved a bellicose set, bullying the Plymouth traders who had preceded them in the area and also the neighboring Indians. In this situation, Uncas became a catalyst for trouble. Although the disgruntled Mohegan lived some distance away, he curried favor with the English on the Connecticut, persuading them that he—in contrast to Sassacus, the "treacherous" Pequot—was their friend; he ingratiated himself particularly with traders who visited his Mohegan village near the Thames River.

In June 1636, one of the Plymouth traders reported to the Puritans at Fort Saybrook that Uncas—who, he explained, was a sachem "faithfull to the English"—had informed him that "indiscreet" settlers on the Connecticut River had warned the Pequots that "the English will shortly come against them" and that "out of desperate madnesse" the Pequots were therefore threatening to attack the settlers and other Indians "joyntly." In addition, the trader passed on the news that Uncas had revealed to him that Sassacus had been "an actor in the death of Stone" and was harboring some of the murderers in the Pequots' country. Uncas was not above making up such stories in the hope of provoking the English to destroy his hated enemy, Sassacus, whom he would then succeed. But it is possible, also, that the Connecticut settlers, whom the Massachusetts authorities had forbidden to wage any war save a defensive one, had actually aroused resentments among the Pequots and had then threatened them with war.

Uncas' reports had other ramifications once they reached Boston. The Bay Colony officials had been chafing over a growing disposition of the Connecticut colonists to disregard the authority of Massachusetts and govern themselves as a new and independent colony. If they were now allowed to handle their own relations with the Pequots, it would not only give support to their ambitions but would risk having the wampum-rich Pequots become tributaries to a new Connecticut colony rather than to Massachusetts. The Bay officials had no way of knowing the truth of Uncas' information, but they felt obliged to assert their authority over the Connecticut settlers, and the way to do that was to take immediate charge of their relations with the Pequots. Several motives, including the Puritans' religious convictions about themselves and the Indians, their growing concern about the control of wampum, and their need to maintain authority over Connecticut, began to merge in Boston into a stern and uninhibited hostility toward the Pequots.

In July 1636, representatives of the Bay Colony summoned the Pequots and their allies, the Western Nehantics, to a conference at Fort Saybrook and, accepting Uncas' information as truth, delivered an ultimatum to the Pequots, demanding that they comply at once with the provisions of the covenant document that they had had the sagamores sign in Boston in 1634—the payment of four hundred fathoms of wampum as restitution for Stone's murder, and the delivery of his killers—or the English would "revenge the blood of our Countrimen as occasion shall serve." It was strong language to the Indians, who were bewildered by the Whites' sudden belligerence. Although the last thing they wanted was a war with the English, the Pequot conferees were in a quandary. Once again, they said that they could not speak for their council, but they promised to take the ultimatum back to their people. On the matter of delivering up Stone's murderers, Sassious, the chief sachem of the Western Nehantics, suddenly announced that he wished to "give" his country to John Winthrop, Jr., the Saybrook governor who was conducting the conference. It was a clever piece of expedient diplomacy because, in the view of the Indians, it would make the Western Nehantics a protectorate and ally of the English rather than the Pequots, who no longer would be responsible for the apprehension of the two Nehantics. For some reason —possibly because he did not understand the Indians' motives and thought that the Nehantics were actually granting him possession of their lands—Winthrop accepted the offer, and the Pequots, who made no objection to the transfer of the Nehantics' alliance, returned home to tell their council what had happened.

The Puritans in Boston waited impatiently for the Pequots to comply with their ultimatum. But shortly after the Saybrook conference ended, word reached the Bay Colony of the murder of another English trader, the Captain John Oldham who in 1633 had been the first Englishman to visit the Connecticut River valley, and the Puritans' wrath exploded. The documentary record of Oldham's death is so full of contradictory details, puzzling omissions, self-serving explanations, and obvious deceptions by John Winthrop, Sr., and other contemporary chroniclers that it is impossible to know who killed Oldham and for what reason. The Puritans in Boston used his death as their excuse, at last, to make war on the Pequots, but the excuse was so flimsy and unjustified that it must be assumed that the Bay Colony authorities had now lost patience and were anxious for any provocation, real or manufactured, that would give them an opportunity to force submission from the Pequots.

Since 1633, Oldham had been an active and well-known trader in Connecticut and Rhode Island, and until his death he appeared to be liked by the Indians, in particular the Narragansetts. In addition, though he had once been in ill repute in the Bay Colony, he had eventually gained status there, carrying out missions to the Indians for the Puritan government and apparently engaging in private business with the Winthrops. It seems that he had played an important role at the Saybrook conference with the Pequots and Western Nehantics and, with two English youths and two Narragansett Indian employees, had then sailed to Block Island to conduct trade. There, Indians had come aboard his pinnace and suddenly killed him, decapitating and mutilating his body in what seems to have been an abrupt and furious action caused by some unexplained personal offense against them. His murderers had then tried to sail his ship to Rhode Island, but had been met by the vessel of another trader who, realizing what had happened, attacked the Indians and after a short fight frightened most of them into jumping into the water, where they drowned. The trader managed to take one prisoner to Saybrook, and two other Indians, hidden on Oldham's craft, finally drifted to Rhode Island, where they were brought to Canonicus, the head sachem of the Narragansetts. At Block Island, Oldham's two Narragansett employees had escaped during the attack on the trader, and they, in addition, eventually got to Rhode Island and were also taken to Canonicus.

The Narragansett sachem realized the seriousness of what had happened and immediately dispatched a party of 200 men in seventeen canoes, led by Miantonomo, his nephew and the tribe's principal war leader, to punish the Block Island Indians and secure the release of the two White youths who had been with Oldham and taken captive. At the same time, he sent one of the murderers who had drifted ashore and Oldham's two Indian employees to Boston to persuade the English that he was innocent of the crime. The group also carried a letter written for Canonicus by the Separatist clergyman Roger Williams, who a few months earlier had left Massachusetts and purchased land from the Narragansett sachem for a new settlement in Rhode Island. Williams explained to the Boston authorities that Canonicus had not been implicated in the murder.

None of the eyewitness accounts, given at Saybrook and Boston by survivors or prisoners, exists, and the secondhand accounts are contradictory. Different contemporary versions had Oldham killed for his property; because he had played a leading role in effecting peace between the Pequots and Narragansetts and had then angered the Narragansetts by trading with the Pequots; and because in some personal way he had offended the individuals who had murdered him. In the various stories, Narragansetts, Pequots, and Block Island Indians were each blamed. The Block Island inhabitants had earlier paid tribute to the Pequots, but in 1634 had become subject to the Eastern Nehantics and their allies, the Narragansetts, who had taken them under their protection, and, according to Roger Williams, the murderer had fled to the Eastern Nehantics for sanctuary. Williams was also told by his Narragansett friends that Miantonomo paid six fathoms of wampum to have the guilty man slain.

But another version, circulated excitedly in Boston, said that the actual murderer—or murderers—had found shelter among the Pequots, the same Indians who, they believed, were refusing to produce the slayers of Captain Stone, and the Bay Colony authorities, leaping to accept this account, were soon convinced that the Pequots were the real perpetrators of the crime against Oldham.

A clamor arose in Boston for revenge, and after an investigation cleared Canonicus, the Narragansett grand sachem, of complicity in the affair, a council of the Bay Colony's magistrates, ministers, and the governor and his council decreed harsh punishment for the inhabitants of Block Island *and the Pequots.* Led by John Endecott, a brutal, irascible man who had been in charge of the Bay Colony's initial settlement prior to the main group's arrival in 1630 and who was known for his extreme religious fanaticism, a punitive expedition of ninety volunteers, imbued with a crusading spirit, set sail from Boston on August 24, 1636, with orders to kill every male Indian on Block Island, bring back all the women and children to sell as slaves, and then go on to the Pequots and force those people, according to the account of John Winthrop, Sr., to give up "the murderers of Capt. Stone and other English, and one thousand fathom of wampum for damages, etc., and some of their children as hostages, which if they should refuse, they were to obtain it by force." The aggressive intentions of the Puritans were astounding. Retribution for the death of Oldham had already been exacted by the trader who had come on his pinnace, as well as by Miantonomo, who had carried out justice according to the Indians' custom. The Narragansetts thought that the matter ought now to be closed. The Pequots had no idea that they were being blamed for anything. For more than a century before the arrival of the Pilgrims, Indians and traders had clashed often, but in each case wrongs had been righted, and the conflicts had been little more than temporary interruptions of a state of coexistence of equals who respected and dealt peaceably with each other. None of the Indians could know that the Whites now intended to change that relationship with them.

To the Puritan colonists and the religious leaders who helped arouse their aggressive fever, the war was morally just, because it would be waged against the children of Satan, and since it would be fought against savages at God's command and under His direction, the Lord would be on their side. To the leaders of the colony, who had now raised their wampum demand of the Pequots from four hundred fathoms to the incredible figure of a thousand and intended to get it this time by holding Pequot children as hostages, the war would have practical results: wealth from slaves and the wampum tribute; the breaking of the Pequots' control of much of the wampum supply and the transferal of that control to the

Bay Colony; and the thwarting of the Connecticut settlers' ambitions to make the Pequots tributaries to themselves and remove their lands from the authority of Massachusetts.

None of the Puritans' aims was achieved by Endecott's expedition. His blustering volunteers, their pay coming only from what they could plunder from the Indians, met brief resistance from a small number of Block Island inhabitants who then disappeared in the woods and swamps. The English scoured the small island, but managed to kill only one Indian. In frustration, they burned two deserted villages, destroyed 200 acres of corn, killed a few dogs, and, taking the only loot they could find —some baskets and mats—sailed angrily for the Pequots' country. On the way they stopped at Fort Saybrook. Their arrival and their announced mission, as bewildering to Lieutenant Gardiner as it would be to the Pequots, dismayed the English officer, who pleaded with Endecott to give up the mad venture, which, he argued, would "raise a hornet's nest about our ears" and force those at Fort Saybrook to face the Indians' vengeance after the Massachusetts men had returned home. Endecott would not be dissuaded, however, and Gardiner and twenty of his men finally agreed to accompany the expedition against the Pequots.

The English set off in boats for the Thames River, sailing close to shore past the Western Nehantics' country. Members of that tribe discovered them and first in wonder and then in alarm ran along the shore, following the ships, calling out, "What cheer, Englishmen, what cheer, what do you come for? . . . What cheer, what cheer, are you hoggery, will you cram us [are you angry, will you kill us, do you come to fight]?" The English made no response, which increased the Indians' fear. Word of the expedition finally ran ahead of them to the Pequots, and when they reached the Thames River, a tall, elderly Pequot sagamore paddled out to ask them what they wanted. When Endecott informed him of the English demands for the wampum, the slayers of Stone, and the hostages, the sagamore argued that the Pequots had done nothing wrong, that Stone had been killed in retribution for Wopigwooit's murder, and that although the grand sachem had been slain by the Dutch, the Indians at that time had not been able to distinguish between the two types of Whites. Endecott refused to believe him, and when he sternly demanded that the Pequots bring him the heads of Stone's murderers or he would go ashore and make war, the old man promised to take his message to his people and return with their reply.

As soon as the sagamore had left, the English decided to land and eventually made their way to the top of a hill where they were soon surrounded by some 300 Pequots, most of whom were unarmed and who milled about anxiously, apparently trying to understand what the White men wanted. When the old man returned, he informed Endecott that Sassacus and another important Pequot sachem, Mononotto, were on Long Island, and since they would have to participate in giving the English their answer, nothing could be done till they came back. Endecott brushed aside the explanation and told the sagamore to find someone else with authority quickly, or he would attack. For several hours, various Pequot leaders, desperately trying to decide what to do but knowing that they had to get everyone but their warriors to some place of safety, used delaying tactics, announcing to the English that a spokesman was on his way, then that their council had convened, and finally that they were preparing to hand over the Block Island Indian who had participated in Oldham's murder. As darkness approached, Endecott at last lost patience and ordered his men to attack the Indians. A brief skirmish ensued in which one Pequot was killed. The rest of the Indians ran into the woods, and the English in their heavy armor were unable to overtake them before they vanished. Frustrated again, Endecott ordered his men into a nearby evacuated Pequot village. After burning the wigwams and destroying the cornfields, the troops crossed the Thames, leveled another empty village, and with almost nothing to show for their venture, returned to Boston. Gardiner's men were held up by contrary winds, and while waiting, stole some corn from another village. A group of Pequots discovered them in the act, and the Connecticut men had to fight off the enraged Indians until nightfall, when the Pequots withdrew and the English could get back in their boats and return to Fort Saybrook.

Endecott's aggression stunned the Indians, who must have been hard put to understand the White men's motives. The Pequots had invited the English to come and trade with them, and they had given up their authority over the Connecticut River sachems so the English could settle in that country. Now their own villages had been burned, their food supplies destroyed, and their people attacked. The confederation's council called for retribution; for the honor and safety of the Pequots, the English would have to be taught to respect them. As Gardiner had foreseen, Pequot war parties, bent on vengeance, were soon attacking Whites in the fields and waters around Fort Saybrook, harassing White travelers in the Connecticut Valley, and at length besieging Fort Saybrook itself. At the same time, Sassacus sent emissaries to the Narragansetts to propose an alliance against the English. The Pequot messengers tried to persuade their old enemies that the English could not be trusted and that if they defeated the Pequots they would then make war on the Narragansetts. The Pequots appear to have been on the verge of convincing Canonicus and his council, but the Bay Colony, having learned of what was occurring, pleaded with Roger Williams to disrupt the meeting. In a hurried visit to Canonicus' village, Williams was able to dissuade the Narragansetts from joining the Pequots, and Sassacus' envoys returned home without their alliance. Soon afterward, at the invitation of the Massachusetts authorities, Canonicus sent a party of Narragansetts led by Miantonomo to Boston, where they signed a covenant with the English, declaring that the Pequots were their mutual enemy.

Meanwhile, the Pequots continued their siege of Fort Saybrook and their ambushing of Whites. Though the Connecticut River settlers asked Massachusetts for help, the Bay Colony delayed sending troops, and in the spring of 1637, Captain John Mason and seven Connecticut settlers went downriver to reinforce Gardiner's garrison. Soon afterward, twenty men under Captain John Underhill, dispatched by the Associates of the Saybrook Company, the backers of the Fort Saybrook establishment, arrived from Boston, and Mason and his men returned to the upriver settlements. At some point, a fateful development occurred. Apparently tiring of the war and thinking that they had achieved their aims and that Gardiner—as White traders had previously done—would be willing to end hostilities and agree to respect the Pequots in the future, the Indians asked Fort Saybrook for a council. Gardiner accepted a temporary truce, but when the Pequots asked him if he had "fought enough," he dismayed them by showing no inclination for peace. They then asked him, Gardiner later reported, "if we did use to kill women and children?"

It was a key moment in American history, for intertribal warfare in New England was not yet total warfare, and war parties did not kill women and children. But Endecott's expedition had hinted at the start of a new ruthlessness against the Indians, and if hostilities were to be continued, the Pequots wanted to know what kind of a war the English intended to wage against them. In his response, Gardiner may have thought he was noncommittal. "We said," he noted, "that they should see that here-after." It was a tragic reply. "So they were silent a small space," he went on, "and then they said, We are Pequits, and have killed Englishmen, and can kill them as mosquetoes, and we will go to Conectecott [River] and kill men, women, and children, and we will take away the horses, cows, and hogs." The door had been opened to a new kind of conflict in New England, one that thereafter would travel westward from frontier to frontier—a war against noncombatants for which the English would be responsible, but the Indians in the eyes of their conquerors would be blamed.

On April 23, 1637, the Pequots carried out their threat. Earlier, the belligerent settlers at Wethersfield had picked a quarrel with the Sicaog sachem, Sequassen, who had originally sold them the land on which they had established their settlement, and they had forcibly driven him away.

Sequassen had appealed for help to his former protectors, the Pequots, and a war party of the latter now attacked Wethersfield, killing six men, three women, twenty cows, and a horse and taking two women captive. The upriver settlers reacted with alarm and a desire for revenge, which seems to have been furthered with great fervor by friendly Indians —led apparently by Uncas, the Mohegan. On May 1, the Connecticut General Court at Hartford declared an "offensive warr" against the Pequots, which Thomas Hooker of Connecticut justified to the Massachusetts authorities in a letter that read: "The Indians here our friends were so importunate with us to make warr presently that unlesse we had attempted some thing we had delivered our persons unto contempt of base fears and cowardise, and caused them to turne enemyse agaynst us. . . ."

Uncas now had his war, with the English against Sassacus, and there seems little doubt that Hooker's letter was referring to the Mohegan and his followers. When a new force of ninety men commanded by John Mason set out from the Connecticut settlements bound for Fort Saybrook and an attack on Sassacus' principal village, Uncas went with them, leading thirty Mohegan warriors and forty Connecticut River Indians as allies of the English against the Pequots—the thirty Mohegans reflecting the relative size and strength of a dissident Indian element which, eventually under Uncas, would be recognized as a new tribe. On their way to Fort Saybrook, the Mohegans demonstrated their loyalty to the English by ambushing and killing a group of seven Pequots. At the fort, however, Gardiner was still skeptical about trusting Indians who had been members of the Pequot confederation, and once again, Uncas had to prove his loyalty by treacherously killing four more Pequots and bringing another one into the fort, where either he or the English colonists—John Winthrop, Sr., said it was the English—tortured him to death.

The news of Connecticut's war declaration and the dispatch of Mason's large force finally moved Massachusetts to action. Still determined to assert the Bay Colony's authority over Connecticut by giving leadership in the war against the Pequots, Winthrop, newly elected as governor at Boston, sent a company of forty men under Captain Daniel Patrick to the Pequot country. The rivalry between Connecticut and Massachusetts led to conflicting stories about Patrick's movements. One version said that Winthrop directed him first to stop at Block Island and seize the Pequot women, children, and old men who the Boston authorities understood from the Narragansetts had been sent to that island by their leaders for safety during the hostilities. It proved to be false information, and it delayed Patrick's arrival at the theater of war until the Connecticut troops and their Indian allies had begun their campaign.

Whether or not that story was true, Patrick and his men were tardy in reaching the Pequot country, which did not displease Mason, the Connecticut leader, who wrote sharply of the Massachusetts commander when he finally did arrive: "We did not desire or delight in his Company, and so we plainly told him."

By that time, the war against the Pequots was well underway. At Fort Saybrook, Mason devised a plan to sail eastward past the Pequots' country to the Narragansetts' country and then march back overland to take the Pequots by surprise. Historians have argued over his motives, some maintaining that if he had landed in Pequot country for a direct assault, he would have forfeited the element of surprise and risked failure; others insisting that his real objective was the complete extermination of the Pequots, which he could accomplish only if he first allayed their fears and then struck them all—men, women, and children—without warning. Mason himself wrote that "we had formerly concluded to destroy them by the Sword and save the Plunder," implying the horrendous goal of totally wiping out the Pequots. The "we" included members of Gardiner's garrison, the Saybrook Company men under John Underhill, and Uncas' Mohegans and Connecticut River Indians, all of whom were to accompany the expedition. Whatever Mason's aim was, Underhill and Gardiner at first opposed his strategy. It is possible that what they questioned was the morality of the unprecedented idea of massacring the Indians, for they only agreed after the expedition's chaplain prayed throughout a night for divine guidance and reported in the morning in favor of Mason's plan.

The expedition then got underway, sailing from Fort Saybrook on May 20, 1637. Western Nehantics and Pequots on the shore kept the vessels under observation, fearing that another attack like that of Endecott's troops was in the offing. This time, however, the English were seen to sail past the Thames River and the Pequots' country, and the ruse worked. Assuming that the English were on another mission, the Pequots let down their guard and permitted the Whites to get out of sight. Landing at length in the country of the Narragansetts, Massachusetts' allies, Mason marched his men in their heavy armor to Canonicus' village, where he informed the surprised sachem that the English were on their way to fight the Pequots for not having lived up to their promises. Replying for the Narragansetts, the war leader Miantonomo told the English that his people approved of what they were doing but feared that the Pequots were too powerful for such a small force to overcome. The boastful, overbearing Uncas, moreover, was no friend of the Narragansetts, and while they knew of his hostility to Sassacus, it is probable that Canonicus and Miantonomo observed with some apprehension the close attachment between the Mohegans and the English and—especially when Uncas blustered that he and the English would defeat Sassacus—resented the new prestige and power the English were bestowing on the ambitious Mohegan. Nevertheless, Canonicus and his council gave Mason permission to march through Narragansett country, and after remaining in the village overnight, the expedition members returned briefly to their ships, which were ordered to sail to the mouth of the Thames River, where the soldiers would meet them in two days after the attack on the Pequots.

At the Narragansett village, a runner had brought a message from Patrick to Mason, asking the troops to wait for the Massachusetts commander and his force. The Connecticut leader had no intention of doing so, and now hurried his army overland toward the Pequots' country, guided by a growing number of Narragansett warriors whose leaders had decided to prove themselves abler and more valuable allies than the pretentious Uncas and his Mohegans. The route westward lay through the lands of the Eastern Nehantics, and after covering twenty miles, the expedition reached the village of Ninigret, the Nehantics' head sachem, who was startled by the sudden appearance of the English troops and was suspicious of their motives. His fears and coolness were interpreted as haughtiness and "insolence," and when the Nehantic sachem refused to let the intruders enter his palisaded village, Mason indignantly put soldiers around the walls with orders to let no Indians leave the town lest they slip away to warn the Pequots.

In the morning Miantonomo, determined to quash Uncas' ambitions, arrived with two hundred Narragansett warriors to join the English. Ninigret, who was an ally of the Narragansetts, now changed his mind, and announced that a number of Eastern Nehantics would also go to fight the Pequots. With a force of some five hundred Indians, the expedition marched another twelve miles to a Pequot fishing site on the Mystic River, where the Narragansetts discovered evidence that the Pequots had dressed a large number of fish the previous day and guessed that a feast or celebration must be underway in their villages. As the troops entered the Pequots' lands, groups of Narragansetts and Eastern Nehantics, recognizing an increase in the belligerent ardor of the English that foretold a truly fierce fight ahead which could result in a ferocious retaliation by the Pequots, decided that it was not their affair and abandoned the expedition. Uncas was able to make capital of their defection and send his reputation soaring among the English as a man of great courage by assuring them that, no matter what the other Indians did, the Mohegans would remain steadfast to the end.

Farther on, Mason held a council, and Uncas and others told him that the Pequots had two strongly defended towns, one nearby known as

Mystic, and the other, where Sassacus lived, still far distant, near the Thames River. Hoping to participate in the attack on Sassacus' village and personally kill his rival, Uncas pleaded for simultaneous assaults on both villages. He was overruled, however, by Mason, who decided to concentrate his entire force first against the nearest village and then go on and attack Sassacus.

The troops camped a couple of miles from the Mystic village that night, and sentries could hear the sounds of celebration coming from within its walls. Before daybreak, Mason deployed the English soldiers before the two entrances in the palisades and, telling the Indian allies that they would now see how the English could fight, ordered them to form an outer circle around the village at the rear of the soldiers. As the sky brightened, the Whites moved forward. A dog barked, and a Pequot lookout, suddenly making out the advancing armored figures, shouted, "Owanuks! Owanuks! [Englishmen! Englishmen!]" He was too late. The English pulled aside brush guarding the entranceways and rushed pell-mell into the village, awakening Indians in the wigwams. At first, many cowered in panic in the lodges, but the English stormed in, hacking at people with their swords and firing blindly at knots of screaming men, women, and children. In the wild terror and confusion, some Indians fought back with knives and anything else they could grab, but most tried desperately to hide or tumbled over each other in an attempt to scramble to safety. Exhilarated and out of breath, the English raced in and out of the wigwams, pulling people from hiding places and swinging and jabbing their swords at everything that moved. Above the turmoil, Mason suddenly shouted, "We must burn them," and grabbing a flaming brand from a fireplace in one of the wigwams, he set alight the mats covering the dwelling. Others followed his example, and soon the whole village was a roaring furnace. Gradually withdrawing from the blazing town, the English encircled the palisades, establishing a line within that of their Indian allies, and continued to cut down desperate Pequots who rushed out of the smoke and fire.

The massacre was soon over. No one knows how many Pequots were killed, but almost the entire population of the village—perhaps as many as 700 men, women, and children—died in the flames or by the Puritans' muskets and swords. Uncas' followers and the Narragansetts, many of whom had undoubtedly been caught up in the frenzy and had joined in the final carnage outside the walls, had never seen any killing like this before and, when it was over, were suddenly appalled and riddled with guilt. "It is naught [bad or wicked], it is naught, because it is too furious, and slays too many men," the Narragansetts cried out to the English. Seven Pequots were known to have escaped, and fear now ran among the colonists and their Indian allies that Sassacus would appear with the main body of Pequot warriors from the other village and fall on them in fury. The English, who had had two men killed and twenty wounded, started hastily for their ships at the mouth of the Thames, while some of the Narragansetts headed back fearfully toward their own country. Before Mason's men reached the ships, about 300 Pequot fighting men appeared and fired arrows at them from a distance. Breaking off the attack, the Pequots then hurried to the village that the English had burned. The scene of slaughter and fire enraged them, and they raced back after the retreating English again, trying to cut them off before they could reach their ships. A series of furious fights occurred, but the Pequots were finally forced to withdraw, and Mason's men, together with Uncas and his detachment and a small number of Narragansetts, got safely aboard their vessels, on one of which they found Patrick and his Massachusetts troops. After returning the Narragansetts to their home country, Mason and his Connecticut soldiers sailed back to Hartford, and Underhill took his Saybrook Company unit back to Boston.

The departure of most of the English troops left Uncas in an exposed position. Sassacus was believed to be still strong, and the Mohegan leader, still at the head of only a small number of Indian followers, faced the possibility of terrible retribution. But the English war against the Pequots was far from over. In Massachusetts, the merciless wiping out of the Pequot village and its inhabitants set off a fanatic clamor to finish the job and exterminate the whole Pequot nation, whose members were denounced with more hatred than ever as satanic enemies and killers of Englishmen. That the Pequots had been attacked unjustly in the first place—that, even if they had been thought to deserve punishment, they had already received far more than their alleged acts merited—could only be seen from a later perspective. To the Puritans, the genocidal conflict was a holy crusade. "We have sufficient light from the Word of God for our proceedings," Underhill said in justifying the massacre of noncombatants at Mystic in which he had participated. With public opinion whipped up, the Bay Colony authorities, who were still driven also by political and economic motives, directed that the war go on until the Pequot nation was wiped from the face of the earth, and Massachusetts —and not the Connecticut settlers—had full control of the Pequots' lands, as well as, undoubtedly, their tributary Indians and their power over sources of wampum. Within a few weeks of the attack at Mystic, a new, aggressive force of 120 Massachusetts fighting men led by Israel Stoughton, a magistrate with military experience, landed at the Thames River from Boston to join Patrick's forty-man unit and continue the fight against the Pequots.

Unknown to the English, meanwhile, the Pequot confederacy, on its own, had begun to disintegrate. Immediately after Mason's men had got away, the Pequots, shaken and mad with grief, had gathered in council at Sassacus' village. Their first act was to order the killing of every Mohegan in the town. In the ensuing tumult, seven Mohegans, all of whom were now regarded as potential spies and traitors, managed to escape and join Uncas. The Pequot council then came apart in storm and dissension. Many of its members attacked Sassacus for the disaster at Mystic and demanded his death. The sachem's supporters successfully defended him, but then were unable to win approval of a proposal by Sassacus that the Pequots seek revenge by attacking the English settlements on the Connecticut River. The majority of the council, thoroughly frightened by the barbarity and power of the English, and concerned for the safety of the people, argued instead that the Pequots abandon their country at once and seek safety with the Mahicans or Munsee Delawares on the Hudson River. Sassacus finally accepted their entreaties, and the entire population, after hastily burning their wigwams and destroying everything they could not take with them, set off along wooded trails to the west. After going a short distance, one group of about forty warriors and many women and children decided that they would rather remain in their home country and risk death. They went back to their burned village and erected a makeshift settlement in the recesses of a nearby swamp. At the same time, hundreds of other Pequots in smaller villages in southeastern Connecticut, learning what was happening, took fright and began to seek safety, some of them searching for hiding places and others fleeing desperately to Long Island and elsewhere.

The main group of Pequots, including Sassacus, Mononotto, and many lesser sachems and sagamores, continued westward, crossing the Connecticut River, where they killed three Englishmen, two of whom they tortured to death and hanged on trees. In the lands of once-tributary sachems west of the Connecticut River, they turned south to Long Island Sound, then trailed westward along the shore, living on fish, shellfish, roots, berries, and wild greens. From time to time, they lost stragglers and small groups, who wandered off to find food for themselves. Many of the people began to despair, especially when they found their former tributaries unfriendly to them, but at length, after crossing the country of the Quinnipiacs near present-day New Haven, they entered the territory of another group, the Wepawaugs, and at present-day Fairfield, Connecticut, forced a local sachem to give them shelter and food in a village partially surrounded by a swamp.

Meanwhile, pursuit had begun. In the Pequot country, Narragansetts had soon discovered the group of Pequots who had chosen to remain on their own lands and were hiding in their new settlement in a swamp. Though the Narragansetts felt compassion for them, they told Stoughton of their presence, and the Massachusetts commander seized all of them. He brutally put to death every male save two, who told him they knew where Sassacus had gone and could lead the English in following the fleeing main body of Pequots, gave about thirty women and children to the Narragansetts, three to some Massachuset Indians who were with his force, and sent the rest—about fifty women and children—to Boston to be sold as slaves.

Then, joined by Patrick's detachment and by Uncas—whose prestige and force of Mohegans had both swelled following the Indians' realization that Sassacus had taken flight—he set out after the Pequot sachem. While most of the English troops moved westward aboard their ships close to the coast, Uncas and his men, accompanied by the two Pequot informers and a small number of English soldiers, went by land, searching out and killing Pequot stragglers. At one point, the Pequot informers had an attack of conscience and announced they would go no farther, and Uncas murdered them. At another place, the Mohegans captured and put to death a group of Pequots, one of whom was a sachem who had opposed Uncas when the Pequot council had originally named Sassacus as head sachem. Uncas cut off his head and placed it in the crotch of an oak tree, where English colonists found it at a later time and named the site Sachem's Head.

At Quinnipiac, the Mohegans captured another Pequot and spared his life when he told them that he would learn where Sassacus was and then guide the English and Mohegans to him. He was as good as his word and, after discovering Sassacus' location, he returned to report it to Uncas. Stoughton, meanwhile, landed his English troops, and the combined force now advanced on Sassacus' hiding place at Fairfield. Although the ensuing attack did not take the Pequots by surprise, it dealt the death blow to their once proud and powerful confederacy.

At the approach of the English, the Pequots plunged into the neighboring wooded swamp, turning to fight off the English and Mohegans who pursued them. After desperate skirmishes and hand-to-hand struggles, the Pequots managed to drive back their enemies long enough to disappear into hiding places deeper in the swamp. Throwing a siege line around the bog, Stoughton called on them, through an interpreter, to give themselves up, promising no injury or punishment to those who could prove that they had not killed Englishmen. The local sachem and some of his frightened people finally emerged, followed by groups of Pequot women, children, and old men. When none of the Pequot fighting men came out, Stoughton tightened his siege line, and maintained it firmly during the night, although some of his men were struck in the darkness by Pequot arrows. Under cover of a heavy fog in the morning, the Pequots finally tried to break out, charging with increasing desperation at different parts of the English line and being driven back each time by heavy fire. At last, one of their fierce rushes succeeded in piercing the English line, and some seventy Pequots raced to freedom and disappeared.

As the second massacre ended, Stoughton and Uncas learned with disappointment that Sassacus was not among the dead or the captives. Actually, the head sachem, taking the wealth of the Pequots—five hundred fathoms of wampum—and accompanied by Mononotto and forty warriors, had left the village before the fight had started, intending to travel to the Hudson River and purchase a secure new homesite for the refugee Pequots from one of the native peoples in that region. Later, it became known that a war party of Mohawks had ambushed them, killing Sassacus and most of his followers. Mononotto and a small group got away, and eventually they made their way back to Connecticut, but nothing more is known of them after that.

The savagery and speed of the Puritans' destruction of the Pequots threw every Indian village in southern New England into fear and confusion. Overnight, sachems and their councils recognized that their world had become unsettled and that the English, with their guns and ruthless methods of war, had the power to subject them and make them tributaries. Within weeks, one of the Bay Colony's war aims had been achieved: sachems of wampum-producing peoples on eastern Long Island, who had been tributaries of the Pequots, transferred their loyalties, voluntarily submitting themselves to the "protection" of the English and offering to pay them tribute, "as we did the Pequits." At the same time, Stoughton sailed back from Fairfield and. again attacking the Block Island Indians, who the Bay Colony authorities felt were still unpunished for Oldham's murder, forced them to submit to Massachusetts and pay one hundred fathoms of wampum and promise an annual tribute thereafter of ten fathoms.

It was only the beginning. Hundreds of Pequots were scattered and in hiding, and the English directed the Mohegans, Eastern Nehantics, and Narragansetts to search them out, kill any they found, and send their heads and hands to the colonial authorities. For months, the tribal leaders obliged them. Nevertheless, many Pequots managed to survive. Some fled to the Nipmucks, and others traveled south or to the Hudson River and beyond, finding safety with peoples as far away as North Carolina. Still others eventually received a secret and unexpected welcome from Uncas, as well as from the Narragansetts and the Eastern Nehantic sachem, Ninigret, all of whom decided that they could build up their own ranks by quietly adopting Pequots who would accept their authority and add their spiritual strength to that of their own people. The old rivalry between the Narragansetts and Eastern Nehantics on the one hand and the Pequots on the other was revived, with Uncas and his Mohegans filling the former role of the Pequots. As unquestioned head of all the Mohegans and of a growing group of refugee Pequots, Uncas became, in fact, the inheritor of the vanished Pequot confederacy, as well as the founder of a new Mohegan tribe, or nation, built around the core of the old Mohegan faction. Ambitious and threatening, he soon became involved in quarrels with the Eastern Nehantics and Narragansetts over hunting and fishing rights in the former Pequot lands, power over tribute-paying groups, and other matters, and Miantonomo finally complained to the English about him, at the same time revealing to the Puritans that the Mohegans were secretly harboring Pequots.

Jealous of the Narragansetts' power as allies of the Bay Colony, and unaware that he was suspect, Uncas, in July 1638, traveled to Boston with thirty-seven of his warriors, intending to wean the support of Massachusetts from the Narragansetts to himself. When he obsequiously offered the colony's governor a gift of twenty fathoms of wampum, however, he was startled by a demand for an explanation as to whether or not he was harboring Pequots. He denied the charge and, placing his hand on his breast, proclaimed hotly, "This heart is not mine: it is yours. . . . Command me any hard thing and I will do it. I will never believe any Indian's words against the English. If any Indian shall kill an Englishman, I will put him to death be he never so dear to me."

The governor believed him and accepted his gift, and for a time the question of the sheltered Pequots was dropped. The English, meanwhile, had other concerns, for they too were quarreling over the void left by the Pequots. Both the Bay Colony and the Connecticut settlers claimed the Pequots' country. Despite Uncas' visit to them, the Massachusetts authorities continued to back Miantonomo, regarding the Narragansetts as their agents in securing the Pequots' lands for the Bay Colony. Uncas at the same time made himself subject to Connecticut, collecting and paying huge tributes of wampum to his protector-friends in Hartford, and they considered that he was serving their purpose when he opposed the Massachusetts-backed Narragansetts. Thus, the two colonies almost immediately used the Indians as proxies in their struggle to possess the Pequots' country. But at length, in September 1638, the Connecticut authorities took decisive action. A number of Pequots, who had been living in hiding and fear, sent word to Hartford that they wished to surrender and would serve the English loyally if their lives were spared. The Connecticut government accepted their offer and took the occasion to persuade both Uncas and Miantonomo to come to Hartford and agree to a tripartite treaty with that colony. Some 200 Pequots were divided among Uncas, Miantonomo, and the Eastern Nehantic sachem, Ninigret, all of whom promised to pay the English an annual tribute in wampum for each Pequot either assigned to them or otherwise harbored in their villages. In addition, the sachems recognized the Pequot country as the property of Connecticut and waived all claims to it for themselves.

The levying of tribute by the colony was part of a widespread development. As they had planned, the English lost little time in extending their control over the production and supply of wampum, not only asserting dominance over the Indian producers but accumulating for themselves a massive treasury of the shell beads by exploiting every opportunity to exact annual payments of tribute from native groups and impose fines on individual Indians for a long list of offenses, ranging from half a fathom for handling a firearm to 560 fathoms for the murder of an Englishman. By November 1637, only a few months after the destruction of the Pequots, Massachusetts, in declaring wampum legal tender, had at last achieved control of its money supply and could regulate its value.

Acquisition of so much wampum, like the opening of the Pequots' lands, inevitably spurred the growth and expansion of the English colonists' power. New English settlements spread rapidly across eastern Long Island and westward along the Connecticut coast toward the Dutch holdings at New Amsterdam. Connecticut eventually won formal possession of the Pequots' country, after first apparently giving Uncas—whose own territory lay to the north and west—secret permission to occupy it.

Unctuous and deceitful to the English and aggressive and bullying toward other Indians, Uncas caused constant trouble. His feud with Miantonomo erupted into war in 1643 when the Narragansett took the side of his ally, Sequassen, the Connecticut River Sicaog, whose village Uncas plundered and burned. Treacherously attacking the Narragansetts during a parley, the Mohegans routed Miantonomo's warriors, and a Mohegan sagamore named Tantaquidgeon captured the sachem. Uncas took Miantonomo to Hartford, where the Commissioners of the United Colonies were meeting, and a council of Puritan clergymen shamelessly ordered the Narragansett's death. Uncas was pleased to carry out the execution, supposedly cutting a piece of flesh from his victim's shoulder and eating it to acquire the dead man's strength, exclaiming, according to the English, "It is the sweetest meat I ever ate. It makes my heart strong."

Later, Uncas was besieged in a fort near his village by Miantonomo's successor and was only saved by the English. His attempts to secure the dominant role in the dealings of all the Indian groups in southern New

England with the Whites continued unabated, however, and through the years he aroused endless turmoil, engendering quarrels and conflicts with the Narragansetts and Eastern Nehantics, the Long Island Indians, the sachems of the Connecticut River, and even with the Nipmucks and Massachusets tribes under the protection of the Puritans' Wampanoag ally, Massasoit. The hectored Indians complained again and again to the English, who intervened repeatedly. Each time, Uncas wheedled the colonists, asserted his innocence, and used his English friends to escape punishment. But the Indians' hatred of him increased, and at one point he was wounded while aboard an English ship by a Narragansett who ran a sword into him.

Two Pequot groups, both under Uncas' jurisdiction but living separate from his villages, had meanwhile come into existence, one residing insecurely in former Pequot settlements at the mouth of the Thames River under a Pequot named Cassasinamon, and the other, led by an Indian named Wequashcuk (corrupted by the English to Wequash Cook) of Pequot and Eastern Nehantic parents, trying to eke an existence farther east near the territory of the Eastern Nehantics. In time, most of the Pequots living with Uncas, no longer able to endure his tyranny, stole away to join one or the other of the two bands, and in 1647 Cassasinamon's group petitioned the colonists to be placed under English, rather than Mohegan, jurisdiction and to be given land on which they could live peaceably. The English became sympathetic to their plight, and in 1655, after the Pequots had dutifully paid all the wampum tribute demanded of them, they were removed from Uncas' power and given formal permission to stay where they were. In 1667, however, pressure from colonists forced their removal, and they were given a reservation known as Masshantuxet, at the headwaters of the Mystic River near the site of the village that the English had burned during the Pequot War. For many years, Wequash Cook's band continued as landless squatters, but in 1683 these eastern Pequots received a reservation north of Stonington.

The last desperate resistance of the New England Indians to White expansion, led by the Wampanoags under Massasoit's son, Metacom, known to the English as King Philip, occurred in 1675–76. Once more, Uncas, now grown fat and alcoholic, aided the English, sending his son, Oweneco, at the head of a detachment of Mohegans to aid in the routing of Philip and his Narragansett allies. For fifty years, the English settlers had been able to divide the Indian nations and conquer them one by one. It worked again. With Indian help, the Narragansetts were destroyed in another massacre reminiscent of the one at Mystic, and the Wampanoags and their other allies were crushed.

The English were now free to overrun New England. Every method, including bribery, trickery, coercion, and murder, was employed to dispossess the Indians. One of the most pathetic victims was the aged and venal Uncas. He repeatedly sold his people's land from under them or gave it away while he was drunk, always attesting to his love and affection for the English. Finally, in 1682 or 1683, he died, hated as a traitor by the survivors of the tribes he had helped destroy, resented by many of his own people, and honored by the Whites as their great friend and ally.

Despite pressure from the increasing White population and years of quarrels and litigation over land deeds and boundaries, the Mohegans continued living where they were, their holdings constantly shrinking and becoming cut up into separate homesites for individual families. Exemplifying the Whites' indifference to the Indians' knowledgeability and sensibilities about themselves, and making fiction more real than truth, James Fenimore Cooper in 1826 appropriated the name of Uncas (in actuality, the *first* of the historical Mohegans) for that of the "good Indian" title character of his book *The Last of the Mohicans.* Putting his version of a noble savage and friend of the Whites in a northern New York setting far from his true homeland and a century after his actual time, and clouding his tribal identity, Cooper convinced generations of Americans, even until today, that with the death of the fictional Uncas—whoever he was—the Mohicans, or Mohegans, became extinct. But they still exist, a few hundred of them residing in the Mohegans' homeland in southeastern Connecticut, in and around the town of Uncasville, and perhaps several thousand more with some Mohegan ancestry elsewhere in the United States and different parts of the world. In the 1970's some of them made known their presence to those who had forgotten them by instituting a suit against Connecticut for reparation for 600 acres of land in the Thames River valley, part of a total of 2,500 acres which they claimed had been taken illegally from their people since the days of the real Uncas.

The Pequots and Narragansetts, too, demonstrated that they had not disappeared. Victims of the same pressures and adversities that had beset the Mohegans, the Pequots had managed to maintain the two reservations the English had given them in the seventeenth century, though the boundaries, the size, and even the Indians' rights to the lands had been contested time and again, and the amount of acreage had been eroded repeatedly by aggressive Whites. Then, in the 1970's, the Western Pequots, the descendants of the Cassasinamon band, with their wooded Masshantuxet reservation near Ledyard down to 164 acres, sued for the return of 800 acres. In Rhode Island, at the same time, Narragansett Indians sued for 3,200 acres at Charlestown in their ancient homeland and in 1979 settled with the state and federal governments for the return of 1,800 acres. All the Indian suits were based on the same claim as that of the Penobscots and Passamaquoddies in Maine—that the taking of their lands had violated the Trade and Intercourse Act passed by Congress in 1790, which non-Indians had long ago ceased to observe, though it had expressly forbidden the conveyance of Indian-owned land without the federal government's approval, and was still the law in the 1970's.

With the close of King Philip's War, the major setting of Indian-White relations moved westward away from the Pequots, Mohegans, Narragansetts, and other native peoples of New England to new frontiers farther inland. Despite all else that may be said about the Puritan legacy, in regard to the Pequot War it always had, still has, and always will have much for which to answer. The telling of American history has been constructed on the foundation of the Puritan version of New England's beginnings, and few White historians have recognized the attack on the Pequots as a deliberate act of genocide which left an unhappy heritage of attitudes for both Indians and Whites. Historians may have dismissed the so-called war, but the Indians cannot do so. The Puritans' treatment of the Pequots was terrible in itself, but to native peoples struggling for understanding and just treatment from the expanding non-Indian population, the harsh and often false images engendered by the fury and fanaticism of the Puritans lived on. From one frontier to another, Whites carried with them notions and fears of Indians which the Puritans had bequeathed to them. Even before their own contact with unconquered tribes, they expected the Indians to prove as hostile and vicious as their forebears had reported them to be, and were predisposed to believe that "the only good Indian" was a dead one.

Two examples illuminate a long history of misunderstandings that —aside from all other reasons for friction and conflict—made tragedy inevitable. In the 1840's, farm families taking the Oregon Trail to the Northwest and adventurers following the California Trail to the gold country left the East and Midwest with preconceived fears about the Indians whom they would meet along the routes. They knew little or nothing about the western tribes, but were steeped in the vivid and gory lore of the colonial Indian wars, the French and Indian War, the Revolutionary struggles with tribes that had sided with the British, the "dark and bloody ground" of Daniel Boone's Kentucky, the wars with the Ohio Valley tribes under Tecumseh, and the Black Hawk conflict in Illinois, all of which, they believed from what they had been taught, had been attended by Indian outrages against civilized humanity.

All Indians, to their thinking, were cruel and bloodthirsty savages, and when they entered Indian country along the western trails, they rode with rifles at the ready, expecting the worst. It so happened that in present-day Nevada the California Trail passed directly through the food-gathering grounds of families of Northern Paiutes, a people so unwarlike and inoffensive that the American fur trappers who had first established the route through their country had hunted them down like rabbits and shot them for sport. Many of the Paiute families lived in terror of the Whites and did their best to hide from them. When the stream of traffic increased on the Trail after the discovery of gold, the Indians' problem of survival became acute, for they often had to get across the White man's road. Indian families hid themselves during the day and scurried fearfully across the road at night, mothers and fathers cautioning their children to silence until they reached safety in the sage and brush on the other side of the road, beyond earshot of the Whites in their camps.

The White travelers on the Trail had their own notions of what was going on. They were sure that they were being surrounded by scheming Indians, watching them from concealment by day and ready to pounce on them under cover of darkness. Sure enough, on guard and listening intently at night, they often heard the sounds of the movements of the Indian families in the dark, and believing that they were about to be attacked and robbed by treacherous "redskins," set up an alarm and fired into the blackness. Many Indians were killed in this way, and when their bodies were found the next day, it was believed—even though children were among them—that the Indians had deserved their death.

A second example, dating almost from the same time, occurred farther north, in eastern Oregon's Grande Ronde Valley, a resting place on the Oregon Trail. There, members of the Nez Perce, Cayuse, and other tribes visited the camps of the covered-wagon trains, intending to trade in friendly fashion with the travel-worn emigrants. These Indians had already had a long history of close and amicable relations with British, French, and American fur traders. Some of them had been converted to Christianity by missionaries who lived peaceably in their midst, and they had established settled homesteads, farms, and cattle herds of their own. When they arrived to trade vegetables, fruit, milk cows, and fresh horses to the emigrants, however, they were greeted by many of the White families with icy hostility, itchy trigger fingers, and attitudes of superiority and high-handedness. The Indians were unused to such treatment from Whites, and came to resent the arrogance and enmity with which their friendliness was rebuffed. The misunderstandings were never resolved, and ultimately tensions between the settlers and the tribes became so great that the violence and warfare always expected by the Whites finally erupted. Officials of Great Britain's Hudson's Bay Company, which for many years had maintained posts among the tribes, were appalled. "I am of opinion," wrote James Douglas, the company's Chief Factor in Oregon, "that there must have been some great mismanagement on the part of the American authorities or it is hardly credible that the natives of Oregon, whose character has been softened and improved by fifty years of commercial intercourse with the establishment of the Hudson's Bay Company, would otherwise exhibit so determined a Spirit of hostility against any white people."

That was history of yesterday, but simplistic movies, television programs, books, and other forms of modern-day communication still keep alive such Indian stereotypes as that of the skulking savage who tomahawked and raped defenseless White women, scalped innocent farmers, and bashed babies' brains out against a rock, all for the orgiastic thrill of it. Those images still feed age-old prejudices and animosities. Where Native Americans and Whites live near one another and Whites covet what the tribes still own, Indians of today know that there are continued racism and genocidal instincts:

In Gordon, Nebraska, near the Pine Ridge, South Dakota, reservation of the Sioux, a mixed assemblage of Whites at a town dance forced an elderly Sioux man to take off his pants and cavort like a naked animal to their hoots and jeers. Then some of them shot him dead and stuffed his body in the cab of a pickup truck.

On the Nisqually River in western Washington, White state officials and private citizens brutalized Indian fishermen and their families, beating them savagely and burning their possessions, while in eastern Washington, at the Walla Walla state penitentiary, guards hysterically choked and battered manacled Indian inmates, shrieking at them obscenely because they wanted to practice their native religions.

At Gallup, New Mexico, anti-Indian prejudice was marked by the humiliation and murder of Navajos; at Elko, Nevada, White officials and citizens threatened Shoshone and Paiute men, women, and children of the Duck Valley reservation, whose agricultural water they wanted for their own recreational use; and in southeastern Idaho, the Power County deputy prosecutor railed publicly at the Indians of the Fort Hall reservation who were trying to zone the use of their lands: "When the Indians talk about rights, they should remember it's like a master-servant relationship. The Lord giveth and the Lord taketh away. This is the white man's case: there are more of us than there are of them."

That was in 1979, 342 years after the Puritans' massacres of the Pequots.

3

"GIVE THE PAPOOSE
A CHANCE"

The Native Americans'
Efforts to Retain Their Spirituality

I n 1889, President Benjamin Harrison appointed one Thomas Jefferson Morgan Commissioner of Indian Affairs in the Department of the Interior. Like many of his predecessors and successors in that office, Morgan knew little about Indians or their needs as they themselves perceived them. After serving in the Civil War, he had been a Baptist minister and had then turned to the field of public education, becoming head of a normal school in Rhode Island. A firm advocate of education's role in making America great, he believed almost fanatically in assimilating Indians, in mixing them as quickly as possible in the nation's melting pot— at the point of bayonets, if necessary—so that they would become like all other Americans, able to share equally in the country's benefits and opportunities.

"The Indians," he announced soon after he took office, "must conform to 'the white man's ways,' peaceably if they will, forcibly if they must. They must adjust themselves to their environment, and conform their mode of living substantially to our civilization. This civilization may not be the best possible, but it is the best the Indians can get. They can not escape it, and must either conform to it or be crushed by it."

The fastest—the only—way to assimilation, as he saw it, was to get the young Indians off their reservations, away from their benighted elders, and into White-run schools. This meant, most importantly, getting Indian youths away from the influence and teachings of their religious leaders, the "medicine men," whom Morgan regarded as a principal force obstructing assimilation. The tribes were no longer a military threat; their ablest chiefs and warriors were dead or powerless; even the traditional political and economic structures of their societies were in tatters and disintegrating. It was the religious leaders, mostly, who were keeping Indianness alive.

Pretending to speak for Indian babies, Morgan told one of his audiences, "These helpless little ones cry out to us: If you leave us here to grow up in our present surroundings, what can we hope for? . . . Our lives will be at the mercy of the 'medicine man'; our religion will be a vile mixture of superstition, legends and meaningless ceremonies." Contrasting the doleful lot of young Indians on reservations with the blessings that would come to them with White men's education, he asked, "Shall they be disappointed? Shall their hopes be blasted? . . . Justice, philanthropy, patriotism, Christianity answer No! And let all the people, speaking through their representatives in Congress, answer No!! *Give the papoose a chance.*"

Morgan exemplified the overwhelming non-Indian sentiment about Native Americans and their cultures in the years following the last of the wars with Indians, and gave explicit voice to a policy of forced assimilation that wreaked havoc on Indians and their societies during the end of the nineteenth century and the first three decades of the twentieth. However, there was nothing new or original in his pronouncements. He was the inheritor of a long legacy of assimilationists, most of whom considered themselves well intentioned, with the best interests of the Indians at heart. What is astonishing is that they still exist today in large numbers. Like their antecedents, they would get rid of Indians by getting rid of Indianness.

Indianness may be many things, and mean something different, to different persons—the possession of certain cultural traits, blood relationships, beliefs and values, or a membership on a tribe's roll—but at its core there is, and always has been, a strong sense of the spiritual and the sacred. Whites rarely, if ever, were able to comprehend fully the religions of individual tribes. Though they probed and inquired, few of them could equate what they heard or observed with anything that was familiar in their own religious systems, and what the great majority could not fathom, it dismissed as something other than what it knew as religion. It was heathenism, superstition, fakery, witchcraft—all of it barbaric and contemptible. Yet, as Morgan and many others sensed, the Native Americans' religion, whatever it was, was the force that held Indian societies together, and the natives' religious leaders were the principal agents in keeping them Indian.

Historically, there was no such thing as a single Indian religion;

spiritual concepts and systems differed from tribe to tribe. All of them, however, served the same individual and collective purposes, working for the survival, unity, and well-being of the people, ensuring order, balance, and harmony, and providing answers to such basic questions of life as: "Who am I?" "Where did I come from?" "Where am I going?" "What are the meaning and purpose of my existence?" "What is my relationship to others, to my group, to the rest of creation, and to the unseen world?"

Some of the systems were relatively simple in outward form, resting on traditionally defined relationships between individuals or communities and their shamans—men and women with strong spiritual powers that enabled them to communicate or intercede with the supernatural world and assist the people as foreseers of the future, as agents who could achieve desired ends through supernatural means, or as curers of ailments. (Thus the derogatory White terms for them such as "witch doctor" and "medicine man," despite the fact that most of them combined the practice of presently accepted psychosomatic medicine with the use of plants and other products of nature upon which modern-day medicine itself now relies.) But other Indian spiritual systems were so remarkably elaborate and complex that it was beyond the power of their participants to explain them fully to outsiders, even if they wished to do so—which they usually did not. Evolving over centuries, they combined, in wondrously sophisticated formulas, precise and intricate levels of concepts, beliefs, prayers, and rituals that, under methodically structured religious leadership and teaching, united the group and each individual with their universe and tied together in meaningful harmony humans, the landscape, the forces and creatures of nature, the heavens, and the supernatural.

Most, if not all, of the different systems stemmed from the peoples' origin myths. They taught that everything in the universe, including man, had a spiritual power, or life force, that all spiritual forces were interconnected, and that man therefore had a responsibility to that interconnection. The earth, which provided life and from which humans came, was sacred, and so was much else in Indian existence. Almost everywhere in the present-day United States there are locations, landmarks, and sites that were sacred to one or another tribe because they marked the boundaries of the tribe's universe, which was sacred, or were associated with sacred events or concepts, or with the departed souls of ancestors. Where a tribe still knows the sites, even though Whites have built upon them or flooded or plowed them over, they are still deemed sacred, though desecrated.

Legends, ceremonies, songs, dances, and arts were integrated parts of the spiritual systems, instructing the people not only in sacred matters but about many of the ends and purposes of the systems themselves—what the group expected of an individual, right and wrong behavior, and the position and obligations of each person within the group. The systems were further strengthened by sacred symbols—fetishes, pipes, painted designs, medicine bundles, shrines, the first runs of fish, and the first fruits of the harvest—that with the help of prayers and rituals made real and living the spiritual attachments between man and the seen and unseen world and assured food, well-being, and the satisfaction of the needs and wants of the society and its members.

The various Indian religions, in short, were awesomely pervasive and relentless, the inner skein of collective and individual life. As a daily community force, the spiritual content of a group, along with government and culture, formed what some tribes referred to as the sacred circle, or hoop, that held a people together. To individual Indians, deep spiritual feelings and reverence for all of creation were as much a part of their being as their physical features and personality. Spiritual power flowed like energy from their bodies, guiding their thoughts and actions by day and entering their dreams at night. It counseled and directed them throughout their lives, endowing them with values and a world view that gave meaning to their existence.

In light of the fundamentally religious nature of Indians and their societies, it was grimly ironic that Whites failed not only to appreciate the sophistication and role of Native American spiritual systems, but even to acknowledge their validity as religions, fulfilling for the Indians what their own religions provided for themselves. It was enough to know that Indians were heathens and savages: what passed for religion among them, it was deemed, were only meaningless practices, superficial and without substance, observed because of the fear of malevolent medicine men, and easily abandoned once the religion of the White man was made known to them. In their earnestness to convert Indians to Christianity, few early missionaries ever recognized the extent of the dependence of Indian societies on their religious systems and the consequent enormity of what the Whites expected the Indians to give up. In a way, it was something like urging them to shed their own skin and fit their flesh and frame into a new one.

Indians by the thousands did accept Christianity, usually under duress and especially after the defeat and collapse of their societies, the deaths of their leaders, and the decimation of their populations by White men's aggressions and diseases. But even after such disasters, many of the Native Americans struggled only to don the new skin of Christianity over the old one of their own spiritual system, retaining both. In time, what occurred was another form of genocide. White pressures mounted inexorably, and determined assimilationists like Morgan strove with unrestrained power and every method possible to wipe out Native American spiritualism as the fountainhead of continued Indianness.

The roots of the assimilationists' aggression against Indian religions went back to colonial days. From the prejudices and fears of the first atrocity-filled wars with Native Americans in Virginia and New England emerged the conviction among the settler-invaders and their descendants that Indians in their native state and Whites could not live together in peace because the Indian, unconquered, was a hostile savage. If the Indian submitted, cut his hair, dressed like a White, lived as a White, became a Christian—in short, was assimilated and no longer an Indian —he might survive. Otherwise, he was to be pushed a safe distance away from White society, isolated and rendered harmless, both physically and in his capacity to influence White society; or he was to be annihilated.

These three options ran thereafter like threads through the course of White-Indian relations and, with slight variations and disguises, continue to confront Native Americans today. The goal of ultimate assimilation is still the taproot of government policy, supported by general American opinion. Indian uniqueness amid the body politic, reservation islands with different beliefs, values, and lifeways within state boundaries, and frictions over land, water, and other resources between tribes and their neighbors are still disturbing to White populations, but there no longer exists a safe place of exile to which to remove the Indians. The policy of extermination, epitomized in the saying "The only good Indian is a dead Indian," gradually lost its acceptance after the final pacification of the western tribes, but in its place have come police and government terrorism and imprisonment of Indian nationalists and "troublemakers" and a widely shared belief that those who refuse to shed their Indianness and become fully assimilated will be annihilated anyway, rotting away in poverty, backwardness, and self-chosen deprivation on their reservations, and eventually dying off.

Throughout the years, missionaries and the churches played a central role in the assimilation process. Their ostensible goal was to convert the heathen and save souls, but inevitably that aim, which implied the wrenching away of Indians from their own religious leaders and systems, was a solid and indispensable first step to getting the Native Americans to stop being Indians and become Whites. Numerous bold and zealous missionaries, including Spanish and French priests in the Southwest, the Great Lakes region, and the Mississippi Valley and such Protestants as John Eliot in Massachusetts and Marcus Whitman in Oregon, are celebrated in histories as bringers of the light to Indians, but the light was usually more than religion alone.

Although some of the missionaries were content simply to contest shamans and native priests for Indian souls, most of them, with various motives, became full-fledged assimilationists. Many of them felt that religious conversion would be made easier or, indeed, would only be possible if the Indians first, or simultaneously, were settled down, peaceably or forcibly, around a mission or, in isolated centers, made to live like Whites and adopt the skills and arts of civilization and be given education. Others in different parts of the continent turned piety into greed and used assimilation unabashedly as a means to dispossess the Indians and acquire their lands and resources. Still other missionaries, driven by what they regarded as humanitarian feeling, tried to turn Indians into Whites as quickly as possible in the belief that it would protect the Indians not only from the erroneous ways of their false prophets but from annihilation by Indian-hating Whites. If they became Whites themselves, they would, it was assumed, be safe from White aggressors.

In times of stress, however, it often turned out that Christianized Indians, well on their way to missionary-guided assimilation, were not safe. John Eliot's converts, isolated in towns of "praying Indians" in Massachusetts, fell victim to the wrath of New England settlers during King Philip's War in 1675–76, and many of them were murdered or sold into slavery. At Lancaster, Pennsylvania, exasperated frontiersmen massacred a settlement of peaceful, Christianized Conestoga Indians during the height of border warfare in 1763. Christianity, also, proved of little help to the Cherokee and other so-called civilized tribes who were driven by troops from their homes and farms in the Southeast in the early nineteenth century. Numerous similar instances could be cited.

Whatever their personal motives, the missionaries helped the assimilationists. They disrupted Indian societies and sowed seeds of doubt and friction among the native peoples. They caused factions, feuds, and schisms, discredited popular leaders and imposed new ones on the Indians, and in scores of ways (including the inadvertent introduction of European diseases) undermined and weakened the unity of the tribes and their ability to resist the White man and protect their lands and resources. Wherever the missionary worked, the Indian spiritual system, the heart of tribal life, was his target. Whatever success he scored eroded that system, caused confusion, and made it easier for White traders, military men, and government agents to make further inroads on the tribal structure and the Indianness of the people.

After the establishment of the United States, the government recognized most missionaries as able allies in dealings with tribes. Believing them to be charitable, politically disinterested, reliable interpreters of the language as well as of Indian ways, and apt to be trusted by the Indians, government agents, soldiers, and treaty commissioners found many uses for them and, in return, generally supported their activities. If there was fault to be found with them, it was in their tendency to take the Indians' side in conflicts with aggressive White frontiersmen and with such government policies as the forced removal of the eastern tribes to the western side of the Mississippi River—actions that interfered with the missionaries' goal of conversion. But, in general, Congress and the administrations in Washington regarded them as the best civilizing influence and came to rely on them increasingly as agents to guide the Indians toward assimilation.

Inevitably, as missionaries and the churches that backed them assumed or were assigned a greater role in Indian relations in the field, the powers of church and state became mixed, and missionary activities were sometimes subsidized by the federal government. Doubling as teachers, agricultural and mechanical arts instructors, doctors, advisers, and, at times, spokesmen for some of the tribes, many missionaries intruded more authoritatively in Indian affairs than the official agents of the government. They dabbled in intratribal matters, interfered in family and clan concerns, assisted favorites to leadership and tried to destroy those who opposed them, continued to create schisms, and worked tirelessly to undermine the traditional cultures of tribes and "civilize" their members.

In the years after the Civil War, their power over Indians reached a dramatic climax. Responding to the pressure of well-meaning reformers, humanitarians, and prominent churchmen who were scandalized by the continuing Indian wars in the West and by revelations of graft and corruption among government reservation agents, President Grant in 1869 began turning over the full responsibility for the administration of Indian agencies to American churches and missionary bodies, whose assumed honesty and charitable motives were expected to give them more success in achieving the pacification and assimilation of the tribes. Contrary to the Constitution, though nobody seemed to mind or to notice it, a power of the state, in this unprecedented development, was delegated to the church. Within three years, some seventy-three Indian agencies had been apportioned among the Presbyterians, Methodists, Catholics, Lutherans, Quakers, Congregationalists, Reformed Dutch, Episcopalians, Baptists, and other denominations whose missionaries and representatives filled the office of agent and were in full charge of educational and other activities on the reservations.

On the whole, it was a disaster for most of the tribes. Some of the new agents lived up to expectations and acquitted themselves honorably. Others proved as corrupt and incompetent as their predecessors. But on many reservations the missionary agents, fanatically determined to Christianize their wards and destroy everything they considered heathenish, reigned without restraint as bigoted dictators. With their authority backed by troops, they tyrannized the Indians with orders that banned Indian ceremonies and dances, the telling of Indian legends and myths, and all other manifestations of Indian religion. Offenders, particularly medicine men who tried to resist them, were treated sternly, subjected to harassment and to a variety of harsh punishments that ranged from the withholding of rations to imprisonment, exile to the Indian Territory, or death.

The policy of entrusting reservations to the churches ultimately failed, but not because of opposition by the Indians or the public's concern about what the missionaries were doing to them. The different denominations took to fighting in unseemly fashion among themselves over the disposition of the reservations, making no secret of their resentment at the real or imagined favoring of rivals. Some failed to raise enough money each year to support their agents and abandoned or lost interest in the undertaking. In Washington, it was seen that many of the missionary agents were no improvement over the government ones, and during the Hayes administration politicians, eager to regain control of jobs and boodle on the reservations, killed the policy.

This, however, did not end the assault on Indian religion, institutions, or culture. The harsh era of missionary control set patterns for the treatment of Indians under the policy of forced assimilation that ensued during the next fifty years. Civil agents, still supported during most of that period by the military, continued to look for help from missionaries, and the alliance of agent, soldier, and missionary subjected Indians to an even tighter and more effective dictatorship than before, doing everything that the government felt necessary to break down and destroy Indianness, including Indian religion.

The government's official mandate to force a final solution of "the Indian problem" was clear. "If it is the purpose of the Government to civilize the Indians," said Secretary of the Interior Henry M. Teller in 1883, "they must be compelled to desist from the savage and barbarous practices that are calculated to continue them in savagery . . . nonprogressive degraded Indians are allowed to exhibit before the young and susceptible children all the debauchery, diabolism, and savagery of the worst state of the Indian race. Every man familiar with Indian life will bear witness to the pernicious influence of these savage rites and heathenish customs. . . . These dances, or feasts, as they are sometimes called, ought, in my judgment, to be discontinued, and if the Indians now supported by the Government are not willing to discontinue them, the agents should be instructed to compel such discontinuance. . . . [A] great hindrance to the civilization of the Indian is the influence of the medicine men, who are always found with the anti-progressive party. The medicine men resort to various artifices and devices to keep the people under their influence. . . . Steps should be taken to compel these impostors to abandon this deception and discontinue their practices, which are not only without benefit to the Indians but positively injurious to them."

Government regulations, promulgated in Washington, included the following: "Any Indian who shall engage in the sun dance, scalp dance, or war dance, or in any other similar feast, so called, shall be deemed guilty of an offense, and upon conviction thereof shall be punished for the first offense by the withholding of his rations for not exceeding ten days or by imprisonment for not exceeding ten days. . . . Any Indian who shall engage in the practices of so-called medicine men, or who shall resort to any artifice or device to keep the Indians of the reservation from adopting and following civilized habits and pursuits, or shall adopt any means to prevent the attendance of children at school, or shall use any arts of a conjurer to prevent Indians from abandoning their barbarous rites and customs, shall be deemed to be guilty of an offense, and upon conviction thereof, for the first offense shall be imprisoned for not less than ten nor more than thirty days. . . ."

At the agencies, enthusiastic missionaries zealously helped implement these orders. Indian children were taken forcibly from their families and sent off to schools, many of them far distant from their reservations. When tribal leaders objected, they were held back by troops or thrown into jail. The structure of Indian societies was undermined and dismantled, and traditional Indian cultural traits were ridiculed and banned. People were taught to be ashamed of their ancestors (savages), of their heritage (barbarism), and of their own Indianness (inferior to Whites). Every overt manifestation of the spiritual content that had held Indian society together was banned by an encompassing Religious Crimes Code that effectively ended freedom of religion for the Indians. The great legacy of Indian myth and legend, music, dance, and art was derided and almost wiped out. Indian philosophy and knowledge were regarded as worthless. Indian children were even beaten and punished for speaking their own languages in school.

Throughout this period, Indians objected, resisted, and suffered. Under such relentless pressure, the religions and cultures of many of the tribes were shorn of their strength. Some people, whom the Whites termed "progressives," accepted the steadily hammered lesson that the day of the Indian was over, and became willing to try to follow the White man's road. The rate of conversion to Christianity differed from one reservation to another, according to the abilities and methods of the missionaries. The Episcopalians and Catholics counted many converts among the Sioux tribes, as did the Presbyterians among the Nez Perces in Idaho. But after fifteen years of effort among the Gila Pimas in Arizona, a Presbyterian had baptized only one convert.

At the same time, oppression was largely counterproductive, alienating great numbers of Indians, stiffening their determination to resist adopting the White man's ways, and turning them against acceptance of government programs. Some of their own religions went underground, many underwent changes and were adapted to new conditions and new ideas, and some new religions like the Native American Church, combining aspects of Christianity and traditional native systems, arose. But wholesale assimilation failed, and the basic spiritual nature of Indians— inherited from generations of ancestors and still providing Native Americans with the principal source and meaning of their identity as Indians and as members of their individual tribes and groups—survived. As late as the 1920's, awareness that Indian spiritual systems still existed set off another wave of hysteria among assimilationists, in and out of government, against "obscene" Indian religions. Missionaries redoubled their efforts, and churches, Gospel missions, and Bible societies multiplied on the reservations, the old established denominations being forced to compete with such new arrivals as the Holiness Church, the Assembly of God, the Church of the Nazarene, the Brethren in Christ, and the Mennonites.

By then, however, American public opinion was beginning to change concerning the Indians' constitutional right to practice their own religions, and many intellectuals and White supporters of the Indians, including John Collier, a scrappy young social reformer who had settled in New Mexico, ridiculed the assimilationists' bigotry, and fought against the new wave of repression. Finally, in 1934, the New Deal administration of Franklin D. Roosevelt, with Collier as Commissioner of Indian Affairs, secured the passage of an Indian Reorganization Act, which, among other reforms, at last restored to the tribes freedom of religion and the right to revive their own cultures.

But assimilationism was not dead, and attacks on Indian religion continued. In the 1950's, a reversal in national Indian policy occurred, and the Eisenhower administration supported congressional efforts to revive and hurry along the assimilation process by terminating all federal relations with the tribes, ending treaty obligations, and turning the reservations over to the states in which they were located. Throughout this "termination" period—which was halted in 1958 because of the injustices and economic hardships suffered by the first tribes on which the new policy was imposed—assimilation-minded senators and others condemned defenders of the Indian Reorganization Act, including its guarantee of the Indians' right to practice their own religion, as "culturists" who insisted on keeping the Indians in a state of backwardness and ignorance. On many reservations, even after the government abandoned the termination policy, Indian freedom of religion was neither enforced nor observed. Agents of the Bureau of Indian Affairs looked away from, or even encouraged, missionaries who continued to break up Indian ceremonies or interfere with and punish individual Indians and their families when they tried to revive languages, arts, and other aspects of their traditional cultures. Clashes with missionaries, attempting to disrupt native-style weddings, dances, and other old-time customs, occurred among the Apaches in Arizona and the Northern Cheyennes in Montana. Mormon missionaries, interfering with the Menominees in Wisconsin, were ejected by the people from the reservation, and in 1965 a Catholic priest who tried to halt traditional Indian dances was led out of Isleta pueblo in New Mexico in handcuffs by the angry native governor of the town.

Even today, many Native Americans experience the hostility toward their religious beliefs and practices that is the continued hallmark of those who still wish to force their assimilation. But the freedoms proclaimed by the Indian Reorganization Act in 1934 were a turning point, and the stage was set for what, in fact, by the 1970's became a remarkable revival of the vitality and influence of Indian spiritualism, with significance not alone for Native Americans, but for the whole United States. In the ferment of the rights revolution of the 1950's and 1960's, of the questioning of the values, superiority, and solidity of the dominant White American culture, including its religious institutions, and of the Indians' own struggle for self-determination, Indians in great numbers—particularly, at first, young people, and then also their parents—began to seek out and turn back to old ways and beliefs. Surprisingly, they found that much had never died, that large parts of many tribes still lived in a traditional manner, and that numerous Indian spiritual leaders and counselors still existed who could instruct them.

Among the Iroquois people of New York State, who had been engulfed by Whites for almost two centuries, the traditional chiefs and religious instructors of the Longhouse acquired new followers and influence, and the institutions and heritage of the Confederacy of the Six Nations, which united traditional Iroquois of the United States and Canada, gained new vitality and strength. "Indians are confused in the White man's world," said Ray Fadden, a Mohawk traditionalist teacher in 1973, "and an Indian who is confused is the most confused. They are questioning the White men's values that their parents accepted and are searching for something different. They [Mohawks, Senecas, and other Iroquois] have found it in the Longhouse. In the Longhouse, they feel like an Indian—people all together—brotherhood. They no longer feel defeated. The Indian spirit is still there, unbroken. We are glad that they are coming back, because coming back means refusing to become a vanishing people. They are finding their personal identity. They see that for them Christian values are inferior to Indian ways. They are reaffirming Indian traditional values, and they are becoming strong again because they know who they are."

Similar revivals of Indian spiritual strength occurred in all parts of the country during the 1970's. Around Puget Sound in Washington State, members of small tribes that had lost most of their ancestral lands, and had become, to their White neighbors, almost indistinguishable as Indians sought instruction in old ways and values from the few remaining traditionalists among them, demanded respect for Indian children and Indian cultures in the public schools, and formed a spiritually based "Indian survival" association that gave leadership to the fight for fishing rights and to a "Trail of Broken Treaties" protest trek across the United States to the nation's capital in 1972. Among the Chippewas of Minnesota and the Sioux of the Dakotas, the number of Indians seeking spiritual assistance from the holy people on their reservations swelled. Sioux medicine men, often the most influential force among local communities on their reservations, not only provided spiritual purpose and strength to the movements for tribal self-determination and sovereignty, but found many people, including Christian Indians, coming back to them for cultural teaching and medical assistance.

Indian prisoners, at the same time, in penitentiaries and state prisons in Oklahoma, Nevada, Wyoming, Washington, South Dakota, and other states, who for years had been forced to accept the ministries of Catholic and Protestant chaplains, argued for and won the right to have sweat lodges in the prisons in which they could worship, pray, and purify themselves in the traditional Indian manner, to be visited by tribal holy men, and to have access to the Sacred Pipe and wear their hair long, according to the traditional and sacred tenets of their tribes. On the reservations themselves, religious dances and ceremonies like the Sun Dance were revived, and the people supported their religious teachers' demands to be allowed to employ the traditional objects and symbols that would give them integrity and make them effective.

"We need to get mescal, sumacs, berries, and cane from the mosquero," a Mescalero Apache told government officials in 1979. "We use that for religious purposes. And for the Indian [eagle] feathers which are not free to us, we have to steal them to get it, and that's not fair. As for the white person, they don't have to steal for their religion; they don't have to fight for their religion. But our Indian people have to fight, and that's not fair. We should be free to get our eagle feathers as we wish, as we did a long time ago."

On the plains, various tribal members, also in 1979, explained to the government that they still needed buffalo meat for certain religious feasts: "Some ceremonies require the presence of a live buffalo among the participants. In other religions, certain ceremonies cannot begin until the participants have eaten buffalo tongue, and some cannot continue unless a buffalo skull is available." Some religious counselors also told of a "spiritual sickness" that occurred when their people were unable to see and live near buffalo.

In Alaska and the Northwest, Athapascans, Yakimas, Colvilles, and others, complaining of fishing and hunting restrictions, recounted the need for salmon, moose, and deer in their religious ceremonies. Such pleas won support within the government, and by the start of the 1980's the BIA and other federal agencies made formal efforts to provide at least some of the tribes with what they required for religious purposes.

The strengthening of Indian spiritualism was accompanied by the growth of a new, almost Pan-Indian influence among the traditional chiefs and religious teachers. Some of them provided spiritual counsel and comfort to the activist participants, who came from many different tribes, at Alcatraz, the takeover of the Bureau of Indian Affairs Building in Washington, D.C., the siege at Wounded Knee, and other headline-making confrontations in the 1960's and 1970's. Many of them, like Oren Lyons, an Onondaga traditionalist chief and teacher, Philip Deere, a Creek medicine man, Thomas Banyacya, interpreter for the Hopi traditional chiefs, and Franklin Fools Crow, Leonard Crow Dog, and John Fire, Sioux medicine men, became known and influential among Indian peoples throughout the country. Moreover, the religious leaders and medicine societies of different native groups often worked together to further Indianness and assist certain all-Indian causes. In 1978, some of them traveled to Geneva with members of the International Indian Treaty Council, a Pan-Indian group, to urge the United Nations Commission on Human Rights to halt the genocide of all native peoples. Two years later, the members of the large Medicine Men Association on the Sioux Rosebud reservation in South Dakota won support from other traditional Indians and their native spiritual counselors for their effort to halt the making of a TV film based on the book *Hanta Yo,* which they asserted distorted Sioux traditional religion and culture and would reinforce assimilationist bigotry and pressure against the Sioux peoples.

Indian spiritualism was also spread by the proliferation of tribally operated elementary and high schools, using Indian teachers and tribally prepared histories and teaching materials, and by Indian-run colleges like the Deganawidah-Quetzalcoatl University (part Indian, part Chicano) at Davis, California, the Navajo Community College in Arizona, and Sinte Gleska College of the Lakotas (Teton Sioux Brulés) at Rosebud, South Dakota. But a major influence, also, was the tribes' own struggles for rights and justice, which aroused patriotic sentiments among the people, especially when they involved spiritual matters.

Tribes fought—and are still fighting—to protect cemeteries and sacred sites on reservations from coal and uranium strip mines, power plants, reservoirs, railroads, highways, transmission lines, and other desecrating developments. They opposed pothunters, collectors, museum expeditions, and archaeologists who dug up their ancestors' graves and carried away their remains and artifacts without tribal permission or supervision. But, increasingly, they sought to protect sacred sites off the reservations, objecting to ski resorts, lumber operations, and other activities that defiled sacred mountains and other terrain features or locations which they still deemed holy and used in the practice of their religions. In 1979, the Sioux and Northern Cheyennes were able, after a protracted struggle, to save Bear Butte, a ceremonial and religious site near the Black Hills in South Dakota, from real estate developers by persuading the Bureau of Indian Affairs to buy it and hold it in trust for the tribes. Wichitas and other Indians in Oklahoma fought for permission to worship at a site on the Fort Sill firing range where the Indians claimed their ancestors had first seen the Great Spirit. And in Arizona, Hopis, Zuñis, and Navajos contested zealously the desecration by recreationists of their sacred San Francisco Peaks, the abode of spiritual beings upon whom the tribes depend for life, the source of many of the physical objects used by healers and medicine men, a place for Indian prayer and ceremony, and the possessors of an "inner form" that makes them deities themselves who preserve the traditions, songs, prayers, and culture of the tribes for future generations. Such spiritually based struggles have inevitably done much to revive and spread Indian religious feeling and the appeal and influence of native spiritual leaders, and at the same time have raised tribal and Indian consciousness and pride.

In view of the many years of stern religious oppression endured by the tribes, it is remarkable that so many followers of traditional ways and religions survived long enough to shepherd today's spiritual revival. If anything, however, most non-Indian Americans still overrate the appeal that their own culture and religious systems have for others, permitting the obvious conclusion that lessons not learned from relations with Indians have contributed to more recent grievous lessons in Vietnam, Islamic lands, and elsewhere overseas. Among the Papago Indians in Arizona, it was found in 1972 that only eleven of fifty-one villages or settlements on the reservation could be considered "modern" and acculturated, even by minimum White standards. Twenty-eight were still strongholds of traditionalism, with native healers, ritual structures, traditional-type dwellings, and an ingrained resistance to modernization and outside influence. The remaining twelve villages were somewhere in between the old and the new. Even in Oklahoma, some 30 percent of the Cherokees, generally regarded as among the most "civilized" and acculturated of all major American tribes, are not Christian but practice their own traditional religion at stomp grounds. Another 40 to 50 percent attend Cherokee churches, which are basically Cherokee institutions with services conducted in the Cherokee language, and with native prayers and hymns. Most of the deacons are Cherokee medicine men and traditional leaders.

Within the United States of the 1980's, this is only the tip of an iceberg. Traditional peoples, still following the counsel and teachings of shamans, native priests, and medicine men, exist in scores of tribes, sometimes forming the majority of those populations. In addition, there are tens of thousands of others who outwardly seem wholly or partly assimilated but who share the beliefs and values of the traditionalists, often participate with them in traditional tribal functions and ceremonies, support traditional leaders and teachers, and seek their spiritual aid. The fact that they continue to be so numerous may be either galling or wondrous to Whites, depending on their point of view, but behind that fact in every case is the universal phenomenon of man's determined will to fight for his way of life, a force that gives meaning and direction to human existence. If the history of Indian-White relations has been one of unending attempts to assimilate the Indians, it has also been one of continued struggles by the Indians to preserve their religions and spiritual unity and strength. Among all such chronicles of resistance, one of the longest and most persevering and dramatic has been that of the Indians of Taos pueblo in northeastern New Mexico. They were among the first Native Americans in the present-day United States to be forced to defend their religion, and they have had to continue to fight for it to this day. Yet the Taos spiritual system remains largely what it was when the Spaniards first came on Taos and marked its people for conversion to Christianity almost 450 years ago.

Taos—whose history this chapter will examine—is one of twenty autonomous Pueblo groups in the Southwest, including the Hopis in Arizona, the Zuñis, Acomas, and Lagunas in western New Mexico, and sixteen others in the valleys of the Rio Grande and some of its tributaries north and south of Albuquerque. Taos, with a modern-day population of about 1,500, is the most northerly, lying just outside of the non-Indian town of Taos and extending upward from a 7,000-foot-high arid plateau of cottonwoods, willows, and rabbit brush to the dark, pine-covered slopes of the Sangre de Cristo Mountains. The Spaniards gave them the name Pueblos because they found them living a settled existence in towns. Taos' name is a Spanish corruption of the native Tua or Teo, and the original name of its townsite was Teotho, meaning roughly the "village" or "houses of the people."

To many non-Indian artists, writers, and tourists, Taos pueblo has long had an unusual appeal, not only because its people have been able to keep intact so much of their native culture, but because of the timeless feeling of their earthen-colored town, which continues to retain a centuries-old appearance. Within its adobe walls, dominating the pueblo, are two large, classic-style Pueblo houses, each rising for several stories in terraced tiers and containing numerous apartment-like rooms on each level. The two large buildings, known as the North House and the South House, and belonging to the two moieties, or halves (the Winter People and the Summer People) into which the tribe is divided, face each other across a large plaza, bisected by a stream, the Rio Pueblo de Taos, that comes down from the mountains with life-giving water for the pueblo.

There are many similarities among all the Pueblos, but also many cultural and linguistic differences. Reflecting a variety of ancestral strains in their backgrounds, they speak a number of different, mutually unintelligible languages. The Hopis speak Hopi, derived from the Uto-Aztecan language stock of many other southwestern and Mexican tribes; the Zuñis speak Zuñi, which has not yet been satisfactorily related to any other language; and the rest speak Keresan tongues or Tiwa, Tewa, or Towa dialects of the family of Tanoan languages. The people of Taos are Tiwa-speaking Tanoans.

All of the Pueblo peoples are descended from some of the oldest-known inhabitants of the hemisphere, originally big-game hunters and gatherers who made their way south from Alaska and have lived in the Southwest for at least 12,000 years. When the large Ice Age animals disappeared from the region, the people adapted to a pattern of life known as the Desert Culture, which extended into the Southwest from the Great Basin and which persisted, almost without change, for thousands of years. Roaming in small groups within limited areas, they hunted and trapped small animals, rodents, birds, and reptiles and gathered grass seeds, mesquite beans, yucca fruits, pine nuts, berries, certain insects, and anything else that was edible. They used hides, vegetable fibers, and rabbit fur for blankets and articles of clothing, developed the use of stone milling implements like metates and manos to grind wild foods, and dwelt in rock overhangs, caves, and dome-shaped wickiups. One widespread sequence of gatherers in the eastern half of the region, known to archaeologists for their particular traits as people of the Cochise tradition, eventually developed several cultures that led or contributed to that of the Pueblos.

The earliest of these was the Mogollon, which emerged about 300 B.C. in the higher country east and west of the southern part of the border between present-day Arizona and New Mexico. Knowledge of how to grow corn, diffusing north from Mexico, had reached groups in that region around 3000 B.C. But the corn was too primitive a type for effective agriculture, and it was not until about 500 B.C. that a new strain—together with beans and squash, which had appeared about 1000 B.C.—enabled some of the peoples to make cultivated crops an important part of their diet. By 300 B.C. agriculture had spread, and many groups were settling down near their plots in small settlements of round, and later quadrangular, semi-subterranean pit houses. At the same time, the skill of pottery-making reached them, also from Mexico.

Although larger and more secure food supplies and the clustering of families in settled village life led to an increase in population, the start of complex social and religious organizations, and an advance in the fashioning of a variety of functional articles, the Mogollon people retained many of their Desert Culture traits, still gathering wild foods and hunting animals and birds. After A.D. 1, the atlatl, or spear-thrower, a hunting weapon of great antiquity, was supplanted by the bow and arrow, which seems to have been introduced from the north. For more than 1,000 years after that, however, there were few significant changes in the Mogollon culture, save for the development of a series of more sophisticated pottery styles. Then, about A.D. 1100, the Mogollon Indians began to construct Pueblo-style buildings—aboveground structures of contiguous rooms, built principally of stone. This new practice came to them from the Anasazi, a second and more dynamic culture that had arisen over a large area farther north, on the arid plateau of the Four Corners country (where present-day Colorado, Utah, Arizona, and New Mexico meet), centered on the drainages of the San Juan, Little Colorado, and northern Rio Grande rivers. From then on, the Mogollon people generally adopted Anasazi ways and, except for certain different regional patterns, the two cultures became essentially alike.

The name "Anasazi" is a Navajo word meaning "ancient ones," and was applied by the Navajos to the ruins and remains of a people who had disappeared from the Four Corners region when the Navajos first reached it sometime between A.D. 1300 and 1500 and made it their home.

By then, however, the people who had disappeared—the Anasazis—had become Pueblos and were living elsewhere.

Although the Anasazi culture started later than the Mogollon and received knowledge of agriculture and other important traits from the Mogollon people, its pace of development eventually far outstripped that of the southerners. From their beginning, about A.D. 1, the Anasazis were particularly adept at weaving basketry containers, sandals, and other goods of vegetable fibers, and archaeologists often refer to them as "Basket Makers" during the period of their transition from the Desert Culture. By A.D. 100, some of the groups had begun to settle down in permanent or semi-permanent domed shelters of logs and mud mortar, and during the next fifty years they acquired the knowledge of pottery-making, probably from the Mogollons. Agriculture, however, did not become important among them until A.D. 400–450.

Between A.D. 400 and 700, they made great strides. The cultivation of corn and squash intensified, and increasing numbers of people drew together in permanent clusters of circular pit houses, lined with stone, roofed with wood, and entered via an antechamber or through a hole in the roof. The houses were built in rock overhangs of cliffs or in large caves. New strains of corn increased productivity, and beans and cotton were also planted. As the years passed, development quickened: turkeys were domesticated and their feathers sewn into feather cloth and cloaks; the stone ax and bow and arrow came into use; skills in basketry and textile production increased; and various religious and decorative ornaments were made of wood, shell, turquoise, seeds, stone, and lignite.

After A.D. 700, architectural skills and innovations increased, and the foundations of the Pueblo culture became so strong that the Anasazis thereafter are referred to as Pueblos. Buildings of contiguous rooms, arranged in straight lines or crescents, were erected aboveground, most of them of stone plastered with adobe, others with walls of poles and adobe. As population grew, demanding more extensive communal activity and leadership, religious and social organizations became more elaborate. Family members of clans and village societies drew together in the buildings of contiguous rooms, and pit houses were turned into round or D-shaped subterranean kivas, ceremonial centers and meeting rooms for the men, entered by a ladder leading down from a smoke hole in the roof. With surplus crops, some people had leisure time to satisfy aesthetic impulses. More beautiful and creative spiritual and personal articles were made, and craftsmen and artisans proliferated.

Pueblo culture continued to develop until about A.D. 1300, reaching a climactic period of radiance and widespread influence after A.D. 1100. Pueblo population expanded rapidly and spread into new areas. Some villages grew into large, compact towns of several thousand people, and in places like Chaco Canyon in northwestern New Mexico, the busy centers were connected by thirty-foot-wide roads to scores of smaller outlying settlements. Buildings increased in size, and both architecture and town planning were formalized, designed to harmonize with spiritual systems. Towns were built on mesa tops and in the recesses of cliff walls, as well as on canyon floors, and some of them possessed multi-tiered buildings of up to four stories. Kiva architecture reflected religious concepts, and for a time a single large ceremonial chamber, or Great Kiva, came into use in different towns.

In the canyons and valleys, as well as on open flatlands near the settlements, gardens flourished. In a land of sparse rain and near-desert conditions, the Pueblos became skilled agriculturists, learning where and how to plant to get the most benefit from the moisture of snow and what little rain there was and from the periodic flooding of intermittent streams. Some people practiced small-scale irrigation, diverting stream water to their crops, and there is evidence, also, of the use of sophisticated methods of astronomical observation that told the towns' leaders the proper times to plant, cultivate, and harvest. Nevertheless, the production of corn was a major preoccupation and concern, and the lives of the people revolved around a cyclical pattern of community prayers and thanksgiving dances for rain, snow, and bountiful crops.

The sphere of Pueblo influence extended across almost the entire Southwest. Trade and other contacts with peoples of different cultures, including the Hohokams and Sinaguas of southern and central Arizona, introduced new ideas and traits to the Pueblos, adding to the richness of their culture (irrigation was probably learned from the Hohokams, who had developed massive canal systems). But most of the other peoples adopted far more from the Pueblos, so that in time their lifeways came increasingly to resemble those of the Pueblo peoples. In some places, there were migrations and mixings of populations. Outsiders from other tribes farther west and in the Great Basin adopted various Pueblo traits or joined Pueblo communities, losing their previous identity but adding to the diverse strains making up the Pueblos. At the same time, the trade routes from Mexico brought parrots, copper bells, and other items, as well as certain Mexican ideas and influences, into the Pueblo country. It was a classic age of high civilization and activity. Pueblo skill and artistry produced outpourings of beautiful painted pottery, among the finest the world has ever known, turquoise jewelry, colored cotton and feather cloth, bracelets, necklaces, and other decorative objects—some created in rich mosaic work—girdles, belts, robes, and clay figurines, possibly effigies associated with spiritual beliefs.

This period of vitality and splendor gradually came to an end. Even as it reached its height, Pueblo influence had begun to wane and disappear on the northern and western edges of the Pueblos' country; their settlements, for reasons not yet known, began to withdraw and consolidate with those of other peoples, shrinking the boundaries of Pueblo territory. In the last quarter of the thirteenth century, the abandonment of villages and towns accelerated rapidly, probably because of a severe twenty-three-year drought from 1276 to 1299 that eroded the farmlands with arroyos and brought agricultural disaster. In one area after another, Pueblo groups left their great centers like Mesa Verde and Chaco Canyon and, guided by spiritual counsel, commenced new migrations to different locations, where they settled down among people who were already there or built new towns of their own.

Scattered over a wide area at their new sites, the Pueblos experienced a reflowering of their culture, particularly in central and southern Arizona, northern Mexico, the Hopi villages (composed of a mixture of people from different areas), the Zuñi country, Acoma, and the Rio Grande Valley. Old ways of life were carried on, and new traits appeared. Towns were designed with one or more large open spaces, or plazas, for outdoor ceremonies and dances, kivas were painted with murals of mythological figures and masked dancers—associated perhaps with the beginning of the Pueblos' Kachina cult—and glazed decorated pottery, as well as unglazed polychrome pottery, was introduced.

About 1450, a new wave of withdrawals and migrations occurred. Once more, towns and entire districts were abandoned, and by 1540, when the Spaniards entered their country, Pueblo peoples had left all parts of the Southwest save areas in and near the Rio Grande Valley and Acoma, the Zuñi country, and the Hopi villages farther west. At these consolidated sites, their culture persisted, differing in many details from one pueblo to the next, but based, among each people, on spiritual beliefs that had evolved and been developed to ensure their survival during the many centuries of their past.

At the heart of Pueblo spiritual life were the lessons, directions, and prophecies of their traditional histories, conveyed from one generation to the next in reverent oral narrations, ceremonies, sacred dances, and mime. Though the traditions differed in details and particulars that had special meaning for each group, they were all similar in their broad outlines. They told of the earliest ancestors entering this world from an underworld, emerging by a passage through the waters of a lake at a place in the north known as Sipapu, or a variant of that word. Guided by the Great Spirit, or the Creator and One above all others, who had helped them in their efforts to reach this world, they had begun a long period of migrations, led by war gods, other spirit forces, and war chiefs and their assistants. During their journeys, the Great Spirit had made them acquainted with how they must live and everything they must believe and do in order to have life continue beneficially for them. They had also been told what would befall them if they ignored or deviated from the instructions.

At length, the Creator had guided the individual groups to where they should live, and they had settled down in those places. They had built towns, taken up agriculture, which was also a gift from the spirit world, and had scrupulously followed the counsel that the Great Spirit had given them. Struggling for good against evil and keeping their lives in harmony with nature, they had overcome the obstacles of the harsh environment in which they had been placed, and had created good lives for themselves. But after hundreds of years, a drought had come, and, to save the people, the Great Spirit had impelled them to move again. In small groups, they had once more gone in different directions, and finally the Creator had given them their new homesites in which they were now dwelling. Again, they were told to live according to the Great Spirit's directions and were warned of new catastrophes if they failed to do so.

The lessons of history permeated and guided every aspect of Pueblo lives. Their principal teaching was the necessity of maintaining a harmonious relationship with everything in the world in which they lived. Everything—the land, the trees, the corn, the people, and all seen and unseen creatures and natural phenomena—was part of a great living force that held the world together. Each had a spirit, and the people's welfare demanded harmony between themselves and the entire spirit world. If it was maintained according to the Creator's directions, the interrelationship of man and the rest of the universe would stay in balance, undisturbed, and spirits of nature would provide the people with their necessities. Only man could upset the balance by doing something wrong. To avoid this, Pueblo society was tightly knit and rigidly conformist, ever watchful against any activity that might violate the Creator's directions. Institutions existed to carry out the routines of daily life and conduct ceremonies in a way that would ensure continued harmony with the spirit world. The people were expected to join the institutions and participate in the ceremonies in a proper way, for the slightest failure to conduct oneself correctly could upset the balance with nature and harm the whole community. Such harm could come from many things, including harboring bad thoughts, refusing to join in a ceremony, or failing to follow the precise details of costuming and movement which the ceremonies required.

Nevertheless, nonconformity and disputes over religious matters were not uncommon, and often, they led to factionalism and divisions among the people. When these disputes occurred, however, they could not be tolerated, for the safety of everyone was imperiled. They would be solved by the eviction of the malcontents, or by their voluntary departure to live with others or establish new settlements of their own.

Such insistence on conformity made the pueblos something of religious despotisms, with various leaders who possessed absolute authority over secular and religious affairs. The precise organization of life differed considerably from one pueblo to another, especially between those in the east and the west. Among the Hopis and other western pueblos, clan heads, both male and female, usually coming from a single household or lineage within each clan, ran the government, which was generally preoccupied with religious matters, particularly the prayers, ceremonies, and behavior that would ensure successful harvests in their near-desert country. At the head of each town or village was a hereditary chief who came from one specific clan. Though he did not have as much authority as the town chiefs in the east, he was an important and respected figure who provided counsel, settled arguments, apportioned the use of land among the families and clans, and could make final decisions.

In the east, along the Rio Grande, either clans did not exist or their authority and principal responsibilities had been supplanted by those of the elders of powerful religious-political associations, or societies, each one charged with the direction and conduct of an aspect of community life, such as the curing of illness, the control of weather, religious affairs, hunting, or warfare. It is thought that the development of large-scale irrigation works among the Rio Grande Valley pueblos, which required organized communal labor, had much to do with the growth of the societies' authority. Clans could not easily construct or maintain such big, jointly used projects, and after a non-kinship group, representing and mobilizing the whole pueblo, took over that responsibility, other associations may have gradually assumed the functions of various clans.

Everyone in a community belonged to one of the societies, which were headed by spiritual leaders and their assistants, and which differed among the various pueblos. The associations had specific areas of concern, such as medicine, hunting, and war, and conducted all activities and ceremonies related to their fields. Where there were moieties, as at Taos and among other Tanoans, the moieties also each had their own associations, whose leaders kept watch against evil spirits that brought sickness and death, served as curers and healers for their members, and supervised numerous aspects of community life. Alone, or working with other associations, they set dates for ceremonies and organized and directed them, coordinated purification rites conducted by the medicine societies, conducted communal hunts, coordinated and conducted war ceremonies, organized and directed the planting and harvesting of crops and the construction and cleaning of irrigation ditches, repaired and maintained the kivas, cleaned the plaza for dances and ceremonies, and nominated and installed town secular officers.

A Kachina cult, which originated among pueblos in the west, was also prevalent in many of the towns. Kachinas were beneficent supernatural beings, sometimes considered to be messengers of the gods, who visited the pueblos for a period of time and had the power to bring rain, good health, and community well-being if the people greeted them with proper, cheerfully observed ceremonies. They appeared in the form of birds, animals, and ancestral spirits with distinctive characteristics, and they were portrayed by masked, vividly garbed members of the cult. Their dances were often accompanied by the cavortings of members of a clown association, who, as town disciplinarians, ridiculed, censured, and even whipped those who had been guilty of offensive conduct.

Clans, societies, moieties, and the Kachina cult usually each had their own kivas, which were sometimes underground or partly so, but could also be round or square rooms built aboveground. Only men were allowed inside of them, entering by ladders lowered through openings in the roof. They were generally the holiest buildings in the pueblo, often containing altars that could be set up for religious observances and that served also as storage places for fetishes, sacred objects, and ceremonial costumes and paraphernalia. In the center of the floor of many kivas was a small hole, symbolizing Sipapu, the sacred passageway through which the first people had emerged on earth from the underworld. The kivas were used as meeting places for the men, as well as for religious discussions, decisions, and rituals. What went on inside of them was generally considered private and secret. At times of Kachina ceremonies, the male members of the cult entered the kiva and donned brilliantly painted and decorated costumes and masks that endowed them with the spirits and powers of the supernatural beings they impersonated. When they came streaming back up the ladder, the townspeople greeted them as spiritual beings who had returned for a visit through the sacred hole of Sipapu. There was no deception, for everyone, including the dancers, understood that the masks conveyed the spirits, and that the dances were necessary to bring good fortune.

The town chiefs in the east, to whom the Spaniards later gave the title *cacique,* the term for headman which they had learned from the Arawak Indians in the Caribbean, served for life and were exempt from ordinary town duties. They were the chief spiritual and ceremonial officers, usually came from a specific socioreligious association that ruled the day-to-day affairs of the village and whose members chose the *cacique,* and were the community's final word of religious counsel. They were expected to be humble, wise, and just, and conduct themselves in an honorable, spiritual manner, refraining from involvement in quarrels, and, by example, instructing the people in how to behave to keep their town in harmony with the spiritual world. Their assistants, often convened in councils, were usually powerful war chiefs, who were the living counterparts of the war gods, and the leaders of the medicine, and sometimes other, societies.

The centralized authority and crosscutting of society by kinship clans, moieties, and associations of the general population worked to tighten and solidify the populations of the towns and avoid serious schisms. Kinship groups might disagree with each other, but their members were also members of the same associations, which held them together. Parents, grandparents, the clown societies, and—as a last resort —the town leaders taught and enforced discipline. But the principal force for unity was the daily reminders of the people's ties to the spiritual world on which their survival depended. On their horizons they could see terrain landmarks that were sacred because the gods dwelled in them or because the Creator had designated them as the boundaries of the land he had given them. Immensely intricate patterns of relationships, developed from their history and religious instructions, bound them intimately, as individuals and groups, to scores of shrines and other sacred places on their lands, where prayer and the use of religious objects brought them into communion with the spiritual world and helped them maintain harmony, balance, and well-being. Religious obedience, the people understood, was the key to their existence. In a sense, as the members of the Indian Claims Commission noted when ruling on a Taos Indian case as recently as 1965, it created "a symbiotic relationship—the people, by their prayers and their religious functions, keep the land producing; and the land keeps the people."

It is believed that the modern-day Taos inhabitants are descendants of Tanoan-speaking Pueblo migrants from the Piedra or nearby Mesa Verde area in southwestern Colorado. Tanoan-speaking people were in the Rio Grande Valley before A.D. 1000, but there were additional Tanoan thrusts and major movements into the valley after that, and it is not certain when Taos was first settled. However, it is known that by 1300, the Taos Indians were already established in a village now referred to as Cornfield Taos near their present town. Their own history says that the Creator had led them there and designated the boundaries of the new homeland he was giving them. Like the other migrants to the Rio Grande, they kept their culture intact, obeyed the Great Spirit's instructions, planted new fields, and prospered. Sometime before 1400, they shifted their townsite from Cornfield Taos to its present location.

Though they cultivated corn, beans, and squash, the high altitude of their country made growing seasons short, and they had to rely on hunting and the gathering of wild foods to supplement their harvests. Altogether, they used and occupied some 300,000 acres. In the semi-arid country west of the Rio Grande, they pursued deer, antelope, rabbits, and other small game. In the wooded mountains to the north and east of their town, they hunted elk, bear, deer, mountain lions, bobcats, grouse, turkeys, hawks, eagles, and ducks, fished for trout, and gathered wild plants, roots, nuts, and berries, as well as wood for building and for fires. The flora and fauna supplied them with material for clothing, household utensils, and medicinal and religious needs, in addition to food.

Tucked within the mountains were many lakes, including Blue Lake, the source of the Rio Pueblo de Taos, which ran through their town and watered their gardens. To the Indians, many of the lakes were sacred for different reasons, but Blue Lake was especially holy. The Creator had given it to them as the source of their life and of the spiritual force of which they were a part. From the lake to the pueblo, the river was the tribe's heartline, and the whole mountain area that it drained was sacred and covered with shrines where the people prayed, paid honor to the spirits of animals, trees, and other elements of creation, gathered clay, plants, and other products for rituals, and conducted their most sacred ceremonies to maintain harmony with the spiritual world and keep the universe in balance. The canyons, wooded slopes, and meadows were used throughout the year for hunting, gathering, communion with nature, and other activities, but annually, toward the end of summer, the entire adult population of the pueblo made a pilgrimage up the river, from the town to Blue Lake, conducting ceremonies at one of the shrines along the way and at the lake. The yearly journey signified a return to their spiritual origins and bore witness to the Creator's teaching that the water, the land, and the people formed one interrelated and living whole.

In their northern location, the Taos Indians were also close to the plains, and over the years became familiar with some of the nomadic, buffalo-hunting peoples of the southern plains, who occasionally came on foot to the pueblo, sometimes to trade peacefully and at other times to raid for corn and various other products. When such trade-and-raid contacts began is not known, but the first of the nomadic visitors of record seem to have been bands of pedestrian Apaches. Even as the Pueblos were migrating to the Rio Grande, the Athapascan-speaking Apaches, in many different groups, were moving southward through the plains in a migration of their own that had begun in northwestern Canada and Alaska. By at least 1525 some of them were periodically raiding the easternmost pueblos, including Taos. On such occasions, the town walls and tall, fortresslike buildings honeycombed with rooms helped protect the pueblo inhabitants, whose warriors, led by the war chiefs, fought off the attackers with bows and arrows, wooden maces, and rocks. At times, also, groups from Taos trekked to Texas' Staked Plains and to western Kansas to hunt buffalo and antelope and met and camped peacefully with Apaches, Wichitas, and other plains peoples.

Such contacts led to the adoption by the Taos people of various plains cultural traits. They took to using certain articles of plains dress and wearing their hair in braids instead of tying it behind the head in the traditional Pueblo knot, or *chongo.* Some of the plains Indian dances were incorporated into their repertoire of social dances, and they also adopted the plains institution of relay races.

Even before then, however, they had developed certain cultural characteristics that differed more or less from those of other Pueblos. They were not alone in being divided into moieties, but in contrast to the usual practice elsewhere, their town chieftainship did not rotate between the moieties; the chief of their northside division was always the head chief of the town. They had no clans, the Kachina cult was only weakly developed among them, and they had a single joint communal kiva, as well as at least six separate ones, three belonging to the associations of each moiety.

In 1540, the first White men the Indians had ever seen, the treasure-seeking expedition of Francisco de Coronado, burst into the ordered world of the Pueblos. Searching for the rumored cities of Cíbola, whose wealth, it was hoped, would rival that of the conquered Aztec empire, Coronado, with 292 armored soldiers, hundreds of Christianized Mexican Indians, and a company of Franciscan friars and their assistants, marched through the Pueblo country. There were sixty or seventy Pueblo towns, with a total population of about 60,000, strung through the Rio Grande Valley and to the west, and the Spaniards visited many of them. In the fall of 1540, one of Coronado's captains, Hernando de Alvarado, leading twenty soldiers, rode up to Taos and was received with curiosity and friendship. It was the townspeople's first sight not only of White men but of horses, crossbows, and firearms. The Spaniards camped briefly outside the town, then went on to explore the plains farther east.

Coronado had intended a peaceable conquest of the region. But by the time he left it in disillusionment in 1542 and returned to Mexico, he had disrupted many of the pueblos and left a trail of violence and atrocities. The intruders outraged the Pueblos, requisitioning food, supplies, and the warm clothing off the Indians' backs; occupying Indian towns and forcing the inhabitants out of them; taking no action against the Spanish violator of a married Indian woman; burning scores of Indians at the stake and dragging others in chains and steel collars; and venting their wrath on whole towns by leveling them. Taos was outside the principal sphere of Coronado's movements and so was spared the Spaniards' brutalities. But the Whites became embroiled in battles with the Zuñis and Hopis in the west, as well as with some of the Rio Grande towns south of Taos. Though the Indians resisted stoutly, their weapons were no match for the harquebuses and steel swords of the Spaniards, who charged at them on their horses and, in a new type of all-out warfare, did not stop fighting until all resistance ended.

Wherever the newcomers went, they demanded formal submission to the Spanish Crown, erected wooden crosses, and tried to get the Indians to venerate them. It is doubtful that any of the Pueblos understood what they were being told about the White men's religion; in some towns, they sprinkled sacred cornmeal in front of the crosses and hung them with prayer sticks of feathers and flowers. Because of the Spaniards' viciousness, the whole region finally turned hostile to them, and the Pueblos were glad to see the intruders depart. With a number of assistants, the friars stayed behind, determined to continue the effort to convert the Indians. According to three survivors who managed to get back to Mexico several years later, one friar was killed when he ventured into present-day Kansas. The fate of the others was never learned.

Coronado's failure to find riches discouraged further interest in the country he had explored, and for almost forty years the Pueblos were free of White invaders. By 1580, however, a new generation of Spaniards in Mexico was again stirred by rumors of wealthy, unconverted Indians in the north. The next year, a small party of soldiers and friars made their way to the Rio Grande and explored the Pueblos' country, finding the people still filled with fearful memories of the Coronado expedition. The Pueblos gave the newcomers food, but were wary of them. When one of the friars decided to return to Mexico alone to report on the good qualities of the country, some Indians, possibly fearing that he was going to bring more Spaniards back with him, killed him along the way. The rest of the group finally headed for home, but left behind two friars and their assistants who planned to settle among the Pueblos and convert them.

The following year, another Spanish expedition entered the Pueblos' country and discovered that the friars and their assistants had been killed. The new group, though a small one, was bold and aggressive. It searched the Pueblo region for minerals, engaged in conflict with several towns, and brutally killed a number of Indians. It was followed by two filibustering expeditions of adventurers from the rough frontier provinces of northern Mexico. The first, in 1591, was bent on making profits by catching Indians to sell as slaves and also by establishing a colony in the Pueblos' country. The Crown had not given it permission to set up a colony, however, and Spanish troops pursued the group and dispersed the settlement it had begun in one of the Rio Grande pueblos. The second group, in 1593, disintegrated when one of its members murdered its leader somewhere on the Kansas plains.

None of these expeditions seems to have visited Taos, though news of their presence and activities undoubtedly reached the town. At the same time, none of them made a lasting impact on Pueblo life. Like Coronado's army, they aroused among some of the Indians a desire for various of their material possessions, including manufactured trade items, metal weapons and utensils, guns, and horses, goats, and cattle, but the Whites' sins and disruptions outweighed the benefits of their presence. The Pueblos knew enough about the Spaniards to fear and dislike them. Their approach to a town was usually the signal for its inhabitants to prepare for trouble, or to flee to a hiding place until the Spaniards left. But none of the intruders, including the friars who had talked against the Indians' spiritual beliefs, had done more than throw the Pueblo world temporarily on the defensive. The spiritual systems, the foundations on which Pueblo life rested, were still undisturbed.

Peril to those systems finally became real when the Spanish court at last authorized the colonizing of the Pueblos' country and the conversion of its inhabitants. Such an expedition, approved by the Crown and led by Don Juan de Oñate, heir to a Mexican mining fortune and the husband of a granddaughter of Cortez, traveled up the Rio Grande in 1598 and took possession of all the "lands, pueblos, cities, villas, of whatsoever nature now founded in the kingdom and province of New Mexico . . . and all its native Indians." Oñate's long, sprawling column included 129 Spanish colonists, soldiers in helmets and metal and leather armor, eight Franciscan friars and two lay brothers, seven thousand cattle, and a train of carts filled with supplies. After sacking Acoma and two other pueblos that tried to resist his rule, and meting out cruel punishments to the survivors as an example to all the pueblos, Oñate succeeded in establishing a permanent colony with a capital, first at a pueblo which he requisitioned and renamed San Juan and later, in 1610, at a town which his successors built and called Santa Fe. For some eighty years, the colony fastened on the Indians a stern, exploitive tyranny, administered principally by missionary friars and enforced by soldiers.

Oñate commenced his rule by convening two large conferences of representatives of the Rio Grande pueblos, including Taos, and using as interpreters two Mexican Indians whom one of the earlier expeditions had left behind and who had been living since then among the Pueblos. After winning from the Indians a promise of loyalty to the King of Spain, Oñate and the Father President of the friars expounded on the great joys and benefits that would come to the Pueblos if they accepted the White man's God. The Indian leaders were confused, but believing perhaps that there would be no danger to their people's way of life if they learned about the spiritual being that made the White men so strong, agreed to permit the friars to visit their towns and instruct the inhabitants. The pueblos were then apportioned among the friars, who began visiting and living in the towns, erecting large crosses, and preaching to the people about Christ and the White man's religion.

Although the missionaries were guarded by soldiers, their boldness and dedication, as well as the novelty and drama of their services and teachings, gradually gained the interest and respect of large numbers of people in many of the towns. In some of them, it was perceived that the brown-robed strangers were challenging the spiritual systems that kept the world in balance, and they were opposed by the leaders of the medicine societies and other pueblo authorities. But elsewhere the conflict was not readily apparent; a town, it was thought, could accept what the friars were teaching as something different and separate from their own beliefs, which they would continue to follow as the basis of their life. In time, increasing numbers of Pueblos knelt for conversion and, possibly with more curiosity and expectancy than understanding, participated in the friars' rituals and ceremonies. As reinforcements of missionaries arrived from Mexico and their influence and following grew, the converts eagerly accepted other things that the friars and priests introduced, using hoes and metal tools that the Whites gave them and learning crafts, music, and Spanish methods of agriculture and livestock raising. By 1608, the missionaries had baptized seven thousand Pueblos, and during the next two decades, marshaling Indian labor, they built mission churches at fifty towns, including Taos, where the church was named San Geronimo.

At the same time, many towns began to feel the heavy hand of Spanish regimentation. The usual Spanish policy of forcing all Indians to cluster around one or several missions, where they could be closely controlled, was impractical among the Pueblos: there were too many towns, too far apart from each other, and too few Spanish officials and soldiers to dare to attempt such a wholesale moving of people. But within each town, the mission system worked in microcosm. The missionaries exerted increasing control and authority over the social and economic life of the people, centering much of the Indians' existence on the mission and keeping them busy supporting the church and the friars by working in the gardens and paying tribute in supplies and labor. Their influence and control, in turn, weakened the political independence of the towns and undermined their leaders' ability to resist the growing authority of the Spaniards' secular government.

As a result, when the Indians were not working for the friars, they were being exploited by the colony's governor and the settlers. To facilitate relations with the many different pueblos—each one independent and possessing its own form of native government, which was religious in nature and not always loyal to the Whites—the Spaniards in 1620 created a new group of Indian civil officials in each town. They included a governor, who represented the town in all important dealings with the colonial government and who was given a silver-headed cane as a symbol of his position and authority; a lieutenant governor, who assisted the town governor and took his place when he was absent; an *alguacil*, or sheriff, who was responsible for maintaining law and order; a *sacristán*, who aided the missionary as a church assistant; *mayordomos*, who were irrigation ditch superintendents; *fiscales*, who were charged with maintaining mission discipline; and, later, war captains, who were usually the war chiefs and were in charge of defending the town against attacks by Apaches and other nomadic raiders.

From the Indians' point of view, the new system resulted in a dual set of town authorities, for they still looked to leadership from their traditional town, moiety, and clan and association chiefs, who—also in parallel with the religion of the missionaries—maintained the towns' ancient native socioreligious systems. In theory, the new civil officials were supposed to be elected by the townspeople, but in many pueblos, including Taos, the choice of governor required the approval of the traditional town chief, who was becoming known as the *cacique,* and who was still regarded by the Pueblos as their most important person. Although the civil officers recognized the continued primacy of the chiefs and elders of the native system and the town governor knew that he had lesser stature among the people than the *cacique,* the dual system created competition and discord. The traditional leaders struggled increasingly to counter the work of the missionaries, and the Spanish-appointed officers, doing their best to satisfy the Spanish religious and secular authorities to whom they were responsible, often came to be looked upon as spies and informers.

To the colony's leaders, intent on making profits for themselves, the province's only source of wealth was the enforced labor of the Indians. The governor granted *encomiendas,* tracts of land seized from the Pueblos, to favored men in the colony and bound their native inhabitants to the grants as serfs. In addition, every inhabitant in each pueblo was forced to pay annual tribute of corn, cloth, and personal labor to the colony. As slave laborers, Indians were soon working the Spaniards' fields, tending their cattle and sheep, and producing clothing and numerous articles of hides, cloth, and wood, which the Spaniards sent to Mexico to be sold for their own profit. The chief exploiters were the Spanish governors themselves, who looked upon their office as a means to acquire a fortune and often vied with the missionaries for the labor of the Indians.

From time to time, Pueblo religious leaders warned the people that, under Spanish influence, they were offending their own spiritual world and upsetting their balance with nature, and occasionally revolts flickered briefly in some of the towns. Taos, on the northern fringe of the Spanish province, was among the first pueblos to try to protect its religion from the destructive presence of the Whites. In 1608, ten years after Oñate established his colony, Taos secretly urged other towns to join in ridding the area of the Spaniards; then, with Picurís and Pecos pueblos and some nearby Apaches, they threatened a war against the towns that would not fight to oust the White men and their missionaries. Nothing came of this, however, and the Spaniards continued to strengthen their hold, even at Taos. With a growing sense of security, the friars attacked the native religions, whipping Indians for "pagan" and "satanic" practices, seizing prayer sticks and other spiritual objects, banning ceremonies and Kachina dances, and invading the kivas to break up meetings and destroy sacred masks, fetishes, and altars. When a protracted drought struck the region, followed by famine, epidemics of smallpox, and increased raids by hungry bands of nomadic Indians, the people of Taos and several other pueblos were certain that the missionaries had angered their spiritual world and disrupted the harmony of the universe.

By 1639, the Taos and Jemez pueblos had had enough. Both of them revolted, killed their friars, and destroyed much of the missions' property. A punitive expedition was sent to Taos, but many of the people fled, probably taking some horses with them. Under the leadership of their war and medicine chiefs, they trekked to the plains and established a new pueblo in what is now Scott County in western Kansas. The Spaniards looted Taos, but made no immediate attempt to pursue the refugees. Two years later, they learned that the Taos people were being troubled by the Apaches and other plains tribes—some of whom now owned horses derived from stock stolen from the pueblos and Spanish settlements on the Rio Grande—and that they were homesick and wanted to return. A Spanish force, accompanied by Pueblo auxiliaries, marched across the plains and brought most of them back. The last of them did not return to Taos until 1662.

Spanish tyranny in the Rio Grande Valley was as unbearable as ever, and in 1650 the Taos religious leaders joined with those of several other pueblos in again planning a revolt. Their efforts to enlist more towns failed, and their plans were discovered. The Spaniards were quick to crush them, hanging nine of the leaders and selling others into slavery. Having now learned the need for unity among all the pueblos, the frustrated towns bided their time. As the years passed, many factors combined to create that unity. The pueblos suffered new droughts, famines, and epidemics that reduced their population to a total of about 16,000. Many of them were struck repeatedly by plains raiders, and the Spaniards were often too weak to protect them. Greed for greater profits led the Spaniards to intensify pressures on the Indians, and unseemly quarrels broke out between the missionaries and the governors over the use of the Pueblos' labor. The governors made demands or gave orders, and the priests ignored or countermanded them. In retaliation, the governors sent troops to arrest the priests, and the priests denounced the governors as heretics and excommunicated them.

The converted Indians were appalled, and many of them began to listen more seriously to their medicine leaders, certain now that they had displeased the spirit world. Such defections angered the priests, who increased their oppression. As if in reaction, a number of priests and several settlers died mysteriously. Rumors ran among the colonists that the Indian medicine chiefs were practicing witchcraft. At the same time, the friars at Taos and other pueblos reported that "idolatry" had become so strong that they could not carry on with their work. Fearing an Indian revolt, the governor dispatched soldiers to the pueblos to seize the religious leaders, burn the kivas, and destroy all native religious objects. Chiefs were hanged at three pueblos, and forty-seven others were taken back to Sante Fe, where they were publicly whipped, jailed, and sentenced to be sold into slavery.

It was this action that finally united the Pueblos. Masses of them, including Christianized Indians, appeared fully armed in Santa Fe. A delegation of seventy, representing many different towns, entered the Governor's Palace and announced angrily that unless their religious leaders were freed by sundown, every town in the province would rise in revolt and kill all the Spaniards in New Mexico. The governor and his advisers recognized that the Indians meant what they said and that the colonists, who numbered about 2,500, could not defend themselves against 16,000 Indians. Reluctantly, he freed the prisoners.

Among them was an old but vigorous Tewa Indian named Popé, who was the chief of the Summer moiety at San Juan pueblo. All his life he had resisted the missionaries, trying to keep his people loyal to their traditional spiritual beliefs. On numerous occasions, the Spaniards had harassed him and denied him the right to hold ceremonies. As punishment, they had finally seized and enslaved his older brother. Even that had had no effect, and Popé had become a symbol of uncompromising opposition to the oppressors. In secret meetings in the kivas, he had told the people that the Spaniards must leave the Pueblo country. His audiences had become larger, and his influence had spread to other pueblos. The friars' complaints about him had finally induced the authorities in Santa Fe to seize him. He had been flogged in the plaza of the capital, jailed for a few days, and then allowed to return to his pueblo. Shortly afterward, he had again been arrested, whipped, and released. Still, it had failed to quiet him. The Spaniards had heard that his continued preachings were being repeated in towns throughout the province. In the general roundup of religious leaders, he had once more been arrested.

Now, Popé went back to San Juan, determined to organize a revolt. The episode at Santa Fe had taught the Pueblos a lesson. They had stood up to the Spanish governor, and he had retreated, showing the weakness of the Whites' position. Traveling to other pueblos, Popé counseled with the traditional religious leaders and won their alliance. For his own safety from the Spaniards, he eventually had to hide in a kiva at Taos, whose leaders helped him meet with chiefs from other towns and prepare a joint uprising. It came on August 10, 1680.

In a whirlwind of fury, the united Pueblos, from the Rio Grande to the Zuñis and Hopis in the west, killed or ousted their missionaries, captured Santa Fe, and drove every Spaniard in headlong flight out of their country. Popé was the main inspirational force of the revolt, but there were other notable Pueblo leaders, including Jaca of Taos, Governor Luis Tupatu of Picurís, Alonso Catiti of Santo Domingo, Bartolomé de Ojeda of Zia, and Domingo Naranjo of Santa Clara. In Taos, the planning center, only two Spanish soldiers escaped the initial uprising; having cleared the town of Whites, the Taos warriors then hurried to Santa Fe to join in the siege and capture of the colonists' capital.

Eleven days after it began, the revolt was over. Some 400 Spaniards, including twenty-one of the thirty-three Franciscan friars in the territory, had been slain in what had been a great American Indian revolution for the restoration of freedom to practice their own religion and follow the ways of their ancestors. It had also been a revolt against political and economic oppression and exploitation, but its principal stimulus had come from the urgent need to restore balance and harmony between the Pueblos and their spiritual world. In each newly freed pueblo, the chiefs held ceremonies in which the Christianized Indians were washed clean of their baptisms and purified with yucca suds. The churches and mission buildings were burned or left to crumble, and every object and relic of the friars' religion was defaced or destroyed. A year after the revolt, reports reached the Spanish refugees, who were clustered at the site of present-day Juárez, Mexico, that the Pueblos "have been found to be so pleased with liberty of conscience and so attached to the belief in the worship of Satan that up to the present not a sign has been visible of their ever having been Christians."

The period of freedom and unity was short-lived. Popé ordered the people to rid their lives of everything the Spaniards had introduced or taught them. He demanded that they abandon their horses, mules, oxen, and sheep, cut down their fruit trees and no longer plant wheat, alfalfa, or other crops brought by the Whites, throw away their guns, saddles, sickles, axes, needles, and other European articles, and forget weaving, carpentry, blacksmithing, and other skills that they had learned from the friars. This, however, proved impossible. The people would not give up things that seemed to them useful and desirable and return to a harder and poorer material existence. Soon, the pueblos were resisting Popé's demands and going their own way again. Popé, in turn, seems now to have become something of a tyrant, whose fanatic orders and conduct accelerated divisions within and among the pueblos. Finally, he died. By then, other problems beset the towns. Apaches, Utes, Navajos, and other plains tribes, mounted on horses and stronger and more aggressive than ever, struck at will against the pueblos, which no longer could count on being helped by the firearms of Spanish soldiers. Some of the people began to urge that the Spaniards be asked to come back, and they established contact with Pueblo Indians from the more southerly towns who had refused to join the revolt and had fled to the El Paso area with the Spaniards. Others never wanted to see the Spaniards again, or were afraid of being punished by them if they were invited to return. The feuds and factionalism grew, and quarrels between the pueblos over policy erupted into angry warfare. The intertribal conflict, raids by the plains Indians, and confusion over what to do threw the region into turmoil.

To make matters worse, from time to time Spanish troops began to reappear, marching up the valley, offering pardons to towns that would again swear loyalty to Spain, burning those that refused to do so, and then withdrawing with threats to return. The fighting and fears of the people caused wholesale movements of population. To escape Apaches, Spaniards, or enemy Pueblos, whole towns were abandoned by their inhabitants, who moved into the towns of their allies, built new pueblos in different locations, or fled to the Hopis or even to friendly groups of Apaches and Navajos. The Pueblo religious leaders were helpless; harmony had been lost, and the world was out of balance.

By the late 1680's, it was evident that the Spaniards were coming back. Their constant probes, with offers of peace and forgiveness, had

Saturiwa, a chief of the
Timucua Indians at the time
of the French attempt to
establish a settlement on the
St. John's River in Florida in
1564. Contemporary drawing
by Jacques Le Moyne de
Morgues.

A Seminole village,
"Residence of a Chief."
Engraving by Gray & Jones,
Charleston, S.C., 1837.

The resistance of Osceola to giving up the land of his people in Florida is portrayed in this nineteenth-century engraving re-creating the scene of the treaty-signing.

BELOW *(left)* It is easy to read in the face of this descendant of Osceola the pride and determination that have enabled the Florida Indians to endure as Indians for 500 years under White rule. *(Right)* Ruby Clay in a modern adaptation of the traditional Seminole headdress, sewing under the roof of her chickee.

A woodcut from an early history book depicts New England Indians dying from diseases introduced by Europeans.

Aurelius Piper, Chief Big Eagle, one of the approximately 100 Paugussets still living near Bridgeport, Connecticut.

An Iroquois wampum belt commemorates the unity of the Five Nations in the League.

A woodcut, published a year after the Pequot massacre at Mystic, Connecticut, in 1637, by English Captain John Underhill, to show how he and Captain John Mason slaughtered the Indians. The Puritans and their Narragansett allies circled the Pequot town, which they then set afire, trapping some 800 Pequots inside. Those who tried to escape from the burning town were killed by the besiegers.

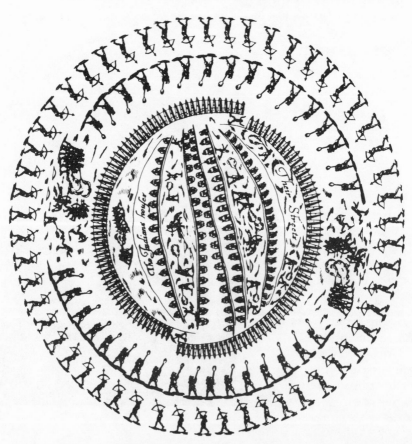

The pueblo of Taos in New Mexico.

Koshares (clowns) and Kachinas prepare for a sacred ceremony at the Hopi village of Oraibi, Arizona, in 1908.

Blue Lake, 1969. This body of water in the mountains of northeastern New Mexico has long been holy to the Taos Indians and an integral part of their spiritual heritage.

A victory celebration at Taos pueblo after the 1970 Senate vote that returned Blue Lake and the surrounding forested lands to the Taos people.

Chief Gaiantwaka, known as "The Cornplanter," a Seneca chief who befriended American frontier families settling in western New York and Pennsylvania after the Revolution.

Basil Williams reading the 1962 Indian Day Proclamation by the then-governor of New York, Nelson Rockefeller, in front of Cornplanter's monument on its old site on the Allegany Reservation.

By 1964, the Senecas had accepted the fact that they would have to move from their old homes on the Allegany Reservation, which was due to be flooded by the Kinzua Dam. Here Kenneth Snow and his wife, son, and mother examine a model of one of the new houses the Corps of Engineers proposed to replace the ones that would be destroyed.

ABOVE *(left)* Paiute women with their food-gathering baskets in the nineteenth century. *(Right)* Paiute men of the 1870's near the site of present-day Las Vegas, Nevada.

The wikiups of a nineteenth-century encampment of Paiute Indians near present-day St. George, Utah.

Pyramid Lake in 1980. It is easy to see how far the water has receded from the former shoreline and from the pyramid rock formation itself since the waters of the Truckee River which feed the lake have been diverted to other uses.

Paiute men catching cui-ui near the mouth of the Truckee River where it enters Pyramid Lake.

Tommy Sopes, a 76-year-old Paiute Indian who has lived his entire life on the Duck Valley Reservation on the Nevada-Idaho border. Here he accompanies himself on a traditional drum as he sings a Paiute prayer honoring the land.

OPPOSITE (*Above*) Marlon Brando and Robert Satiacum stage a "fish-in" on Washington's Puyallup River in March 1964, as part of the campaign to test and preserve Indian treaty rights to fish in the Northwest. (*Below*) Alvin Bridges, his daughter Suzette, another daughter, and his wife, on the bank of the Nisqually River in June 1968, during one of the many fishing conflicts that took place around Frank's Landing.

Janet McCloud—a Tulalip Indian from Puget Sound and a descendant of Sealth, the Duwamish chief who signed an early agreement with the Whites— has been a leader in helping her people retain their treaty rights to fish in the Northwest.

Bob Blacketer, a Nisqually Indian, microtagging chinook as part of a conservation project under the auspices of the Northwest Indian Fisheries Commission.

A Brulé Sioux village near Pine Ridge, South Dakota, March 1891, after the massacre at Wounded Knee. Grabill photograph.

Ration Day on the Pine Ridge Reservation, 1891.

Oglala defense position at Wounded Knee, near Pine Ridge, in 1973.

Maggie Six-Shooter and her granddaughter, modern-day Sioux who live on the Pine Ridge Reservation.

Sioux drummers during a modern-day powwow in South Dakota.

John Trudell, seated, announcing the government's removal of the Indians from Alcatraz Island, which they had occupied in November 1969 to call attention to their desperate conditions.

AIM Treaty Convention in 1974 at Mobridge, South Dakota. *Left to right, foreground:* Philip Deer, Russell Means, Leonard Crow Dog. *At far right:* Vernon Bellecourt.

Indians marching in Washington, D.C., at the end of the "Longest Walk" in 1978.

won over many of the pueblos whose leaders had maintained contact with the Spanish base at present-day Juárez. In 1689, relations had become so warm that representatives of eleven pueblos met with the Spanish governor at his headquarters and were given formal land grants for their towns. In the future, each pueblo, including Taos, would accept such a grant—given in the name of the Crown—for its townsite and the land the people required for their existence. To the Indians of Taos and other pueblos, it was the land the Creator had given them, and both spiritually and legally these grants were viewed as confirmation that it already belonged to them.

With the help of the friendly pueblos and native leaders who acted as intermediaries and pleaded their cause at hostile towns, the Spaniards finally launched their campaign of reconquest in 1692. They got a mixed reaction from the Indians. Some of the towns resisted, some were abandoned in fright, and others swore loyalty and joined the Spanish soldiers in attacks on "rebel" towns. For a time, serious resistance crumbled, and the Spaniards were able to bring about an uneasy truce with most of the pueblos. They offered friendship to each town and ended the hated *encomienda* system that had previously exploited the Indians' labor. But a revival of religious repression by the newly installed friars, together with continued fears of punishment, gave birth to a new revolutionary movement among some of the towns. Taos and other pueblos revolted in 1694 and again in 1696, once more killing their missionaries. Using native intermediaries and a "divide and conquer" policy that pitted the pueblos against each other, the Spaniards crushed the resistance both times, and at last secured their hold over the Rio Grande Valley. Pueblo armed resistance waned and finally disappeared.

The revolt of 1696 taught the Spaniards a lesson. Though religious interference continued, a new generation of friars adopted a more humane and tolerant attitude toward the Indians' beliefs and eventually abandoned any serious effort to stop their ceremonies. The civil government's vigorous defense of the towns against the attacks of the nomadic tribes also pleased the Pueblos, whose leaders the Spaniards brought into a partnership for the mutual defense of the province. Pueblo auxiliaries, led by the war captains, were soon a major part of every Spanish expedition sent against Apaches, Pawnees, and other plains tribes.

The new policies won many converts for the friars. The number of baptisms soared, and many pueblos gradually accepted at least the outward forms of Christianity. Among most of the converts, however, the friars' religion was only skin-deep; their own religion continued to be more meaningful to them, and they remained deeply attached to their own beliefs and spiritual leaders. The latter, now without hope of successful resistance, adjusted to the new state of affairs, taking their religion underground and concealing their medicine association rites and more sacred dances and ceremonies from all non-Pueblo people. The secrecy ensured the survival of their own systems and led to the development of the "compartmentalizing" of the two religions in each pueblo, both of them kept separate and distinct, and both claiming the adherence of the same people. Pueblos could be simultaneously Christian and participate in the friars' rituals and also retain their ancestral native beliefs. Those who went too far in the Christian direction and threatened difficulty for the traditional religion either voluntarily or by persuasion left the pueblo and moved into a Spanish settlement. Over the years, many did so and gradually melded into the province's growing population of Hispanos and mixed-bloods.

The passing years saw other changes. Both the secular government and the missionaries began to pay less attention to the Pueblos. The decline of Spain's power was reflected in New Mexico, where the resources and strength of the governor and his officials also waned. At the same time, increasing attention had to be paid to the defense of the province against raiding plains Indians and threats from the French in the Mississippi Valley. New demands on the Spanish authorities were also created by the growth of the non-Indian population; both the civil government and the friars spent much of their time administering to the proliferating non-Pueblo Christian settlements in the Rio Grande Valley. While a veneer of Spanish culture inevitably spread over the Indians' towns, their inhabitants were left increasingly to themselves, and their spiritual systems, still little changed from pre-White days, regained a large measure of freedom from interference.

During the early part of the nineteenth century, Spanish decay accelerated. In 1821, Mexico, of which the Pueblos' country was a part, won its independence from Spain, and neglect of the Pueblos became complete. The Mexican authorities, more concerned with Texas and the threat of expansion by the United States, left the Pueblos alone. Only five towns had the services of missionaries, and they were no threat to the Indians' religions. Many pueblos relaxed their secrecy and lived amicably with neighboring non-Indian towns, sometimes joining with them in maintaining irrigation canals or in other matters that affected them both. In 1837, showing that they could still fight for their rights, members of Taos pueblo led another uprising, which was joined by some of the Hispanic population, as well as by other Pueblo Indians. The target of their anger was the new governor, who was not a native-born New Mexican and who, it was rumored, was about to levy heavy taxes on the people of the province. Under the leadership of a Taos Indian named José

Gonzales, the rebels killed the governor, captured Santa Fe, and installed Gonzales as governor. It was a remarkable event. For almost six months, a Pueblo Indian presided over New Mexico. Then a Mexican counter-revolutionist, aided by troops from Chihuahua, overthrew his regime and shot him.

Ten years later, in January 1847, the inhabitants of Taos pueblo cooperated with the Mexican population in another uprising, this time against the Americans, who were at war with Mexico and had occupied the Rio Grande area the previous August and installed an American governor. Resentments and fears over mammoth land thefts by the Americans, including the governor, Charles Bent, a well-known fur trader, were stirred up against the invading Anglos, and Governor Bent and other Americans were assassinated in the non-Indian town of Taos, which had grown up during Spanish days on part of the pueblo's land. When an American punitive force marched north from Santa Fe, the Taos Indian population resisted, then took refuge in the Catholic church inside the pueblo's walls. The Americans battered down the walls with their howitzers and killed 150 Indians before the rest surrendered. The leaders of the revolt, including a Taos Indian named Tomás Romero, were put to death.

The next year, by the terms of the Treaty of Guadalupe Hidalgo that ended the Mexican War, the Pueblos' country became officially part of the United States, which, following the example of the Mexicans, recognized the rights of the different pueblos to ownership of the lands the Spaniards had "granted" them. The Pueblos, who were regarded as more civilized than other Indians, were treated the same as the non-Indian population and offered American citizenship, and in 1863 the Lincoln administration presented to the governor of each pueblo a silver-headed cane inscribed with the signature of the President. The governors still possessed the canes presented to them by the Spaniards, and to this day both of them are displayed in the governors' homes and at important pueblo ceremonies.

For many years, the Pueblos felt no serious interference from the Americans and, indeed, were quickly won over to them by the vigorous military action that U.S. troops took against the Navajos, Apaches, Comanches, and other tribes which had been raiding the pueblos. By the 1880's, the military power of those tribes had been broken, and the raids had ceased.

By that time, also, however, the Americans themselves were beginning to become a threat to the Pueblo spiritual systems. Since the last years under the faltering Spaniards, the Pueblo religion had grown strong again, flourishing with little secrecy. Most of the Mexican and

American authorities who observed the native ceremonies generally dismissed them as little more than picturesque and harmless vestiges of an earlier day among people who now seemed to be essentially devout Catholics, and they made only rare and ineffectual attempts to persuade the towns to give up their "paganistic" practices. By the 1880's, however, Baptist, Presbyterian, and other American Protestant missionaries had intruded into some of the pueblos and, with considerable high-handedness and bigotry, were trying to force their own faiths on the Indians. The Catholic priests resisted this competition, but the Protestants learned, with horror and distaste, that the Pueblos' own "heathenism" was stronger than their outward attachment to Christianity, and that it was still their "superstitious" native religious leaders who actually controlled their lives.

The Protestants' complaints of "obscene" and "un-American" ceremonies and of "helpless" Indians who were trying to break away from the "tyranny" of "witch doctors" went up through the hierarchies of the churches, whose leaders in the East were already part of the coalition of reformers and assimilationists that was pressuring the government to end Indianness. Reservations, with local agents, had been established in all the pueblos, and the Department of the Interior responded to the complaints with some of the same policies it was applying to the newly defeated plains tribes. The agents received orders to take Indian children away from their parents and religious teachers and put them in White-run boarding schools far from the Pueblo towns, and at the same time prohibit ceremonies in the pueblos that violated Christian standards and punish leaders who conducted or permitted them.

Thus once more, beginning in the late nineteenth century and lasting well into the twentieth century, oppression came to the pueblos, and the Pueblo chiefs, to save their religions and societies, were forced once again to adopt secrecy as a defensive measure and take the practice of their sacred beliefs underground. Though largely unnoticed or ignored by the rest of the American population, the missionaries and Bureau of Indian Affairs agents brought tension, unhappiness, and conflict to many of the pueblos. Young Indians were wrenched from their parents in tears and sent like captives to distant schools, such as Carlisle in Pennsylvania, to be turned into Whites. Many Indians are still alive who remember their homesickness and the brutalities and beatings administered to them if they spoke their own language at school, indulged in practices of their home towns, or were charged with other infractions. At the pueblos, the government's new Indian Religious Crimes Code gave the agents the authority to end the towns' religious freedom. There were disruptions and clashes, but for a time the Bureau of Indian Affairs agents were too few in number, too inept, lazy, and unknowledgeable, and too lacking in the means of inquiry and enforcement to cow the pueblos' leaders. Meanwhile, the town chiefs and officials managed successfully to conceal their more sacred rites and strengthen the wall of secrecy about their spiritual affairs from all outsiders.

Taos pueblo had other difficulties. In the 1890's, a town youth, who had returned from one of the boarding schools, spread among some of the people an interest in the new Pan-Indian Native American Church religion, which he had learned from other Indians at the school and which involved the use of peyote as a sacrament. While its concepts and practices were helpful to people of other tribes, they ran counter to the still strong and viable ancestral spiritual system of Taos, and their introduction distressed the traditional religious leaders and led to opposition and serious factionalism and violence. In the end, only a few families adopted the new religion, but the episode reflected the coming of a new era of disruptive contacts with the non-Pueblo world that would lure many of the Pueblo peoples away from their own spiritual systems, and even from their towns.

Soon after the start of the new century, however, there began in Taos an epic modern-day struggle which, to the contrary, eventually united all the people of Taos around their native religion, and won for them the support of the other pueblos and all the Indians of the United States. To Whites, who did not understand the religious nature of the conflict, it began and continued as a land problem. Under the Mexican and American regimes, Hispano and Anglo farmers had increasingly encroached on pueblo lands, a few of them paying for the property, but most tricking the Indians in one way or another or simply becoming squatters. By the end of the century, the swelling influx of land-hungry Americans added even more pressure for irrigable land, and they swarmed over large areas of Pueblo property, many of them clouding their right to do so by claiming falsely that they had bought titles from Hispanos who had originally been squatters. When the pueblos tried to regain their lands by having the federal government, as trustee of Indian property, oust the Whites, they could not do so; upholding New Mexican territorial statutes, the Supreme Court in 1876 had ruled that the Pueblos, unlike other reservation Indians, were citizens to whom the trust protections did not apply and who could therefore dispose of their lands as they saw fit. Non-Indians, in other words, did not need the permission of the federal government to acquire Pueblo lands. As a result, the pueblos, by legal and illegal means, continued to lose arable land, as well as valuable water, to the aggressively expanding non-Indians.

All the religious chiefs worried about this, but none more so than those of Taos. The lands being lost or threatened were within the boundaries of what the Creator had given them to sustain their life and to venerate and protect if their existence was to continue. They were filled with meaningful shrines and locations that were interrelated with their spiritual systems, and the Whites were obliterating and desecrating them, threatening the balance that the people were obliged to maintain with nature. They were particularly anxious about the still undefiled mountainous country north and east of their town that contained many of their sacred lakes, including Blue Lake, and the watershed and course of their heartline, the Rio Pueblo de Taos, and were concerned that non-Indian squatters would soon invade the timbered slopes and pollute the waters or turn aside the river to irrigate their own farms.

In 1903, the Taos chiefs learned that the Theodore Roosevelt administration was planning to include this entire region in a national forest reserve that would be barred to entry or settlement. Believing that this might protect Blue Lake and the mountain country from outsiders, they watched the proposal cautiously and on October 21, 1904, petitioned the Department of the Interior to set aside the watershed of the river "for the exclusive use of our tribe" if entry was prohibited in the area. The government ignored the petition, and on November 7, 1906, without consulting the Indians about their property, included some 130,000 acres of their most sacred land, including Blue Lake and the river's watershed, in a Taos Forest Reserve, which in June 1908 an executive order made part of the Carson National Forest, administered by the U.S. Forest Service.

Behind what had happened was something of which the Taos chiefs were unaware and over which they had had no control: a firm belief by the conservation-minded Chief Forester Gifford Pinchot and the Secretary of Agriculture that the Indians and the Bureau of Indian Affairs could not be trusted to care for, or manage, forests, and that all forests on Indian reservations should be treated as public lands and managed for the entire American public by the Forest Service. Neither Pinchot nor anyone in Washington knew how well the Taos people, religiously committed to the protection of their forested land, had preserved it for more than six hundred years, nor did they care to know. An Indian, in their opinion, was by nature incompetent. "I am convinced," the Secretary of Agriculture wrote to the Secretary of the Interior on February 20, 1906, just before the Taos reserve was created, that "portions of Indian reservations should be created into National forest reserves by direct Act of Congress, or, better still, by an Act of Congress giving the President power to make such proclamations when he deems it best for the public interest." There was no concern shown for the Indian interest, and President Roosevelt's proclamation of November 7 that withdrew the new reserve set it apart "as a Public Reservation, for the use and benefit of the people," with no mention of the Indians.

On March 31, 1909, a Forest Service district supervisor in Santa Fe finally replied to the Taos chiefs' petition of 1904: "In as much as no action was taken on this petition and since it is immaterial . . . I beg to inform you that there need be no uneasiness . . . that you will not receive full protection for irrigation and grazing interests in the section of the country to which you refer." No mention was made of exclusive Indian use or of protections required by the Indians' religious ties to the area.

The Taos leaders were greatly disturbed and, after counseling with the *cacique*, determined somehow to reestablish their exclusive rights to their sacred lands and waters. Meanwhile, encroachments by non-Indian squatters on other lands of the pueblo caused so much turmoil that territorial militia were sent to Taos in 1910 to prevent what appeared to be an imminent Indian uprising. In 1912, and again in 1916, the Taos chiefs appealed to the Secretary of the Interior to make the Blue Lake area into an executive-order reservation for the Taos Indians, but both times the Secretary of Agriculture, on the advice of the Forest Service, refused to approve the proposal. In 1913, the confusion concerning the lands of all the pueblos was compounded by a Supreme Court decision that reversed the one of 1876 and now decided that the Pueblos had the same legal status as other Indians, that they could not alienate their lands without the approval of the federal government, and that they were entitled to reclaim lands that had passed out of their hands, legally or illegally. Suddenly, the validity of some 3,000 land claims by 12,000 non-Indians on Pueblo lands was in question.

To avoid threatened bloodshed, Secretary of the Interior Albert B. Fall, on July 20, 1922, induced New Mexican Senator Holm O. Bursum to introduce a bill that heavily favored non-Indians, giving them rights that would have deprived the Pueblos fraudulently of at least 60,000 acres of their land and much of their water, and would have transferred juris-diction over most of their internal town affairs to a federal district court. In response, John Collier and many other White friends of the Indians, working largely through the media, attacked the Bursum bill as an uncon-scionable new robbery of Indian lands. Their campaign raised a national uproar that ultimately defeated the Bursum bill, substituting, instead, the establishment of a Pueblo Lands Board to review the value of each claim and compensate either the Indians or the non-Indians for the lands they gave up. Over the years, most of the non-Indians were then peaceably bought out and removed from the Pueblos' lands.

The defeat of the Bursum bill nettled one of its principal sponsors, Charles H. Burke, a wealthy South Dakota realtor and former Republican congressman, at the time the Commissioner of Indian Affairs. Stung by Collier's fiery defense of the Pueblos' lands, Burke, a rabid assimilationist, made the Pueblos' religion a new ground on which to do battle with Collier. Inevitably, it brought him into conflict with Taos. The chiefs of that town were still determined to regain Blue Lake and their river's watershed. During World War I, they had been further offended by the Forest Service's decision to open the region to non-Indian livestock raisers. The Indians had complained that the users trampled their sacred sites and shrines, polluted the water, and interfered with the privacy of their religious devotions. Friction had increased with the Forest Service personnel, many of whom had consistently treated the Indians with contempt, acted as if the Taos people had no more rights to the area than the non-Indians, and maliciously supported the non-Indian population in spreading rumors of dark and mysterious activities, including ritual murders and sexual orgies that supposedly accompanied the annual Indian ceremonies at Blue Lake.

The rumors merged with a general campaign being waged by missionaries and assimilationists in the early 1920's against the religious ceremonies and practices of all the pueblos. Making use of reports by investigators of the Department of the Interior and such organizations as the Indian Rights Association of Philadelphia, the YWCA, and the Board of Indian Commissioners, which drew their information from non-Indian New Mexicans and Protestant Indians who had turned against their town leaders, Burke issued directives, ordering the reservation superintendents to work with the missionaries in enforcing bans on Pueblo religious activities and stopping "so-called religious ceremonies." On February 24, 1923, he sent his own "Message to All Indians," giving them a year to abandon their "useless and harmful performances."

He was immediately opposed by Collier and other non-Indians, who argued in writings and speeches that the Pueblo ceremonies were secret, not because they were immoral, but because the Indians were trying to preserve them against the attacks of ignorant and bigoted people. Burke was undeterred, and with the help of such persons as William E. "Pussyfoot" Johnson, a former director of the World League of Alcoholism, who charged that the Pueblos withdrew their children from school to give them a two-year course in sodomy, kept up his attack. On April 18, 1924, accompanied by Secretary of the Interior Hubert Work, Burke visited Taos, supposedly the stronghold of "hideous and revolting" Pueblo practices, and, addressing the Taos Pueblo Council of solemn, dignified civil and religious leaders, called them "half animals" and ordered them to return to the government school two of their young men whom they had temporarily withdrawn for instruction in the pueblo's spiritual beliefs. The next month, seventy-four delegates from fifteen pueblos convened angrily in a meeting of the All-Pueblo Council, an inter-pueblo consultative body whose roots went back to the time of the Revolt of 1680, and issued a declaration to all the Indians and other people of the United States, demanding religious liberty for the Pueblos.

Aided by missionaries and supported by Matthew K. Sniffen of the Indian Rights Association and other assimilationists, Burke replied by trying to set up a rival inter-pueblo organization composed of "progressive" Christianized Indians. It had no popular support, however, and soon collapsed. In the meantime, the Taos council sent Burke a letter stating that their religion "was more important to each of us than money, horses, land, or anything else in the world." It taught them "about God and the earth, and about our duty to God, to earth, and to one another." The letter fell on deaf ears.

The following summer, when the Taos religious chiefs disciplined two town members of the Native American Church who had invaded their traditional ceremonies, giving them the choice of paying two-dollar fines or receiving one lash with their clothes and a blanket as protection, Burke gave approval to the local superintendent to arrest all but one member of the Taos governing body just before the annual ceremonial trek to Blue Lake. Nine of the town chiefs were taken by armed guards to Santa Fe and jailed until the next day, when a New Mexico district court freed them. Again, the All-Pueblo Council convened at Santo Domingo and sent a message to the President and Congress protesting the attack on the Taos leaders, which seemed to many of them to be a repetition of what the Spaniards had done to Popé and other Pueblo spiritual chiefs in the years immediately before the Revolt of 1680. In reply to their message, Bureau of Indian Affairs officials suggested to the press that the Pueblos' opposition was being financed by Communist "money from Moscow."

The American people generally paid little attention to the attack on the Indians' religion. Burke, however, was almost at the end of his power. Frustrated by the Indians' opposition, he had a bill introduced in Congress setting up a system under which the courts could enforce his efforts to end religious practices that he found objectionable. Many people joined Collier in opposing the measure as blatantly unconstitutional, and when it died in Congress in 1926, so did Burke's crusade. But in the field, individual agents and reservation superintendents, still working with missionaries, continued to interfere with Indian religions until the passage of the Indian Reorganization Act in 1934, and even long after that.

Meanwhile, the fight to regain Blue Lake continued. In 1926, when the newly constituted Pueblo Lands Board met to settle the land claims quarrels, the Taos Indians offered to waive compensation of almost $300,000 for land taken from them by the non-Indian town of Taos if the government returned the Blue Lake area to them. The members of the Lands Board, in an act of sleight-of-hand that was later questioned by the U.S. Senate and the Indian Claims Commission, led the tribe to believe that it would act to restore Blue Lake to them, then accepted their offer to waive compensation for the Taos land, but of course had no power over what happened to Blue Lake. That matter, Commissioner Burke told them, was "not germane" to the board's jurisdiction. So the Indians were out both their money and the lake.

Still, the pueblo kept trying. In 1927, as a result of their complaints that they had been misled, the Forest Service agreed to give them the non-exclusive use of approximately 31,000 acres, including the Blue Lake area, and an exclusive use permit for the same acreage for three days in August so they could make their annual pilgrimage to the lake in private, provided they applied to the Forest Service at least ten days in advance. The Indians thought they had been given exclusive use year-round, and were horrified when the Forest Service the next year issued ninety-five permits to non-Indians to use the area for camping, recreation, and other activities. Though the agreement was modified a year later to bar the area to mineral prospectors, the Taos chiefs found the whole arrangement unsatisfactory. Whites were still using the watershed, desecrating its shrines and Blue Lake, and the agreement was subject to cancellation or change by the Forest Service at any time. The pueblo still wanted its holy land returned to it.

Senate hearings in 1933 raised the Indians' hopes, but an act passed the same year did little more than formalize the 1927 agreement and grant the pueblo the right to a permit to use the area for fifty years. It took the Department of the Interior seven years, however, to grant the permit (Collier, now Commissioner of Indian Affairs, was trying to increase the acreage the Indians could use), and the pueblo still had exclusive rights for only three days in August. Whites continued to gain entry the rest of the year. In 1951, after years of friction with the Forest Service and appeals to Congress to return the land to them, the Taos council, supported by the town's seventy-six-year-old *cacique*, Juan de Jesús Romero, a patient spiritual leader whose long, determined campaign to regain Blue Lake had given him the status of a patriot among his people, decided to take their case to the Indian Claims Commission. Fourteen years later, on September 8, 1965, that body ruled that the tribe still held legal title to the 130,000 acres that the government had taken from it in 1906, but could only authorize that the Indians be paid for what they had lost.

During the next five years, the Indians tried repeatedly to get Congress to return their land to them, rather than pay them for it. They were willing to settle for 50,000 acres, including Blue Lake, and the House of Representatives supported them. But in the Senate they were bitterly opposed by New Mexico's senior senator, Clinton Anderson, and an influential staff member of the Senate Subcommittee on Indian Affairs, James Gamble. The latter told the Indians' lawyer point-blank that he was "one hundred percent against the return of Blue Lake because anything that supported Indian religion would hold back their development and encourage them to maintain their culture." Anderson, willing at one point to settle for 3,000 acres—"plenty big enough for a church"—could not understand the Indians' religious needs and suspected that the tribe wanted the additional acreage for timber sales and for the development of homesites. He was supported by Forest Service officials, non-Indian timber operators in New Mexico who *did* want to get at the trees in the Carson Forest, and representatives of conservation and sportsmen's organizations, all of whom deprecated the Indians' claim to the land for religious purposes as "a load of bull," "mumbo-jumbo," or sheer fakery. One anti-Indian lobbyist at the Senate hearings in 1968 said that he had secretly searched the forest and Blue Lake for the Indians' shrines, but couldn't find any.

Twice, bills for the return of the land died in the Senate. Taos spokesmen, including the venerable *cacique,* made trips to hearings in the capital and, with the help of non-Indian supporters, gained national sympathy for the pueblo. The issue came to symbolize continued injustice to Indians, and tribes throughout the country sent pleas to the President and Congress in behalf of Taos. Finally, in July 1970, President Nixon informed Congress that he backed the pueblo's cause, and on December 2 the Senate overrode Anderson's objections and by a vote of 70–12 passed a bill returning 48,000 acres and Blue Lake to Taos. The patient *cacique,* Juan de Jesús Romero, and the other pueblo spokesmen went home to a joyous celebration. Taos had won a sixty-four-year fight and had once again saved its traditional religion.

Juan de Jesús Romero died at Taos pueblo on July 30, 1978, at the age of 103, mourned by his people. By then, Indians throughout the country were fighting for the right to practice their own religions and for respect for their sacred lands, objects, and shrines. It was still coming slowly and hard, though certain court cases were aiding them. Largely as a result of Indian persistence, and the accumulating evidence in courts that Indian religions were still not being understood and protected under the Constitution as religions, Congress on August 11, 1978, passed an American Indian Religious Freedom Act, introduced by Senator James

Abourezk of South Dakota and stating that "henceforth it shall be the policy of the United States to protect and preserve for American Indians their inherent right of freedom to believe, express, and exercise the traditional religions of the American Indian, Eskimo, Aleut, and Native Hawaiians, including but not limited to access to sites, use and possession of sacred objects, and the freedom to worship through ceremonials and traditional sites."

As far as the general public was concerned, the Act had no teeth and could only serve as an educational stimulus. But it purported to set policy for the Bureau of Indian Affairs and for every agency of the federal government, each of which was given a year, under a provision of the Act, to evaluate its own policies and procedures "in consultation with native traditional leaders in order to determine appropriate changes necessary to protect and preserve Native American religious cultural rights and practices." A mechanism for such consultations was set up with the assistance of the Native American Rights Fund in Boulder, Colorado, and Washington, D.C., and the American Indian Law Center in Albuquerque, and each department, agency, and commission of the executive branch of the federal government filed a statement promising adherence to the intent of the new law.

The first test came quickly. On April 12, 1979, the Tennessee Valley Authority filed its statement, reporting that "consideration of Native American religious concerns is being factored into the land management and planning functions. TVA recognizes its responsibilities . . . and will continue to actively evaluate its activities and procedures relevant to the religious needs and concerns of Native Americans." But TVA was building a dam on the Little Tennessee River, and traditional Cherokee Indians had been opposing its construction because its reservoir would flood the original sacred homeland of the Cherokees, including the site of Chota, their ancient capital, sanctuary, and most important town, and would destroy homesites of some of their people, medicine gathering places, shrines, and cemeteries that held the bones of their revered chiefs and ancestors.

Conservationists were also fighting the dam, partly because it threatened an endangered species of fish, the snail darter. The media's coverage of the conflict focused on the snail darter, and said little or nothing about the Cherokees' religious concerns. When the conservationists and the snail darter lost their case, the TVA continued building the dam, condemning the land and removing the inhabitants. Despite its statement of April 12, 1979 (which some Indians felt was a jargonistic, "forked-tongue" attempt to evade the requirements of the Act), TVA found no need to save the source of the Indians' traditional religion. The traditional Cherokees, backed by the National Indian Youth Council, a Pan-Indian organization of young Native Americans battling for traditional rights, took TVA to court. On April 15, 1980, the United States Court of Appeals for the Sixth Circuit ruled for TVA. The dam was finished, the valley was flooded, and to the Indians, the American Indian Religious Freedom Act was just another promise.

After the dam was built, it was proved that the TVA planners had not required all the land that they had condemned. Instead of returning it to the Indians, the agency offered to sell some of it at vastly increased prices to real-estate developers as choice lakefront property. In Washington, D.C., a non-Indian official of the TVA had already called the young Indians of the National Indian Youth Council—the "papooses" who had been educated in White men's schools and had then stirred up trouble about Indian religion—"phonies."

II

TODAY

THE STRUGGLE
TO SURVIVE

4

CORNPLANTER, CAN YOU SWIM?

The Native Americans' Fight to
Hold On to Their Land Base

I N A CEMETERY high on a promontory overlooking the broad waters of
the Allegheny Reservoir in northwestern Pennsylvania stands a stone
monument to a once powerful and celebrated Seneca Indian war chief,
Gaiantwaka, The Cornplanter, who fought with the British against the
Americans during the Revolution and then became a friend of the United
States government and a defender of American frontier families settling
in western New York and Pennsylvania and the upper Ohio River basin.
The monument has not been long at its present site. In 1964, amid
controversy, anger, and the protests of many Seneca Indians, the United
States Army Corps of Engineers moved the memorial shaft, together with
what was left of the earthly remains of The Cornplanter and more than
300 of his followers and descendants, from a hallowed Indian cemetery
("our Arlington," a distraught Seneca woman pleaded) that was about to
be inundated by rising waters of a reservoir created by the new Kinzua
Dam, which the engineers had just built on the Allegheny River.

In the Iroquoian Seneca tongue, which many of the Seneca people
still speak, *kinzua* means "fish on spear" and refers to a site on the river
198 miles upstream from Pittsburgh, just south of the New York state
line, where the dam was constructed. Finished in 1965 at a cost of almost
$120,000,000, it was the largest concrete-and-earth-fill dam in the east-
ern United States, almost 1,900 feet long and 179 feet high. It was
designed to help control floods, as well as to regulate the flow of water
for navigation and for the dilution of polluting waste matter poured into

the river by mills above Pittsburgh. Among the dam's important by-
products were hydroelectric power and the creation of new water sports
facilities in the region. Depending on rainfall and the season of the year,
the reservoir's size fluctuates constantly. At its maximum, in time of
severe flood conditions, the lake extends thirty-five miles upriver from
the dam to the city of Salamanca, New York, and has a water surface of
more than 21,000 acres. But under ordinary conditions, it extends
twenty-seven miles, more or less, covers some 12,000 acres, and has a
shoreline of ninety-one miles in summer. In winter it is a considerably
smaller pool, covering a minimum of about 6,600 acres and exposing
large areas of mud flats. To the summer vacationer, tourist, fisherman,
and lover of lake sports, the reservoir has provided a large new recreation
center in the forested mountain country of western New York and Pennsylvania and has borne out the army engineers' promise that the dam and
its lake would result in the development of a relatively untouched part of
the Northeast in the time-honored tradition of American progress.

But there was a cost beyond the cost of the dam. In creating the
Allegheny Reservoir, the army engineers gutted the Seneca Indians' reservation, drowning approximately 10,000 acres of the Indians' only habitable land, including their ancestral homes, farms, hunting grounds,
fishing sites, community buildings, and burial plots, and deliberately
breaking an Indian treaty in order to do so. In this case, the violated
document was the nation's oldest still-active treaty, made in 1794 with
The Cornplanter's Senecas and the other Iroquois nations at a time when
the new American republic urgently needed their friendship on the turbulent northwest frontier, and resting ever since then on solemn guarantees which were given the Indians by President George Washington and
which were supposed to endure through the life of the United States
itself.

To many non-Indians who were aware of the corps's treaty-breaking
action, it was, as Florida congressman James Haley of the House Interior
and Insular Affairs Committee told the engineers on May 18, 1963, "a
horrible tragedy, a horribly tragic thing," underscored especially by the
fact that the Kennedy administration was, at that same time, insisting that
the Soviet Union and the countries in its camp honor and respect the
sacredness of treaties. To the Senecas and to many other Native Americans, it was, moreover, a shocking reminder not only that the history of
the White man's dispossession of the Indians had not ended, but that in
the second half of the twentieth century the dispossession could be every
bit as callous and ruthless as it had been in the past.

The story of the engineers' seizure of the Senecas' land epitomized
one of the bitterest aspects of Indian-White relations. In the past, nothing

contributed more to Indian-White conflicts than the non-Indians' taking of Indian land, and nothing today keeps Native Americans more wary of the rest of American society than their realization that they must continue to struggle defensively for the little land that is left to them. "Once," Native American elders and teachers remind their youth, "we owned all the land." (Traditionally, Indian communities or tribes, rather than individuals, were deemed to own the land because the Creator had not given it to individuals but to communal groups to live upon, respect, and preserve for future generations. They could share its bounty with others, but they could not sell it.) In the present-day United States, including Alaska, the tribes and individual Indians own approximately 90 million acres, less than 3 percent of what they originally possessed. The importance to the Indians is not in the statistics alone, but in what the loss meant to the losers. "The White man," declared Harriett Pierce, a Seneca descendant of The Cornplanter, during the heat of her tribe's fight with the engineers, "views land for its money value. We Indians have a spiritual tie with the earth, a reverence for it that Whites don't share and can hardly understand."

Through the years, thousands of Indians, members of tribes in all parts of the country, told White men: "The earth is my mother. The earth is part of my body. I belong to the land out of which I came." In the Northwest, Smohalla, a Wanapam Indian holy man on the middle Columbia River, argued with White missionaries, miners, government agents, and soldiers in the nineteenth century: "You ask me to plow the ground! Shall I take a knife and tear my mother's bosom? Then when I die she will not take me to her bosom to rest. You ask me to dig for stone! Shall I dig under her skin for her bones? Then when I die I cannot enter her body to be born again. You ask me to cut grass and make hay and sell it, and be rich like white men! But how dare I cut off my mother's hair?" White negotiators heard such sentiments, reflections of the spiritual bond between Native Americans and the earth and all creation, used to justify Indian refusals to sell their lands at countless treaty meetings. "These lands are ours," thundered the Shawnee chief Tecumseh to General William Henry Harrison in Indiana in 1810. "No tribe has a right to sell. Sell a country! Why not sell the air, the clouds and the great sea, as well as the earth? Did not the Great Spirit make them all for the use of his children?"

The Indians' highly charged religious and emotional bonds with the earth increased the pain and agony of each loss of land. To understand the depth of the wrench is to understand why so many tribes refused to sell their homelands which the Creator spirit had given them and where their ancestors were buried, why they struggled desperately to stay where they were, why the Sioux refused (as some of them still refuse) to accept monetary payment for their sacred Black Hills in South Dakota and Chief Joseph's Nez Perces suffered persecution and death trying to hold on to their home in Oregon's Wallowa Valley. In today's America, the tribes have come to know the economic value of their lands and natural resources, and they fight to retain them for the viability and self-sufficiency they will help to give their people. But the land continues, as well, to have its much greater and deeper meaning for them, and many Indians still refuse to permit their leaders and lawyers to accept title-extinguishment money from the government for lands that were unjustly taken from them in the past and which they claim still belong to them.

History itself has shown the Indians something more. Without a land base, there is no cohesive people, there is no tribe, there are no longer Indians, only lost, wandering individuals being sucked into the non-Indian world. For a tribe to continue to exist, for Indians and Indianness to continue, there must be a recognized, protected, and revered tribal home. By the time of the emergence of the United States after the Revolution, so many Indian nations of the colonial period had lost their lands and disappeared that many of the tribes that were still powerful recognized the need to secure guarantees for the protection of their lands from the White man's new government. Requiring the friendship of the strong tribes, the Congress of the Articles of Confederation fashioned an Indian policy in the Northwest Ordinance of 1787 designed to satisfy the tribes: "The utmost good faith shall always be observed towards the Indians," the Congress declared. "Their lands and property shall never be taken from them without their consent; and, in their property, rights, and liberty, they shall never be invaded or disturbed, unless in just and lawful wars authorized by Congress; but laws founded in justice and humanity shall from time to time be made for preventing wrongs being done to them, and for preserving peace and friendship with them."

Largely at the insistence of the Iroquois tribes and those of the Ohio Valley, the first administration of George Washington adopted the same policy, but with additions. Finances for the new government would come, in large part, from the sale of western land to settlers. While the federal government maintained political sovereignty over all the land within the territorial boundaries of the United States, it recognized that the Indians held title to the lands that they occupied. Therefore, as the White settlers advanced westward, the government would send out commissioners ahead of them, buy required lands—by congressionally approved treaties made with the Indian owners—survey the purchased lands, and then sell them to the settlers. No one but the treaty-making agents of the federal government could deal with the Indians, and no Indian land could pass directly from a tribe to a private citizen or a state. Furthermore, in various negotiations with the Iroquois Six Nations, Washington's administration promised to protect tribal land rights against states and private individuals; pay for land cessions with annuities, grants to Indian headmen, and educational, technical, and agricultural assistance; and provide justice for the Indians in federal courts when they were aggrieved by Whites.

The shape of federal-Indian relations from then on stemmed, theoretically at least, from these policies. Like the provision of the Northwest Ordinance, some of the policies were rooted in those of the British government and the royal colonies before the Revolution—and, like them, some were merely good intentions that frequently were neither observed nor enforced. Settlers and land speculators often went ahead of federal treaty commissioners and usurped Indian lands or violated the law and made their own, often dishonest, deals. Friction and conflict developed, and by the time government land purchasers arrived on the scene, there was little they could do, for their own political health, but cajole, bribe, coerce, or deceive the tribes into signing formal cession documents for lands already overrun or threatened by Whites. If the Indians refused to sign, the commissioners worked on them with alcohol, forged X's next to their names on the documents, got more pliant and venal Indians to sign, even if the land in question did not belong to them, or called in troops, who destroyed the tribes and forced the defeated and demoralized survivors to hand over the desired lands.

In this fashion, the promises of the Northwest Ordinance became forgotten words; the national policy of extinguishing Indian land titles fairly and justly was rhetoric heard only in Washington, D.C.; tribes were cut up, removed from their homelands and forced to move again and again, reduced to impotent remnants on reservations, and absorbed by other tribes and deprived of their identity; and the Whites acquired most of the land and resources of the present-day United States. When all Indian military resistance ended, the goal of assimilating the survivors served as a vehicle for stripping the tribes, even more quickly, of whatever lands they still possessed. With Indians assimilated and living as individual breadwinners like everyone else, there would be no tribes, and without tribes, there would be no tribal lands. All such property, save for bits and pieces allotted as the private homesteads of individual Indians, would pass finally into the public domain to be purchased and used by non-Indians.

In 1887, the Dawes Allotment Act, providing for the end of tribal relationships and stipulating that reservations were to be divided into family-sized farms which would be allotted to each Indian, inaugurated this policy. Each adult Indian was to receive 160 acres, each minor child

80 acres, and whatever was left over would be declared surplus and sold to Whites. The policy remained in force until 1934, when it was seen to have been a catastrophe for the Indians and was ended. In the intervening years, some 90 million acres of the most productive and valuable Indian lands passed into White ownership. The government was not able to implement the policy on every reservation, but even where it was carried out, it failed to break up the tribes, convert large numbers of Indians into independent farmers, or hasten assimilation. Many of the Indians, without the cultural background or training for the new way of life, and lacking financial credit or assistance of any kind, leased or sold their allotments to Whites at bargain prices. Others were cheated out of their holdings, and still others merely gave up on land too poor to farm. Poverty increased, and reservation life became marked by disease and hopelessness.

For a time, under the New Deal in the 1930's, meager funds were made available to try to rebuild the land base of some of the tribes. Most of the land purchased for the Indians was submarginal, however, and the program was soon abandoned. In the early 1950's Congress and the Eisenhower administration took up where the Dawes Allotment Act had stopped and, hoping to end "the Indian problem," launched the "termination" policy designed to sever relationships between the federal government and the tribes. Several tribes were terminated, their lands stripped of government trust protection, and their members deprived of treaty rights. Thrown on their own as subjects of the states in which they resided, the Indians were quickly victimized. Unable to pay taxes or meet their needs, they were reminded that they now had the rights of all citizens to dispose of their lands and resources as they wished. Once again, Whites, by purchase or trickery, acquired large amounts of Indian land.

The termination policy was too harsh and abrupt. Gradually, the Indians resisted, with new pride and patriotism flowing out of their resistance. In 1958 the government was forced to abort further implementation of the policy, and by the early 1960's Native Americans throughout the country were at last asserting the need to stand and fight for what land was left to them. "Everything is tied to our homeland," D'Arcy McNickle, a Flathead Indian anthropologist, reminded other Indians at a Chicago Indian conference in 1961. "Our language, religion, songs, beliefs—everything. Without our homeland, we are nothing." In Alaska, an Eskimo woman from Bethel told a senate committee during hearings on a Native Land Claims bill: "Take our land, take our life." And in western New York and Pennsylvania, an inspiring example of resistance to the further erosion of their land base was being provided to all tribes by the fight the Senecas were waging against the flooding of their reservation by the Corps of Engineers.

From the beginning, when army lawyers first looked into the problem of acquiring the Senecas' land for the Kinzua Dam's reservoir, the engineers had little concern for the uniqueness of the Indians' treaty-secured position. The corps is a highly efficient and capable expression of the modern technological age, able to build great dams, move mountains, control roaring rivers, and alter any manner of landscape. But to many the corps exemplifies, at the same time, the big, self-propelled, faceless juggernauts of the world that grind ahead, seemingly unmoved by the outcries of the people whose lives they affect. As an autocratically tinged bureaucracy and one of the most irresistible lobbies in the nation, relying on the "pork barrel" support of political groups everywhere who sooner or later want public works for their own areas, it befriends the American people in the mass and in the abstract, and makes war on the same people when, as individuals or in small numbers (including not a few Indian tribes who have lost land to the engineers' water projects along the Missouri and other western rivers), they get in the way. In 1966 a special study group composed of two colonels and a civilian official of the corps reported that "too often the [engineers'] planning effort is confined to refining the concept and proving the justification for one or a few promising projects. Too few reports contain evidence that adequate consideration was given to alternatives and to all factors pertinent to producing an optimum solution." In the case of the building of the Kinzua Dam, an "optimum solution" required that the engineers possess enough of an understanding of, and a concern for, the Indians' close spiritual tie to their land and the Senecas' 1794 treaty to deter them from breaking the pact.

The Senecas, whom the engineers confronted in the 1950's, are descendants of the westernmost of the five confederated Iroquois tribes who for numerous centuries had occupied present-day upper New York State from Lake Champlain to the Genesee River. From east to west they are, in order, the Mohawks, Oneidas, Onondagas, Cayugas, and Senecas, the latter being known (as they still are) as the western anchor, or keeper of the western door, of the Iroquois Confederacy. Joined in the early eighteenth century by Tuscarora refugees, Iroquoian relatives who had been driven out of North Carolina by Whites, the confederacy thereafter became known as the League of the Six Nations. In the late 1600's, several groups of Senecas had moved southwestward from the Genesee River to the upper Allegheny Valley, and during the ensuing years those western Senecas maintained domination over a large area of western New York and Pennsylvania and eastern Ohio, swelling their own numbers and power by absorbing many Indian refugee groups and Indian and non-Indian captives. From time to time, French, English, or Dutch traders were welcomed in the region, but no White settlement was permitted.

Toward the mid-1700's, trouble came for the western Senecas when English and French military groups began to fight for authority over the upper Ohio Valley. The Senecas, who guarded and wielded power in that area in behalf of the League, were caught between the two groups of warring Whites, but when the struggle erupted into the full-fledged French and Indian War, most of them sided with the French, participating in Braddock's defeat and other battles. With the final victory of the British and the withdrawal of the French from the continent in 1763, the still powerful Senecas joined more westerly Indians under Pontiac and tried unsuccessfully to oust the English forces and all settlers from the country west of the Appalachian Mountains. After the collapse of Pontiac's alliance, the western Senecas retired up the Allegheny River to their towns in the woods along the New York–Pennsylvania border.

With the coming of the American Revolution, pressure was again exerted on individual Iroquois tribes, this time by both the British and the colonists, who, between them, finally split the League. Many of the Senecas and Cayugas joined Joseph Brant and his Mohawks as allies of the British, the Oneidas and some of the Tuscaroras threw in with the Americans, and other groups tried to remain neutral.

Under The Cornplanter, whom they elected as their war leader and whom the British commissioned as a captain, the western Senecas from the Genesee and Allegheny valleys fought American troops at Oriskany and elsewhere and raided American posts and settlements. The Cornplanter, then only about twenty-five years old, was already one of the best known and most respected of all the Iroquois war chiefs. Born at the Seneca village of Canawaugus near present-day Avon, New York, about 1750, he was the son of a Seneca mother of chiefly lineage and a Dutch trader from Albany named John Abeel. He had grown to manhood as a bold warrior, distinguishing himself in the border warfare of the times, and by the outbreak of the Revolution he was the principal war chief and a leading spokesman of the western Senecas.

The Revolution was disastrous for the Iroquois. In retaliation for their raids and for the help the Indians had given the British, American punitive forces invaded the countries of the Senecas and other tribes in 1779, burning towns, destroying crops, and driving the people from their homelands. Many of the pro-British Senecas joined Brant at Fort Niagara, an English post. In 1781, following great hardships, some of the people drifted back to their homes. Others formed a large permanent settlement at Buffalo Creek near Fort Niagara. Cornplanter and those who returned to the country of the Genesee and Allegheny rivers found their villages in ruins. Settling down on the Allegheny, Cornplanter took over the civil leadership of his people from an elderly uncle, Kiasutha.

The League was divided, but the individual tribes were still deemed dangerous by the Americans. With a pro-British group of Iroquois, Brant moved to Canada, where, in the post-Revolutionary years, he continued to intrigue with the British and threaten the American frontier. Under the protection of the British along the Niagara, where English troops and traders remained on American soil until Jay's Treaty of 1794, the displaced eastern Senecas kept up a bitter hostility to the Americans. And along the Allegheny, Cornplanter and the western Senecas were a threat closer to the White settlements in New York and Pennsylvania. Farther west, American families were pushing into the Ohio country and were being resisted by Shawnees, Miamis, and other confederated tribes in that area. The peril to the non-Indians was acute, for at any time one or all of the disaffected Iroquois groups, under the influence of the British, could join the Ohio country Indians in an all-out, catastrophic war on the settlers.

To counteract the danger, American peace commissioners met time and again with both the eastern and western Senecas, offering concessions, compromises, and gifts. The diplomatic efforts, together with his own need for amicable relations with nearby American traders and troops, finally induced Cornplanter to adopt a policy of reconciliation with the United States, and the Seneca chief's influence was decisive with most of the Iroquois. By 1794, when General Anthony Wayne crushed the Ohio tribes with finality at the Battle of Fallen Timbers, Cornplanter had not only immobilized the Senecas and other Iroquois so that they remained out of the conflict, but had participated in the sale of large areas of Seneca land in western Pennsylvania and New York to the Americans. His actions had been angrily opposed by many Iroquois chiefs, including Red Jacket, a fiery eastern Seneca orator at Buffalo Creek, but Cornplanter had ignored them, saying, "If we do not sell the land, the whites will take it anyway."

The Americans were not unaware of the many good services Cornplanter had rendered them, often at the risk of his life. Time and again, they had been informed of his travels to Buffalo Creek, to the Ohio country, and to the various Iroquois groups to argue with sachems and chiefs in behalf of the Americans. On other occasions, he had gone to Albany, Philadelphia, and New York to meet with White officials. In December 1790, he had met President Washington in Philadelphia and had told him that his people were beginning to fear the loss of their own lands to White settlers. On December 29, Washington responded to him in a letter that was to have little meaning to the Army Corps of Engineers when the Senecas presented it to them more than a century and a half later. Washington wrote:

". . . Your great object seems to be the security of your remaining lands, and I have therefore upon this point, meant to be sufficiently strong and clear. That in future you cannot be defrauded of your lands. That you possess the right to sell, and the right of refusing to sell your lands. That therefore the sale of your lands in future, will depend entirely upon yourselves."

In 1791 the state of Pennsylvania, in acknowledgment of Cornplanter's friendship, and "to fix his attachment to the state," granted him and his heirs "in perpetuity" three tracts of land on the upper Allegheny River in Pennsylvania. One of these, near present-day West Hickory, the chief sold in 1795 to a White friend. Another, at what is now Oil City, he sold to two White men in 1818, but claimed he was paid in worthless money and notes. The third tract, approximately 780 acres, was on the western bank of the Allegheny about three miles south of the New York state line. It included Cornplanter's own town of Jenuchshadago, or The Burnt House, and two islands in the river that comprised another 120 acres. Cornplanter made it his headquarters, settling down there with his followers, who in time built thirty houses for about 400 people on the grant.

In 1794, after Wayne's victory over the Ohio tribes, the federal government sent Timothy Pickering of Massachusetts as commissioner to meet with the chiefs of the Six Nations at Canandaigua, New York, and to try to establish a lasting peace with all the Iroquois. Pickering's mission was successful: on November 11, 1794, he signed a treaty with fifty-nine sachems and war chiefs, including Cornplanter, Fish Carrier, Red Jacket, Half Town, and Handsome Lake for the western and eastern Senecas, delineating the boundaries of what, in effect, became reservations for the tribes and securing a permanent peace between the United States and the different Iroquois groups.

Article 3 of the treaty, which was signed by Washington, applied only to the Senecas: "Now the United States acknowledge all the land within the aforementioned boundaries, to be the property of the Seneka nation; and the United States will never claim the same, nor disturb the Seneka nation . . . but it shall remain theirs, until they choose to sell the same to the people of the United States, who have the right to purchase."

These were the words which the engineers, a century and a half later, were to brush aside. The solemn promise was "never," and until the 1950's it gave the Senecas security. In their imagery they made it read:

"as long as the grass shall grow and the rivers run," and with that contract they lived in peace.

Cornplanter died on February 18, 1836, and was buried on his grant. That small plot of land in the meantime had taken on added meaning for the Senecas, for there, in 1799, Cornplanter's half-brother, the prophet Ganiodayo, or Handsome Lake, had had the first of his revelations and had preached the Good Message—a set of new religious beliefs and practices—to all the Iroquois. This new religion, which still permeates Iroquois life, was a blending of old Seneca beliefs with an ethical code borrowed largely from the Quakers. Its birth on the Cornplanter grant, from where it spread, endowed the plot with something of the sacredness of a holy shrine. In ensuing years, the burial of Cornplanter and his followers and descendants on the same grounds added to the grant's significance, a fact acknowledged by the state of Pennsylvania in 1866 when it erected the stone monument over Cornplanter's grave.

Under the tutelage of Quakers, who first came to live among the Senecas on the Allegheny River in 1798, the Indians became rapidly acculturated to the White man's way of living. Indians were educated, and Indian men were induced to farm. (The Quakers persuaded the Senecas to end their customary way of living together in extended families in longhouses and to spread out in individually owned homesteads along the river, out of sight of each other, so the men would not be embarrassed by being seen in the fields, doing what had traditionally been considered women's work.) Beginning in 1803, factional disputes on the Cornplanter grant resulted in a gradual movement by Senecas to new communities higher up on the Allegheny River across the New York border, and by 1806 Coldspring, south of present-day Salamanca, had become a new Seneca center.

As a result of various land sales which they continued to make to settlers and land companies, the Senecas' territory eventually dwindled to five, and then four, reservations in western New York. They were the Cattaraugus, close to Lake Erie south of Buffalo; the Tonawanda, slightly northeast of Buffalo; a small plot of some 640 acres near Oil Spring in western New York; and a long, narrow strip along the Allegheny River, from present-day Vandalia, New York, to the Pennsylvania state line. This became known as the Allegany reservation, its name evolving with a different spelling from that of the river. South of this reservation, across the Pennsylvania line, descendants of Cornplanter still dwelled on his grant, which they had inherited as his heirs.

In 1848, after the Ogden Land Company had almost managed to swindle the Senecas out of the last of their holdings in New York by getting drunken, venal, or bogus chiefs to sign papers of sale, a group of young Senecas on the Allegany and Cattaraugus reservations deposed the hereditary chiefs for incompetence and graft and set up a new, republican form of government on those two reservations. Calling themselves the Seneca Nation, they wrote a constitution that separated church and state; provided for a legislative council of eighteen (now sixteen) members and a president and other officers elected annually (now every two years) by all adult males (women now have the vote too); established a judiciary of three "peacemakers" for minor crimes; asked that jurisdiction over serious crimes and major lawsuits be transferred to New York state courts; and detached the two reservations from the League of the Six Nations, which had continued (and still continues) to hold together in brotherhood most of the Iroquois peoples in the United States and Canada. Today, more than 130 years later, the Seneca Nation still exists; it has the same form of government, the office of president rotating every two years between the Allegany and Cattaraugus reservations.

In the middle of the nineteenth century the Erie and Pennsylvania railroads, pushing across New York, bought rights-of-way from the Senecas and established a junction on the Allegany reservation. The site grew into a village, originally called Hemlock but renamed for Don Jose Salamanca Mayel, a large stockholder in the Erie Railroad. The rights-of-way purchases, plus certain leases granted by the Senecas to private citizens, were confirmed by federal statute in 1875 and 1890, when Congress gave the Allegany reservation Senecas the right to grant thereafter ninety-nine-year leases to all White homeowners and businesses in Salamanca and in four other White towns established on the reservation. The leases brought ridiculously small returns to the Indians (in 1970 the entire city of Salamanca, with a population of a little more than 9,000, paid the Senecas a total of only about $16,000 in annual rent), but all the leases will be renegotiated by 1991, and the new rents will unquestionably be higher, more in line with their market worth.

As the years rolled on, the different Iroquois peoples in New York, surrounded by a sea of Whites, were all but forgotten. Living quietly on their reservations, they continued to hunt, fish, and farm, educate their children, and in many cases take jobs in the White man's world. A large number of Allegany Senecas worked in furniture factories or for the railroads in Salamanca. Others, along with Mohawks, became structural steelworkers, traveling to distant cities for periods of time to help build bridges and skyscrapers. While most of the Iroquois became Christians, many continued to observe the beliefs and practices of the Handsome Lake religion, participating in annual cycles of thanksgiving and other ceremonies. These were held in Longhouses, rectangular frame buildings which served as both social and religious centers, as well as meeting places, for the Handsome Lake followers. But even the Christians, still holding themselves apart from the Whites around them, continued to have pride in their Indian ancestry, and it was said that every Iroquois still had "one foot in the Longhouse."

In the years after World War II, several of the Six Nations were beset by sudden new threats to their reservations, upon whose land base their continued existence as tribal groups depended. In 1954, when the St. Lawrence Seaway was under construction, its builders wanted to place some of their facilities on the St. Regis reservation belonging to the Mohawks. The needed land was condemned, and though the Indians received $100,000 in compensation, they were left with less of their property and with the uneasy feeling that one day their entire reservation could be taken from them.

Three years later the Tuscaroras, whose reservation lies near Niagara Falls, were treated even more high-handedly by Robert Moses, chairman of the New York Power Authority. Part of his plan for the giant Niagara Power Project was a pump-storage reservoir to be located on the Tuscaroras' reservation. Their resistance to his original demand for 1,300 acres forced him to scale the reservoir down to 550 acres and to pay the Tuscaroras $886,000 for the land, plus the costs of relocating the nine Indian families who were living on it.

Considering the amount of land and the number of Indian families involved, however, none of these incursions matched the assault which the army engineers made on the Senecas' Allegany reservation and the Cornplanter grant.

The idea for Kinzua Dam was born in 1928, following disastrous floods in the Ohio Valley. In 1938 and again in 1941, the chief of engineers asked for and received authorization from Congress to build Kinzua and a number of other dams as part of a general program of flood control for Pittsburgh and the Ohio River basin. The Senecas were not informed by the engineers of their proposal to construct a dam that would inundate a large part of their reservation, and the engineers, in turn, were so unconcerned about the existence of a treaty which they would have to break if they built the dam that they failed to make much of a point of it in their presentation to Congress. To the corps, it seemed, land was land, no matter who lived on it. Proceeding on the assumption that the acquisition of land, ultimately, would be the usual matter of paying individual owners, engineers appeared on the Allegany Reservation in 1939 and 1940. The president and the council of the Seneca Nation, thinking that the engineers were making some studies of the river, offered no objection when they began to make surveys along the banks.

Interruptions by Secretary of the Interior Harold Ickes, who wanted Pennsylvania to pay part of the cost of the dam, and then by World War II, temporarily sidetracked the Kinzua project. Through sources other than the Corps of Engineers, however, the Senecas began to learn of the plan for the dam, and by 1955, when the engineers again appeared before the Seneca council to ask permission to continue their surveys on the reservation, the Indians were nervous. The engineers allayed their fears, however, by assuring them that they did not yet know if they wished to build the dam and would not know until they had completed their surveys. Assuming that the engineers would keep them informed, the Indians once more let them make their studies.

The members of the Seneca Nation by this time numbered approximately 4,300, of whom perhaps 1,800 lived on the Allegany reservation, 2,200 on the Cattaraugus reservation thirty miles away, and the rest off the reservations. The Allegany reservation, on which the engineers were focusing their attention, totaled 30,469 acres in a slender, forty-two-mile-long strip, averaging a mile wide, on both sides of the Allegheny River in New York as it wound through a valley to the Pennsylvania border. Some 12,000 acres of the reservation were occupied by Salamanca and the other White towns or were taken by rights-of-way for roads and railroads, and much of the rest of the land was steep, rocky, forested hillside and therefore uninhabitable. Most of the Indians lived in frame houses or hemlock-board shanties strung out in a long line in clearings and wooded areas on the lower hills and bottomlands along the river. Though individuals owned the surface portions of land "a plowshare deep," legal title to the entire reservation was held by the Seneca Nation. A plot could only be sold by its owner to another enrolled member of the Nation, and a lease to a non-Seneca required the approval of the tribal council. The average annual income of an Indian family was about $3,000 (as against $5,000 for a White family in Salamanca), but the Senecas generally lived in contentment, with fish, game, and firewood close at hand, and with a privacy and a closeness to nature that many a White visitor envied. South of the Pennsylvania line and separated from the reservation by three miles, about fifteen of The Cornplanter's descendants still lived on his grant, close to the burial ground where his monument stood. Also on the grant were a schoolhouse, a church, several barns, and aged, overgrown fields and orchards, as well as the homes of the inhabitants.

The engineers made their surveys and left, and in 1956 the Senecas were startled to learn that Congress had appropriated funds for plans for Kinzua Dam. Hearings had been held in Washington, and the engineers had testified, although the Indians had neither been invited to the hearings nor been informed that they were occurring. Now thoroughly alarmed, the Senecas and their tribal attorney moved quickly on two fronts. First, they sought an injunction to keep the engineers off their land. Next, recognizing the need for flood control, they proposed an alternative dam site that would not involve the flooding of their lands and hired two eminent private engineers, Dr. Arthur E. Morgan, first chairman of the Tennessee Valley Authority, and Barton M. Jones, who had built TVA's Norris Dam, to make an independent study of the feasibility of the alternative site.

The cat was now out of the bag. Newspapers began to publicize the attempted new seizure of Indian lands in violation of a treaty, and sympathetic congressmen claimed that the engineers had misled them, that they had not been informed about the treaty. But if the engineers were chagrined, they failed to show it. Early in 1957, ignoring their critics, they got federal courts to uphold their right to continue to make surveys on the reservation. And that same year, when Morgan and Jones gave their support to the Senecas' alternative plan for diverting Allegheny flood waters into Lake Erie, showing, also, that it would be cheaper than the cost of the Kinzua project, the engineers testified successfully against the Indians' proposal in Congress (with "explicit misstatements and misrepresentations," according to Dr. Morgan) and won another million-dollar appropriation to complete the planning and begin the construction of Kinzua Dam.

The Indians had friends, within and outside of Congress, but not enough of them. Dr. Morgan produced still another alternative proposal —a dam site that would not involve any Indian lands—but a study sponsored by the engineers concluded that Dr. Morgan's dam would cost more money and take longer to build. Morgan and the Senecas did not agree, and sought an independent evaluation, but the engineers prevailed on the Senate to turn aside this request. Treaty or no treaty, the engineers were not going to risk a reversal of their plan, which now, it was revealed, would necessitate the condemnation of slightly more than 10,000 acres of the Indians' habitable land (leaving them only 2,300 on which they could live); the moving of 134 families, or about 700 people, more than one-third of the population of the reservation; the relocation of about 3,000 Seneca graves; and the inundation of the Cornplanter grant in Pennsylvania.

Falling back on the 1794 treaty, which promised that the United States would never claim the Senecas' land and guaranteed that it would be theirs until they chose to sell it, the Indians, in a case against the Secretary of the Army, now sought to halt construction of the Kinzua project, hoping to force the adoption, instead, of the Morgan plan. On

April 14, 1958, the U.S. District Court for the District of Columbia ruled that the engineers could take reservation land, the same as any other, by the right of eminent domain, implying, in effect (although the court did not condone it), that the government of the United States, which could make a treaty, could also break it if it wished to do so. The case went on to the U.S. Court of Appeals for the District of Columbia and to the Supreme Court, but the judgment stood. Whether by their own ignorance or by the withholding of information from Congress, the engineers had maneuvered Congress into a position of voting, in the 1950's, to break still another Indian treaty, which it had the constitutional, if not the moral, right to do. By the time Congress realized what it had done, it was too late. The engineers had too many friends on Capitol Hill, and there was no one strong enough to induce the bureaucratic wheels within the corps to reverse themselves.

That this was true became painfully clear to the Senecas when, as a last desperate measure, they appealed to President Kennedy in 1961, hoping that he would use his prerogative to withhold funds appropriated for the dam. On August 9, 1961, Kennedy replied to Basil Williams, the president of the Seneca Nation: "I have now had an opportunity to review the subject and have concluded that it is not possible to halt the construction of Kinzua Dam. . . . Impounding of the funds appropriated by the Congress after long and exhaustive congressional review, and after resolution by our judicial process of the legal right of the Federal Government to acquire the property necessary to the construction of the reservoir, would not be proper."

And so the dam was built. In his letter to Williams, President Kennedy had added that he would direct federal agencies to assist the Senecas by considering the possibility of finding new land to exchange with the Nation for the area it would lose; by reviewing the recreational potential of the reservoir and methods by which the Senecas could share in that potential; by determining the special damages suffered by the Nation's loss of so much of its land; by aiding those Senecas who had to give up their homes; and by preparing recommendations for whatever legislation might be required to achieve those ends. The White House sent a copy of the letter two days later with a covering memorandum to Major General William F. Cassidy, director of civil works, Corps of Engineers, ordering the corps to "look into these questions without delay."

The letter was bucked down through the corps, and although meetings, begun two months later, were held with other government agencies such as the Bureau of Indian Affairs, as well as with representatives of the Senecas, the corps behaved as if it were thoroughly irritated with the

Indians and had no intention of doing anything for them. The corps did pay the salary of an able and dedicated representative of the Bureau of Indian Affairs, Sidney Carney, a Choctaw Indian who was sent to work among the Senecas. But except for that, two full years later, with the dam nearing completion and the Indians still living in homes that were threatened by the reservoir, so little had been done by Cassidy and the engineers to carry out Kennedy's order that some members of Congress, on their own, introduced bills authorizing payments for the relocation and rehabilitation of the Indians. Even then, corps representatives, appearing before Congress, were so intent on not being billed for any but the normal charges of building the dam (payments to Indians, charged to the corps, would certainly make Kinzua more expensive than Dr. Morgan's and the Senecas' alternative proposals), and showed so little recognition that, in this case perhaps, the nation owed something extra for breaking a treaty, that many congressmen were moved to anger. "Apparently you don't want to try to do anything for this Indian tribe," Congressman John P. Saylor of Pennsylvania berated a stony-faced corps witness. "Apparently you have become so calloused and so crass that the breaking of the oldest treaty that the United States has is a matter of little concern to you. . . . the Corps of Engineers has never intended to do anything whatsoever with regard to the Seneca Indians, and they have intended from the very beginning to treat this as just any other dam and leave the Indians only their recourse in the courts."

On August 31, 1964, after months of disagreement between the House and Senate over how much to pay the Senecas—a disagreement caused to some extent by the corps' influence in urging the Senate to cut down the original House figures and not pay the Indians except via the usual court proceedings—Congress passed a $15,000,573 reparations bill for the Senecas. But added to the bill was a disturbing amendment, inserted by termination-minded legislators, requiring the Secretary of the Interior to present to Congress within three years a plan for the termination of the Senecas' relations with the federal government—in effect imperiling the future of the tribe by bringing to an end such things as the tax-exempt status of the reservation and federal approval of leases and trusteeship of Seneca land. (As required, the plan was submitted in 1967, but by then the termination policy had been so discredited that Congress never acted on it.)

Meanwhile, shortly after President Kennedy had shut the final door on them, the Senecas, who had fought hard to save their land, set about determinedly to prepare for the coming disruption. Under the leadership of George Heron, a past president of the Nation, they set up committees to pick relocation areas for new homes and cemeteries, to plan housing and new community centers, and to propose economic development projects that would aid the people in their new situation. When Congress' appropriation became available in September 1964, the Senecas were ready to move quickly. New ranch-type houses of varying designs were built during the wet and wintry months in two tightly compressed areas that totalled 500 acres. One of them, named Jimersontown, near Salamanca, was laid out in 145 one-acre plots; the other, Steamburg, near the southern end of the reservation, had 160 plots of the same size. The Corps of Engineers built the streets in both of the new settlements. A family could own as many as three plots, but even so, the shift to suburban-type living, with houses close to each other, was a sharp and unhappy change for people who had been used to privacy and a closeness to the woods and wild game. Other money was used to move 3,000 Seneca graves to two new cemeteries; to build a community center and tribal council headquarters on each reservation; to develop a sixty-acre industrial park on the Cattaraugus Reservation for industry that, it was hoped, would employ Indians; and to set up a 1.8-million-dollar educational fund for college and business and vocational school scholarships for young Senecas. In addition, twenty-five public housing rental units on the Allegany reservation and thirty-five at Cattaraugus were erected with other federal funds.

The hubbub of moving was accentuated by constant harassment from the engineers, whose plans called for completion of the dam in 1965 and who kept posting deadlines for the Indians to get out of the condemned area. In working with the leadership of the Senecas, the engineers behaved properly and according to orders and regulations, but many Senecas today remember only their cold and officious manner and recall them as the Sioux recall Custer.

It has been traditional for the federal government, when it has wanted something from an Indian tribe, to make promises to its leadership and then let others at a later date worry about carrying out the promises—which, more often than not, was never done. In the case of the Senecas, the government continued the tradition. By 1968, with the dam built and the engineers gone from the scene, the Senecas were well on their way to adjustment to a new life on their smaller reservation. But in scores of ways, hopes that the Indians had once held high were still unrealized. Complaints ranged from new houses left unfinished (front steps not provided from the porch to the ground) or already showing signs of shoddy construction, to frustrated attempts to bring revenue to the Nation through use of the area's new recreational potential. Although the engineers, in response to President Kennedy's letter, had led the Senecas to believe that they could profit from concessions on the reservoir, the Indians were indefinitely stalled: the water level at their end of the reservoir, the upper portion, rose and fell the most and through much of the year contained great mud flats. Solving the problem by channeling or other means would have cost much more than the Indians could afford, especially since their concessions would be competing economically with other facilities (some of them free to the public) prepared by the engineers at the taxpayers' expense lower down on the lake, where the water level was more constant.

The owners and residents of the Cornplanter grant across the state line in Pennsylvania were treated even more roughly by the engineers, who maintained that the treaty of 1794 had never applied to the land that Pennsylvania had given to Cornplanter. Even so, acquiring that plot, sacred to the chief's descendants and to the followers of the Handsome Lake religion, should have dictated sensitive negotiations by the engineers; instead, its owners were treated like any other citizens whose property was being condemned. As early as February 1961, the Cornplanter heirs, organized as the Cornplanter Indian Landowners Corporation, accepted the fact that most of the grant would have to be given up to the reservoir and that Cornplanter's grave and monument would have to be moved. (Consider what White opposition might have been, said some of the Cornplanter heirs, if an engineers' project had forced the relocation of the tomb of George Washington or Abraham Lincoln.) As a means of persuading the Senecas to accept the decision quickly and without a legal contest, the engineers promised Merrill W. Bowen, president of the Cornplanter group, that the cemetery would be moved to a place of the Indians' choice.

Anxious to maintain the burial ground of the chief and their ancestors on communal property where the heirs could continue to meet with a reverential sense of the spiritual link to their past, the Senecas first selected a site on the highest part of the grant, which would not be flooded, but the engineers turned it down with the assertion that they could not build an access road to it. Then, on August 28, 1963, the Senecas were offered a sixty-five-acre tract above the level of the reservoir by the sympathetic family of Latham B. Weber, a non-Indian and the publisher of the Salamanca *Republican-Press*. The site was ideal. It was on the west side of the river, close to the old grant and contiguous to the southern boundary of the Allegany reservation. But no sooner had the newspaper announced the gift than the engineers informed both Bowen and the Webers that they needed that tract too, not for the reservoir but for public recreation purposes! "It is essential to the needs of the project," the engineers insisted.

There then began a protracted attempt by the Senecas to change the engineers' minds, an attempt that floundered in a sea of deafness, evasion, and red tape. On October 1, 1963, despite their original promise to relocate Cornplanter's grave in a place of the Indians' choice, the engineers announced in a newspaper release that all the graves on the grant would be moved to a new cemetery on a hill across the river, which the Indians would have to share with some Whites who were also losing their cemetery. More than 150 Cornplanter heirs, realizing that they were to be separated from the symbolic presence of the chief, signed a petition in protest, but the engineers were unmoved and on March 31, 1964, received authority from a federal court in Erie, Pennsylvania, to relocate the Indian graves wherever they wished. The relocation to the site across the river, which began on August 26, was attended by threats, rumors, and charges. Fearful of trouble, the engineers were overly secretive about the matter, and on the day that the grave of Cornplanter was to be opened, only two heirs were notified to be present as witnesses. Two others showed up, however, and accusations later appeared in newspapers and were filed with the engineers and with the office of Senator Joseph S. Clark of Pennsylvania, charging rough and irreverent handling of the remains, mixing of bones of different Indians, and other alleged misdeeds by those carrying out the work. Though these allegations were false, they reflected the state of tension and hostility between the Cornplanter heirs and the engineers.

The conflict was not over, for the Cornplanters still had no land for a memorial and meeting grounds to take the place of the old grant. In December 1964, Senator Clark made a personal appeal to Colonel James C. Hammer, the district engineer in Pittsburgh, to allow the Indians to keep the Weber tract. Hammer first told Clark's office that the Webers had given the land to the Senecas only after they had known it was to be condemned, which was untrue and which the Webers and Bowen were quick to deny (the Webers had offered the tract to the Indians on August 28, 1963, and had only been informed of the government's interest in acquiring the tract by Colonel Bert de Melker of the army engineers on September 24). Hammer then replied formally on January 27, 1965, suggesting that the corps meet with the Indians to try to help them find a suitable site, but implying that they could not have the Weber tract, which provided "a prime location for recreational facilities" on the new reservoir. In February, Curtis F. Hunter, a corps representative in Warren, Pennsylvania, near the dam site, met with Bowen and the Webers' attorney in Salamanca, proposed certain alternative possibilities, including the Indians' use of the Weber tract by license rather than by ownership, and suggested that they all meet with Colonel Hammer the next time that officer was in the area. On March 14 Hunter called for a meeting on the following day. Hammer did not show up, and instead of talking about the Weber tract, Hunter, according to the Senecas, seemed anxious to pressure the Indians into acceptance of the use of an alternative site across the river. When an impasse was reached, he promised to write Colonel Hammer a letter explaining the Indians' reasons for wanting to retain the Weber tract and told Bowen he would send him a copy. He failed to do this; instead, on April 1, one of his colleagues in Warren, a real estate official named Stanley O'Hopp, asked the Senecas for another meeting on April 5. At that conference, O'Hopp told them that they could not have the Weber property, but he offered them three alternative sites, the biggest of which, across the river, totaled about sixty-three acres. When the Indians again argued for the Weber tract, he told them to state their position on paper and submit it to the corps for consideration.

On April 21, Bowen followed up the suggestion and wrote to Colonel Hammer, telling him that O'Hopp's alternative proposals did not reflect a "clear understanding" of the needs and desires of the Cornplanter descendants, and then explained in detail why the Indians wished to retain the Weber tract, which adjoined the Seneca reservation. On receipt of the letter, Hammer decided that nothing could come of further discussions with the Cornplanter heirs, and he ordered condemnation proceedings to be started against the Weber property. Withholding this information from the Cornplanters, Hammer wrote Bowen on May 13 a curt note stating, "I have carefully considered the contents of your letter, but I am unable to find a valid basis for changing the determination . . . that the Weber tract in its entirety is essential to the needs of the Project."

When Bowen got the letter, he telegraphed Hammer, asking for a meeting with him personally. On May 21 Hammer's deputy, Lieutenant Colonel Bruce W. Jamison, replied evasively in a letter that "the Corps" would be pleased to be "represented at such conference as you may arrange," and also notified the Seneca, almost as an afterthought, that "in line with" Colonel Hammer's letter of May 13, the corps was commencing eminent domain proceedings for the acquisition of the Weber tract. "As you know," Jamison concluded, "the negotiations for acquisition by purchase were not productive of a mutually agreeable price." The Indians could not have known such a thing, because there had never been any negotiations with them over a price.

President Kennedy was now dead, Congress had lost interest in the dam controversy, and the Senecas were almost alone in coping with the forgotten promises. Distressed by the way the Cornplanters were being pushed around, Walter Taylor, a Quaker representative assisting the Senecas to relocate, wrote a letter to President Lyndon Johnson, appealing for his assistance in behalf of the Indians. The letter was referred routinely by the White House to Lieutenant General W. K. Wilson, Jr., chief of engineers, in Washington, who sent it to Colonel Hammer in Pittsburgh for his comments. On May 27 General Wilson replied to the Quaker representative, passing on several pieces of misinformation, among them that Hammer "had met with Mr. Bowen on several occasions to negotiate the acquisition of the land for the project" (they had not met face to face once, despite Bowen's request for such a meeting), and that when the Webers had given the land to the Indians, "it was well known that the 'Weber' tract was scheduled for acquisition by the Corps" (an untruth that Bowen and the Webers had already set straight). "The entire 'Weber' tract is essential to the needs of the project and must be acquired," General Wilson concluded, employing the same words that Hammer had used in his note of May 13 to Bowen.

The Army had its back up, and neither General Wilson nor anyone else in the corps could see the silliness of their bureaucratic rigidity. Insisting that a small, sixty-five-acre tract for recreational use was essential to the success of the Kinzua Dam project would have been farcical had it not been so unhappy for the victimized Indians. Nor did the Army stop there. From its point of view, the Quaker representative had made a grievous error in writing to the President, and now the Senecas would pay for it.

On May 28, in reply to another telegraphed appeal from Bowen, Colonel Hammer let the Cornplanter leader know that there was nothing more to discuss about the Weber property and that the Army had already instituted eminent domain proceedings. Recognizing that the engineers could not be stopped, the Cornplanter heirs finally surrendered on June 15, writing Colonel Hammer that they would give up the Weber land but wished to discuss use of the sixty-three acres across the river that Hunter and O'Hopp had mentioned the previous March and April. Hammer replied, asking Bowen to set up the meeting, but shortly afterward Bowen's wife died, and the conference did not occur until September 16. It proved to be the last straw. Hunter and O'Hopp appeared for the engineers and announced that, because of the Indians' "procrastination," the offer of sixty-three acres had been reduced to 8.42 acres, almost entirely hillside, covered with trees and brush. The Indians were shocked, but got nowhere with the corps's negotiators. In a last pitiful appeal, Bowen asked if Hunter could get the engineers to tack on another two acres at the bottom of the hill where the ground was level and the Cornplanters could hold their meetings without danger of sliding. Hunter said he would try, but the next day he called back and reported that the answer was no. Someday, he said, there might be a ski development "back in that direction," and the level land would be needed for a road on which to get in.

So the Cornplanters, in the end, accepted an exclusive but revokable license to use the 8.42 isolated acres of steep land. On September 24, 1965, Bowen wrote a final letter to Senator Clark, who, although an insistent advocate of the building of Kinzua Dam, had also tried to help the Cornplanters. Telling the Pennsylvania senator of the outcome of their struggle, Bowen urged him to make no further effort in their behalf. "We have been informed," he said, "that our prior efforts to obtain your assistance and that of President Johnson have merely irritated the Corps of Engineers and possibly damaged our case. Your intervention now might only bring about some excuse to take away the few crumbs still offered to us."

His reason for writing the senator, Bowen went on, was "to give you the benefit of our sad experience as you may find legislative opportunities to improve the approach of the Corps of Engineers to other people in the future—people who may be as inexperienced, poor, and lacking in shrewdness and legal services as we have been."

Kinzua Dam was formally dedicated on September 16, 1966. Two hundred and eighty-three years after William Penn had signed his famous treaty that had purchased land justly and honorably from Native Americans, the last Indian-owned property in Pennsylvania disappeared under the waters of what the Senecas were calling Lake Perfidy. At a gala luncheon in the local high school after the ceremonies at the dam, a quartet of non-Indian girls known as the Kinzua Damsels entertained Governor William Scranton and the other guests with the song "This Is My Country."

The Cornplanters have never received adequate restitution for the land that was taken from them. Generations of non-Indians had taken such seizures for granted. "Since most treaties are instruments of political expediency, used by a particular generation to serve their peculiar ends, there are those who believe that succeeding generations should be permitted to make their own agreements, since their problems will undoubtedly be entirely different." So ran the argument in defense of what had happened, in a letter to a Pennsylvania newspaper written by one of the non-Indians who had exhumed the remains of the Senecas in the old Cornplanter burial ground.

Times, however, were already changing. A few years later, in the 1970's, New York State tried to condemn another slice of the Senecas' land for a four-lane superhighway that would run through much of what was left of the shrunken Allegany reservation. Once again, the Senecas opposed the incursion. This time, a federal court ruled that the state had to negotiate with the tribe as equal sovereigns. In 1981 New York finally agreed to give the Seneca Nation title to 795 acres of state land and $2 million in cash in exchange for a permanent easement to 795 acres in the reservation. Some Indians opposed the transaction, but others felt it was worthwhile, for it had created a precedent for the tribe as an equal sovereign in its future relations with the state. Seizures of its land could no longer be taken for granted.

By that time, the resistance of other tribes to assaults on their lands and resources was making dramatic headlines elsewhere. In Montana, Wyoming, Utah, New Mexico, and Arizona, tribes were contesting federal agencies and energy companies over coal and uranium strip mines, power plants, pipelines, and rights-of-way that imperiled the continued existence of their reservations. Along southern and western rivers, other tribes were fighting new battles with the Corps of Engineers and the Bureau of Reclamation over dams and water projects that would flood them out or take water away from them, and in Alaska Eskimos and Indians were struggling to retain lands on which they depended for their food supplies. Still other tribes were holding off railroads, real estate and industrial developers, and planners of military and other installations that threatened to overwhelm them.

All the newfound will of Native Americans to draw the line against the further dwindling of their land base owed something to the Kinzua Dam struggle. Tribes throughout the country tried to help the Senecas, and when the Senecas' efforts failed, they were alarmed. In May 1964, the leaders of a dozen of the largest tribes, meeting at a conference on Indian poverty in Washington, D.C., called in a body on senators and members of the House of Representatives to let them know that the injustice to the Senecas had been felt by all Indians and that the breaking of the 1794 treaty would stiffen the determination of all the tribes to defend what was theirs. In a way, it was a turning point in Indian affairs.

Today, the Senecas live with memories of a lovely valley smelling of wild grapes and of an untamed river filled with trout and bordered by deep woods which the people shared with deer, bear, rabbits, and raccoons. The wilderness is gone. Above the fluctuating waters and mud flats of the engineers' reservoir, so isolated from the Indians that it seems no more to have anything to do with them, stands the transplanted Cornplanter monument in the part-Indian, part-White cemetery. Because of the secretive way in which the remains were moved from the old burial ground, no Seneca knows for sure who lies beneath the shaft. The great chief Cornplanter, say many of them, may now rest under the waters of the lake.

5

"LIKE GIVING HEROIN TO AN ADDICT"

The Reassertion of Native American Water Rights

IN THE 1970'S, a crisis came to the states of the northern plains. In that semi-arid part of the United States, where water is a fought-over commodity, a sudden burst of coal strip mining and energy-producing developments, spurred by the international oil shortage, precipitated a new era of fiercely competitive quarrels over possession of the region's limited water resources. Almost overnight, farmers and ranchers were in confrontations with acquisitive, water-consuming energy conglomerates; both contested the worried demands of municipalities and local industrial and domestic water users; and all three threatened the water supplies of the area's numerous Indian reservations.

In the apportioning of western water, the life-and-death needs of the Indians have historically been given short shrift. "Water is our lifeblood. Without it, our homeland is useless, our people will die, and we will cease to exist," more than one western tribal leader has pointed out. Moreover, Indians were there first, the original owners and the first users of the water. Yet, in carrying out the nation's Manifest Destiny policy of opening up the West to White population and development, the federal government, despite its responsibilities as trustee of the Indians' property, for more than a century led the way in taking water from the Indians and giving it to the Whites. Many tribes, as a result, were reduced to poverty and suffering, especially in the critically dry Southwest. The record in Arizona, where incoming farmers, with government support, simply dammed rivers above the irrigated fields of such industrious and self-supporting agricultural tribes as the Pimas and Papagos, cutting off their water supply and condemning them to ruin and starvation, was particularly odious. There, today, the attitude behind such callousness is still strong. The contemporary growth of central Arizona, the refusal to meter the groundwater by water-wasteful cotton-growing corporations, and the greed of land and tract-building speculators in Phoenix, Tucson, Scottsdale, and other communities are still supported in large measure by an indifference to the needs of the water-starved tribes and their reservations and by the use of such refined methods of robbery as the stealthy oblique pumping of water from declining water tables beneath Indian reservations for pipeline delivery to the lawns and faucets of burgeoning real estate developments for newly arrived Whites.

But amid the impact of the energy crisis on the northern plains there were signs that a new day was dawning for Indian water rights. The situation was, still is, and for a long time to come will be, rancorous and tied in the knots of legalistic procedures (there is no branch of American law more susceptible to complexity and confusion than that of water rights). Nevertheless, as the result of new Indian assertiveness, various tribes by the mid-1970's had managed to expose, and inspire judicial condemnation of, the derelictions of their trustee, impelling the federal government, finally in 1979, to move over to the Indians' side in Montana, where conflicts resulting from energy developments had become the hottest. In that year, the Justice Department filed suits to try to safeguard the threatened water resources of the Flathead, Blackfeet, Rocky Boys, Fort Peck, and Fort Belknap reservations by asking a federal court to establish the amount of water to which they had rights prior to all others from the Flathead, Milk, Marias, and Poplar rivers in that state.

The suits surprised both Indians and Whites and caused immediate controversy. Many non-Indians foresaw a loss of water to the reservations and were angered. The suits were "unfair to non-Indians and non-federal water users," complained Montana's senior senator, John Melcher. "This strong-arm tactic by the Justice Department must be met with strong resistance by Montanans." It may not have occurred to him that he was upholding Indian sovereignty by implying that the Native Americans were not also Montanans, but the tribes, too, were upset. The Justice Department had filed the suits without adequately consulting them, an affront to their struggle for self-determination and the right to make decisions about their own affairs. Moreover, in view of the federal government's long record of selling out the tribes, of losing Indian rights by the use of second-rate government lawyers and ill-prepared cases, and of forcing injurious settlements on the Indians, the tribes were suspicious of the Justice Department's intent. If there were to be suits, they wished to use their own lawyers and pursue the cases themselves. In addition, they were not sure that they wanted their water rights established, or "quantified"—not yet, anyway. It would limit them to all the water they would get now and forever into the future—for all foreseeable and unforeseeable needs of their children and their children's children. They knew that under already established law they possessed treaty-guaranteed claims to all the water ever required to carry out the function of their reservations. "Quantification," to them, implied another stealing of their property by putting a permanent limit on what water they could claim and use.

But the government went ahead with the suits. Interior Department officials reminded the Indians that representatives from all of Montana's seven reservations had tried to negotiate with the state legislature, but the state had snubbed them and the legislature had passed a bill putting all water users, including the tribes, under state authority. Montana's next step would have been to haul the tribes into a state court for an enforced settlement of their water rights, and the tribes knew, said the Interior Department, that they could not get as fair a hearing in a state court as in a federal court. From experience, the tribes readily agreed with that and recognized, at length, that the federal government had raced the state to litigation and had successfully gotten the issue into a federal court. So the Montana water-rights cases, which would inevitably be drawn-out and might land ultimately in the Supreme Court, started toward a decision that would take years to resolve.

How well the government would do for the Montana tribes could not be foreseen. But there was good reason for the Indians to be wary. Courts, not public opinion—and certainly not Congress, a national administration, or state governments—had forced the Justice Department to reach its new, protective position. In particular, a case in Nevada, affecting a small, relatively little-known tribe, the Pyramid Lake Paiutes, was familiar to many of the Indians. More than most other cases, it had dramatized for the courts, as well as for Native Americans throughout the country, the historic role of the trustee as a robber of Indian rights.

There were political and legal backdrops to that history, all of them familiar to tribes that were trying to protect their water rights, but not well understood by most non-Indians. Under the Commerce Clause of the Constitution, the federal government, specifically Congress, is charged with conducting all affairs with Indians. Until 1871, those affairs were generally formalized by treaties, as with foreign powers, which under another constitutional provision were recognized as "the supreme Law of the Land." No state, save by the express authority of Congress, ever had the constitutional right to deal with the affairs of Indians within its borders—nor do they yet have that right. This injunction was sustained forcibly by Justice John Marshall in *Worcester* v. *Georgia* in 1832 (". . . all intercourse with them [the Indians] shall be carried on exclusively by the government of the Union") and by numerous subsequent statutes and court decisions. In addition, new states, on acceptance into the Union, were frequently required to accept a congressional reminder that Indian lands within the state "shall remain under the absolute jurisdiction and control of the Congress of the United States." To the Indians, therefore, the question of the settling of their water rights has rightly been considered a matter between them and the federal government, including its judiciary branch, whose courts—not without considerable significance—have been freer than state courts from the anti-Indian political and economic pressures of those Whites within a state who covet Indian resources.

During the nineteenth century, many reservations were created, most of them by treaty between the federal government and the tribes, but some (for tribes whose lands had already been overrun) by special executive or congressional order that often gave landless peoples a home in lieu of what had been taken from them. At the same time, and into the twentieth century, statutes and court decisions confirmed treaty rights, as well as services owed to the tribes in return for the lands they had given up or lost, and, also, defined responsibilities of the federal government to the tribes, including the obligation to act as trustee over Indian property. In the face of non-Indian political pressures, the carrying out of the trust function left much to be desired. As a matter of practice, the government acted more often as the agent of non-Indian interests intent on acquiring or using Indian lands or resources, usually at bargain rates, than as protector of what the Indians owned. With the connivance of the government, through the Department of the Interior, tribes were cheated and robbed, their assets were mishandled and subjected to fraud, and it became a habit not even to inform them of developments and agreements made in their name that would adversely affect their resources. Compounding the injustices was a conflict of interest within the Department of the Interior itself. While one agency of the Department, the Bureau of Indian Affairs, was charged with the responsibility for the trust function, other Department agencies, including the Bureau of Reclamation, the Bureau of Land Management, the National Park Service, and the Fish and Wildlife Service—looking out for the interests of the American people as a whole—often appropriated Indian lands and their resources for their own projects or trampled on Indian rights. Having more support from the non-Indian population than the BIA, the latter agencies generally found it easy to persuade Interior's Solicitor and the Department of Justice lawyers to side with them and refuse to go to court in the Indians' behalf, and the BIA, in turn, found it politically expedient to let the Indians lose.

Though the tribes, on the whole, were unable to protect themselves and were not only illegally unrepresented but—also in violation of the Constitution—were permitted to suffer losses without due process of law, their water interests occasionally did surface in significant law cases, particularly *Winters* v. *United States* in 1908, *United States* v. *Ahtanum Irrigation District* in 1956, and *Arizona* v. *California* in 1963. Those cases established for Indians what became known as the Winters' Doctrine (after the name of the first case), which held that when the United States government created Indian reservations, it also reserved, by implication, sufficient water in any streams running through or bordering on a reservation to carry out the purposes of that reservation—that is, to make the reservation livable by reserving, also, whatever water "may be reasonably necessary, not only for present uses, but for future requirements." Moreover, since it was ruled that treaties were "not a grant of rights to the Indians, but a grant of rights from them—a reservation of those not granted," the Indians, rather than the government, had reserved the water, which like the land was their property, and they were generally deemed to possess a paramount and first-priority right, ahead of any rights a state might grant, to all the water necessary for a reservation's purposes.

In theory, this would appear to have been an answer to the tribes' water problems. The Winters' Doctrine, dating from as long ago as 1908, seemed to have offered the reservations sound legal grounds to retain, maintain, and safeguard whatever water they required, for then and for the future. But to most tribes whose water rights had already been taken from them or were still being threatened, the difficulty was to make the law of the Winters' Doctrine apply to themselves. Waging a long, complicated, and costly water-rights case on their own was beyond the means or capability of impoverished and legally unsophisticated peoples, and there were dozens of reasons—including the prospect of exposing its own culpability and thereby becoming a defendant—why their trustee, the Department of the Interior, refused to have the Justice Department initiate Winters' Doctrine suits for them. The years thus went by, with the Department doing little to stem the theft of Indian water resources—until the fate of one body of tribally owned water, Nevada's Pyramid Lake, possessed by a small group of Northern Paiutes, suddenly in the 1960's became too big a national scandal for the government to ignore.

The "Pathfinder," Lieutenant John C. Frémont of the Army's Corps of Topographical Engineers, was the first White man to describe Pyramid Lake. Exploring southward from Oregon at the head of a party of twenty-five men, including the veteran trappers and guides Kit Carson and Tom

Fitzpatrick, he reached the summit of a range of barren hills in northwestern Nevada on January 10, 1844, and sighted in the desert "a sheet of green" breaking "upon our eyes like the ocean." "The waves were curling in the breeze," Frémont reported, "and their dark-green color showed it to be a body of deep water. For a long time we sat enjoying the view. . . . It was set like a gem in the mountains."

The explorers found a well-used Indian trail and, following it south along the eastern shore of the great inland lake, passed herds of mountain sheep, flocks of ducks, and odd tufa formations—calcium carbonate deposits precipitated from the water along the lake's edge mostly by the timeless action of algae and waves, and resembling castles, domes, and needles of varicolored stone. One of them particularly, an island rising almost three hundred feet above the surface of the water, caught their fancy. It "presented a pretty exact outline of the great pyramid of Cheops," Frémont said. "This striking feature suggested a name for the lake, and I called it Pyramid Lake."

At the southern end of the lake the explorers came on a camp of Cui-ui Ticutta Indians (eaters of the cui-ui fish—pronounced *kwee-wee*), a band of a widespread Great Basin tribe which called itself Numa (the People), who are known today as Northern Paiutes. The Indians greeted the Whites in friendship and supplied them with great quantities of fish —"magnificent salmon trout," said Frémont's cartographer, Charles Preuss, who wrote in his diary, "I gorged myself until I almost choked." The fish were giant Lahontan cutthroat trout, a species found in no other part of the world. "Their flavor was excellent," Frémont reported, "superior, in fact, to that of any fish I have ever known. They were of extraordinary size—about as large as the Columbia River Salmon—generally from two to four feet in length." There were ample supplies of them, taken from the lake and a river that flowed into it beside the Indian camp, and the people, who, Frémont noted, "appeared to live an easy and happy life," gave the visitors "a salmon-trout feast as is seldom seen . . . every variety of manner in which fish could be prepared—boiled, fried, and roasted in the ashes—was put into requisition; and every few minutes an Indian would be seen running off to spear a fresh one."

That was almost a century and a half ago. To the modern-day visitor who catches his first sight of the huge body of water in the desert, Pyramid Lake is still as breathtakingly dramatic as it was to Frémont. Shaped like a partly opened fan, a little more than thirty miles long on its north-south axis, some eleven miles wide at its broadest expanse in the north and less than four miles wide in the south, it lies in a long, hidden basin near the Nevada-California border. Ranges of arid mountains, rising as high as four thousand feet above the water, surround the lake, descending toward it in steep declines and long, sloping benches and flats covered with sagebrush and other desert plants. On the south the mountains conceal the lake from travelers hurrying by on the east-west railroad or Interstate 80, as well as from the busy urban centers of Reno and Sparks, only thirty miles to the southwest.

The color of the lake, deep blue, green, or gray, changes to reflect the hues of the desert sky but depends also on the density and movement of concentrations of plankton in its waters. Along the shore there are still relatively few signs of development or of man's presence, and the great sheet of water and the hills around it are overwhelmingly quiet save for the sounds of wildlife. California gulls, Caspian terns, and blue herons flap and soar across the sky. Ducks ride the swells, and approximately 7,500 white pelicans, probably the largest colony of that species in North America, nest on Anaho Island, a 750-acre National Wildlife Refuge three hundred yards off the eastern shore. The curled-horned mountain sheep that Frémont saw are gone, but coyotes, mule deer, jackrabbits, and bobcats are abundant, as are armies of ground squirrels, lizards, and other rodents and reptiles that make their home in the desert cover.

Despite its large size, the lake is fragile. A remnant of a bigger prehistoric body of water known as Lake Lahontan that filled much of the western Great Basin during the Ice Age, it has only one principal source of water, the Truckee River, which starts at Lake Tahoe in the High Sierras on the Nevada-California border, almost one hundred miles to the southwest. The river runs down the eastern slope of the Sierras, through Reno and Sparks, and empties into the southern end of the lake near the present town of Nixon, on the site of the Indian camp that Frémont visited in 1844. Pyramid has a maximum depth of about 335 feet, and no outlet, but it loses approximately 147 billion gallons, or about four and a half feet, of water a year by evaporation. It receives a small amount of water from underground sources, from surface runoff, and from occasional desert rains; but in the main it is dependent on the Truckee River, whose replenishments historically kept it at a somewhat fixed level.

The National Park Service terms Pyramid Lake "the most beautiful desert lake in the United States . . . perhaps the most beautiful of its kind in North America"; conservationists and lovers of outdoor beauty have regarded its wild solitude as one of the few remaining unspoiled natural wonders in the American West; and the state of Nevada touts the lake as among its prized attractions for tourists and sportsmen. But the lake is still the property of the descendants of the Native American Cui-ui Ticutta, who are now known officially as the Pyramid Lake Paiute tribe. Save for a narrow strip of barren and mountainous country entirely surrounding the lake and a panhandle of land extending seventeen miles along the lower Truckee, the lake presently constitutes their entire reservation and all they possess on which to exist. Since 1905, however, the lake—and therefore the tribe, numbering today about 1,000 people—has been threatened with wanton destruction.

The Paiutes, occupiers of the area since ancient times, traditionally lived on rabbits, mud hens, pine nuts, seeds, and other creatures and wild foods of their desert environment. But, as Frémont noted, fish from the lake—notably the big Lahontan trout and the cui-ui, the latter a valuable food fish, growing up to nine pounds and, like the Lahontan trout, found in no other region in the world—were the band's principal item of diet. Since the people lived principally on fish, the federal government in 1859 set aside the lake and the lower river for them as the main part of an otherwise almost barren reservation, with the intent that it serve as their major means of life. Through the years, federal courts confirmed the lake as the Indians' property, and the tribe kept it unspoiled and productive.

In 1905, however, the Reclamation Service of the Department of the Interior built Derby Dam across the Truckee River twenty miles east of Reno, diverting approximately half of the flow of the river, considerably more in dry years, away from Pyramid Lake and into a government irrigation project, newly constructed for White settlers in the Nevada desert around present-day Fallon. No one appears to have considered what would happen to Pyramid Lake or to the reservation and the people who lived on it, once their water was taken from them. No one consulted the Indians or asked them for it, and no one, not even in the Bureau of Indian Affairs, told them that the water was going to be taken. Voiceless and powerless in a White man's world at the time, the Paiutes were in every sense of the word wards of the government. But when Nevada's political leaders asked Congress to authorize the irrigation project, the Department of the Interior raised not a murmur in defense of the Indians' water. In a conflict between the interests of the Indians and those of the White farmers who were "opening up" the West, the Department's solicitors, as was their habit, turned their back on the "vanishing race," and with the building of Derby Dam, Pyramid Lake began to receive only that water which the dam did not divert for the irrigation project (now known as the Newlands Project, for Nevada's reclamation-minded Senator Francis G. Newlands).

The results at the lake were as dramatic as they were predictable. By the 1960's, the great sheet of water had dropped an average of fifteen inches a year, for a total of more than eighty feet. Its shoreline had receded an average of ten feet a year; a sister body of water, Lake Winnemucca, once also about thirty miles long and fed by overflow water from Pyramid Lake, had entirely dried up and disappeared. Pyramid Lake's length had shrunk by several miles, and its surface area had contracted by more than fifty square miles. Frémont's pyramid, now rising 365 feet above the lake, had ceased to be an island, being connected to the shore; and Anaho Island, facing the same prospect, seemed destined to lose its famed pelicans once coyotes and other predators could cross on dry land to the rookeries. At the south end of the lake, moreover, sandbars clogged the mouth of the Truckee, and fish could no longer get up the river to spawn. About 1938, the giant Lahontan trout disappeared from the lake, and the cui-ui faced extinction.

The future of the Pyramid Lake Paiutes had clearly become endangered. Gaining new voice, unity, and self-assertiveness, the Indians determined, in the mid-1950's, to commence an eleventh-hour fight to save their lake. The alternative, as they saw it, was the slow death of the tribe, for without the fish, people would have to abandon the reservation to seek homes elsewhere, and the tribe would disintegrate and vanish. "It is a matter of life and death, not just a question of getting what rightfully belongs to us," the elected tribal chairman, James Vidovich, told the people. And, added Vidovich—an electrical worker then in his thirties, and the descendant of a Paiute who had received the family's surname from an employer of Yugoslav origins—"It may be a long, hard fight."

To the Pyramid Lake Paiutes, there was nothing new about that. They were only there, he could have recalled to them, because of other long, hard fights for their existence that their fathers had waged in the past. The first Whites who came on them, fur trappers and emigrants to California, before and after Frémont's visit, had crossed their lands and killed them. They were then small groups of extended families who lived in conical brush-covered wickiups, employing the spiritual help of shamans and praying to Numanah, the Creator of All Things, following seasonal rounds of fishing, hunting, and gathering wild foods, and in winter combining in larger band-sized groups in sheltered locations. The apparent poverty of their land, resources, and way of life, together with their small numbers and weakness as compared to the power and strength of the plains tribes, drew the bullying of many Whites, who, with contempt, termed them Digger Indians, for the stick with which they dug roots, and killed them on sight for sport.

After the discovery of silver in Nevada, miners and settlers crowded in among them, appropriating their lands, destroying the wild game and pine-nut groves, and continuing to murder them. The creation of the reservation for the Indians in 1859 failed to give them security, and in 1860 they fought back boldly under Numaga, one of their band leaders. They ambushed and whipped one force of Whites on the southern border of Pyramid Lake, but were then outnumbered by a larger, punitive army and forced to flee for safety among other bands in the northern Great Basin. Colonel Frederick W. Lander, an Indian superintendent, at length negotiated a peace, and the Paiutes, winning an end to the armed aggressions against them, regained their lake and reservation.

But there were other struggles. They resisted missionaries, government agents, and teachers who tried to stamp out their religion and culture. Unable to follow seasonal rounds of hunting and gathering beyond their reservation, they were forced into the White man's cash economy for their necessities and went to work for Whites, attempting to steel themselves against prejudice and unfair treatment in their jobs by retaining their dignity and Paiute identity. Their longest fight was waged against White squatters who in 1865 began settling along the lower Truckee River, on the reservation's only irrigable land. That struggle, waged in courts and the Congress, lasted almost one hundred years, but finally ended in partial victory for the Paiutes and the ousting of some of the squatter families in the 1950's. By that time, the town of Nixon at the foot of the lake had become established as their tribal center, and the Indians, outwardly, were largely assimilated. Inwardly, however, they were still Paiutes and were ready for the battle for their lake.

Although most of the Paiutes' land surface was arid, with irrigation some of the panhandle strip south of the lake could be farmed and grazed. Through the years, the Indians had opened somewhat less than 800 acres of bottomland along the Truckee to irrigation, principally for raising hay for cattle and horses; but the tribe was unable to afford to irrigate the higher land, and the federal government would not grant them financial assistance, despite promises to do so. Moreover, the Paiutes at heart were not farmers or stockmen.

Thus the lake, with its cui-ui and artificially planted fish that required periodic restocking and produced only a small fraction of the lake's former output, was still in the mid-1950's their major resource, and along with fish for food, provided 75 percent of their tribal income through the sale of fishing and boating permits to Whites. Other income was derived from cattle and from part-time jobs on ranches or in the cities. Still, as late as 1967, almost 70 percent of the Pyramid Lake Paiutes were unemployed, and 52 percent of their families had incomes of under $2,000 a year. If the lake could be preserved, there was an additional promise for the future: the orderly development of recreation facilities, strictly controlled by the tribe in limited areas on the lake, could, according to a survey made for the Paiutes, provide steady jobs for the unemployed and make the reservation economically self-sustaining. Outside capital was available for such development, but not for a lake whose shoreline was steadily declining.

The tribe's principal rival for the Truckee's water, the Newlands Project, was originally planned by the government to irrigate 232,800 acres of desert with water from the Truckee, and another 137,000 acres with water from the Carson River, which runs somewhat parallel to, and to the south and east of, the Truckee. The available supply of water, as well as the agricultural capability of the soils, however, was grossly overestimated by the Reclamation Service, and from its inception, the project never had more than 50,000 to 65,000 acres under irrigation with water from both rivers. Fifty years after its beginning, the project looked like an old, settled farm area, with many grassy pastures, fields, gardens, and stands of trees, all watered by canals, and new and old barns and farm and ranch houses shaded by trees and fronting on highways and secondary roads that laced the district. Except at its edges, where the project bordered on the dusty sagebrush desert and muddy flats where temporary runoff flooding occurred, a visitor could imagine that he was almost anywhere in the rural Midwest.

Altogether, the water diverted from the Truckee to the project served about 1,025 farms on which dwelled approximately 5,800 people. The farmers produced mainly hay and alfalfa for cattle; some barley, wheat, and other grains; corn silage; and a small amount of vegetables and fruits, including potatoes and melons. In the winter thousands of cattle and sheep were brought in from the ranges to be fattened for market. In addition, some farmers maintained dairy herds, raised turkeys and other poultry, and kept bees. Most of the Whites, typically industrious, middle-income farm families, lived on the lands of the project, but many who owned uneconomical one- and two-acre lots with water rights leased their land to bigger operators and lived in the town of Fallon. The latter, with a population close to 3,000, was the principal shopping and marketing town on the project and, except for a garish gambling casino, might, with its wide streets and easy, friendly pace, have passed for any county seat in the agricultural West.

The average gross crop value of the Newlands Project amounted to no more than $4,500,000 per year, and from 1909 until 1965 the value of all crops produced during those fifty-six years totaled only $104,-500,000. Those figures assumed significance when matched as achievements of "progress" against what was being denied to the Indians. A 1964 report by a federal task force concluded, for example, that if the decline of the lake were halted and recreational facilities built on its shores, recreational income at the lake would soon exceed the annual crop value of the irrigation project and within fifteen years this income would increase to more than three times the annual value of the project. A later National Park Service study even upped that figure considerably.

Many people on the project were not unsympathetic to the plight of Pyramid Lake, but they argued bitterly that they and their families had long since acquired legal rights to the water, and it was just too bad if there was not enough in the Truckee for the lake as well. One of the largest landowners on the project, Carl F. Dodge, a Nevada state senator whose 1,400 acres had been owned by his family for fifty years, reflected the attitude of many of the Whites when the Paiutes began their fight. If the water was more valuable for the purpose of keeping Pyramid Lake alive than for keeping the project's farms producing, Dodge said, "then let them buy the water rights and take them over. All I can say about it is if they feel that way, money talks."

No one believed that such a course was economically or, in Nevada, politically practicable. Ranchers and farmers formed a powerful element in the state's political life, and with few areas in Nevada able to support agriculture, it was a safe bet that the state would vigorously resist permitting one of its biggest agricultural districts to return to desert. Moreover, the farms were no longer the only users of the project's water. Through the years, excess "tail water" draining off the farms had built up previously existing marshes in the adjoining desert. Like Pyramid Lake, these became the habitat of large flocks of ducks and other waterfowl and attracted gun clubs. At the same time, other waste water created a partly irrigated pasture, which farmers of the project put to use as a common grazing ground. In 1948 the Department of the Interior's Fish and Wildlife Service made a pact with the irrigators on the Newlands Project and Nevada's Fish and Game Commission. Out of the waterfowl marshlands were created the Stillwater Wildlife Management area (a public shooting ground) and the Stillwater National Wildlife Refuge (a protected area), and the Interior Department's Bureau of Land Management also agreed to develop and improve the pasture. Once established, both the government's wildlife area and the pasture became recognized "users" of Truckee water. The effect, therefore, was to provide water for Stillwater ducks and project cows, while continuing to deny it to the Indians and Pyramid Lake. And in still another development, Lahontan Reservoir, a large storage lake dammed up by the Bureau of Reclamation to feed the Truckee and Carson river waters to the project as they were needed, had begun to thrive as a recreational center. The very water diverted away from the Indians' lake was being used by Whites for boating, fishing, and swimming on an artificially created lake less than thirty-five miles away.

All of this had to be reckoned with by the Paiutes in their late-hour attempt to save Pyramid Lake, and it was further complicated by non-Indian users of water upstream from the lake on both the Truckee and the Carson. The number of those users, including other farmers as well as domestic and industrial interests around Reno, had increased greatly since 1905, and not surprisingly their competitive claims to the limited supply of water had grown more complex. A determined Indian fight for their right to water would threaten all non-Indian users, becoming capable of unsettling many, if not all, of the recognized water rights on the two rivers.

On the Truckee those rights were firmly established in 1944 by a federal district court decision known as the Orr Water Ditch Company decree. The Departments of Interior and Justice did represent the Paiutes at that time, but actually worsened the Indians' position by permitting what amounted to the legalization of Pyramid Lake's destruction. The Winters' Doctrine by then had been in existence for many years; the government clearly had the opportunity to right an old wrong by insisting on a court grant of adequate water, under the doctrine, for the lake. But the government asked for no water right at all for the lake, and it got none. The decree gave the Paiutes a right to only a meager amount of water, but with the provision that it could be used only for irrigation or stock and domestic purposes. Moreover, the amount of water which they could draw in any year was based on how much land they had under irrigation, and since they were never able to irrigate more than the small strip along the lower Truckee bottomlands, they never thereafter had the legal right to draw more than a fifth of the water granted to them—and none of it, legally, could be used for Pyramid Lake!

In actuality, Pyramid Lake continued to receive water from springs and underground sources below Derby Dam, from leaks in the dam and in the first section of the project's canal, and particularly from floodwater from heavy snowpacks in the Sierras, which the Newlands Project did not need and could not divert and which flowed past the dam to the lower Truckee. Under the Orr Ditch decree, however, the Indians had no right even to the unused floodwater, and so in 1955, when the Bureau of Reclamation announced plans to build new dams on the headwaters of the Truckee and Carson rivers to control and use the floodwaters, it stated specifically that none of the new project's saved floodwater would be made available to the Indians. This was too much for the Paiutes, who, despite their sparse resources, sought local legal help and began their fight.

On their own, rather than relying on the Bureau of Indian Affairs, they took their case to the Interior and Insular Affairs committees of both the House of Representatives and the Senate, which were then considering the Washoe Project, of which the proposed new flood-control dams were a part. Both committees responded with reports that noted officially for the first time that Pyramid Lake's crisis was due largely to acts of the federal government, and that the government had never undertaken compensatory measures to maintain the lake as a fishery and now ought to do so. When the bill authorizing the Washoe Project passed Congress on August 1, 1956, it directed that facilities be provided to increase water releases to Pyramid Lake to restore its fishery.

By 1963, however, when the Bureau of Reclamation finally firmed up its plans for the project, it revealed, on the contrary, that the new dams would cause the lake to go down even more rapidly. In April 1964, responding to protests by the Paiutes, Secretary of the Interior Stewart Udall appointed an intradepartmental task force to examine the claims of everyone, including the Indians. A preliminary report, completed in September, indicated concern over how to increase, rather than decrease, the water going to Pyramid Lake. It proposed certain modifications in the Washoe Project's plan and economies in the use of water by the Newlands Project. But it recommended no specified grant of water to the lake, nor did it guarantee that the lake would not suffer from the Washoe Project. Ignoring the possibility of a Winters' Doctrine suit on behalf of the tribe, it said only that the government should exercise "every effort to maintain the greatest practicable flow of water into Pyramid Lake."

When public hearings on the report were held in Reno, the Paiutes and various Indian and White supporters, who were beginning to be attracted to the cause of the tribe, argued angrily against the omission of a guaranteed grant of water to build up and stabilize the lake.

"Why tell us you will give us as much water as possible?" demanded Avery Winnemucca, a descendant of one of the tribe's best-known leaders after whom Nevada Whites, ironically, had named one of their cities. "Why don't you be specific? At least you did that with others. You've got figures to prove that there is so much allocation for this and so much for that, all in figures. But Pyramid Lake, no. You give us as much as possible."

Other pro-lake, pro-Indian speakers went further, telling Udall's task force members that any discussion of the Washoe Project was premature until the government, under the Winters' Doctrine, took steps to guarantee the lake's preservation. "Here in Nevada a terrible crime has been committed against Nevada's first citizens," charged the Reverend H. Clyde Mathews, chairman of the Nevada Advisory Committee to the United States Commission on Civil Rights. Then he added what few others in Nevada had previously admitted openly:

"If this property had been owned by six hundred White stockholders in an irrigation company, would this property have been taken without compensation, *or at all?* . . . The United States government itself has been discriminatory on the basis of race, creed, and national origin in the manner in which the Nevada Indians' water and fishery rights have been allowed to be denied, ignored, manipulated, and in effect destroyed."

Despite such pleas, the task force's final report, reflecting the powerful influence of the Bureau of Reclamation, refused to recommend that the government go to court to seek a water grant for the lake. There was no time for a long, complex water-rights case. A water users' vote of approval for the Washoe Project was waiting to be held. In addition, the Department of the Interior feared that litigation on behalf of the Paiutes might lead to an internal conflict of mammoth proportions within the Department: the successful prosecution of the Indians' case could endanger not only the Newlands Project but other reclamation projects that Indian tribes elsewhere might claim had overridden their rights. All the Department could do for Pyramid Lake, the task force noted, was to undertake certain measures—including the salvaging of excess water, the elimination of seepage and waste in the Newlands Project's canals, and the imposition of regulations and controls at the project—that would increase the amount of water available to the lake. The carrying out of the recommendations would guarantee a considerable increase of water to the lake, Udall told the Indians, and with that promise they withdrew their opposition to the Washoe Project. On November 3, 1964, the White voters in the affected Nevada river basins approved it.

The Bureau of Reclamation did make efforts to conserve Truckee River water by setting up certain minimal controls on the Newlands Project, but it soon became questionable whether the Indians would benefit. Despite the Paiutes' appeals for a statement of a legal basis for the water Udall had promised them, the Department of the Interior refused to assert that the United States owned, controlled, and had the right to deliver to Pyramid Lake the water it was going to save on the Newlands Project, and thus left that water open to appropriation by non-Indian users. In 1968 that threat surfaced with a vengeance. Since 1955, California and Nevada had been working on a settlement that would divide between the two states the waters flowing from Lake Tahoe. All the water in question (including the Truckee and Carson) passed through California before entering Nevada, so California, too, had a claim to it. After thirteen years of work, a document was drafted that not only limited the Indians' water to what the Orr Ditch decree gave them in 1944, but *went beyond that by expressly preventing the federal government and the Indians from ever going to court to seek more water for Pyramid Lake.* Henceforth, the Paiutes would have to apply to Nevada for any water saved by the Newlands Project, and the threat of the Winters' Doctrine to the Whites would disappear.

The compact was too raw even for the Department of the Interior, which did not care to turn over the fate of federal water rights to the states. The Department registered its objections, with the implied threat that Congress would not ratify an agreement that gave up federal rights. But the Nevada legislature took up the document all the same, and after brief hearings, approved the compact. In California it was a different story. Unwilling to risk rejection by Congress, and appealed to by the Northern Paiute Indians, the National Congress of American Indians (the case had now become a national Indian cause), and many Indian and White friends, the California Assembly Committee on Natural Resources and Conservation refused to approve the compact in the form adopted by Nevada.

On July 6, 1969, the new Secretary of the Interior, Walter J. Hickel, met at Lake Tahoe with governors Ronald Reagan of California and Paul Laxalt of Nevada to try to break the deadlock. Their solution, announced to the press after a ninety-minute meeting on the lake in the cabin of a cruiser owned by Reno gambler William Harrah, made matters worse. Without consulting the Indians, they had agreed that engineers should hasten Pyramid Lake's gradual decline by draining it down to a level at which it would stabilize.

As Vine Deloria, Jr., the Sioux Indian author of *Custer Died for Your Sins,* charged at the time: "It was the same logic used by the Army to destroy a Vietnamese village—'We had to destroy the village to save it.' It naturally followed that the only way to save Pyramid Lake was to drain it."

This weird proposal, which would have dropped the lake abruptly by 152 feet and left it a salt lake in a huge basin of mud flats, outraged not only the Paiutes, who could not believe that the three governments would commit such a flagrant robbery of their property, but large numbers of non-Indians in Nevada, who suddenly saw Pyramid Lake as a priceless gem of the desert and an important recreational asset for the whole state. The public outcry forced the three officials to drop the plan hurriedly and, instead, set up another task force of federal and state appointees who would try to satisfy the supporters of the lake so that a new version of the compact could be written. Even that task force got off to a controversial start, when Governor Laxalt claimed the right to name a Paiute representative to the body. Knowing that the group would be dominated by the Bureau of Reclamation and "stacked" against them, and that any Indian on the body would be participating in the tribe's destruction, the Paiutes refused to have anything to do with it. In their view, their only hope lay now in persuading the government to file a Winters' Doctrine suit for their water. Repeated appeals to the Department of the Interior to do so, however, fell on deaf ears. Meanwhile, the Bureau of Reclamation hurried ahead with its Washoe Project, and the interstate compact task force worked out a compromise agreement which tried to eliminate some of the most objectionable features of the original document. The Paiutes still opposed it, since it offered no solution to the lake's problem, but the two states finally sent it off to Congress, which has still not approved it.

By 1970, the Paiutes appeared to have reached the end of the road. A tangle of decrees, statutes, regulations, and water rights and laws had been used by the Nevada and federal governments to ensure the continued taking of their water. They were almost out of money for legal fees and, on their own, could go no further. In January 1970—as a result of a request for some information and advice from their lawyer, Robert D. Stitser of Reno, to the California Indian Legal Services, an Office of Economic Opportunity public service group of attorneys who had worked successfully on cases with California tribes and were knowledgeable on Indian and water law—new help was suddenly offered them. With the assistance of Robert Pelcyger, one of the CILS lawyers, Stitser and the tribe began to prepare a Winters' Doctrine suit, which the tribe would file on its own, and to look for money with which to enlist the services of hydrologists and other expert witnesses. In June, financial aid became available when the Ford Foundation in New York gave California Indian Legal Services a large planning grant to develop a national non-profit organization known as the Native American Rights Fund, which would provide legal services to Indians without charge. On August 22, 1970, the Paiutes, represented by Stitser and Pelcyger, who had become a staff member of the Native American Rights Fund—and also supported by a national Indian-interest organization, the Association on American Indian Affairs—filed a suit in the U.S. District Court for the District of Columbia against the Secretary of the Interior and the Attorney General of the United States, asking that the former be ordered to deliver enough water to Pyramid Lake to stabilize it by eliminating the wasteful use of water in the Truckee and Carson rivers, and that the latter be required to seek "a judicial determination" of the Indians' right to Truckee water.

The first priority was to get enough water to the lake as quickly as possible in order to halt its further decline. The suit held that that could be done simply by stopping the waste of Truckee and Carson river waters by the Whites and making the saved water available to the lake. The facts concerning the waste were set forth compellingly to the court. For one thing, the tribe's attorneys revealed, the Bureau of Reclamation had for years permitted the Newlands Project to receive up to nine feet of water for each of its acres, when under the Orr Ditch decree and another decree known as the Alpine decree, which related to the use of Carson River water, it should only have received from 2.92 to 4.5 feet per acre. Much of this illegally taken water, which could have gone to the lake, had been wasted. Moreover, Secretary Udall's promise to the Indians to impose regulations and controls on the project to stop the greedy waste and make the saved water available to the lake had been subverted.

It was estimated that to stabilize Pyramid Lake at its present level, the lake needed to receive an annual average of 135,000 acre-feet of water more than it had been getting from the Truckee (an acre-foot being enough water to cover one acre with one foot of water). For approximately fifty years, said the suit, the Secretary of the Interior's agents (the Bureau of Reclamation) had been permitting the waste of up to 200,000 acre-feet of water annually. If the court ordered the Secretary to stop the waste and send the saved water down the Truckee, Pyramid Lake could, at least, be stabilized, without forcing anyone to give up water to which they had a legal right under the Orr decree.

The Whites of the Newlands Project saw it otherwise. Orr decree or not, the Bureau of Reclamation had permitted them to receive 406,000 acre-feet of water a year (far in excess of the decree's limitations), and they wanted that figure adhered to. Their pressure, and that of the Nevada state government, which supported them against the Indians, registered strongly in the Interior Department in Washington. At first, Judge Gerhard A. Gesell of the District Court urged the Secretary and the Indians' attorneys to try to settle the Paiutes' suit by negotiation. It proved impossible. The government's lawyers promised that the Department would issue new regulations concerning the Newlands Project's use of water in 1972, after first consulting the tribe. The promise was not observed. In April 1972, without notice to the Indians, new government regulations appeared that made the situation worse than before. All they said was that measures would be taken to ensure that the water would be put to better use. There was, however, no mention of how much water the Newlands Project could receive, thus permitting the irrigators to draw all the water they wanted, without limit.

The Paiutes' lawyers immediately obtained an order from Judge Gesell voiding the new "non-regulations" and, for the moment, reimposing the 406,000 acre-feet limit, which the project had been using. At the same time, the judge decided that the case must now go to trial. But there were other government manipulations. Trying to halt the litigation, Secretary of the Interior Rogers C. B. Morton announced that he had, at last, requested the Attorney General to institute a suit "for the recognition and protection of a water right for the maintenance of Pyramid Lake"— after seventy years, the government would finally go to court for the Paiutes' Winters' Doctrine water rights. It was obvious to Judge Gesell, however, that such a suit might take ten to fifteen years before a final decree was issued. There was no need to wait, he said, "to resolve what seems to me to be a matter that requires more immediate attention"— the question of saving the lake with water that the government could make available to it. Complaining that the Interior Department's actions in handling the Paiutes' case that was before him had "bamboozled" him —"I suppose that is the politest word," he said—he scheduled the trial for July.

The Department's "bamboozling," in truth, was an attempt to get out of a situation that was beginning to concern the Nixon administration, which prided itself on its good relations with Native Americans. Largely as a result of the Pyramid Lake case, presidential advisers in the White House had recognized the conflict of interest within the Department of the Interior that had worked against Indians, and in 1970 the Administration had sent to Congress a bill to establish an Indian Trust Counsel Authority that would be independent of the Departments of the Interior and Justice, and would be expressly empowered to bring suits for Indians, even against branches of the United States government, in cases involving land, water, or other natural resource rights. With such an Authority, the Paiutes would not have to be dependent for legal action on the Department of the Interior, whose policy makers and solicitors had been torn between them and the Bureau of Reclamation. Congress, however, had done nothing about the Trust Counsel bill, the Administration had failed to press it, and the legislation had been buried and forgotten. But publicity about the Pyramid Lake case had increased, and the White House and the Secretary of the Interior were receiving criticism from the public and the media. In January 1972, Democratic Senators Edward M. Kennedy of Massachusetts and John Tunney of California had held a public hearing in Nevada on the plight of the Paiutes and their lake, and their lambasting of the Bureau of Reclamation had received ample coverage by the press. Moreover, the interstate task force had completed the writing of new recommendations, which had urged the elimination of waste to make available about 95,000 acre-feet of water for the lake, less than it needed, but had suggested, also, that the only way to solve the Paiutes' problem was to go to court and settle their right to water.

All this was in the background of Secretary Morton's decision to file a Winters' Doctrine suit for the tribe. It did not halt the Paiutes' case against the Secretary in Judge Gesell's court, but the Interior Department hoped that it would demonstrate the good intentions of the Administration. In addition, because of the length of time the suit would take, it would further stall an unpopular readjustment of the amount of water the Newlands Project could receive and confer on a future administration the problem of facing the consequences of a decision that might give the Paiutes water that was now being used by somebody else.

On June 5, 1972, a month before the District Court trial was to begin, Secretary Morton announced that new regulations for the salvaging of water going to the Newlands Project—as well as a decision about how much water the Project would receive after the saving and how much, therefore, would be available to Pyramid Lake—would be made public in September. The trial was postponed to await these decisions, and in September the Secretary made his announcement. Once more, it was a disappointment to the Paiutes and the court: The regulations were to be voluntary, rather than mandatory, and would only reduce the amount of water going to the Newlands Project from 406,000 to 378,000 acre-feet a year, still much more than the Project's entitlement under the applicable decrees. The total saving for use by Pyramid Lake would be a mere 28,000 acre-feet a year, far short of what it required if it were to be stabilized.

The tribal lawyers' protests to the Secretary met with rebuffs. Instead, the Department went ahead with the Winters' Doctrine case. On September 22, the Solicitor General of the United States, going directly to the Supreme Court, asked that body to exercise original jurisdiction and hear a complaint of the United States against the states of Nevada and California, which sought a decree "declaring the right of the United States for the benefit of the Pyramid Lake Paiute Tribe of Indians to the use of sufficient waters of the Truckee River to fulfill the purposes for which the Pyramid Lake Reservation was created, including the maintenance and preservation of Pyramid Lake and the maintenance of the lower reaches of the Truckee River as a natural spawning ground for fish and other purposes beneficial to and satisfying such use to be with a priority of November 29, 1859."

With the government thus finally pursuing the long-range rights case, the tribe commenced its own action for immediate water for the lake in Judge Gesell's district court. After a four-day trial in October, Judge Gesell, on November 8, ruled decisively for the Paiutes, calling the Secretary's September decision on the amount of water the Newlands Project could have "an abuse of discretion and not in accordance with law," and adding that "the effect was to deprive the Tribe of water without legal justification." He ordered the Secretary to submit to him by January 1, 1973, new regulations that would result in the Newlands Project's receipt of an amount of water "wholly consistent with the Secretary's fiduciary duty to the Tribe."

The decision was historic. Not only did it direct the delivery of adequate water to stabilize Pyramid Lake until the Paiutes' full water rights could be ruled upon in the Winters' Doctrine case, but it set a legal precedent for all other American Indian tribes in their conflicts with the federal government as trustee of their property. All previous cases against the government had been limited to the seeking of damages after the fact for Indian property that had already been lost, mismanaged, or damaged. This was the first litigation brought by Indians that successfully forced the government as trustee and fiduciary to carry out its obligation to protect Indian property. The government decided not to appeal Judge Gesell's decision, and the Department of the Interior set about implementing the court's directive, ordering more thorough and effective waste controls and freeing some of the Washoe Project's water for Pyramid Lake. At the same time, the court ordered the Newlands Project to be limited to the use of 350,000 acre-feet of water in 1973 and 288,129 acre-feet in 1974.

Though the government observed the court's decision, the farmers of the Newlands Project did not. Entering Nevada courts, they contested the limits which the federal court had placed on their water supply, and year after year continued to draw what they wanted. By the early 1980's, they were still receiving up to 400,000 acre-feet annually, and it was clear that they would try to continue to do so until the Winters' Doctrine suit, or some additional litigation in the future, firmly established the amount of water to which they had a right. Nevertheless, the Bureau of Reclamation's measures, together with the good fortune of a series of years in which the volume of water in the Truckee was above average, helped the lake, which remained relatively stable. In the absence of a definitely specified water right of its own, however, its fate continued to be uncertain. In good years, the level of its water rose dramatically—even providing sufficient inflow to the lower river to permit the fish to ascend to their old spawning grounds—but in bad years it fell. Pursuing a fisheries restoration program, the tribe contracted first with the Nevada Fish and Game Department and then with the U.S. Fish and Wildlife Service for the annual planting of the lake with Lahontan trout fingerlings and other species from state and federal hatcheries, and eventually obtained federal funds for two hatcheries of its own on the reservation. The maintenance of the lake as a popular family recreational area and a fishery for sportsmen brought increasing income to the Paiutes through the 1970's and inspired new hope that the reservation could ultimately become self-sufficient. Organizing a Pyramid Lake Indian Tribal Enterprises, the Indians trained tribal members to manage the expanding fisheries restoration program, which included—when there was adequate flow—the maintenance of the lower Truckee as a revived spawning ground for the natural propagation of the fish. The success of that project, however, rested on the fate of the government's suit for their water right, which they hoped would ensure the spawning grounds enough water each year.

As foreseen, the Winters' Doctrine case was a protracted one. The Supreme Court, in June 1973, declined to exercise original jurisdiction, saying that the case should be filed in a lower federal court in Nevada. In December, the Justice Department did so, initiating a suit in the District Court against the Truckee-Carson Irrigation District, the state of Nevada, the cities of Reno and Sparks, and approximately 17,000 individually named persons, firms, partnerships, and corporations, all users of Truckee river water, to reopen the Orr Ditch decree of 1944 and establish a permanent water right for Pyramid Lake and the lower Truckee River fishery. The tribe, represented by Robert Stitser and the Native American Rights Fund, joined the United States as plaintiff.

The case, however, did not at first go well for the Indians. On December 8, 1977, the court dismissed the suit, holding that the failure of the government to claim a water right for the lake and the fishery during the Orr Ditch adjudications had effectively ended that right, and that the United States and the Paiutes were now barred by the 1944 decree from claiming a right. In other words, the Department of the Interior's dereliction of its trust duty in 1944 had lost the Paiutes their water rights, and it was now too late to reopen the matter. But the government and the tribe appealed to the Ninth Circuit Court of Appeals, and on June 15, 1981, that court upheld the right of the tribe to sufficient water for its fishery, ruling that the Secretary of the Interior was not authorized to take Indian water rights for a reclamation project, and that when the United States represented Indians in litigation, it was obligated to act as a trustee and not compromise the Indians' interests because of conflicting obligations.

The Native American Rights Fund hailed this as a landmark decision for Indians in general, but it was only another step along the road for the Paiutes. Their opponents immediately petitioned the Circuit Court for a rehearing. By early 1982, they had not received an answer, but it seemed certain that, one way or the other, the case would eventually go to the Supreme Court. Meanwhile, facing the prospect of continued lengthy litigation and a possibility that in the end they might not be able to reopen the Orr decree, the tribal and government attorneys worked together on what they hoped might become an alternative solution—a final negotiated settlement of all the Pyramid Lake water litigation.

Whatever occurred ultimately, however, one fact loomed large. The doughty fight of the small Pauite tribe in the Nevada desert had not been in vain. At a minimum, it had saved Pyramid Lake, at least for a time, had given its trustee a sobering lesson, and had demonstrated to other tribes that they could put an end to the continuing theft of their resources, including water. By 1977, the struggle to regain and preserve tribal water rights had become one of the foremost phenomena of Indian affairs throughout the western half of the country. Dozens of tribes were in some type of litigation to hold on to water they owned, or to get back what had been taken illegally from them. Addressing a meeting of tribal leaders in October of that year, the Assistant Secretary of the Interior for Indian Affairs, Forrest J. Gerard, a Blackfoot Indian, read off a list of tribes that were battling with non-Indian society over rights to water. It was an imposing roll call of large and small tribes in every part of the West: the Yakimas, Crows, Arapahos, the Jicarilla, White Mountain, and Mescalero Apaches, the Zuñis, Blackfeet, and Northern Cheyennes, the Moapa, Hoopa, Navajo, Cocopah, and Agua Caliente of Palm Springs, the Osages, Colvilles, Duck Valley Shoshone-Paiutes, and Crow Creek Sioux, the Spokans, Muckleshoots, Umatillas, and Pawnees, the Cherokees, Chemehuevis, three Ute tribes in Utah, various Pueblos in New Mexico, the Pimas and Papagos in Arizona, and on and on.

The sudden Indian assertiveness frightened and angered both urban and rural Whites in the West, who saw a threat to the water they had been using and the water they planned on having for future needs. Upholding the Winters' Doctrine for a tribe seemed to imply to non-Indians the disintegration of all western water law, the voiding or clouding of all established water claims, and a new start with new rules and disastrously reduced rights to water. At the same time, corporations, drawn to the West to develop energy resources or for other reasons, as well as military and other branches of the government, with plans for large-scale facilities in sparsely populated parts of the West, viewed the new Indian water claims as obstacles and nuisances that made it harder for them to acquire the water they needed for their operations. The fears and frustrations of all these groups led to political and legal counterthrusts, designed to halt the tribes in their tracks.

As early as 1973, a National Water Commission report foresaw the coming conflict, but recognizing the growing non-Indian municipal, agricultural, industrial, and recreational needs for water in the West, recommended policies that, in effect, justified by expediency the seizure of Indian water rights. Nothing was done with the report, but its recommendations were not forgotten. In 1976, the courts dealt the Indians a setback. A piece of legislation known as the McCarran Amendment (for the

Nevada senator, Pat McCarran) had earlier given states the right to liti-
gate against the federal government in state courts in cases affecting
federal water rights—that is, rights to water which the federal government
claimed it owned. In a suit known as the Akin case, involving some Indian
water rights, it was now established that states, under the McCarran
Amendment, could also pursue cases affecting *Indian* water rights in state
courts. To the Indians, this seemed a violation of the Constitution, but
it stuck. Though Indian water cases could also be tried in federal courts,
the right to decide them now depended, in part, on who got to which
court first. But the possibility of a trial in a state court was a damaging
development for the tribes, for, as noted earlier, the odds were that the
Indians would receive less equitable treatment there than in a more
independent federal court.

Opposition to the Indians' water offensives continued, and in 1977
President Jimmy Carter, aware of the growing competition for the resource, issued a national water management policy. As a step toward its
implementation, his Water Resources Council, headed by Secretary of
the Interior Cecil Andrus, set up a policy committee within the Interior
Department, chaired by Guy Martin, Assistant Secretary for Land and
Water Resources, to carry out a nine-point plan. One of the points was
to determine, or quantify, federal and Indian water rights in the country.
The tribes immediately objected, both to having their water rights
lumped again with federal rights and to having the Department, which
experience had taught them to distrust, quantify their rights for them.
Many tribes did not yet know their future water needs, were not ready to
have their rights declared and made public, and, when they were ready,
preferred to go into a federal court with their own lawyers and have their
rights established under the Winters' Doctrine. Moreover, they were
angry that the Interior Department had not consulted them.

The Secretary's Water Resources Council backtracked slightly,
agreeing to keep federal and Indian water rights separated (they were
"not the same," the Council admitted), and promised not to publish a
paper on Indian rights to the use of water. But a presidential water policy
message on June 6, 1978, again implied the sameness of federal and
Indian water rights and called on the tribes to quantify their rights by
negotiation with the states. The message further disturbed many tribes,
as well as national Indian organizations, showing not only an ignorance
of the tribes' constitutional and historical reliance on dealing exclusively
with the federal government, but a lack of sensitivity on the part of their
trustee by asking them to negotiate with their principal adversaries.
Negotiations, moreover, they pointed out, would only be about giving up
some of the water they then owned, or to which they had a right. In

negotiations, the states could only win, and the Indians could only lose. Other tribes, however, believing that negotiation might be the only practical way to obtain federal financial assistance for water development projects, decided to engage in the settlement process, for without such projects their paper water rights would be virtually worthless. In addition, negotiation was working beneficially for some tribes, like the Ak-Chin in Arizona, and was viewed by others, like the Pyramid Lake Paiutes, as perhaps providing the best prospect for getting a maximum of what they sought.

Nevertheless, the pressure of western business, agricultural, and political interests to limit the Indians' water rights and establish those limits permanently continued to be felt by the Department of the Interior, and on August 28, 1978, Assistant Secretary for Indian Affairs Gerard, one of the Department's policy committee members, compliantly circulated a memorandum to the tribes, stating that negotiations with the states should proceed, and under the lead of the Department. Tribal resistance forced a temporary shelving of the policy, and on April 5, 1979, the Department again took to litigation, filing suits in the federal district court in Montana, as mentioned at the beginning of this chapter, to determine the Winters' Doctrine water rights of five tribes in that state.

Montana scored a temporary victory when later that year, the federal court dismissed the suits on the ground that they must be heard in the state courts, where Montana had wanted them to be tried in the first place. The federal government, however, appealed to the Ninth Circuit Court, and the cases continued into the 1980's at the federal level. In 1979, also, the Montana legislature created a nine-member Reserved Water Rights Compact Commission whose designated task was to try to settle the state's water conflicts with the tribes, as well as with the federal government, by negotiation, rather than litigation. Like many tribes elsewhere, the Montana tribes considered which course would serve them best—litigation, negotiation, or congressional legislation—and four of them (later reduced to three, when the Flatheads backed away) entered negotiations with the state, though with such skepticism of results that they also continued the court cases.

As long as Indians continue to assert their water rights, and courts recognize them as their rightful property, conflict and confrontation will go on. The Indians need their water to survive. The Whites want not only to keep the water they have, but to secure as much Indian water as they can get for their expanding needs. The federal government satisfies neither side, and in the impasse, Whites in some states have begun to urge their representatives in Congress to introduce legislation that, by one method or another, would simply seize Indian-owned water. One such bill, drafted by Senator Slade Gorton of Washington in the fall of 1981, got nowhere, but others are sure to be introduced in succeeding sessions of Congress. The Indians have pointed out that this approach is fool-hardy, for it will result in enormous litigation in which, under due process, the tribes will ask for billions of dollars in damages.

And so, the bitterness—and confusion—build. On March 24, 1981, the Supreme Court opened a whole new Pandora's box of potential conflicts with its ruling in another Montana case that the state owned, and could regulate the use of, the bed and banks of the Bighorn River as it flowed through the Crows' reservation. This decision, giving to the state rights to, and jurisdiction over, property within the reservation which the tribe felt was its own according to treaties, raised a storm among the Indians. The state, and not the tribe, could now apparently control the use of the property inside the reservation for fishing, recreation, mining, energy development, and any other activity by non-Indians as well as Indians. The decision, said the Native American Rights Fund, affected tribes everywhere in the country, throwing "the issue of title ownership to riverbeds, lake beds, and tidelands on reservations up in the air, suggesting dozens of treaties nationwide could now be contested by non-Indians desiring control of these waterways." Most immediately threatened were the Flatheads, who were pressing a similar case in Montana over the right of ownership of the bed of Flathead Lake on their reservation.

At almost the same time, in Arizona, where in 1935 protesting Pima Indians had been barred from a Phoenix courtroom in which U.S. attorneys—supposedly representing them as their trustee—shamelessly gave away their water to a copper company and other White users, there was also turmoil. As one of his last acts in office, in December 1980, Secretary of the Interior Andrus made a first gesture of recompense to the Pimas, as well as to the Papagos and other Arizona Indians, who for so long had been callously robbed of their water and reduced to poverty, by signing contracts for annual allocations of a total of 309,828 acre-feet of water to be delivered to their reservations from the mammoth Central Arizona Project when it is completed in the mid-1980's. Among much of Arizona's White population, an explosion of fury followed. The irate protests included a large advertisement in the December 7 issue of the Arizona *Republic*, headlined in bold black letters: "LIKE GIVING HEROIN TO AN ADDICT."

6

THE GREAT NORTHWEST FISHING WAR

The Clashes over Native American Fishing and Hunting Claims

IN JANUARY 1961, James and Louis Starr, Jr., two Muckleshoot Indian fishermen in western Washington State, and Leonard Wayne, a Puyallup Indian who had been raised as a Muckleshoot, set their gill nets in the Green River, a stream that flows from the Cascade Mountains into the southern part of Puget Sound. The next morning, they returned and hauled in their catch—a single coho, or silver, salmon. Suddenly, seven Washington game wardens, with drawn revolvers, burst from hiding places along the bank and arrested the three men for the double crime of fishing out of season and using nets. They were taken to a Seattle court, given suspended fines of $250 apiece, and held in jail for two weeks until other Indians managed to bail them out. Their cases were appealed, and twenty-two months later, in November 1962, they were acquitted by Judge James W. Hodson of Washington's King County Superior Court, who decided that they had been fishing legally in accordance with rights contained in a treaty which their ancestors had made with the federal government.

The episode was not unprecedented. Throughout the Northwest, as well as in Michigan and other parts of the United States, fishing-oriented tribes had had histories of tense and inconclusive conflicts with state and local officials over whether their treaties gave them fishing rights not possessed by others. The 1961 Muckleshoot case, however, had a special significance, for despite its outcome, it signaled the start of a sustained, determined drive by northwestern state agencies and non-Indian sport and commercial fishermen to end Indian treaty fishing rights in that part of the nation once and for all. The struggle lasted for years around Puget Sound and on the Columbia River and became increasingly sensational. It was marked by violent battles, hundreds of arrests, demonstrations, the intercession of sympathetic non-Indian celebrities, conflicting court rulings, and, ultimately, by landmark judicial decisions that affected not only fisheries in the Northwest but the future of Indian fishing rights everywhere. In a broader context, additionally, its impact on Indian-White relations was historic: It helped to give rise to an anti-Indian backlash movement whose political influence was felt by tribes in all parts of the country. But, also, it became a catalyst for Indian militancy in the late 1960's and the 1970's, feeding the flames of Red Power activism, ushering in an era of such confrontations as those at Alcatraz, the Bureau of Indian Affairs Building in Washington, D.C., and Wounded Knee, and providing inspiration and strength to a developing thrust among all tribes for self-determination and sovereignty.

To those Indians who were involved in it, the fishing rights struggle was a fight for survival. During its course, they suffered physical attacks and beatings, jailings, the confiscation of their boats, fishing gear, and other property, the loss of their livelihood, and bitter persecution and abuse. Though most of them were members of some of the smallest and weakest tribes in the country, they were arrayed against almost the entire White population and the full power of the administrative and judicial establishments of their states. Sometimes they were opposed also by the elected leaders and other members of their own tribes. But they persisted, and in the war of long odds that was waged against them, they came, in time, to loom as modern-day Native American patriots.

The issue of Indian treaty fishing rights has often been attended more by emotion and racist prejudice than by understanding. In the beginning, when abundant fish filled the lakes and rivers of all the continent, there was enough for everyone, and conflicts over fishing rights between Indians and non-Indians were rare. But as the number of commercial and sport fishermen multiplied, as their catch increased, as logging, pollution, dams, and other works of man combined to deplete the fish population, the competition for what remained became intense. States issued fishing rules and regulations, instituted conservation measures, and embarked on hatchery and restocking programs. Often, those programs, as well as the state fish and game agencies that administered them, were fully or partly financed by the fees and licenses paid by the non-Indian fishermen, who established a close rapport with the agencies and felt a vested interest in the fish for which they were paying. Still, demand exceeded supply, the commercial and sport fishermen competed for what was available, and the agencies struggled to maximize the product for both groups.

In view of modern-day realities, it seemed natural and justifiable to Whites to treat Indian fishers like everyone else, making them abide by state regulations as either sport or commercial fishermen. On or off their reservations, it appeared fair that they should respect legal seasons and limitations of catch and employ the same gear that others were forced to use. But the Indians believed differently: Because of their special relations with the federal government, they insisted, first of all, that state rules, regulations, and conservation measures did not apply to them when they fished according to their treaty rights. Secondly, they maintained that the validity of those rights stemmed from the fact that in their treaties, by which they had ceded lands, resources, and grants to the government, they had specifically reserved certain rights, including fishing and hunting, for themselves. The treaties had defined the nature of those rights, the government had guaranteed them, and the tribes had clung to them as property, never giving them away. Moreover, as the fish supply dwindled, the Indians felt aggrieved. Knowing that their existence depended on fish, they had always practiced conservation, and they considered themselves instinctively abler and more dedicated conservationists than non-Indian fishermen. It was plain to them who was polluting the rivers and whose dams were cutting off access to spawning beds. Constituting only a small fraction of the total number of fishermen, they not only balked at being made the scapegoat for the disappearing fish, but complained that White men's actions were nullifying their treaties by depriving them of fish to which they had a right. And they felt, by the same token, that the Whites had a treaty obligation to maintain a fish supply for them, even by restocking programs.

Their reasoning, however, was not appreciated by non-Indians, and fell on deaf ears. It no longer mattered to Whites what the treaties said; in contemporary America, such agreements were out of date—and, besides, Whites argued, one could interpret the wording of the treaties any way one wished. In this impasse, and under pressure from non-Indian fishermen, state agencies refused to acknowledge any obligation to a separate Indian fishery. In effect, by ignoring its right to exist, they also helped their own problem, adding the Indians' share of fish to the total supply available for division between the sport and commercial fisheries.

The fight that erupted in the Northwest was a clash of these opposing points of view and centered, initially, on the Muckleshoots, Puyallups, and Nisquallies, three of a number of small tribes whose reservations bordered Puget Sound and the waters of northwestern Washington. By the mid-twentieth century, most Whites in the region were scarcely aware of the Indians who lived among them. Many of the tiny tribal landholdings were lost in the industrial and urban developments that sprawled along the shores of the Sound, and most of the tribal members, whose families had been acculturated for generations, could hardly be distinguished from their non-Indian neighbors. They dressed and lived like Whites—many of them off their small reservations and in White residential areas—sent their children to public schools, and competed economically with non-Indians for jobs and a livelihood.

Their Indianness and pride of identity as tribal members, however, were still strong. In each tribe, elders, clan members, and traditional teachers kept alive cultural traits and knowledge of their group's history, language, and spiritual values and beliefs. Only a minority of the Indian families still derived their income from fishing, but among most of the people fish were still important, not only as food but as a symbol of their group's spiritual cohesiveness. Fish had meant survival for their ancestors, who welcomed their seasonal appearances with ceremonies of thanksgiving. The symbiotic relationship between the people and the fish kept the world in harmony, and the Indians' lives, cultures, and spiritual values revolved around that relationship. Despite acculturation and assimilation, the sense of that bond still remained deeply ingrained among them, as if the disappearance of the fish would mean, also, the disappearance of the Indians.

The Muckleshoots, Puyallups, and Nisquallies fished primarily for salmon and steelhead, in pre-White days using canoes of various sizes that were fashioned from cedar logs, and different types of nets, weirs, and traps, as well as spears and hook and line. They caught five species of Pacific salmon: chinook, the largest, also called king or tyee, which averaged from twelve to twenty-five pounds but could weigh up to one hundred pounds; silver, or coho; sockeye, or blueback; pink, or humpy; and chum, or dog. The annual runs of the salmon past the Indians' fishing camps on their way up the rivers from the Pacific to the upper-tributary spawning grounds generally occurred between May 1 and November 30, with the Indians gathering in most of their catch from July to early November. The steelhead, a sea-run rainbow trout, made its welcomed appearance the rest of the year and was harvested between the beginning of December and the end of April. The fish were once so plentiful that an early White settler in the Northwest declared that a person could almost walk across a stream on their backs. Though the Indians in aboriginal times also hunted game and gathered berries, roots, and other wild foods in season, the fish were their staple. That part of their catch that was not consumed at once was air-dried or smoked for later use or for trade with other tribes. The fishing sites belonged to the people in whose territories they were located, but social visiting and intermarriage among members of different groups were common, and the sites were usually shared with relatives and friends from other villages, bands, and tribes.

It is estimated that when Whites first began to settle in northwestern Washington in the 1840's, the total Native American population along Puget Sound was more than 10,000. While many of the villages seem to have been politically autonomous, most were culturally, socially, and linguistically associated in bands and acknowledged the leadership of particular headmen who possessed outstanding qualities and capabilities. The Nisquallies, whose numbers have been variously estimated at between 600 and 2,000, occupied a large area from the region of present-day Olympia at the southern end of the Sound to Mount Rainier in the Cascades. Most of their villages were along the lower Nisqually River, which they shared with their neighbors, the Puyallups. The latter, whose population appears to have been between 500 and 1,000, were centered along the Puyallup and White rivers and possessed the country from present-day Tacoma to the heights of the Cascades. There was, at the time, no people known as Muckleshoots. But just to the north of the Puyallups, principally along the White and Green rivers, lived several bands, including the Skope-ahmish, or Sko-bobch (meaning Green River), whom the Whites later called the Muckleshoots, for the name of the region which became their reservation. All of the groups were members of the Coastal Salish language family and were somewhat interrelated among themselves and with other Puget Sound peoples.

In the early 1850's, White population grew to several thousand, and in 1853 Congress created Washington Territory. Late that same year, Isaac I. Stevens, a former army officer in the Mexican War, arrived as the first governor. Politically ambitious and in a hurry to make a mark for himself by turning Washington into a thriving part of the Union, Stevens hastened to acquire the lush and fertile lands of the Puget Sound Indians for the settlers whom he intended to lure to the territory. With little regard for the rights and sensibilities of the Indians, he and his aides called together the various bands, and in a whirlwind series of treaty meetings with different groups cajoled and threatened their headmen into ceding large parts of their territories and agreeing to cluster together in a number of small, unwanted areas which Stevens had selected for them.

The first treaty, signed at Medicine Creek on December 26, 1854, with the Nisquallies, Puyallups, and seven other tribes and bands, set the pattern for the others. Stevens, drunk and impatient, ordered the proceedings to be conducted in the limited vocabulary of the Chinook jargon, a mixture of some three hundred French, English, Chinookan and other Indian words used in negotiations between White fur traders and the northwestern tribes. It has been maintained that the employment of the jargon instead of the Indians' own tongues was intended to ease Stevens' task of persuasion by obscuring precisely what he was asking the headmen to sign; but it is clear that they understood enough to know that they were being ordered to move away from the fertile, watered valleys of their fishing rivers, which the White settlers wanted, to three small, undesirable areas where it would be hard, if not impossible, to catch fish. Having been apprised, however, that the Indians would insist that their survival depended on the retention of their right to fish, Stevens gave them a guarantee of access to, and use of, their old fishing stations, and the final treaty contained a section specifically reserving that right for the bands, reading: "The right of taking fish at all usual and accustomed grounds and stations is further secured to said Indians in common with all citizens of the Territory." Despite this assurance, Leschi, a principal headman of the Nisquallies, and a number of other Indians refused to relinquish their ancestral lands and sign the treaty. But Stevens bullied the others into doing so and, according to some of those who refused to sign, forged X's and thumbprints next to their names and that of Leschi. Altogether, the bands and tribes ceded about 2,240,000 acres for $32,500 to be paid to them over a twenty-year period. None of them was happy with what had occurred, and they left the council in confusion and anxiety.

On January 22, 1855, under much the same circumstances, Stevens hurried the Duwamish and five other Puget Sound tribes into signing a somewhat similar treaty at Point Elliott. The Duwamish, whose territory included the site of present-day Seattle, were led by Chief Sealth ("Seattle" being a corruption of his name), an imposing and eloquent man who was already well known as friendly to the Whites. Among those present, also, were the Skope-ahmish and other bands that later became known as the Muckleshoots. They did not sign, but apparently accepted Sealth as their spokesman and he signed for them. The treaty contained the same words securing their fishing rights that Stevens had included in the Medicine Creek Treaty, but, again, there was unhappiness. Resigned to the White men's dominion, Sealth made an impassioned speech to Stevens and his aides, concluding movingly: "When the last Red Man shall have perished, and the memory of my tribe shall have become a myth among the white man, these shores will swarm with the invisible dead of my tribe, and when your children's children think themselves alone in the field, the store, the shop, upon the highway, or in the silence of the pathless woods, they will not be alone. . . . At night when the streets of your cities and villages are silent and you think them deserted, they will throng with the returning hosts that once filled them and still love this beautiful land. The White Man will never be alone."

Stevens brushed aside such Indian sentiments and within the following month met three times more with other tribes, signing treaties at two of the gatherings, but tearing up the treaty paper at the final meeting after receiving angry opposition from one of the headmen. Each of the treaties he signed contained the provision assuring the Indians the right to take fish "at all usual and accustomed grounds and stations . . . in common with all citizens of the Territory." Meanwhile, on December 30, 1854, he sent the Medicine Creek Treaty to Washington for ratification. With it went a letter containing an explanation of the Indians' reservation of their fishing rights and illuminating not only the Indians' dependence on fish but the Whites' reliance on the Indian fishermen for their own local consumption and commercial export of fish. "They [the Indians] catch most of our fish," Stevens wrote, "supplying not only our people with clams and oysters but salmon to those who cure and export it . . . their principal food is fish and roots and berries. . . . The provisions as to reserves and as to taking fish . . . had strict reference to their conditions as above, to their actual wants and to the part they play and ought to play in the labor and prosperity of the Territory. It may be here observed that their mode of taking fish differs so essentially from that of the whites that it will not interfere with the latter." The Medicine Creek Treaty, which included agreements with the Nisquallies and Puyallups, was ratified by the Senate on March 3, 1855, and signed by President Franklin Pierce on April 10 of the same year.

In the Northwest, however, trouble was brewing. Impatient settlers, not waiting for the ratification of the treaties, overran the Indians' lands, angering the bands and embarrassing the headmen who had signed Stevens' papers. Fearing conflict, Stevens' Indian agent at the new territorial capital of Olympia rounded up thousands of members of many different bands and tribes and interned them, under the eyes of the militia, in seven temporary holding areas scattered along Puget Sound. This provocative action made the situation worse, and war suddenly broke out in October 1855 when the Whites tried to take the Nisqually leader, Leschi, and his brother into protective custody. The two men escaped to the mountains, joined a large group of refugees from Nisqually, Puyallup, and other tribal villages, and commenced to fight back defensively against the Whites, even threatening Seattle with a foray that sent frightened settlers rushing to the safety of blockhouses. Employing ruthless measures, Stevens and the militia finally stamped out the Indians' resistance and drove Leschi to the eastern side of the Cascades. Later, when he returned, he was captured, tried for the murder of a White man, and hanged, though many Whites considered him innocent of the killing and urged his acquittal.

The conflict effectively ended the Indians' ability to defend themselves against the increasing White population in western Washington, but it convinced the federal government that the tribes had legitimate grievances against Stevens' hasty and high-handed treaties. Under instructions from his superiors, Stevens met with the interned Nisquallies and Puyallups at Fox Island near Tacoma, where they were being held, and readjusted the permanent reservations he had previously assigned to them, giving them back many of their old fishing sites. The Nisquallies received 4,717 acres on both sides of the Nisqually River, several miles above its mouth at the southern end of the Sound, and the Puyallups, who had complained that the original site designated for them at the mouth of the Puyallup River was too small to hold all their people, were granted additional land along both sides of the river to form a reservation which, after another change in its boundaries in 1873, comprised about 18,000 acres.

At the same time, Stevens took note of the dissatisfaction of the Skope-ahmish and a number of other bands whom Sealth, the Duwamish leader, had represented at the Point Elliott treaty meeting. Those bands resented being forced to move out of their own country and onto a reservation with the coastal Duwamish and wanted their riverine fishing sites restored to them. A military post was being abandoned on the Muckleshoot Prairie in their homeland, and Stevens now returned that site to them, establishing a reservation of approximately 3,500 acres that encompassed portions of the Green and White rivers. Shared by many of the small bands, it was named the Muckleshoot reservation after the prairie and post that had stood there. By 1870, all the various groups on the reserve were known collectively to the Whites as Muckleshoot Indians. The three reservations, newly defined by Stevens, were duly approved by executive order in Washington, D.C., on January 20, 1857, and the tribes and bands were moved onto them.

In the years that followed, Whites continued to stream into the Puget Sound region, and the Indians lost ownership of much of the lands within their reservation boundaries. The area at the mouth of the Puyallup River grew into the city of Tacoma (after the Indians' name for Mount Rainier), and in the 1870's, the federal government began eroding the Puyallups' holdings by granting rights-of-way on their reservation to railroads and other industrial and commercial applicants.

The Dawes Allotment Act, passed in 1887, was quickly implemented on all three reservations; the Indians were given individual family-sized allotments, and the rest of their lands were opened to Whites, who poured onto the reservations and established farms and homes on former tribal holdings. In order to protect the Indians, the Dawes Act prohibited the selling of an Indian's allotment for twenty-five years, when presumably the owner would be competent to deal with Whites as an equal and defend himself against fraud. The pressure for Indian land and resources at Puget Sound became so great, however, that many of the Indians' most desirable allotments were permitted to be sold after ten years, and, by fair means and foul, the transference of Indian property into White hands accelerated.

In 1893, Congress helped the expanding city of Tacoma all but obliterate the Puyallup reservation by specifically ordering the sale of all the reservation's land, save what had been allotted for Indian homes and an Indian school and burying ground. Similarly, in 1917, during World War I, the government condemned all of the Nisquallies' land on the eastern side of the Nisqually River for use by the Army's Fort Lewis. At a stroke, the tribe lost 3,300 acres, or more than 70 percent of its reservation. The ousted Nisqually families were eventually paid a total of $160,-840 for their lands and improvements and for the loss of their hunting rights and access to the lakes and streams on the condemned property. Some of the money was used to purchase other land for tribal members who had lost their allotments. A number of them resettled on the west bank of the Nisqually River, and though they were outside of the reservation's boundaries, their new property was given trust status by the federal government, just as if they were within the reservation.

By the 1960's, the continuing inroads on the reservations and the intermixing within their boundaries of Indian and White property owners, together with the acculturation of most of the Indians and the disappearance of traditional tribal and band political structures, made many non-Indians think that it no longer mattered knowing when they were on or off a reservation, or who was and was not an Indian. In their view, reservations were outmoded and would soon disappear entirely, and Indians were, or should be, no different from anyone else. Actually, at the time, 1,200 acres of the Muckleshoot reservation were still in Indian hands, and of the total Muckleshoot tribal enrollment of 340, about 270 lived on the reservation. The Nisquallies possessed 816 acres and about 190 of them lived on trust land. The original tribally owned 18,000 acres of the Puyallups had been whittled down to 33, most of them used for their cemetery, but another 200 or 300 acres were privately owned within the reservation by descendants of the Indian allottees. The total Puyallup tribal enrollment was about 450, some 170 of whom lived on these old allotments.

The many changes that had come to the region had also affected the Indians' fisheries. Many of their usual and accustomed fishing sites had disappeared to farms and White settlements or had been destroyed by towns, cities, and riverside commerce and industry. Others had been ruined by loggers and pulp mills, municipal and industrial pollution, dams, and the rearranging of river channels. As Whites took over more of the land, the Indians found it increasingly difficult to gain access to many of the fishing sites that remained. For a time, after the period of the treaties, the Indians, as Stevens had observed, had supplied a large share of the fish consumed by Whites. In the 1880's, however, the burgeoning of salmon canneries encouraged the growth of commercial fishing among the Whites, and their competitiveness with the tribal fishers produced the first quarrels. The conflicts became so bad that in 1886 federal troops were sent to some of the fishing sites to protect the Indians.

As sport fishing became popular, the Indians faced another form of competition, and conflicts increased. Treaty rights became blurred and subject to argument. By the beginning of the twentieth century, there was a widespread disregard for Indian rights, which became more prevalent as the fish runs dwindled and competition grew. To conserve the fish, state regulations were adopted applying to Indians, as well as to non-Indians, and state agencies came into existence to enforce the codes. In 1905, when the federal government contested the right of the state of Washington to grant a private company an exclusive license to use a traditional Indian fishing ground, the Supreme Court in *U.S.* v. *Winans* ruled it a violation of Indian treaty rights, but created confusion by recognizing that the state had some regulatory authority over Indian fishermen, without defining the nature and extent of that authority. On many occasions, thereafter, Indians were arrested for violations of state fishing regulations, and three times, twice in 1916 and once in 1921, the Washington State Supreme Court ruled that the Indians had no greater fishing rights than the Whites and must comply with the state laws. In none of the cases did the federal government live up to its trust obligation and appeal the decisions to a federal court in behalf of the Indians.

At the same time, there were doubts. In 1941, the Washington Supreme Court upheld the conviction of a Yakima Indian for fishing without a license. This time, the federal government appealed, and the U.S. Supreme Court decided that the state could not require Indians to buy a license to exercise their treaty right to fish, though again it left confusion by adding that a state could regulate Indian fishing for conservation purposes. When, however, the state in 1951 tried to stop some Makah

Indians from fishing with nets, a federal court ruled that the regulation which the Makahs were alleged to have violated was not necessary for conservation purposes.

The rights of the state versus those of the Indians were thus left unclear throughout the first half of the twentieth century. In actual practice, Washington's Department of Fisheries, which had jurisdiction over salmon as a commercial food fish, and its Department of Game, which enforced the regulations affecting steelhead as essentially a game, or sport, fish (the two agencies were originally one department), viewed the White fishermen as their clients and were contemptuous of any special exemptions claimed by the Indians. Judges of the state's lower courts, also, were susceptible to the pleas and pressures of the non-Indian fishermen and found it hard to accept the argument that Indians could break a state law that everyone else had to obey. If it was illegal to use nets to catch game fish, including steelhead, and to sell or ship game fish, then that was the law, and, as they saw it, it applied equally to Whites and Indians.

But when Indians were arrested, there were sometimes perplexing arguments, and it was often apparent that neither agencies nor judges were exactly sure of what, if any, protection the treaties actually gave the Indians from the state's police power in the matter of fishing. Could the state enforce its rules on a reservation? Did "usual and accustomed grounds" mean that Indians could catch fish outside of their reservations with the same disregard for state laws that they evidenced on their reservations? What were the boundaries of the reservations—the original ones established by Stevens, or those of the Indians' present shrunken holdings? Did the treaty phrase "in common with all citizens" mean that the Indians had to accept the same regulations as everyone else, or did it refer to the amount of fish to which they were entitled? Such were among the numerous questions asked, and various judges differed among themselves about the answers, eventually coming to recognize that only the U.S. Supreme Court could settle these issues. But since the Indians were so poor that they often could not raise bail money for themselves, and the federal government only rarely defended them, the likelihood of a definitive, encompassing case ever going that far, helpful as it might be, seemed remote.

Though most White public opinion firmly assumed that the phrase "in common with all citizens" committed Indians to observance of the state laws, the doubts throughout the years were strong enough to inhibit a full-scale campaign to make the Indians accept the state's rules or stop fishing. The fishery officials and game wardens, frustrated by the uncertainty, and frequently exhibiting crude racism in their anger against the tribal fishermen, harassed the Indians on the Green, Puyallup, and other rivers and made just enough arrests to maintain their authority. Occasionally, judges let the Indians go with a warning, but more often gave them a fine and sixty days in jail. Indians frequently did not even attempt to argue that they had been fishing according to their treaty rights; experience taught them that the judges would simply declare they were wrong. As an added penalty, they sometimes lost their boats and fishing gear: the fish and game officers would impound them during their raids to bring to court "as evidence," but no boat was ever brought to a court hearing, and when the Indians were unable to get them back, they had to find another job to scrape up enough money to reequip themselves.

Such confiscations, to some Indians, seemed part of a plan to drive them off the rivers by taking away their means of livelihood, somewhat as Whites had crippled the plains Indians by killing the buffalo. These suspicions were not without substance. Through the years, the White men's impact, interference, and competition had made many of the Indians abandon fishing. To the survivors, the loss of gear and boats—especially their old dugouts, which were irreplaceable—was a heavy blow. The Indians, generally, were among the poorest of the state's poor, and every year, some of those who were arrested could not meet the expense of buying new nets and outboard motorboats and had to borrow boats, join others, or else give up fishing.

In 1954, an Indian arrest that was appealed to a higher court made it appear for a time that the question of Indian fishing rights might be settled. The case involved a rugged Indian entrepreneur named Robert Satiacum, who was part Puyallup and part Yakima. He had grown up among Whites at Fife, a suburb of Tacoma, had worked in the construction industry, and at times ran several fishing boats on the lower Puyallup River. Satiacum looked and behaved like a two-fisted prizefighter and was not afraid of the fish and game officials. He was arrested and charged with being in possession of game fish (steelhead) during a closed season, and with having used fixed gill nets to catch game fish at two locations, one of them outside the Puyallup reservation and the other within the original boundaries of the reservation but on land that had passed into White ownership.

Satiacum had the means and determination to appeal his conviction to a Washington Superior Court, which ruled in his favor on the grounds that he had been within his treaty rights by fishing at usual and accustomed fishing sites of the Puyallups in accordance with the immemorial customs of his tribe, and that the state regulations illegally deprived him of those treaty rights. The state appealed the decision to the Washington Supreme Court, which in 1957 sustained the Superior Court, but split,

4–4, half of its members agreeing with the Superior Court and half saying that the state would have had the right to arrest Satiacum if it had first proved that enforcement of the regulations had been necessary for conservation purposes. Satiacum's case was dismissed, but the split decision left the Indians' rights issues still unsettled.

Proving that the conserving of the Northwest fisheries depended on halting the activities of Indian fishermen was impossible, as well as ludicrous. The total of all the Indian fishers was estimated to be about 800, as against approximately 6,600 non-Indian commercial fishermen and some 283,000 non-Indian sport fishermen. About 4,000 White ocean-going trollers, supplying fish to large packing corporations, as well as huge fleets of commercial charter boats, harvested the largest part of the salmon runs, each year hauling in more than two million tons of the fish offshore before they ever got to the rivers to reproduce. Once in the rivers, the salmon and steelhead runs were cut down by the barriers and pollution of the Whites. Moreover, the Indians were as distressed as the Whites by the fall-off in fish and were not recklessly trying to speed the depletion, which hurt them as much as the non-Indians. Though the state wardens cultivated the impression that the Indians had no interest in conservation, the opposite, in fact, was true. Most Indian fishermen limited their catches by carefully policing themselves, and on a number of occasions the tribes proposed that the state agencies and White fishermen join them in designing and implementing a comprehensive and effective conservation program. The state agencies refused to take them seriously, or even meet with them for discussions. The truth was that a meaningful program for the restoration of the fisheries was regarded by the state officials as politically and economically unrealistic, since it implied such unacceptable measures as drastically reducing the number of White fishermen and their catch, forcing cities and industries to clean up and clear the rivers, and prohibiting new developments that would further degrade the environmental habitat of the fish. In the wake of the Satiacum decision, therefore, the fish and game authorities realized that they could not build a logical case against the Indians, and for a time they halted their arrests.

Simplistic arguments, however, continued to be used to rouse public sentiment and prejudice against the Indian fishers. Some of the campaign was deliberately furthered by irritated state game wardens who spied on the Indian fishermen and made secret movies of them catching steelhead in nets out of season to show at meetings of sport fishermen's clubs. Such provocations had their intended effect. Anger continued to build, editorial writers and politicans seethed, and in 1961 the atmosphere was right for state officials to move once more against the Indians. This time, they did so with a determination to bring a final halt to their violations of the state laws. The first of a number of arrests and harassments were of the two Muckleshoots and the Puyallup on the Green River who were later acquitted for being within their treaty rights—the same reason that the Superior Court had used in ruling in favor of Satiacum. Soon afterward, the wardens cracked down on Indian fishermen on the Nisqually River. On January 6, 1962, a small army of three dozen officers with walkie-talkies and a reconnaissance spotter plane overhead closed in on six Indians and, confiscating their boats, motors, and gear, arrested them for fishing with gill nets. Two Seattle attorneys took the case of the Indians, who pleaded not guilty on the grounds that they had been fishing on Indian trust land, which they claimed was part of the Nisqually reservation, and were thus within their treaty rights. The Game Department then charged that they were not pure-blood Nisquallies and therefore had no treaty rights, and the trial became a "pedigree" case, in which the Indians had to gather a stack of affidavits, with the help of Billy Frank, Jr., the tribe's vice-president, to try to prove that they were recognized Nisquallies. In the end, three of the fishermen were freed, but the other three were fined $10 each.

The acquittal of the three men did not deter the fish and game agents. What appeared to be a serious legal obstacle to their efforts, however, occurred suddenly in 1963 with a federal court decision concerning a treaty fishing rights case in the neighboring state of Oregon. In *Maison v. Confederated Tribes of the Umatilla Indian Reservation,* the U.S. Ninth Circuit Court of Appeals in San Francisco echoed Washington's Satiacum decision in favor of the Indians, ruling that Oregon could only regulate off-reservation fishing by Indians at their usual and accustomed sites to the extent that the regulation was necessary for the conservation of fish, but it went beyond the Satiacum decision by adding, also, that the state could only carry out the regulation if it could not attain the conservation objective by *first* resorting to all other methods, including the restriction of the fishing rights of the non-Indians alone. In other words, a state must first prohibit pollution, sport fishing, and everything else depleting the fish before interfering with Indian treaties. Oregon appealed the decision, but the U.S. Supreme Court declined to review it, and the Circuit Court's ruling stood.

The federal court's decision heartened the Puget Sound Indians, but caused only temporary consternation among Washington's officials. If anything, it turned more Whites against the tribal fishermen along the Sound, and the Indians soon realized that the state of Washington intended to ignore the Oregon ruling as impractical. On September 27, 1963, the Fish and Game Departments got a temporary injunction closing the entire Green River to net fishing, and on the same day arrested fifteen Muckleshoots who had been netting salmon. The latter were able to raise enough money to get lawyers, and they pleaded not guilty. Their appeal, *State* v. *Herman Moses et al.* (for one of the arrested fishermen), destined to become the first of a series of test cases, was sent to the King County Superior Court.

If Oregon's Umatilla decision had originally raised the Indians' hopes, another one, this time in Washington, now thoroughly dashed them and made the tribal fishermen on all the rivers feel that a real crisis was approaching. On December 17, 1963, the Washington State Supreme Court, appearing to many to violate the U.S. Constitution by ignoring the federal court's Umatilla ruling, decided, in a case affecting a Swinomish Indian in Washington who had been arrested for gill netting off the mouth of the Skagit River (the case was *State* v. *McCoy*), that Washington State did have the power to regulate Indian fishing for conservation purposes. Nothing was said about first having to try every other conservation measure possible, including the restriction of non-Indian fishing, and the decision, in fact, also conflicted with the same court's action in the Satiacum case, in which four of its members at the time had decided that the state could not interfere with treaty rights at all and the other four had said that the state had to prove that regulations were necessary for conservation.

The McCoy decision gave Washington State fish and game officials a clear go-ahead. With the steelhead season already underway, the Indian fishermen knew that the game wardens would soon be coming after them in earnest. Hopes for their cause now seemed dim. Nonetheless, they decided that they had no alternative but to continue exercising their rights, hoping that public sentiment might eventually support them or that another test case might develop and give them a more favorable decision. Though they faced the prospect of more arrests, jailings, economic hardships, and perhaps physical violence against them, they persuaded themselves that right was on their side and that, in the end, if they kept fishing, they would win.

Measures for resistance were first organized by a determined group of families whose members fished regularly on the Nisqually River at Frank's Landing, a brushy tract that had been purchased years before for Billy Frank, Sr., one of the tribal members whose allotment on the opposite side of the river had been condemned in 1917 for Fort Lewis. Though the new site was outside the original boundaries of the Nisqually reservation, it had been given trust status, and the Indians—but, by 1963, not the state—considered it to be part of the reservation. Fishing was better there than on the original reservation, where the Nisqually River ran faster and more turbulently, and Frank's location, a usual and accustomed tribal fishing site, was frequented by many Indians. Billy Frank, Sr., a Nisqually elder who lived on the tract with his wife, was still alive, and other fishing relatives and friends included Don and Pauline Matheson, Alvin and Maiselle Bridges and their daughters, Valerie, Alison, and Suzette, Billy Frank, Jr., the tribal vice-president, Nugent Kautz, Don George, Jr., and Donald and Janet McCloud. Don McCloud was a Puyallup who had been reared among the Nisquallies, and Janet, the mother of eight children, was a Tulalip Indian from farther north on Puget Sound and a descendant of Sealth, the Duwamish chief. An energetic and forceful traditionalist, she believed in brotherhood between Indians and Whites, but fought to get Indians to maintain pride in their Indianness as well. In the nearby town of Yelm, where the McClouds lived, she crusaded against the White-run public school system, demanding that the administrators and teachers end their prejudice against Indian students and include course materials that would encourage understanding and respect for Indian history and culture.

Immediately after the McCoy decision, the Frank's Landing fishers called an emergency meeting. Word of it was circulated along Puget Sound by Dewey Sigo, a Squaxim Indian who bought fish from Indians to sell to non-Indian commercial markets, and some fifty persons attended the gathering, including Indians from the upper Skagit River, Nooksacks, Quilleutes, and Puyallups. Deciding, first, to make a direct plea to the governor, who they hoped might intervene with the state agencies in their behalf, they made signs reading "No salmon—no Santa," and on December 23, just before Christmas, drove to Olympia and demonstrated at the state capitol. Governor Albert Rosellini invited them in, listened to them politely, but dismissed them with a patronizing "Nice to hear your problems. Come back again."

The appeal focused media attention on them, but also drew the ire of the Fish and Game Departments. On January 1, 1964, George Smallwood of the Game Department appeared at Frank's Landing, where some of the Indians were fishing for dog salmon and steelhead, and ordered them to fish only within the boundaries of the original reservation seven miles farther up the river, where the state was willing to recognize that it had no jurisdiction. The Indians insisted that this was part of the reservation, and an area where Indians had always fished, and they refused to pull in their nets. It was the start of a war. The state officials got an injunction from Judge Robert H. Jaques of the Pierce County Superior Court, closing the Nisqually River below the state-recognized Nisqually reservation to net fishing by the twelve male Indians who regularly fished at Frank's Landing, and the wardens immediately moved in and arrested the Indians. The Bureau of Indian Affairs ignored the Indians' plight, and even the leaders of the Nisqually tribe, who thought the fishermen's resistance was foolish and would only breed more anti-Indian feeling, refused to help with defense funds. To raise legal fees and support the families of the arrested men, as well as to strengthen their own unity, the fishing families formed an organization called the Survival of American Indians Association and put out a mimeographed newsletter, written and edited largely by Janet McCloud, which told their side of the story. By fishbakes and other means, they raised fifty dollars and enlisted the aid of Jack Tanner, a Tacoma attorney and president of the northwestern division of the National Association for the Advancement of Colored People.

After the first arrests, the fishermen called a truce and moved to Medicine Creek, where they continued to fish quietly. The truce lasted only a brief time. They returned to Frank's Landing, and were again arrested, this time receiving suspended sentences. In the meantime, the arrests spread to the Puyallup and other rivers, and once again fishermen like Robert Satiacum were in conflict with the enforcement officials. The newspapers and radio gave coverage to the fishing war, and reports of what was occurring began to reach other parts of the country, raising sympathy for the embattled fishermen of the small, impoverished Washington tribes, whose struggle was likened by some to that of a David against an unjust Goliath. Members of the activist National Indian Youth Council, as well as traditional Indian leaders from other tribes, traveled to Puget Sound, offering to help the fishing families, join protest "fish-ins," and risk being arrested. The struggle made a particular impact on a soft-spoken, politically astute young Indian named Hank Adams, who had been born twenty years before on the Fort Peck reservation in Montana to Assiniboine and Sioux parents, but who had been raised by his mother and her second husband on the Quinault reservation in Washington. In time, he became a leading figure at Frank's Landing, raising the struggle's level of militancy and making it a symbol of the Native Americans' new determination to stand up against White men for their rights.

Help also came from some non-Indians, including the motion-picture actor Marlon Brando, who arrived to lend support to a protest march on the state capitol, which the NIYC planned in behalf of the fishermen. Prior to the march, Brando decided not to join the group at Frank's Landing because of the opposition of the Nisqually tribal leaders, but staged a demonstration fish-in, instead, with Satiacum on the Puyallup River on March 2. He was arrested for net fishing, but was released on a technicality and not tried. The next day, he participated in the march on Olympia with some 1,000 Indians, non-Indian supporters, and curiosity seekers. At the capitol, he and some of the Indians had a fruitless meeting with Governor Rosellini, after which Brando left the state.

The actor's presence gave the Indians' cause dramatic nationwide publicity, but the arrests continued. At Frank's Landing, on March 11, six fishermen, including Bill Frank, Jr., Don McCloud, Al Bridges, and Nugent Kautz, who had earlier received suspended sentences on condition that they stop fishing, fished again, were rearrested, and were ordered to jail for thirty days. After a hearing in Superior Court, their case was appealed to the State Supreme Court. With their own test case finally underway, the Frank's Landing fishermen, including those whose case was on appeal, staged another series of fish-ins, trying to continue to earn a living, and the war went on. Indians were arrested, received jail terms, and then went back to the river to fish and be rearrested. While the fishermen were in jail, women, children, and other men took their places. The Indians taunted the enforcement officers, and the latter pushed the Indians around and roughed them up. During their arrests, as well as in court, the Indians were subjected to obscenities and racist treatment. "We had the power and force to exterminate these people from the face of the earth, instead of making treaties with them," a Pierce County assistant prosecutor exclaimed during a hearing after one of the arrests. "Perhaps we should have! We certainly wouldn't be having all this trouble with them today." At another time, Judge Jaques was accused of telling the Indians, "They never meant for you people to be free like everyone else." The bigotry and violence horrified old Billy Frank, Sr., who unsuccessfully petitioned a federal court for an investigation of the brutality and disregard for the Indians' civil rights.

During the summer of 1964, Senator Warren G. Magnuson of Washington tried to solve the dispute and end the adverse attention the state was receiving by introducing two measures in Congress. Both of them advocated compromises that would have been unfavorable to the Indian fishermen, and after hearings on them in August, they died in a Senate committee. In the state, the conflict continued, marked by a picketing of the state's fisheries office in Seattle; by vain attempts by the Intertribal Council of Western Washington Indians and the National Congress of American Indians, representing tribes throughout the country, to gain support for an impartial study, involving federal and state agencies, to determine sound methods for managing and conserving the fish supply; and, in February 1965, by another demonstration at Olympia.

Meanwhile, in December 1964, Judge F. A. Walterskirchen of the King County Superior Court finally ruled on the test case of *State* v. *Herman Moses et al.*, affecting the fifteen Muckleshoot Indians who had been arrested on the Green River in September 1963. His decision, dealing the Muckleshoots an unexpected blow, was that the Muckleshoots had no treaty rights at all: no people listed as Muckleshoots had signed the 1855 Point Elliott Treaty with Stevens, and therefore the Muckleshoots could not claim any fishing rights under the treaty. He followed this decision by making permanent the injunction against net fishing on the Green River. The Muckleshoots immediately appealed his decision to the Washington State Supreme Court on the grounds that the Indians had not been permitted an opportunity to prove that the Muckleshoots were descendants of bands like the Skope-ahmish that had been at the treaty meeting and been represented by Chief Sealth of the Duwamish, who had signed the document for them, and that the Bureau of Indian Affairs itself recognized the Muckleshoots as a treaty tribe.

Thereafter, the issue followed a tortured course of its own, reflecting to the Indians the lengths to which the state would resort in order to deprive them of their fishing rights. The State Supreme Court, on January 12, 1967, dismissed the Indians' evidence on a technicality and sustained Judge Walterskirchen's opinion. The Muckleshoots, moreover, were barred from a further appeal, thus ending the case. But in March 1966, in another, and deliberate, test fish-in demonstration, four Muckleshoots gill-netted in the Green River in defiance of the injunction and were arrested. They were convicted in a lower court, but their case was taken by an attorney representing the American Civil Liberties Union, as well as by two lawyers supplied by the U.S. Department of Justice—which had finally been asked by the Interior Department to support the Muckleshoots' treaty rights—and was appealed to the King County Superior Court, the same one that had ruled that the tribe had no treaty rights. Expert evidence was again introduced, and the court, now presided over by Judge Lloyd Shorett, finally agreed that the Muckleshoots were a federally recognized treaty tribe. But it was not a total victory. Though the Indians had fished in a usual and accustomed place, the court sustained their conviction for using gill nets. The case was appealed to the State Supreme Court, which affirmed Judge Shorett, and then to the U.S. Supreme Court, where it joined other fishing rights cases that by then had reached the highest court.

Amid the confusions of the varied issues that were being raised by the different cases, still other Washington courts in 1965 began to vacillate and render conflicting opinions, all of them making the Indians' struggle more frustrating and difficult. In a case affecting Satiacum and other Puyallup fishermen, who were being arrested for violating state fishing regulations on the Puyallup River and Commencement Bay, Judge John D. Cochran of the Pierce County Superior Court, in May, astounded the Puyallups, as well as the Bureau of Indian Affairs, by ruling that there was no longer a Puyallup tribe or a Puyallup reservation, and that all Indian fishermen on the river must therefore observe the state's fishing rules and regulations. The reservation, said Judge Cochran, had, in effect, been abolished by the breakup and loss of tribally owned lands under the Allotment Act of 1887. There were now only 33 acres of trust land left, most of it a cemetery, and there was no tribe to succeed in interest to the rights of the Puyallup signers of the 1854 Treaty of Medicine Creek.

The tribe was forced to appeal this remarkable decision to the State Supreme Court, claiming that it still existed and enjoyed federal recognition as a treaty tribe, that its treaty rights still applied to all lands within the original boundaries of the reservation, and that tribal members still had the right to fish at usual and accustomed places. On January 12, 1967, the Washington Supreme Court decided that there was a Puyallup tribe, but not a reservation, that treaty rights were not absolute, and that they did not extend to the right "to take fish with such gear and at such times as would destroy the fishery." In other words, the Puyallups were deemed not to have any on-reservation rights, since there was no reservation, and only the same off-reservation rights as were accorded everyone else. In addition, the court finally noted that it thought the federal judge of the Ninth Circuit Court had been wrong in the Oregon Umatilla case in ordering a state not to infringe on Indian treaty rights unless it was indispensable for conservation, and introduced more puzzlement by differing entirely with its own previous decision in the Satiacum case of 1957, which had declared that the state regulations had deprived Satiacum of his treaty fishing rights. This decision, too, was appealed to the U.S. Supreme Court.

The initial decision of Judge Cochran, meanwhile, had angered the Puyallup fishermen, and conflict erupted off and on throughout the year as they defied his injunction closing the river to their net fishing. Indians, as well as state officers and Tacoma policemen, were bruised and hurt in scuffles, and Satiacum, threatening to use arms to defend his boats, was arrested twice. A sixty-day jail term kept him off the river, but one of the charges against him, tried as a criminal rather than a civil case, ended in his acquittal by a six-member jury. While he was imprisoned, his attractive twenty-three-year-old wife, Suzanne—a fiery Kaw Indian and grand-niece of Herbert Hoover's Vice-President, Charles Curtis—provided sensational headlines, together with a sister-in-law, Clara Satiacum, by continuing to run his fishing boats, taunting the enforcement officials and engaging in a series of melees with them, including one wild episode on the night of September 21, when the two women, using one of the boats, led eighteen Tacoma police in a frenzied chase up and down the river for an hour-and-a-half. They were finally cornered by police in a commandeered tugboat but, though arrested and given sentences, were released without having to serve time in jail.

The continued resistance of the Indians and their defiance on the rivers frustrated the fish and game wardens and wore down their patience. Hatred for the Indians, whose calm persistence made the wardens' riverbank stakeouts and sudden lunges at the fishermen seem like the antics of Toonerville cops, increased the tension, and violence of an uglier nature finally broke out at Frank's Landing on the Nisqually River. On the night of October 7, the lights of a warden's patrol boat picked up two Indians, Bill Frank, Jr., and Al Bridges, setting their nets from a dugout canoe. Gunning their motor, the wardens rammed the canoe, dumping both men into the river and almost drowning them. Two nights later, about one in the morning, the wardens came on two Indian boys on a logjam in the middle of the river. As they cornered the youths and began to harass them, word spread along the shore. Indians flocked to the scene, surrounded the wardens, and a fight broke out. More police arrived, including state police and even Fort Lewis military policemen armed with submachine guns, and a riot, with possible heavy casualties, was averted only by the forceful intercession of the county sheriff, whom the Indians regarded as a friend.

The damage, however, had been done. On October 13, the angry Nisquallies held a widely publicized protest fish-in, intending to make it the basis for a legal challenge to the state's injunction against their fishing. Newspaper reporters, photographers, television cameramen, and observers from such organizations as the American Friends Service Committee showed up, as did some eighty state game wardens, some of them carrying nightsticks, blackjacks, and long, seven-celled flashlights. The wardens stationed themselves on both sides of the river and waited for the Indians to do something. Finally, the Indians, who totaled eight men and nineteen women and children, put a dugout into the river, carrying two Indian fishermen, two little boys, their dog, and a newspaper cameraman. As the fishermen began to lower a net, a warden hollered, "Get 'em," and a powerboat roared out and crashed into the dugout, pitching everyone into the water. In an instant, Indians rushed into the river to save the children, the wardens descended on them from both banks, and a free-swinging battle was underway. Rocks were thrown, people were hit with clubs and sticks, and children were dragged by their hair and knocked down. When it was over, several people had been hurt, including Indians, White reporters and cameramen, and some of the wardens. Indian boats and canoes, nets, and outboard motors were confiscated, and seven Indians, including Janet and Donald McCloud, Alvin and Mai-selle Bridges, and Suzanne Satiacum, who had come to give moral support, were arrested for resisting the officers. The newsmen, however, had dramatic stories to write and pictures to show of the wardens' brutality, and some of the non-Indian observers had lurid, pro-Indian accounts to relate (including the smell of whiskey on the breath of some of the wardens). When the Indians were finally tried by a jury almost three-and-a-half years later, on January 1, 1969, they were acquitted on the grounds that they had been justifiably defending themselves.

For a long time, the Nisquallies and Puyallups had been trying to get the federal government to help them, both by defending their fishing rights as their trustee and by protecting their civil rights against the state officials. Appeals to the Attorney General for help in February 1965 had been brusquely turned down by Assistant Attorney General John Doar. A new plea to Secretary of the Interior Stewart Udall was now also rejected for much the same reason: pending court clarification of the tribes' treaty fishing rights, the executive branch was too uncertain of the Indians' complicated legal position to intervene. A march on the Seattle federal courthouse to seek help by members and supporters of the Survival of American Indians Association on October 26, after the attack at Frank's Landing, also failed in its purpose. The Indians were still on their own, and the wardens' surveillances and interferences continued. On December 19, Al Bridges was again arrested on the Nisqually, and a few weeks later, two more Indian fishermen were seized.

In February 1966, the Black comedian and civil rights figure Dick Gregory and his wife, Lillian, drew more publicity to the Indians' fight by participating in a series of fish-ins with the Indians. Gregory was arrested and convicted on three counts of illegal net fishing. He appealed his conviction to the State Supreme Court in March 1968, but lost and served forty days in jail, fasting during his confinement, and announcing, on his release, "If more people went to jail for rights, fewer would go for wrongs."

The fishing rights struggle, meanwhile, was spreading to the Columbia River, where in the spring of 1966 Washington and Oregon officials began arresting Yakima Indian fishermen, sometimes at gunpoint and with considerable savagery, for fishing for chinook salmon with set-nets at a fishing site known as Cooks Landing above Bonneville Dam. After more than thirty-two arrests had been made, with the Yakimas receiving suspended sentences and then going back to fishing, the Yakimas armed themselves for defense. On July 27, when five Washington State wardens tried to make two more arrests, a Yakima named Clarence Tahkeal interfered with the arrest, training his rifle on the wardens until he could turn them over to the state police in a citizen's arrest that charged the wardens with trespassing.

The conflict on the Columbia spelled new problems for Washington State. The Yakimas, unlike the small groups along Puget Sound, were a large and politically powerful tribe. Moreover, they were associated with a number of other large interior tribes, including the Umatillas, the Warm Springs Indians, and the Nez Perces of Idaho, in asserting treaty fishing rights, similar to those of the Puget Sound Indians, stemming from treaties which they, too, had made with Stevens in 1855. The sudden campaign against the Yakima fishermen at Cooks Landing contributed to the raising of questions among all those tribes about the observance of their own fishing rights, and on August 19 and 20, 1966, they held a meeting at the White Swan Longhouse on the Yakima reservation. It was attended by thirty-eight Indian delegates, as well as tribal attorneys, the assistant area director of the Bureau of Indian Affairs in Portland, and a regional solicitor for the Bureau, who announced that the Department of the Interior would now, upon request, have the U.S. Department of Justice defend their treaty rights and assist the tribes in upholding the self-regulation of their own fishing. The promise encouraged the Indians, who formed a Columbia River Indian Fishing Council and prepared to defend their fishing rights on the Columbia and its tributaries.

The solicitor's assurance of federal support, reflecting growing concern by the Interior Department over the conflict in the Northwest, was the beginning of a change in the recognition of its obligation to the fishing Indians. Early in May, Assistant Attorney General Edwin L. Weisl, Jr., arrived in Portland from Washington, D.C., to look into the arrests of the Yakima fishermen and announced that the federal government was "determined to fight in the courts to uphold the solemn obligation" of the treaties made with the Columbia River fishing tribes. He added, however, that the government would furnish counsel only for those defendants who fished in compliance with tribal council fishing rules.

It was a first step, but a second one followed quickly. Having made known its intention to support any Indian arrested by a state while fishing in accordance with treaty rights and tribally approved regulations, the Department of Justice, on May 31, entered, as *amicus curiae*, the case in which the Puyallups were trying to prove that they were still a treaty tribe and still owned a reservation, which was then before the Washington State Supreme Court. As noted earlier, tribal recognition was won, but despite the government's assistance, the court ruled against the existence of a Puyallup reservation and supported the state's right to regulate the Puyallups' fishing. If only as an outside supporting friend, however, the federal government had now intervened for the first time in years in a Washington fishing rights case.

The tribe's lawyers appealed the Washington court's decision to the

U.S. Supreme Court, and on December 18, 1967, the Court agreed to hear it, but combined it with the Nisqually case, mentioned earlier, that had begun on March 11, 1964, with the arrests of Nugent Kautz, Bill Frank, Jr., Donald McCloud, Al Bridges, and two other Indians for defying the injunction against net fishing at Frank's Landing. In the Washington State Supreme Court, on January 12, 1967, that case had gone against the Indians, and had been appealed to the U.S. Supreme Court. One of the basic issues in both cases—the state's right to regulate treaty Indian fishing at usual and accustomed sites off the reservation—was essentially the same.

On May 27, 1968, the U.S. Supreme Court, in a decision written by Justice William O. Douglas in the combined case known as *Department of Game* v. *Puyallup Tribe,* agreed unanimously that, while the treaty Indians did have special rights, separate and distinct from those of others, to fish at usual and accustomed places off the reservation, the state had the power to regulate the fishing, providing the regulation was reasonable and necessary and did not discriminate against the Indians. The case was sent back to the state courts to clarify, in accordance with the Court's decision, what was "reasonable and necessary." Moreover, though the Puyallups were confirmed as a recognized tribe, the question of whether their reservation had been extinguished was not settled.

It was an ambiguous and unsatisfactory decision, which, if anything, worsened the Indians' position. The Court had ignored the concept of the earlier Umatilla decision, in which a federal Circuit Court had ruled that Indians should only be regulated after a limitation or prohibition of non-Indian fishing, and which the Supreme Court at the time had let stand by declining to review it. Now, not only could the state set and enforce fishing rules against the Indians, which courts would be willing to accept as "reasonable and necessary" in themselves, without taking other conservation measures, but the Indians, having got their case to the Supreme Court, seemed at the end of their road.

As the Indians feared, the state viewed the decision as vindication of its asserted right to continue regulating Indian fishing as it saw fit, maintaining that its rules were reasonable and necessary and not discriminatory against the treaty tribes. The Puyallup reservation was still deemed nonexistent, and another injunction again closed the Puyallup River to the Indian fishermen. The Nisqually River was also closed outside the boundaries of the Nisqually reservation, and at Frank's Landing, whose fishermen were angered by a BIA decision in October that the site was not considered part of the reservation, there were renewed demonstrations and an escalation of violence and tension.

In 1966, Janet McCloud had viewed the fishing rights struggle as only one phase of a larger, overall fight by Native Americans for their rights throughout the United States, and she had left the Survival of American Indians Association to enlarge the scope of her activities and join Hopi and other Indian traditionalist leaders and teachers. Traveling to other tribes, she urged their members to revive pride in their Indian-ness and return to the traditional values of their peoples. Gradually, as she became known nationally among Indians, she took up the leadership of such causes as the just treatment of Indian inmates of federal and state prisons, and became a member of the national steering committee of the Native American Rights Fund. Hank Adams eventually took over the direction of the Survival Association at Frank's Landing and strove to merge its struggle with those of activist Indian and non-Indian groups elsewhere in the country. Early in 1968, after meeting with Martin Luther King and then attending the assassinated Black leader's funeral in At-lanta, he became one of the leaders of the Poor People's march on Washington and, with Al Bridges and a delegation of Puget Sound fishing Indians, was in the national capital when the Supreme Court ruled on the Puyallup case. The decision incensed Adams and the Indians with him, and joined by non-Indian members of the Poor People's group, he led a protest march on the Supreme Court Building. During the demonstra-tion, a window of the building was broken, and Adams and the western Washington Indians pledged to return to their homes and "fish every season every year from now on," declaring that "no power of the United States, whether political, administrative, legislative, judicial, or military, may extinguish these rights so long as an Indian lives."

Adams and the others returned to Frank's Landing and began fishing again. Their defiance, accompanied by press releases and fiery broad-sides, received wide publicity and helped stoke a growing militancy among young Indians in San Francisco—where, in 1969, they occupied Alcatraz Island—and other parts of the nation. A few of them came to Frank's Landing, among them Sidney Mills, a nineteen-year-old Yakima Indian paratrooper, who had returned from Vietnam for hospitalization for wounds and had become so disturbed by the attack on his own peo-ple's fishing rights that he went AWOL. Later, after serving time in a stockade, he received a discharge. He settled at Frank's Landing as a sort of liaison between the Yakima and Puget Sound fishermen, worked with Adams, and eventually married Al Bridges' daughter Suzette (Adams married another daughter, Alison). The fishermen's militancy, at the same time, won considerable support from non-Indian students and counterculture young people in the Northwest, and many of them came to Frank's Landing to try to help the Indians.

The state officials accepted the challenge, and by the beginning of

October 1968, after the Supreme Court decision, raids and arrests had begun again. The fishermen established several camps along the Nisqually River and fished at all of them. On October 13, the anniversary of the 1965 battle on the river, fifteen Indians and about two hundred non-Indians staged a protest rally against the new arrests at the Temple of Justice at the capitol in Olympia. The next day, some fifty wardens and sheriffs' officers appeared at Frank's Landing and, after a scuffle with the Indians and their student allies, arrested two non-Indians and seized a net. Anti-Indian sport fishermen were now also showing up, threatening the Indians with violence, and after the raid Adams accused one of them of firing a shot at an Indian. To protect the camp, Adams posted a guard at the perimeter of Frank's Landing, armed himself, Sid Mills, and another Indian, and announced that thereafter the weapons would be used against any trespasser or state officer who interfered with the Indians' fishing. The threat had no effect. Three days later, the wardens and police struck again, this time attacking Indians who were fishing at one of the other sites on the river. They arrested six fishermen, including the indestructible Al Bridges, and manhandled his daughter Valerie. Though Adams waged a tireless press campaign, accusing the state of discriminating against the Indians and violating the Supreme Court decision by not proving that their interference with the Indians' fishing was reasonable and necessary, the conflict and violence went on.

Meanwhile, arrests of Yakima Indians had also continued on the Columbia River, and in July a group known as the National Office for the Rights of the Indigent (NORI) was asked by Edgar Cahn, the executive director of the Citizens Advocate Center in Washington, D.C., and an attorney interested in Indian affairs, to help the Yakimas. NORI obtained the legal-aid services of three lawyers, who filed a case against the Oregon Fish and Game Commissions in behalf of fourteen Yakimas, including members of the Sohappy family, who had been subjected to arrests, seeking to define their treaty fishing rights, as well as the extent to which Oregon could regulate Indian fishing. Two months after the filing of the suit, known as *Sohappy* v. *Smith,* the Department of Justice followed through on the government's earlier assurance to the Columbia River tribes and filed a suit against the state of Oregon for itself, the Yakimas, the Umatillas, and the Nez Perces, seeking an injunction to enforce Indian off-reservation fishing rights in the Columbia River watershed. Later, the three tribes, as well as the Warm Springs tribe, intervened in their own behalf in the case, which was known as *The United States* v. *Oregon.*

The two cases, which ran concurrently, were filed in the U.S. District Court in Oregon. The opinion, handed down on July 8, 1969, by District

Judge Robert C. Belloni, was an echo of the decision in the Umatilla case of 1963, which had been ignored for so long. Ordering the state to recognize Indian treaty fishing interests as "a subject separate and distinct from that of fishing by others," it upheld the right of treaty Indians to fish at usual and accustomed places and to have an opportunity to take a "fair and equitable share of all fish." Before the state could regulate Indian treaty fishing, moreover, it ruled that it must establish by preliminary hearings that the specific regulations were reasonable and necessary and were the least restrictive that could be imposed. To accomplish conservation objectives, the state was reminded to restrict or prohibit non-Indian fishing before interfering with treaty rights and imposing similar restrictions on treaty Indians. In addition, Indians must be given an opportunity to "participate meaningfully in the rule-making process."

The decision startled Oregon and Washington. Its implications, including those of putting Indian rights ahead of those of Whites and giving the Indians a chance to take an "equitable" share of all fish (the court's interpretation of "in common with all citizens"), angered the non-Indian sport and commercial fishermen along Puget Sound, and although Washington State said it would abide by the decision, it failed to implement its rulings. Instead, the fish and game agencies maintained the old injunctions and continued to make arrests. With nothing changed, the Indians went on fishing as a matter of course, both for their livelihood and to assert their rights, and from time to time celebrities like the Indian singer Buffy Sainte-Marie and the actress Jane Fonda came to give them support.

During 1970, violence broke out again on the Puyallup River, where Satiacum and other Puyallups had been complaining that the state was violating the 1968 Supreme Court decision. Since the decision, Washington had done nothing to alter its own opinion that the Puyallups' reservation no longer existed, and it had kept in force an injunction that closed the river to Indian net fishermen. The Puyallups finally decided to fight the injunction as discriminatory against the Indians and unnecessary for conservation purposes and had again begun fishing with setnets for steelhead to sell commercially. Satiacum had been arrested and had appealed his conviction. The Indians, meanwhile, kept fishing, and on August 1, during the salmon season, some of them established a fishing camp and set up a few tipis on a small piece of remaining Puyallup trust land along the river. In the following days, the camp's population increased, as fishermen from Frank's Landing, Indians from different parts of the country, and non-Indian sympathizers joined them.

The blatant net fishing by a large number of people angered White sport fishermen, who began to mutter threats against the Indians. Urged on by the Whites, state fishery officers raided the camp twice, on the nights of August 10 and 11, and on August 12, the fishermen, under the leadership of Satiacum, Ramona Bennett, a Puyallup tribal council member, Charles Cantrell, another Puyallup, and Sid Mills and Al Bridges, established a protective armed guard around the site. Largely to defuse the situation, the state officials offered to let the Indians fish for salmon two days a week, using nets, between September 21 and October 23. The Indians rejected the offer, and on September 9, about seventy-five state officers and twenty-five Tacoma policemen in riot helmets and carrying guns, together with a number of aroused White supporters, showed up at the camp, which was then occupied by about two hundred Indians and non-Indians. When some of the fisheries men in a small boat tried to pull in the Indians' nets, somebody fired several shots, and a wild battle began in the camp and on a trestle that crossed the river. The police and state officers swung clubs and threw tear gas, and one Indian hurled a fire bomb that set the wooden trestle ablaze. The police finally restored peace and, amid the flames, smoke, and the wreckage of the camp, arrested fifty-five adults and five juveniles. The other occupants were dispersed, the camp was bulldozed, and the following year those who had been arrested began to receive jury trials. Four non-Indians were convicted of unlawful assembly, and three Indians and a White woman were acquitted. After that, the trials were halted because of other, and more significant, developments that had resulted from the riot.

During the weeks that had preceded the battle, the Department of the Interior had watched the tension on the Puyallup River with mounting apprehension. The Supreme Court decision was not being observed, and after Satiacum's conviction, Stanley Pitkin, the U.S. Attorney for Western Washington, had been directed by the Justice Department to enter a case in behalf of the tribe's steelhead fishing rights. The case, *Washington Department of Game* v. *Puyallup Tribe,* or *Puyallup II* (because it was the second major Puyallup case), went to the State Supreme Court and then the U.S. Supreme Court, which on November 19, 1973, struck down the state's injunction on the Puyallup River as discriminatory against the Indians and returned the case to Washington State courts to determine a formula for the allocation of steelhead between the Indians and the sport fishermen that would be equitable to both. It still did not settle the central issues of the fishing rights conflict, but for Washington State it was another warning that the winds were beginning to blow in favor of the Indians.

Meanwhile, the battle of September 9 took place. In Washington, D.C., President Nixon and Vice-President Agnew had just launched a new policy of support for tribal self-determination and the achievement of Indian aims and aspirations. The violent assault on the Indians, shown on national television, shocked officials in the White House and the Department of the Interior, and was a catalyst for the filing of a new, comprehensive suit on which the Justice Department had been working in an effort to settle all the issues affecting the Washington tribes' fishing rights. Fulfilling its obligation at last as trustee for the tribes, the government became the plaintiff, and on September 18, nine days after the fight at the river, U.S. Attorney Pitkin filed the case, *The United States* v. *Washington,* in the U.S. District Court in Tacoma. It was soon perceived that the case could lead to a landmark decision, clarifying what the 1968 U.S. Supreme Court decision had ignored or left ambiguous, and fourteen Washington tribes, to whom the case was relevant, intervened as co-plaintiffs with the United States.

In the wake of the destruction of the Indians' camp on the Puyallup, meanwhile, tempers flared between the Indians, who continued to fish, and local sport fishermen, who harassed them and threatened to take the law in their own hands and drive them from the river. Then, in the early morning hours of January 19, 1971, Hank Adams was shot in the stomach while he was dozing in a car after setting a fish net in the Puyallup River. Though an investigation of sorts was launched, the assailants were not found, and the Indians charged the police with a deliberate cover-up, an accusation that one official rebutted by suggesting that Adams had shot himself. Adams recovered, and in the following months he and Sid Mills strengthened the association of the Northwest fishing rights struggle with other Indian causes being pressed elsewhere in the country. In the fall of 1972, Adams was one of the main strategists of the Trail of Broken Treaties, a caravan trek to Washington, D.C., by several thousand Indians from throughout the country that ended in the occupation of the Bureau of Indian Affairs Building. He was one of the authors of the Indians' list of twenty demands, including the restoration of treaty-making between the federal government and the tribes and a review of violations of past treaties, and was then the chief Indian negotiator in the meetings that ended that confrontation, as well as an intermediary in attempts to terminate the siege at Wounded Knee in South Dakota in the following year. In 1977, having become a nationally recognized spokesman on Indian relations with the federal government, he participated in the preparation of the report of the American Indian Policy Review Commission for Congress.

By that time, the case of *The United States* v. *Washington,* which had suspended the trials of those who had been arrested during the battle on the Puyallup River, was history. During its course, the government attorneys were joined by lawyers for the tribes, including David Getches of the Native American Rights Fund, who represented five of the tribes, and by many agencies and organizations that participated as *amici curiae*. District Judge George H. Boldt, an Eisenhower appointee, now seventy-four years old and nearing the end of his career, worried the Indians. He had once told a tribal attorney, "I don't want to hear any more about these damn Indian fishing cases." But he called in his law clerk and told him "to put on that table every single case from the beginning of the country that pertains in any way to the rights of Indians." The two of them then went through every one of them, working tirelessly through weekends. One of his most important conclusions came from his study of nineteenth-century legal dictionaries. The phrase "in common with," he decided, meant that Stevens' treaties had agreed that the Indians had a right to an opportunity to take the same amount of fish as the Whites.

On February 12, 1974, he rendered his decision in a series of rulings that aroused a storm of protest among the Whites in the state. Pointing out that, by the treaties, the Indians had "granted the White settlers the right to fish beside them," he upheld the right of the treaty tribes to fish and manage the fisheries in their traditional fishing places and ordered that they had to be given the opportunity to take 50 percent of the harvestable fish. He declared illegal all state regulations that went beyond conserving fish to affect the time, manner, and volume of off-reservation fishing by treaty Indians at their usual and accustomed sites, and to see that his orders were implemented and enforced, he retained continuing jurisdiction.

A court had finally recognized the Indians' fishing rights. On the Puyallup, Nisqually, Green, and other rivers, the little people of the tribes, who had had the determination and courage not to give up, but to keep fishing, had won. But it was not over. Judge Boldt was burned in effigy, vilified, accused of having an Indian mistress, and attacked by White fishermen, who were spurred on by the anti-Indian rabble-rousing of Washington State's politically ambitious attorney general, Slade Gorton. Despite threats to Judge Boldt's life, his receipt of a stream of "loathsome" letters, and the bombing of the Federal Building in Tacoma, he continued to hand down rulings to implement his decisions. He decided that only Congress could disestablish or diminish an Indian reservation, and until it did so, the Puyallup reservation, with its original boundaries, still existed. To help get the Indians started on managing their fisheries and undertaking conservation and restoration programs, he supported the organizing of a Northwest Indian Fisheries Commission, with representatives from all the fishing tribes and staffs of biologists and other technical and scientific experts. Appointing a Fishery Technical Advisor to the court, he oversaw the drafting of an interim plan to implement the complex elements of his decision. There were many of them, and some would lead to further court cases. Methods, for instance, had to be devised for computing fish allocations and reporting and counting the Indian and non-Indian catch. A "substantially disproportionate" part of the annual fish runs, moreover, were taken by offshore fishermen before they ever got to the Indians' fishing grounds. It prevented the Indians from having an opportunity to take 50 percent of the fish.

From the beginning, the state of Washington refused to accept the decision. The Washington State Supreme Court, holding that the state could not allocate a resource "among races," enjoined the Department of Fisheries from enforcing Judge Boldt's orders, and amid a growing conflict between the state and federal judges, the Boldt decision went to the U.S. Ninth Circuit Court of Appeals. Thirteen more tribes intervened against the state of Washington, and on June 4, 1975, the Court of Appeals upheld Judge Boldt. A month later, Washington appealed for a rehearing, which was denied. The U.S. Supreme Court, on January 26, 1976, declined Washington's petition for a review, and Judge Boldt's decision stood.

Meanwhile, with the state refusing to enforce the decision, the recent history of the South, in which states had refused to enforce integration in defiance of federal court orders, had its counterpart in Washington. Illegal non-Indian fishing, encouraged by Washington's states' rights stance and detrimental to the Indians' interest, was rampant. At one point, the Ninth Circuit Court denounced the machinations of the state and non-Indian fishermen as one of "the most concerted official and private efforts to frustrate a decree of a federal court witnessed in this century," save for some segregation cases. As the state twisted and turned to avoid implementing Judge Boldt's decision, administrative and legal challenges proliferated. Picking up a theme popular with the non-Indian sport fishermen, the state won a ruling by the Pierce County Superior Court that the Puyallups had no treaty right to steelhead that had been produced in hatcheries and must let the artificially propagated steelhead go through their nets, a ruling that was obviously difficult to observe. When the Puyallups appealed the decision to the Washington State Supreme Court, Judge Boldt enjoined the state from carrying out the edict on any other river until the Puyallups' case had been decided.

On April 8, the State Supreme Court upheld the Superior Court decision and asserted the state's right of jurisdiction over Indian fishing, both off and on reservations, to enforce the decision against taking hatchery-produced fish. The decision in the case, known as *Puyallup III*, was appealed, and in 1977 the U.S. Supreme Court held that individual Indians, but not a tribe, could be subjected to regulation by the state both on and off their reservation. It declined, however, to rule on the Indians' right to hatchery fish, and that issue became part of a larger case, known as *The United States* v. *Washington—Phase II*, dealing, also, with another issue that had not been settled by the Boldt decision—the right of protection of fish habitats against environmental degradation so that the ability of the Indians to secure their share of the fish would not be impaired. In September 1980, the two issues were considered by Judge William H. Orrick of the U.S. District Court for Western Washington, who decided against the state on the hatchery issue and ruled that the state had an obligation to protect the Indians' fishery habitats against environmental degradation.

Still, the cases went on. In Oregon, rulings by District Judge Belloni paralleled and supplemented those of Judge Boldt. On May 8, 1974, Judge Belloni allocated 50 percent of the spring chinook salmon harvest to the Columbia River tribes. Washington and Oregon appealed to the Ninth Circuit Court, which affirmed Judge Belloni's order. The next year, Judge Belloni again directed Washington and Oregon to assure the upriver Indians 50 percent of the harvestable salmon. Washington, in both years, failed to take steps to implement his orders by restricting the offshore commercial fishing of non-Indians so that more salmon would reach the Columbia, and in June 1976, the judge enjoined the state from permitting non-Indian commercial troll fishing until July. Criminal contempt charges were filed against forty-eight Washington trollers who defied the order, but the charges against them were dismissed. At the same time, Judge Boldt extended the rulings of *The United States* v. *Washington* to herring fishing, and in 1978, as defiance continued, he seized control of the Puget Sound commercial salmon fisheries.

The actions of the federal judges inflamed the non-Indian trollers and independent gill-netters and sport fishermen. Supported by Washington Fisheries Department officials, they vented their rage on the Indian fishermen, vandalizing their equipment and boats, ramming their craft at fishing sites, and threatening to shoot them. On a larger scale, they proclaimed a "Revolt Against Boldt," marching on the capitol and declaring a war against any state officers who tried to enforce the orders of the federal courts. The principal targets of Judges Boldt and Belloni were the oceangoing trollers, whose huge catches penalized the non-Indian gill-netters and sport fishermen as much as the Indians; but the heritage of anti-Indian demagoguery fostered the continued placing of all blame on the Indians, and many Whites in the state gave their support to the non-Indian fishermen. Their feelings meshed with, and added to, a questioning of Indian treaty rights that was beginning to emerge in many other parts of the country.

Tribes in a number of states were in the news almost daily, pressing claims for land, water, hunting, and mineral rights, and they were winning cases in the federal courts that seemed to give the Indians a disturbing new status and power. Where their victories were not a direct threat to White property owners and vested interests, as in the Maine and Massachusetts land claims cases, there were few complaints, but their resistance to the acquisition of coal, uranium, water, and other tribal properties, as in Utah, Montana, and Arizona, frustrated and angered developers and state officials. Anti-Indian sentiment was already strong in some parts of the country, fostered most notably by an aggressive organization named, ironically, the Interstate Congress for Equal Rights and Responsibilities, with chapters in at least ten states. It was campaigning vigorously for the end of Indian reservations, tribes, and special rights, and wanted the Department of Justice to stop helping the tribes in the courts. It lobbied in Washington, D.C., and state capitals, numbered among its members state attorneys general and county officials, and published books and pamphlets with titles like *Are We Giving America Back to the Indians?* Almost overnight, fourteen organizations of White fishermen and their sympathizers were formed in Washington State and, joining the Interstate Congress, became its most vocal and powerful constituents. Nine anti-Indian bills, with various aims, including the abrogation of Indian treaties and the ending of tribal rights, were introduced in Congress, the most sweeping of them being authored, in reaction to the Boldt decision, by members of the Washington State delegation. One of them, Congressman Lloyd Meeds, had previously been among the Indians' best friends in the House of Representatives. In the elections of 1976, his friendship had almost cost him his seat, and he had turned full tilt against them.

Washington's senators, Henry M. Jackson and Warren G. Magnuson, also felt the fishermen's heat and pressed Attorney General Griffin B. Bell to consider the possibility of ending the government's trustee obligation to defend Indian rights and property in the courts. Nothing came of their proposal, or of the bills in Congress, but the concern of both Indians and Whites moved President Jimmy Carter to appoint, in April 1977, a special Presidential Task Force to try to find solutions to the different fishing rights issues. While the task force worked, conflict worsened between Judge Boldt and the Washington State Supreme Court, which issued orders to the state agencies that countermanded those of the federal judge and encouraged the continued defiance of the non-Indian fishermen. The tense situation was not helped by the task force. Its "Settlement Plan," a feeble effort to persuade all parties to compromise, was published in June 1978, but was rejected by the White fishermen as well as the tribes.

The state, meanwhile, was attempting to get the U.S. Supreme Court to reconsider its 1976 decision not to review the Boldt rulings. As the turmoil in Washington increased, the Carter administration, which had little understanding of the issues and tended to blame the Indians for the conflict, joined the state in its request, and on October 16, 1978, the Supreme Court agreed to intervene and review the controversial case. Its climactic decision, on July 2, 1979, sustained Judge Boldt, adding only slight modifications to his rulings, including an order that the Indians' maximum 50 percent share of the fish include their catch on reservations or at places other than their usual and accustomed sites, as well as fish that they took for subsistence or ceremonial purposes.

The decision at long last ended the rebellion of the Washington state courts, which fell in line with the federal courts to implement the Boldt rulings and halt illegal fishing by Whites. With the collapse of official resistance, a new era arrived for the Indian fishermen in the state. There were still conflicts, a dragging of feet by some, and continuous efforts to undo the Boldt rulings by others. In 1980, Slade Gorton, who as state attorney general had carried the fight against the Indians for a decade and lost every fishing rights case he had waged in a federal court, was elected to the United States Senate, largely as a result of his war against the Indian fishermen. He did not give up. In the Senate, he got himself named to the Committee on Indian Affairs, introduced a bill of questionable constitutionality to void the Boldt decisions as they applied to steelhead fishing, and continued his crusade against the tribes. In the Northwest, at the same time, defiance of the Boldt rulings flared up again among some of the White fishermen, who seemingly hoped that renewed conflict and violence would induce the Reagan administration and Congress to support Gorton's efforts. The courts continued to oppose the rebellious fishermen, however, directing the policing of fishing in Puget Sound, and by 1982 Gorton had won little backing from other Senators.

Meanwhile, as Judge Boldt hoped, a new era had also arrived for the salmon and steelhead. Working with the state Fisheries Department rather than against it, the Northwest Indian Fisheries Commission of the Puget Sound tribes, and a similar organization of the Columbia River fishing tribes, set to work to develop long-term management and enhancement programs that would help restore the depleted fish runs. Given an opportunity, the tribes quickly proved that they were capable and committed conservationists who had always known that their own future lay in the survival of the fish. Indians received technical training and assistance from universities and in cooperative programs with scientists of the U.S. Fish and Wildlife Service, and individual tribes established experimental stations and hatcheries and began programs of releasing millions of salmon into the Washington streams. Congress, in turn, on December 22, 1980, passed a landmark Salmon and Steelhead Conservation and Enhancement Act to help finance restoration programs to increase the Northwest fish supply and assist both Indian and non-Indian fishermen to work together harmoniously with federal and state officials to achieve the goals of the Boldt decision.

At the same time, there were problems still to be met. The big hydroelectric dams of the Columbia River and its tributaries still interfered with the fish runs, and in years when few salmon reached the upper parts of the rivers, fishing was halted or restricted, and members of the interior tribes like the Nez Perces in Idaho fought for their rights under the Boldt and Belloni decisions, insisting that they had a right to a share of the year's total harvestable supply. It was still up to the White man to see to it that adequate fish reached their usual and accustomed fishing grounds. In courts, as well as in Congress, new contests would also have to be waged against nuclear power plants, industrial polluters, pro-energy legislation favoring the proliferation of small hydroelectric projects exempt from protecting the fish runs, and other developments on the Northwest's rivers and streams that would degrade the habitat of the fish, cut off access to spawning grounds, or otherwise impair the fisheries.

But the long fight of the Nisquallies, Puyallups, Muckleshoots, and other Puget Sound Indians had had great impact beyond saving their own fisheries and putting them in a position to share in the restoration of the Northwest fish runs. The Boldt decision, which had vindicated them, had pointed the way also to the protection of treaty fishing rights—as well as treasured hunting and trapping rights—that were still important to many other tribes all over the country as a means of survival and a continued way of life. On May 7, 1979, Chippewa tribes, waging the same kind of struggle that had occurred at Puget Sound, won their own landmark decision in the U.S. District Court for Western Michigan (later sustained by the Sixth U.S. Circuit Court of Appeals and, on December 14, 1981, allowed to stand by the U.S. Supreme Court's denial of an appeal by the state of Michigan), which recognized their right to fish free of state regulation in the areas of Lakes Superior, Michigan, and Huron. By a similar insistence on the observance of treaty guarantees, where they applied, tribes noted that hunting and trapping rights could also be protected.

The small tribes of the Puget Sound area were no longer forgotten, demeaned, or overlooked peoples. The Indians had come back, proud of their heritage and the chapter they had added to their history. The White man, as Sealth, the Duwamish, told Stevens, would never be alone.

III

TOMORROW

WALKING
TALL

7

THE SIOUX
WILL RISE AGAIN

The Native Americans' Modern-Day Quest
to Regain Self-Determination, Sovereignty,
and Control of Their Affairs and Resources

AT APPROXIMATELY SEVEN-THIRTY in the evening of February 27, 1973, a caravan of fifty-four automobiles, carrying 250 Indians of both sexes and all ages, drove into a bleak hamlet on the wintry Pine Ridge reservation in southwestern South Dakota. Most of them were Oglala Sioux, or Lakotas, who lived on the reservation, but some were members of other tribes, and many of them were armed. The first arrivals shot out the dusk-to-dawn lights illuminating the hamlet's tiny cluster of buildings, seized more weapons and ammunition from a trading post, and, herding the few White inhabitants under guard into one of the houses, set up roadblocks and defenses and announced the liberation of the area. The settlement was Wounded Knee, where, in December 1890, U.S. troops had killed almost 300 Sioux men, women, and children.

Twelve years before, at a 1961 conference of Indians of all tribes in Chicago, Robert Burnette, president of the Brulé Sioux, whose Rosebud reservation adjoined Pine Ridge, reminded his audience that the Sioux had been the last of the great tribes of the plains to go down fighting for their freedom. "You mark what I say," he declared. "The Sioux are fighters. We're not going to take it lying down forever. One of these days, you'll see us rise up again, and when we do, we'll be fighting for all tribes, not just our own." In 1973, the Oglalas, heirs of the nineteenth-century patriot chief Crazy Horse, who led in the defeat of Custer at the Little

Bighorn, did just that. Enduring a seventy-one-day siege by U.S. marshals, FBI agents, and various police forces at Wounded Knee, the modern-day Sioux and their allies fought for the rebirth of freedom for all American Indians.

Their rebellion was the climax of a series of other attempts by embittered Indians to call the world's attention to the frustrations of their daily lives. It was preceded by occupations of Alcatraz Island in San Francisco, the Bureau of Indian Affairs Building in Washington, D.C., and many other pieces of land and buildings in different parts of the country. None of them had eased the Indians' plight or long-standing grievances. On most reservations, the people were still treated as incompetents, second-class citizens, and faceless members of a conquered and irrelevant minority. They still suffered from grinding poverty, inadequate housing and health care, chronic unemployment, and neglect, and were still subjected to oppression and discrimination. Many of them, including those who spoke out against their intolerable conditions, were murdered by Whites, and when they died, the non-Indian population paid little or no attention to their deaths or what they had died for, and justice was rarely done to their killers. They were still also being defrauded of their lands, water, and natural resources, which further impoverished them and undermined their ability to survive. In the process, treaty obligations were still ignored; hunting, fishing, and civil rights denied; and their spiritual life and sacred objects and places scorned and destroyed.

All this, in 1973, was in the minds of those who seized and held Wounded Knee. It was another shout to the world for attention by the people whom Burnette, in a book published in 1971, called "the tortured Americans." But the occupiers—reservation members and supporters of the Oglala Sioux Civil Rights Organization and members of the Pan-Indian American Indian Movement, known as AIM, whom the Oglalas had summoned to Pine Ridge to assist them—had a more ambitious goal. They intended to destroy the political bonds in which the federal government held the Oglalas' reservation, and by example inspire other tribes to regain sovereignty and establish responsible governments of their own. The little bit of land they held at Wounded Knee they proclaimed the free nation of the Oglala Lakotas.

Their fight began as a revolt against the Pine Ridge reservation's form of tribal government, a White-imposed system that bred corruption and tyranny and kept its people powerless in their relations with White society. Throughout the country, most Indians deplored the violence of the uprising, and relatively few of them came to Pine Ridge to help the Oglalas. But everywhere Indians who chafed under similar domination understood what was happening and cheered on "the people who are standing up for us and saying the truth." The Oglalas and their AIM supporters, they perceived, were fighting for all of them, striking at what they regarded to be the root cause of all their ills and problems, a colonialist relationship between the federal government and pliant Indian leaders whom the Bureau of Indian Affairs supported and manipulated as virtual puppets. Without governments of their own choosing that were accountable, responsive, and responsible to the tribal members rather than to the BIA, the self-interest of the people suffered. The Indians complained from experience that those who ruled them had no commitment to the improvement of reservation conditions, to programs people needed, to the ending of murders and discrimination, and to the protection of treaty rights and Indian property. "Without the freedom to run and control our own affairs that comes with sovereignty, all the injustices and inequalities of our lives will continue," said a California Indian educator at the time. "It is the answer to everything. What we need is to throw the federal government and our own Uncle Tomahawks off our backs and seize the power to protect ourselves and start solving our problems in our own way." He, as well as members of scores of tribes, recognized that this was what the long siege at Wounded Knee was all about.

To non-Indian Americans who enjoy freedom, with many different forms of local self-government in their towns, counties, and states, and who in some cases know their states as sovereign entities within the body politic of the United States, the yearnings of the Native Americans for accountable governments of their own should not have been hard to understand. In June 1973, after the siege ended, Senator James Abourezk of South Dakota, the chairman of the U.S. Senate Subcommittee on Indian Affairs, held hearings at Pine Ridge to try to discover why the confrontation had occurred. One of those who testified was Ramon Roubideaux, the attorney for Russell Means, an Oglala Sioux and the charismatic national coordinator of AIM who had been one of the leaders at Wounded Knee. "The point that should be made," Roubideaux, who was also a Sioux, told Abourezk, "is that at that time . . . in 1871 which discontinued treaty-making with Indian nations, that at that time we had sovereignty, right of self-government, the right to govern ourselves, the right to choose the type of government we wanted. . . . after the congressional act of 1871, which I am sure you are aware of, the Government passed a series of statutes throughout the years which bit by bit took away the last bit of sovereignty or right to govern ourselves that we had, culminating in the Indian Reorganization Act of 1934. . . . which tried to say they were giving us self-government. But as you know, self-government by permission is no self-government at all. And what that Act did, Senator, is place the Indian people into a prison. It placed us under a situation where we were ruled by a minority of Indian people under the guidance and direction of the Bureau of Indian Affairs. And this has happened in all these years. So that I think this committee should realize that we have got a very serious situation throughout the country."

Roubideaux could have been speaking for many of the more than 250 tribal groups in the country. At one time, all of them, with different forms of government, ruled themselves. As they were conquered, they were deprived of their sovereignty—the supremacy of their own government over themselves—and were subjected to the increasingly pervasive rule of the United States, exercised by agents of the Bureau of Indian Affairs. In 1871, with the conquest of the tribes all but completed, Congress ended further treaty making with them, decreeing that henceforth "no Indian nation or tribe within . . . the United States shall be acknowledged or recognized as an independent nation, tribe or power." Though all existing treaties were considered to be still binding on the government, the relationship of the government to the tribes became defined as that of guardian to ward. Without authority or responsibility, traditional tribal governments withered or went underground, and all power over group and individual affairs was asserted by White men.

Lacking any recognized form of self-government, the tribes languished and their situation deteriorated. By 1934, years of oppression and neglect had made reservation life a national scandal. In response to the prodding of John Collier, the New Deal's Commissioner of Indian Affairs, as well as other reformers, Congress that year passed the Indian Reorganization Act (IRA), which, among other things, enabled tribes to establish limited self-government. Under the legislation, tribes that agreed to accept the Reorganization Act could adopt a constitution and then vote for members of a governing body which their constitution created.

Though the return of any degree of self-government seemed to be a long step forward, it proved not always to be the case. Instead of enabling each tribe to choose its own form of government, which in many instances would have meant a revival or adaptation of a traditional system conforming closely to the cultural heritage of the people, the implementation of the Act resulted in the government unilaterally imposing on the Indians an unfamiliar system that guaranteed continued non-Indian control over them. Many tribes resisted acceptance, but with the zeal of a crusader who knew better than the Indians what was good for them, Collier forced upon a large number of them constitutions that BIA agents and other Whites wrote for them and that set up White-style governments: representative tribal councils, with elected presidents or chairmen, vice-chairmen, secretaries, treasurers, sergeants at arms, and other officers.

The governments, furthermore, were given no real power. The matters with which the councils could deal were strictly circumscribed, and all their decisions and actions were subject to the approval of the BIA. The reservation superintendent, as agent of the Secretary of the Interior, still had full control over the property and financial affairs of the tribe and of individual Indians, as well as almost every aspect of their daily lives, and could veto anything they or their government did of which he disapproved. Even the tribes' selection of a tribal lawyer required the endorsement of the Secretary of the Interior, which was usually not given without the superintendent's approval. At the same time, the governments became convenient vehicles for the superintendents and their staffs, giving them a centralized reservation leadership which served both as a rubber stamp of tribal acceptance of their policies, programs, and administration and as a complaisant subordinate authority over the Indians.

To ensure the acceptance of the constitution and the election of the new governments, all that was required was the approval of a majority of those who voted. Since the constitutions failed to provide true freedom, and in some cases threatened non-recognized but still existing traditional forms of government—such as those guided by clan or spiritual leaders—many people boycotted the voting. Others abstained because of confusion, fear of power-seeking fellow tribesmen, or an inability to get to the voting places. Whatever the reason, the Indian Reorganization Act, from its start, implanted unrepresentative minority governments on many reservations. The experience of the Pine Ridge Sioux typified that of other tribes. Only 13 percent of the eligible Oglala voters accepted the IRA. Twelve percent voted against it. The other 75 percent failed to vote or, from the Indians' point of view, voted in the negative by boycotting the procedure. But a majority of those who voted had said "Yes," and a minority of 13 percent was thus used to foist upon the other 87 percent a form of self-government that White men had chosen for them.

The results could have been foreseen. The superintendent needed compliant Indians with whom to work, and he intruded into intratribal political affairs to support their election. Once they were in office, those who went along with the BIA were accorded favors, honors, and opportunities to benefit financially and build petty political machines of friends and relatives who would loyally serve the BIA's purposes. Those who became troublesome or too independent were undermined and, by one method or another, rendered ineffective. Inevitably, the system created elite cliques of reservation politicians, usually educated half-bloods who were more assimilated and more favorably inclined to the White men's ways than their fellow tribesmen. Sometimes there developed rival factions of "ins" and "outs," often reflecting longtime intratribal feuds. The superintendent generally tried to keep both of them willing to do his bidding. If he failed, he threw his favors to one faction and the weight of his powers and influence against the other one. On the whole, those who held office found it beneficial and worthwhile personally to satisfy the BIA, and became increasingly dependent on, and responsible to, the superintendent and his staff and less responsive or accountable to the membership of the tribe. The latter, in turn, felt contempt for those who were profiting at their expense from the White men's government and in large numbers ignored them and continued to boycott the elections.

The lack of a true self-government caused innumerable conflicts that were often marked by violence and the trampling of human and civil rights. Those in office sometimes carried out their authority with a "big stick," pushing around and punishing the families of those who opposed them, becoming petty bosses and tyrants, and further alienating the people from the tribal government. As the gap between the politicians and the grass-roots people widened, the latter looked increasingly to their spiritual teachers and other traditionalists for guidance and leadership. Though the traditionalists and their followers, who were often the majority on a reservation, had nothing to do with the BIA or the recognized tribal government, their presence was a constant irritant and threat to the council and its officers. At times, their moral force disrupted the elected government, turning individual council members and officers against the BIA and its supporters. On such occasions, the rebels might be excluded from council meetings, denied information and the right to vote, or ousted from office. Frequently, such rifts led to the tightening of authoritarian control; a chairman would fail to hold council meetings and, assisted by a secretary or treasurer who was personally loyal to him, would assume all powers for himself and conduct the tribe's affairs in secrecy, though still reporting to the superintendent. While the situation created the possibility of bribe-taking from contractors and embezzlement of tribal funds on the part of the chairman and his followers, the superintendent rarely interfered, and at times even entered into a collusive partnership with the dictatorial chairman, enjoying a relationship that made his job smoother if it did not, indeed, also give him a share of the graft.

Until the 1960's, the system effectively kept decision-making out of the Indians' hands. Policies and programs were established by Congress and the Department of the Interior in Washington and were imposed on the tribes by BIA area officials and superintendents on the reservations. Both the policies and the programs usually applied to all, or many, of the reservations, and ultimately almost all of them failed because they were not tailored to the specific cultural backgrounds and contemporary needs of the individual tribes. Try as they might, neither the local BIA staff nor the tribal government could successfully implement measures whose unrealism reflected the lack of Indian input. At the same time, failures resulted also from the incompetence of BIA officials, inadequate funding, and the inability of the Bureau to be a super-government, administering all aspects of tribal and individual existence. The Bureau was generally acknowledged to be one of the least efficient and most poorly staffed agencies in the Department of the Interior. Yet its limited staff, often criticized by congressional investigators as being notoriously ill-equipped for its responsibilities, was empowered to manage and control every field of activity for the Indians. The Bureau, in effect, was expected to be almost all the departments of the federal government rolled into one, possessing the modern-day expertise to manage the Indians' irrigation projects, forests, mineral resources, and fisheries, construct their roads and houses, make out their wills, lease their lands, invest their income, run their schools, oversee their law and order, conduct their relations with states, railroads, utilities, corporations, and other non-Indian institutions and individuals, and supervise and regulate a hundred and one other activities in their daily lives. The result was chronic mismanagement, inertia, and—in the absence of accountability to the Indians—maladministration and malfeasance.

A principal victim was reservation property, which the federal government as trustee was obligated to protect. Quite the opposite often occurred. On the Sioux reservations in the Dakotas, as well as on other reservations, superintendents regularly leased Indian grazing lands to White stockmen for a fraction of the standard fees paid to White landowners. Other tribes maintained that they were shortchanged in arrangements the Bureau made for rights-of-way across their lands and for long-term leases of reservation acreage to developers of housing, resort, and recreation projects for Whites. Still others complained (and a few even fought the Department of the Interior in congressional hearings and court cases) of the mismanagement of tribal timber stands, fisheries, hydroelectric power sites, and other resources by BIA "experts."

Though tribes knew that they were being exploited, there was little that most of them could do to protect their property or guarantee the receipt of a fair payment for what they leased or sold. Long before the energy crisis burst upon the nation in 1973, many energy companies and other non-Indian interests acquired permits and leases for the exploration and use of uranium, oil, coal, natural gas, and other energy resources on various western reservations. Analyses in the 1970's of the methods by which most of them had acquired those rights disclosed the helplessness of the tribes in the absence of responsible self-governments with protective powers of their own. Generally, after making initial contacts with federal officials in Washington—frequently members of Congress or the Secretary of the Interior—a company's representatives would be brought together with the tribal lawyer (usually a non-Indian, approved, if not appointed, by the Secretary of the Interior), who, after inducing the tribal chairman to accept what was offered, drew up a contract with the company that was acceptable to the Interior Department. Sometimes the contract was written by the Department's own solicitors or with their help. The lawyer and the BIA reservation superintendent and his staff would then aid the tribal chairman in persuading a majority of the tribal council members to accept the contract. At times, the council sessions resembled treaty meetings of the nineteenth century. Council members felt pressured to agree and often did not understand the legalistically worded provisions of what they were accepting. Sometimes, when their opposition was feared, the contract was not even taken to the council; acceptance by the chairman and one or two of his officers would suffice. Only rarely were the members of the tribe as a whole consulted or permitted to pass on the proposal.

By this kind of rubber-stamp procedure, the Navajo tribal leadership, in the quarter century following World War II, was induced to sign exploration and lease arrangements for coal, oil and natural gas, uranium, and other resources on its huge reservation, which was the size of West Virginia. As early as 1958, the Navajos were receiving $29 million a year in royalties and bonuses for their oil and gas alone. But many of the leases for the different resources, drawn up for the most part by government and corporate technical experts and lawyers, gave the Indians inequitable terms and locked the tribe into a disadvantageous position. Royalties were low, and as prices went up, the Navajos were forced to continue to part with their resources for the originally established price. One contract, signed in 1957, gave Utah International, Inc., the right to strip-mine Navajo coal for royalty payments of from 15 to 37½ cents a ton. In 1977, after the energy crisis had forced prices skyward, the Navajos were still receiving the same royalties, though the retail price of coal had risen to between $15 and $20 per ton. Such long-term contracts, negotiated by the government without escalation clauses, and holding tribes to royalties that ranged generally between 12½ and 17½ cents a ton, were approved for other tribes also and applied to approximately 10 percent of all Indian-owned coal in the nation.

The leases, in addition, adversely affected many tribal interests. Environmental and health protections were ignored; social, economic, and cultural impacts on the tribal members were not considered; and provisions for monitoring against contract violations, cheating, and theft were either nonexistent or minimal. On Navajo and Laguna Pueblo lands in Arizona and New Mexico, neither warning nor protection was given to Indian miners and reservation residents against the perils of uranium dust and tailings, and many Indians eventually contracted cancer. On the Wind River reservation in Wyoming, where the Shoshonis and Arapahos leased part of their land to some thirty different oil companies, the lack of government monitoring permitted the companies to adopt a variety of shabby methods to steal large amounts of the Indians' oil for almost forty years, until the thievery was detected in 1980.

Other tribal rights and resources were also eroded. The availability of the cheap coal on the Navajo reservation led to pressures by corporations for reservation sites for large mine-mouth, highly pollutant power and coal gasification plants and their attendant industrial complexes; for rights-of-way for railroads, transmission, pipe, and slurry lines, and highways; and for Navajo water rights. Leases for these additional rights and resources were also sought, and often acquired, at the expense of the Indians. In December 1968, the Department of the Interior persuaded the Navajo leadership and tribal council to make possible the building of a large public-utility-owned, coal-fueled power plant at Page, Arizona, by signing over the tribe's right to 34,100 acre-feet of water and waiving all its untested rights to Colorado River water other than what the Navajos might be able to get from the limited share of the river's water apportioned to the state of Arizona. The enabling resolution passed by a compliant tribal council was written by attorneys in Washington and was brought to the council meeting by a Department of Interior official. Members of the council later claimed that they had been misled, and tried unsuccessfully to void the resolution, which they asserted had been inadequately explained to them by their tribal leaders and lawyers.

The situation of powerlessness could not go on forever. As early as 1944, a number of BIA Indian employees, as well as leading Indians of different tribes, formed a Pan-Indian organization, the National Congress of American Indians, to deal in a united way with "the broad problems confronting the total Indian population or large segments of it." Membership was open to individuals of Indian ancestry, as well as Indian tribes, bands, and communities. The organization soon had a Washington office and, declaring BIA personnel ineligible for membership, began to lobby on Capitol Hill on major Indian issues. Because the tribes often differed among themselves and wished no one else to speak for their respective peoples, its effectiveness was limited. Nevertheless, though the NCAI was unable to accomplish significant reforms in Indian administration, its lobbying and educational programs helped to halt the federal government's implementation of the disastrous and short-lived "termination" policy of the 1950's, which, as explained in Chapter 3, was intended to hasten the assimilation of Indians by ending all federal relations with them, including treaty and trust obligations, and turning the tribes and their reservations over to the states. After Utes, Klamaths, Menominees, and a number of other tribes were "terminated" against their will, each of them losing lands and resources and suffering large-scale hardships at the hands of aggressive Whites in their states, the NCAI and numerous tribes, together with non-Indian supporters, persuaded the Eisenhower administration and Congress that the policy had proved to be simply a cover for new injuries and injustices to the Indians, and its implementation was stopped.

By the start of the 1960's, new winds were stirring. At a conference at the University of Chicago in June 1961, 420 Indians from sixty-seven tribes, including reservation leaders like Robert Burnette, as well as off-reservation Indians who were pursuing successful careers in the White men's world, produced a "Declaration of Indian Purpose," which, among other things, called for the government's recognition of the right of tribes to participate in the decision-making process for all policies and programs that would affect them. Neither Congress nor the Kennedy administration responded to them, but it was the start of an Indian appeal that grew louder and more demanding as the decade progressed. One of the principal forces for change was the emergence of young Indians who left the reservations to go to college, mixed in the non-Indian world, and in the early 1960's formed their own Pan-Indian organization, the National Indian Youth Council, which gave voice to the discontent on the reservations. At a meeting of the executive council of the National Congress of American Indians in January 1964, Clyde Warrior, a Ponca Indian from Oklahoma and one of the leaders of the National Indian Youth Council, laced into the older tribal leaders for having been willing through the years to let the White man rule the reservations and control the affairs of the Indian people. His accusations sank in. Burnette, who had become executive director of the NCAI, agreed with him. "In fact," Burnette declared, "I had wanted to say some of the same things for the past three years." The NIYC became increasingly militant, spreading its influence among young Indians in the cities, as well as on reservations, and keeping up a steady pressure on tribal leaders, whom it charged with serving the BIA and refusing to protect and represent the people.

Older persons, too, made themselves heard. State and regional inter-tribal organizations proliferated, and reservation Indians traveled to conferences, meetings, and powwows, discussing their impatience with BIA rule and passing resolutions demanding more of a say in their own affairs. Some of the meetings were funded by churches and non-Indian organizations that were sympathetic to the Indians' demand for more self-government. One of the Indians' most active supporters was the Reverend Clifford Samuelson, who headed the Indian work of the national Episcopal Church. In May 1964, he led a coalition of groups that brought some 400 Indians and an equal number of non-Indians who were interested in tribal welfare to a Capital Conference on Indian Poverty in Washington, D.C. Largely as a result of the lobbying efforts of those who attended the conference, Indians were included as beneficiaries of the programs of the Economic Opportunity Act, which the Johnson administration was pushing through Congress as the keystone of its war on poverty. It proved to be a notable breakthrough in giving tribal governments the beginning of a meaningful voice in the decision-making process. Under the Act, tribes could devise their own reservation programs to cope with poverty. Once their proposals and budgets were approved, funds were given to the Indians to run the programs themselves. It was the first time that tribes generally had been permitted to assume full responsibility for the management of, and the use of funds for, programs on the reservations, and, by and large, they demonstrated successfully that they were able to carry out functions which, up till then, the BIA had administered and supervised for them. Part of the success, it was noted, stemmed from the fact that the programs were ones which the Indians themselves wanted and planned according to needs as they saw them.

The lesson was not lost on the tribes, whose elected leaders, feeling the pressure of their people to assert more independence from the BIA, demanded the same opportunities to run their BIA programs. The BIA and its parent, the Department of the Interior, demurred, but on October 13, 1966, Senator George McGovern of South Dakota, who counted the Sioux among his constituents, introduced a resolution in the Senate calling for a new national Indian policy that would give the tribes self-determination and provide them with the programs and services of other federal agencies besides the BIA. The other agencies, he insisted, should follow the Office of Economic Opportunity's example and involve the Indians in the decision-making process and the management and control of their programs.

Nothing came of his appeal for self-determination, because the issue to most congressional leaders, as well as to the White House and such interested agencies as the Bureau of the Budget and the Department of the Interior, was not the ability of the tribes to govern themselves, but the control that the federal government would lose over the Indians and their lands and resources. Nevertheless, the resolution and the Indians' support of it introduced in Washington a new sense of urgency in federal-Indian relations, and Congress soon began to make available to tribes some of the general welfare and development programs of such agencies as the Economic Development Administration and the Departments of Labor, Housing and Urban Development, and Health, Education, and Welfare. Those agencies set up Indian "desks," often staffed by Indians, which considered funding requests from the tribes. The tribal governments, in turn, created tribal authorities, or offices, of their own on the reservations to work with the agencies' field representatives in administering the new programs.

The non-BIA money that had been coming onto the reservations from the Office of Economic Opportunity programs and that now poured in from the other agencies exacerbated the division between the tribal leaders and the part of the population that scorned and stayed aloof from them. Many of the cliques of tribal politicians and their followers, becoming as dependent on the new agencies as they were on the BIA, quarreled over the dispensing of the funds and the many new jobs that the programs provided and jockeyed for control of them by accusing each other—often correctly—of nepotism, misappropriating program money, taking graft from White contractors, or being in collusion with the BIA or the other agencies' field personnel to enrich themselves at the expense of the people. At the same time, conflicts over power broke out in some tribes between the chairmen and the tribal members who took charge of the programs, especially when the latter acted too independently or seemed to be using their positions as steppingstones to running for political office against the chairmen. The corruption and infighting further repelled the opponents of the tribal council form of government and gave them more reason to regard everyone in the tribe's power structure as being captives of the White men's money and pawns of the new agencies, as well as of the BIA.

The opportunities that the new programs gave the Indians to expand their authority at the same time accelerated the trend that had begun at the Chicago conference in 1961. The BIA, only slightly weakened by the intrusion of the other federal agencies on the reservations, still dominated the tribal governments and regulated most reservation affairs, and the conditions of daily life for the bulk of the population were little changed. But in many tribes, the people's antagonism to their tribal leaders, often stimulated by anti-BIA traditionalists, was becoming stronger and was joined by that of some of the younger reservation members who had jobs in the new programs and resented the BIA's continued hold over the Indians and their governments. As voters in tribal elections, their criticism of the Indian politicians, whom they called "apples" (red outside, white inside), could not go unheeded, and a number of the tribal leaders themselves—some genuinely wanting more control over reservation affairs, others merely currying popular support to enable them to run for, or stay in, office—also began to speak out against BIA domination.

At conventions of the NCAI and at hearings and meetings in Washington, their demands for self-determination and the same kind of programmatic relations with the Bureau that they enjoyed with the other agencies began to make an impact on the Johnson administration. In gestures to mollify the tribes, Johnson, in 1967, acknowledged the Indians' right to participate in the making of decisions about policies and programs that were designed for their reservations, and the following year, on March 6, 1968, sent a special message to Congress on Indian affairs, starting with the pronouncement: "I propose a new goal for our Indian programs: A goal that ends the old debate about 'termination' of Indian programs and stresses self-determination."

Though the allusion to self-determination was largely rhetoric, the BIA followed up by agreeing, at last, to experiment with giving tribes the same opportunities to run their programs that they had received from the other agencies. Under a system of contracting, the Bureau began to make direct grants of funds to some of the tribes to enable them to run the individual programs themselves—as many of them as the BIA decided they were capable of administering. Contracting started hesitantly, but eventually two tribes, the Zuñis in New Mexico and the Miccosukees in Florida, held varying degrees of control over all their affairs, and other tribes were taking over the operation of BIA schools and the management of road building and other reservation activities. The reform, however, was only halfhearted and was hobbled by congressional opposition and BIA impediments and limitations. The grants were inadequate, frequently covering only the direct costs of the programs, or parts of them, and not the indirect costs of tribal administration, and were often doled out so late that the tribes could not plan or implement the programs effectively. The Bureau, moreover, monitored the tribe's performance, sometimes managing to maintain actual control, and at any time it could, and did, cancel a contract and reassert its authority. Even the Zuñis never had more than nominal control over their programs, and in time the BIA was again running their affairs.

The moves of the Johnson administration, including the creation of a National Council on Indian Opportunity chaired by the Vice-President and composed of cabinet members and national Indian leaders, were, by and large, sops to the tribes and, if anything, merely supported and strengthened the role of the subordinate tribal officers over their peoples.

On the reservations, the general population perceived no significant improvement in their conditions or in the protection of their rights and property and continued to blame their problems on complicity between corrupt tribal politicians and the BIA. Outside the reservations, there was additional dissatisfaction. More than half a million Indians lived in cities like Chicago, Minneapolis, Denver, Seattle, and San Francisco, where they or their parents had been lured by World War II defense jobs or had been "relocated" during the 1950's by ill-devised BIA programs to ease reservation unemployment. Adjusting to White culture had been difficult for large numbers of them, and their lives were filled with social and economic problems as serious as those on the reservations. Denied the federal services to which they were entitled on the reservations, they existed in poverty, deprivation, and loneliness, and had their own grievances.

During the 1960's, the civil rights movement of the Blacks, the emergence of Third World nations, the Vietnam War protests, and other events had made their impact on the Indians, stirring a pride in their Indianness and arousing a sense of Indian nationalism. Among the young city Indians particularly, as with those at colleges and universities, there developed a fierce loyalty to their individual tribes and to Indian people in general. From that point, it was a short step to militant advocacy of Indian self-determination and hostility toward the BIA and all other White oppressors of the Indians. They met at Indian centers, read Indian newspapers that angered them with reports of conditions on the reservations and injustices to the tribes, conducted conferences and seminars on Indian problems, and listened to activist Indian speakers like Vine Deloria, Jr., a young Standing Rock (Hunkpapa) Sioux who had become executive director of the National Congress of American Indians and would, in 1969, publish *Custer Died for Your Sins*, an explosive, best-selling assault on White exploiters of the Indians and the pliant leaders who ran the tribes.

Within the context of the non-Indian protest movements of the times, it was inevitable that Indian demonstrations would soon occur also. Some of the more activist Indians joined the militant National Indian Youth Council, whose leaders were adept at using the White men's media to proclaim their goal of Red Power, the right of Indians to rule themselves. Others formed new organizations of varying degrees of militancy. Old and new grievances were focused upon: the indifference of the government to long-standing injustices; Washington's deafness to the demand for self-determination; White opposition to the Pyramid Lake Paiutes' right to water, the Taos Pueblos' right to their sacred lands, the Puget Sound Indians' right to fish, the Alaskan Natives' right to settlement of their land claims; the discrimination and violence against Indians; the neglect of urban Indians; the mistreatment of Indians in correctional institutions; and the exploitation and denigration of Indians by promoters, advertisers, and writers. These and other complaints stirred bitter anger.

On November 20, 1969, the frustrations overflowed at San Francisco. A landing party of seventy-eight Indians, calling themselves Indians of All Tribes, suddenly occupied Alcatraz Island, whose federal prison had been abandoned by the government. Pointing out that the original native owners had never ceded the island, the occupiers claimed title to it under a law that permitted certain tribes to reclaim land taken from them by the federal government when the government no longer had use for it. They proclaimed Alcatraz to be Indian Land and announced their twin goals of publicizing the desperate facts of Indian existence and converting the island into a Native American cultural and educational center.

Their boldness electrified Indians throughout the United States and Canada, and many of them hurried from reservations and other cities to join the occupiers. The recently inaugurated Nixon administration, trying to get off on the right foot with Indians, decided to avoid a confrontation and sought instead to end the occupation peacefully through negotiations. The occupiers—though they quickly began to suffer from shortages of water, food, heat, and electricity—settled in for the duration.

The government let them hold the island for more than a year-and-a-half, meanwhile continuing to negotiate unsuccessfully with them. Proposals to lease Alcatraz to them and provide funds for constructing an Indian trading post or Indian-oriented amusement park, or for some other income-producing scheme, were all turned down. "We had no wish to become tourist attractions or public curiosities," said one of the occupiers. "We wanted self-determination, the chance to do for ourselves what the government of these United States had neglected to do since its inception."

With the situation stalemated, the non-Indian public soon lost interest. Many of the occupiers themselves were obliged to return to their reservations or take jobs in San Francisco to pay for food, medicine, and other necessities on the island. On June 11, 1971, the occupation ended as suddenly as it had begun: twenty federal marshals, armed with shotguns and automatic weapons, landed on Alcatraz. Only fifteen Indians—six men, four women, and five children—were present; everyone else was on the mainland, shopping or at their jobs. The marshals removed the few Indians at gunpoint to nearby Treasure Island, and then released them.

Though the occupation was over, its effects endured. Throughout the country, Alcatraz had become a symbol of freedom to many Indians, both on and off the reservations, and had inspired a series of similar occupations and takeovers. In March and April 1970, angrily protesting groups of Native Americans in the Seattle area three times tried to occupy some acreage at Fort Lawton, which was about to be declared surplus. More than a hundred arrests were made, and many of the Indians were beaten by MP's. During the same year, Indians, demonstrating against BIA rule, tried to occupy Bureau offices across the nation. Twenty-one were arrested in Littleton, Colorado, twenty-three in Chicago, twenty-five in Minneapolis, thirty in Philadelphia, and twelve in Alameda, California. Other protests occurred in BIA offices in Cleveland, Los Angeles, and Albuquerque. In the Southwest, tribal members demonstrated for their rights to water from the Colorado River and for protection of their lands against White developers, and in northern California, hundreds of Pomo and Pit River Indians, reoccupying territories that Whites had seized from their ancestors more than a hundred years before, held out against legal and physical attacks by the properties' modern-day government and corporate owners. The spirit of defiance spread to the Midwest and East. In South Dakota's Black Hills, taken from its Sioux owners in the 1870's, young Sioux and other Indians demonstrated atop the carved heads of the Presidents at Mount Rushmore, asserting their reoccupation of the site. In Wisconsin, Chippewas opposed the taking of some of their lands for a new national park and occupied an abandoned Coast Guard station, and in Michigan others fought for their fishing rights and donned war paint and ceremonial clothes to lay claim to a lighthouse and some acreage on Lake Superior. In upper New York State, Mohawks and other Iroquois, rebelling against their White-recognized tribal governments, fought to eject Whites from their reservation lands, while in New York City's harbor, other Indians attempted unsuccessfully to plant themselves on Ellis Island, the former entry point for millions of European immigrants.

Throughout 1970, these manifestations of desperation were signs to the federal government and the non-Indian population that the Indian pot was boiling and the lid was rattling loudly. The great majority of Indians agreed with the protesters and supported their goals, though, fearing violence and possible government retaliation, they maintained a cautious silence. Even so, many of the tribal leaders, as well as BIA and other federal officials, were nervous—revolt was in the air, and a national Indian movement, directed against both of them, seemed to be taking form. "If the government doesn't start living up to its obligations, armed resistance and occupation will have to become a regular thing," a

Chippewa protest leader warned during one of the demonstrations in Michigan.

Such statements, in conjunction with the rash of seizures of government property and flouting of the law, gave concern to state and federal law enforcement agencies. Law enforcement officials, knowing little of the frustrations underlying the protests, or of the protesters' deep roots of support among the general Indian population, regarded the demonstrators as a handful of renegades and trouble-makers, whose conspiratorial activities, like those of the Black Panthers, could be nipped in the bud if the principal agitators were eliminated. This view found support among some Indian political leaders who felt embarrassed or threatened by the demonstrators; they urged the government to clamp down on the protesters, whom they characterized disparagingly as largely "urban Indians" who did not represent anyone but themselves. Other tribal leaders, however, recognized the depth of the unrest on their reservations and, fearing revolts against themselves, appealed to the Nixon administration to quiet the din by taking steps to answer the tribes' complaints against the BIA and the government's policies.

In a somewhat legalistic and inhibited fashion, the Administration had already embarked on this more benign course of treating the discontent. Soon after taking office, Nixon had strengthened the National Council on Indian Opportunity as a coordinating center for the improved delivery of federal programs to the reservations, and had given tribal leaders direct access to the Executive Office of the White House by assigning Bradley Patterson, an aide to Leonard Garment, one of the President's advisers on domestic affairs, as a sort of overall troubleshooter for the Indians' complaints. Patterson was knowledgeable and sympathetic on Indian affairs, and Indian delegations were soon bringing their problems to him. On occasion he was able to help them; more often, however, he could do little to stir the BIA bureaucracy.

On July 8, 1970, Nixon also sent a special message to Congress, proclaiming the Indians' right to self-determination and asking Congress to join him in ending the period of paternalism and termination. The tribes received this news with guarded optimism, recognizing that, again, it was merely a statement of intention. Soon afterward, the Administration raised their hopes higher by sending a package of Indian bills to Congress designed to remove or ameliorate some of the tribes' major grievances. They called for the creation of an independent Indian trust counsel authority to represent the tribes in conflicts involving natural resources and thus end the Interior Department's conflict of interest; the authorization of an Assistant Secretary for Indian Affairs in the Interior Department to give tribal matters more weight within the Department;

increased funding for BIA programs; the right of tribes to take over the control of reservation schools; and the provision of a legal foundation for the system of contracting with tribes, which some members of Congress, as well as of the BIA, were opposing and stifling as an illegal assignment of powers. At the same time, both Nixon and Vice-President Spiro Agnew threw their support behind the Taos pueblo's fight to regain Blue Lake, which to many tribes had become a symbol of governmental injustice to Indians. That support proved decisive; Congress voted, at last, to return the lake and its surrounding lands to the Pueblos, after which the Administration also returned lands which the Warm Springs Indians in Oregon and the Yakimas in Washington had been trying to regain, and brought about a settlement of native land claims in Alaska.

None of these steps disarmed or weakened the protest movement. The package of reform bills became stalled in Congress, and the Administration failed to press for their enactment, so that on the reservations the ills that they were intended to cure remained unhealed. Programs were still underfunded, no trust counsel was created to protect tribal resources, contracting faltered and stopped, and self-determination was still only a goal. The Administration, moreover, displayed a desire to work only with the elected leaders of the reservation tribes and gave short shrift to dissident or urban groups. The latter comprised some of the most militant and articulate leaders of the unrest, and the government's inattention to their grievances, such as their ineligibility for the benefits of Indian health or other reservation programs, further angered them.

In 1971, activities within the BIA fed fuel to the fire. Determined to shake up the Bureau and end its dictatorial hold on the tribes, Louis R. Bruce, a retired New York advertising executive of Mohawk and Sioux ancestry who had become Nixon's Commissioner of Indian Affairs, filled key roles in the Bureau with about a dozen able and dedicated young Indian activists, who went to work to restructure the agency and remove powers from the old bureaucracy, intending to convert it from a directing to a service organization. Those who were being affected, particularly in the BIA area offices where jobs seemed to be threatened, mounted an immediate counterattack, turning various congressmen and tribal political leaders against Bruce and his aides by terming them irresponsible and inexperienced urban Indians who were acting without congressional authority and were imperiling BIA programs for the reservations. Most of the charges were self-serving and false, but complaints from angry members of Congress and fearful reservation leaders soon caused turmoil in the Bureau.

Harrison Loesch, who, as Assistant Secretary of the Interior for Public Land Management, was Bruce's superior, knew little about Indian matters and was already out of sympathy with the reforms that Bruce was trying to accomplish. A hard-nosed Colorado lawyer, he talked about Indians like a nineteenth-century Westerner, and it took little urging for him or Interior Secretary Rogers C. B. Morton to accept the complaints about Bruce's administration. Two old-line BIA Indian bureaucrats, John O. Crow and Wilma L. Victor—both of them notorious among Indians as terminationists, and particularly disliked by younger Indians—were placed in positions where they could control and veto the restructuring of the BIA and the changes that Bruce's aides were bringing about. Although Bruce was trying to carry out the Indian policies that Nixon had enunciated, the White House left him adrift, and he was soon shorn of his authority. His efforts to change things were stopped, and one by one his young assistants became powerless and left the Bureau.

Indians throughout the country learned of what was happening, and the protesters began to focus their attacks on Loesch, Crow, and Victor as symbols of continued government insensitivity to Native Americans. At the same time, to retain the loyalty and support of the disgruntled and fearful tribal leaders, the Administration unabashedly helped organize and fund a National Tribal Chairmen's Association. To those who had been charging collusion between tribal chairmen and the government, the action was another example of the government's ability to buy off and control the reservation leadership. It occurred, moreover, at a time when a number of revolts by traditionalists and grass-roots Indians were beginning to break out against tribal officers and unrepresentative reservation governments, and served further to inflame those who were waging the struggles.

Among some groups, like the Creeks and Cherokees in Oklahoma, challenges were being made to tyrannical authority that was promoted and supported by area BIA officials. "I, Claude Cox, your Principal Chief, and the former chief, W. E. 'Dode' McIntosh, have decided to close the 'stomp grounds,' " announced the government-recognized leader of the Creeks to rebellious traditionalists. "This nonsense should stop and advise you people and so called 'fire chiefs' this paganizism is to old and should be put out-of-date and advise you to become christianized in the Methodist Church." Cox had been elected to his office by less than 25 percent of his people's eligible vote. Other tribes, like the Tesuque Pueblos of New Mexico, were clashing with leaders who, under BIA direction, were making long-term leases for tribal lands, natural resources, and water rights, without consulting their people. In particular, friction of major consequence was developing over contracts and leases with large public utilities and energy companies. Though they involved payments of millions of dollars to the tribes, they were not publicized to the people, and when the agreements were discovered, they aroused bitter charges of payoffs to tribal leaders for developments that threatened the tribes' future.

Several of the cases raised the specter of "termination by corporation," a new peril suddenly perceived as endangering the tribes' survival. In 1970, traditionalist Hopis in Arizona learned of coal and water contracts signed in secret and in violation of the Hopi constitution in the 1960's by energy companies and the head of the Hopi tribal council. Calling for the strip-mining of sacred Hopi lands on Black Mesa and the large-scale use of the Hopis' scarce water supplies, the contracts had been executed under pressure from the Interior Department and the tribe's non-Indian lawyer. The council members were kept as much in the dark as the rest of the tribe, and even in 1970 did not know the terms of the leases or to whom the coal company was making its payments. Disclosures of similar nature were made also by Navajo traditionalists, and angry and protracted conflicts ensued between members of each tribe and their leaders over the desecration and destruction of their shrines and lands by the strip miners; the forced removal of families from areas to be mined; the leasing of rights-of-way that took more of their territory; the building of power and gasification plants that would bring industrialization and numerous White men onto their lands; the pollution of reservation air and water; the lack of cultural and environmental protections; and other threats that could doom the tribes and their reservations.

Across the northern plains there were similar conflicts. On the Northern Cheyenne reservation in Montana, a group of Indians who owned allotments discovered that their tribal council, encouraged by the BIA, had secretly leased to coal developers and speculators the rights to coal under 56 percent of the reservation's entire surface, including their allotments, and was about to sign another agreement with a subsidiary of Conoco that would raise that figure to 72 percent. The leases, moreover, offered the tribe scandalously low royalties for its coal; would open the reservation to a flood of non-Indians who would be permitted to build industrial centers and a city for 30,000 Whites on the Indians' land; and were full of violations of the Code of Federal Regulations. Simultaneously, on the neighboring Crow reservation in Montana, tribal members learned of similar injurious and one-sided deals for Crow coal and water rights, negotiated with different energy companies by their tribal leaders under government sponsorship.

The exposure of the contracts had a profound impact within both tribes. Some of the embarrassed leaders hastily dissociated themselves from the BIA, blaming the government for persuading them to sign the contracts. On the Northern Cheyenne reservation, a genuine unity was established for a time among the tribal officers, the council, and the people in defense of their resources and for the protection of their environment and culture. Enlisting the aid of non-governmental Indian and non-Indian technical experts, lawyers, and environmentalists, the unified tribe eventually forced the Department of the Interior to suspend all the coal contracts, pending renegotiations and mutual agreement between the tribe and the corporations over fair prices and environmental protections. At the same time, the tribe established a Northern Cheyenne Research Project, staffed by social, economic, and environmental experts, to help the Indians decide for themselves how best to develop their coal resources, or whether to do so at all. After much intratribal conflict, the Crows, too, were able to throw out some of their contracts and renegotiate fair terms and improved protection.

The flood of revelations concerning secret contracts, with their threats to the future of reservations and the existence of the tribal peoples, almost instantly made them national Indian causes. The last dam restraining a dramatic Indian outburst broke with a series of murders and outrages committed against Indians. At Tacoma, Hank Adams, the fishing rights leader and head of the Survival of American Indians Association, was shot and seriously wounded, and no one was arrested. In California, Richard Oakes, one of the best-known and most respected leaders of the occupation of Alcatraz Island, was murdered by a White man, whom the law treated lightly. In Philadelphia, Leroy Shenandoah, an Onondaga veteran of the Green Berets and a member of the honor guard at President Kennedy's funeral, was brutally beaten and shot to death by police, who justified the act as "excusable homicide." And in Gordon, Nebraska, near the Pine Ridge and Rosebud reservations, Raymond Yellow Thunder, a fifty-one-year-old Sioux, was stripped of his pants by drunken Whites, humiliated for fun before a White audience of mixed sexes at the American Legion hall, and later was found dead in the cab of a pickup truck.

In August 1972, a number of Indian groups joined Brulé and Oglala Sioux at the annual Sun Dance on the Rosebud reservation. The ceremony was held at Crow Dog's Paradise, the home of the families of Henry and Leonard Crow Dog, who were Sioux medicine men. It was in the heart of the old buffalo country, where the Sioux, under their warrior chiefs and spiritual leaders, had once been a free people. Among those present were some of the members of the American Indian Movement, who had come to visit the medicine men to seek spiritual direction, an element which they felt had been "vitally missing" from their activities.

AIM already had the reputation of being the most militant of all the Pan-Indian organizations. It had been founded in July 1968 by George

Mitchell and Dennis Banks, two Chippewa Indians living in Minneapolis, to try to help that city's many neglected Indians. The group's first demands forced officials of the Office of Economic Opportunity and other agencies to channel funds to Indian-controlled anti-poverty programs and survival schools for Indian children who had dropped out of regular schools. With a grant from a local church, AIM then formed Indian patrols to protect Indians who had been drinking at night from indiscriminate arrests and beatings by the Minneapolis police. The patrols halted fights and took drunken Indians home, and police arrests almost ended.

The group's successes increased its following, and AIM chapters sprang up in other cities. Clyde and Vernon Bellecourt and Russell Means joined the leadership. The Bellecourts, who were also Chippewas, had been in prison, but said they had learned "where that path led" and regarded AIM as an organization devoted to keeping young Indians from walking the same path. Means, a thirty-two-year-old Oglala Sioux, had been raised on the Pine Ridge reservation and in various urban centers. He had attended five colleges but had not graduated, had lived in Los Angeles and then on the Rosebud reservation, where he worked for the tribal council, and had then gone to Cleveland and become the director of the local American Indian Center. A master of fiery rhetoric and at staging events that captured the attention of the media, he led a following of urban Indians in various demonstrations, including the seizure of the *Mayflower II* on Thanksgiving Day 1970 and the temporary occupation of Mount Rushmore in 1971. He and Banks, who was about thirty-eight and had worked for a Minneapolis corporation, became the most inspiring and best known of AIM's leaders.

In December 1970, Banks and other AIM members attended a government conference on the problems of urban Indians at the Airlie House in Warrenton, Virginia. A dispute broke out, and some of the militants vandalized the conference center and stole liquor and cash. The next year, at the height of the BIA bureaucrats' revolt against Commissioner Bruce and his aides, Means tried to come to Bruce's rescue. With a band of AIM members, he invaded the BIA offices in Washington, intending to make a citizen's arrest of John Crow and Wilma Victor, but was hustled out of the building. As a result of such episodes, administration officials like Robert Robertson, the executive director of the National Council on Indian Opportunity, who had had friction with the Alcatraz occupiers, regarded AIM as a potentially dangerous group of revolutionaries, and the Department of Justice had the FBI watch its leaders closely.

Though AIM had started as an urban organization, it had also turned its attention to tribal problems and had gradually acquired followers on different reservations. In February 1972, when nothing was done to punish the tormentors and murderers of Raymond Yellow Thunder, Means and Banks led some 1,300 angry Indians, mostly Sioux from Pine Ridge and Rosebud, into the town of Gordon, occupying it for three days and threatening town and state officials if they failed to carry out justice. To the relief of the frightened townspeople, two Whites were finally jailed in connection with the crime, a policeman was suspended, and the local authorities were persuaded to promise to end discrimination against Indians. Though discrimination continued, AIM's reputation soared among reservation Indians. What tribal leaders had not dared to do to protect their people, AIM had done. A second attempt to assist a tribe did not go so well. In April 1972, an armed group of AIM members showed up at a Chippewa reservation in Minnesota to support the tribe's efforts to make Whites buy tribal fishing licenses. Their menacing attitude upset the tribal leaders, who made them leave the reservation.

In August, AIM members went to the Rosebud Sun Dance. Their visit with the Sioux medicine men was a moving one. If they were to be a true Indian organization, Henry and Leonard Crow Dog told them, they would have to have the spiritual involvement of Indian medicine men and holy people. "That," said one of the AIM leaders later, "is actually when the American Indian Movement was first born. Because we think that the American Indian Movement is not only an advocate for Indian people. It is the spiritual rebirth of our nation. It carries the spirituality of our ancient people and of our elder people. So now the American Indian Movement relies very, very heavily on the traditional leaders and the holy men of the various tribes—to give them the direction they need so they can best help the Indian people."

For Indians who had been raised in the White men's world, the teachings of the medicine men were an emotional experience, confirming that they had been right to turn against White society, which had treated them so badly, and follow, instead, the traditional ways of their own people. The new spiritual drive of the movement gave it more strength and additional rapport with grass-roots people and fired it with the zeal of an Indian crusade against White oppressors. At the same time, the traditionalists and holy men on the reservations gained a formidable ally in their fight against the tribal leaders and the BIA-run governments. AIM, it appeared, might be able to mobilize the people—a threat that many of the tribal chairmen and their followers also recognized.

At the conclusion of the Sun Dance, the leaders of a number of the groups began discussing the recent killings of Indians and the BIA's hold over reservation governments, and decided that they had to do something to "wake up America" to the Indians' grievances. Burnette, the former Rosebud president and NCAI executive director, proposed that all Indian organizations join in a spiritual movement "under the banner of the Trail of Broken Treaties and proceed to Washington, where we will show the world what Indians truly stand for." The others agreed to the proposal, and on September 30 the representatives of nine Indian organizations, as well as individuals from different reservations and cities, met in Denver and planned three automobile caravans that would leave from Los Angeles, San Francisco, and Seattle, crossing the country and picking up more Indians on the way, and meet in Washington late in October, just before the national elections. Burnette and several others would go on ahead, making preparations for their stay in Washington and arranging for meetings with President Nixon, presidential candidate George McGovern, and other political and governmental leaders. The Indians would be peaceful and on their best behavior. "There cannot be any liquor or drugs used by anyone, and our plan should consist of a schedule of peaceful negotiations and religious ceremonies," said Burnette. There was no disagreement.

Despite these intentions, the Trail of Broken Treaties ended in violence and an outburst of destructive fury. Because AIM was participating, Washington officialdom went on the alert. Promises of accommodations, food, and medical supplies for the Indians, as well as of meetings with leading governmental figures, were made to Burnette and then broken. Both Robertson and Assistant Secretary of the Interior Loesch publicly offered cooperation, but secretly ordered it withheld. On October 11, Loesch sent a memo to Commissioner Bruce: "This is to give you very specific instructions that the Bureau is not to provide any assistance or funding either directly or indirectly." Meanwhile, the caravans crossed the country, stopping at reservations and Indian centers to pick up medicine men, mothers and fathers with their children, young couples, old people, anybody who would come. There was no idea of violence. To all of them, it was a chance to tell the heads of the government of the sufferings and needs of the American Indians.

The caravans converged on Minneapolis and St. Paul, where Hank Adams, one of the leaders of the Seattle group, went to work with others on the preparation of a set of twenty demands to present to the government. Based on a program that Adams had framed the previous year calling for a new national Indian policy "to remove the human needs and aspirations of Indian tribes and Indian people from the workings of the general American political system and . . . reinstate a system of bilateral relationships between Indian tribes and the Federal Government," the new document demanded the reinstitution of a treaty-making relationship between the United States and the "Indian Tribes and Nations."

Before they left Minneapolis, word came to them of Loesch's memo to Bruce, which someone had leaked to Burnette, and a number of infuriated members of AIM took over the Minneapolis BIA area office for two hours to protest Loesch's "forked tongue."

In Washington, Burnette at length managed to persuade Loesch that the Indians' intentions were peaceful, and the Assistant Secretary agreed reluctantly to try to help find facilities for the caravan members while they were in Washington and to arrange meetings with top officials—though President Nixon, he told them, would be in California. The caravans arrived in the capital on November 1 and 2 and found that the only accommodation for their hundreds of members was the rat-infested basement of a church. Moreover, the important officials they expected to see turned out to be Loesch, Robertson, and Bradley Patterson, whom they regarded as "underlings." Bitterness reached the boiling point when they were informed that, because they were "political advocates," they could not enter Arlington Cemetery to hold ceremonies at the graves of Indian heroes, including Ira Hayes, a Pima from Arizona who had been one of the Marine flag raisers at Iwo Jima in World War II.

Angered by their reception, and not knowing where to stay, they drove past the White House to the BIA Building, which guards had hastily locked after hearing that they were on their way. The caravan leaders found an unlocked back door and went upstairs to discuss their housing problem with Commissioner Bruce. The meeting was soon joined by Crow and Loesch, whose patronizing and high-handed manner ("Now you listen to me," Loesch kept telling them) increased the tension. Downstairs, meanwhile, someone had opened the doors, and more than 500 Indians came into the building, settling down in the cafeteria and auditorium. Loesch finally left the meeting in the Commissioner's office, and Bruce continued to work with the caravan leaders over where the Indians could stay.

At four o'clock that afternoon, the building's guard was changed, and the new shift tried to clear the Indians out. When the Indians refused to leave because the negotiations were still underway, a scuffle ensued, and helmeted District of Columbia riot police, summoned by an official of the General Services Administration, stormed into the building. After a brief fight, in which a number of people were hurt, the White House was notified of what was happening, and the riot police were ordered to withdraw.

But the damage had been done. Up till then, the Indians had been peaceful, despite the provocative hostility with which the nation's capital had received them. Now, they ousted the guards and took possession of the building, barricading its doors, lower windows, and stairways with office furniture, copying machines, and file cabinets. For almost a week, while friendly groups in Washington supplied them with food and other necessities, the Indians held the building. Loesch, Patterson, Robertson, and other officials met with Means, Banks, the Bellecourts, and other leaders and tried to talk them into leaving, but the Indians would not depart until Interior Secretary Morton or some other high officer of the government discussed with them their twenty-point list of demands. Morton, who regarded the Indians as a "splinter group of militants," refused to agree to such a meeting until the Indians left the government's property, and no one else of equal rank was available.

The caravans' leaders made the Commissioner's office their headquarters, and Bruce and LaDonna Harris, a Comanche Indian and the politically influential head of Americans for Indian Opportunity, each stayed with them for a night to demonstrate their support and try to safeguard them by their presence. Riot police and U.S. marshals were stationed outside the building, and as the occupation continued, it became a media event of high drama, providing the Indians with international attention. To offset the sympathy the Indians were receiving, Robertson persuaded a number of tribal chairmen to send telegrams and letters denouncing the occupiers, and on November 6 he brought some of the members of the National Tribal Chairmen's Association to Washington to tell the press that the general Indian population disapproved of what was going on in the BIA Building. The press conference backfired, however, when Hank Adams and a number of the caravans' leaders appeared and accused the chairmen of being puppets of the government and not representing their people. Reminded that playing the government's game might bring them trouble from their own people back home, the chairmen said that they supported some of the protesters' list of twenty demands, but deplored the caravans' tactics, and then left, some of them angry that the government had put them in such an awkward position.

Robertson and others in the Administration had hoped that the NTCA members would use their authority and influence to persuade the occupiers to go home. When that failed, the Justice Department, acting on the decision of a government interagency group, secured a District Court order permitting the forcible eviction of the Indians that evening. Word of the impending attack reached the Indians, and they prepared to defend themselves, reinforcing the barricades and fashioning homemade weapons out of table legs, broken pieces of sinks, mop handles, and scissor blades, and creating extensive damage to the interior of the building and its furnishings. Late that afternoon, negotiators in behalf of the Indians met for the last time with solicitors of the Interior Department and told them that, on the eve of election day, the Administration was risking a bloody battle with Indian men, women, and children in the capital city, in which many persons on both sides would undoubtedly be killed. The Indians, in truth, had prepared a large store of Molotov cocktails and were ready to set the building afire. The warning was relayed to President Nixon's assistants. At the same time, a ruling by the U.S. Court of Appeals granted attorneys for the Indians a postponement of the attack. That night, after a message was received from the airplane in which Nixon was campaigning, the negotiations, which up till then had been conducted by lesser officials of the Interior Department, were taken over by representatives of the President.

In a series of conferences with Hank Adams and other caravan leaders, Leonard Garment, the President's special assistant, Frank Carlucci, the deputy director of the Office of Management and Budget, and Patterson ended the impasse, promising to set up an interagency task force to respond to the caravans' twenty demands and winning the Indians' agreement to evacuate the BIA Building. The government provided $66,650 from the Office of Economic Opportunity to help get the Indians back home, and on November 8 the occupiers streamed from the building, some of them taking cartons of documents from the BIA files which they claimed contained proof of Bureau corruption and anti-Indian activities. When the press was permitted into the building, the nation was treated to lurid pictures and descriptions of the damage which the Indians had done to the interior, most of which took place at the time when they thought they were going to be attacked.

The nation as a whole was divided over what had occurred. Many persons deplored the Indians' actions, condemned the destruction and trashing inside the building, and wanted the Indians punished. Others viewed the confrontation as a reflection of the Indians' frustrations and desperate plight and blamed the government for not having paid attention to their grievances. In the confusion and recriminations that followed the demonstrators' departure, the country debated what had happened, and to some Indians it appeared that the Trail of Broken Treaties had accomplished its goal, forcing public opinion to consider a change in the government's handling of Indian affairs. But it was only for a moment. On November 13, Patterson informed Hank Adams that the Administration would refuse to discuss the twenty demands or any other subject with representatives of the Trail of Broken Treaties until the Indians returned all the documents and other property that they had taken from the BIA Building. The interagency task force finally did make a response on January 9, 1973, but turned down all the demands as impractical. By that time, the public had lost interest in the affair.

The Indians themselves were as divided over the event as the rest of the country. Many tribal chairmen who toured the building were infuriated by the scattering and destruction of records that pertained to their reservations and joined Robertson and Loesch in blaming it on urban radicals, though caravan records showed that more than 70 percent of the occupiers had been reservation Indians. The anger of most of the chairmen died when several of them, aware of the underlying causes of the building's occupation and the grass-roots strength of the Indian protesters, urged calm and a reasoned approach. Heading an all-Indian inquiry group, Peter MacDonald, the chairman of the Navajo Nation, told television viewers on the program *Face the Nation* that the caravans' action reflected the "rage and frustration all Indian people feel." Other tribal chairmen who complained about the demonstrators, he said, "failed to analyze what really caused our people to rise up in frustration," and he charged that some of the Indian leaders had "been pushed into making statements" by Robert Robertson of the National Council on Indian Opportunity. As to the charge that the protest had been the work of urban Indians, he declared, "I represent the largest tribe in America, about one-third of reservation Indians, and what was expressed [in the protest] is a feeling you have inside. Their demands cut across urban and reservation Indians." The National Congress of American Indians mounted a counterattack also, charging that the Interior Department and the NCIO, "in the most sinister atmosphere imaginable," had worked "clandestinely to muster tribal leaders for the defense of the Administration." Such two-faced actions, it said, "only lend credence to the strong accusations made by the activists."

The Administration was torn between hard-liners like Robertson and Loesch, who had not approved of the settlement and wanted to pursue and punish the militants, and Garment, Carlucci, and Patterson, who better understood some of the causes of the Indians' anger and felt lucky that they had been able to defuse and end a dangerous situation. In an effort to tidy up the BIA and get its relations with the tribes on track again, Morton fired Louis Bruce, who had shown sympathy for the occupiers, and the White House fired Loesch and Crow, who had inflamed and mishandled the caravans' leaders. Under temporary new leadership, the BIA tried to put its records together again and reassert its authority on the reservations. Its breathing spell proved to be a short one.

The Indians who had taken part in the occupation fanned out across the country and returned to their reservations and home cities. The FBI kept many of them under surveillance, but wherever they went, they behaved like victors who had won a notable triumph over the government in behalf of all Indians. Explaining to audiences of reservation and urban

Indians what they had tried to do and what they thought they had accomplished, they extolled the ability of AIM to lead them and urged a widening of their struggle. In many places, the traditionalists, youths, and grass-roots Indian families greeted them with honor ceremonies and dances. Elsewhere, however, the BIA superintendents and reservation leaders roused fear and opposition to them as troublemakers and violence-prone radicals, not typical of real Indians, and did their best to bar them from the reservations and keep their influence from spreading.

Even before the situation had quieted in Washington, trouble began to build among the nearly 12,000 Oglalas on Pine Ridge, Russell Means's home reservation. Because of its action at Gordon, AIM had a respected reputation among many of the Pine Ridge families, who viewed Means as something of a modern-day Crazy Horse, unafraid of the Whites and willing to battle for the people's rights. The local BIA officials and the elected tribal chairman, Richard Wilson, held just the opposite view, regarding Means as a menace and AIM as a dangerous revolutionary force that threatened the status quo on the reservation. Wilson himself compounded the problem. A short, corpulent man who drank heavily, indulged in threats and bullying, and walked around in dark glasses that made him look like a caricature of a rural sheriff, he had become chairman in April 1972, after a campaign in which he was charged with buying hundreds of votes with drinks and payoffs, using money which bootleggers and other Whites allegedly gave him for promises of favors and contracts on the reservation.

His conduct as chairman immediately plunged the reservation into turmoil. He fired old-time and efficient Indian jobholders and replaced them with relatives, friends, and strong-arm supporters, and raised their salaries as well as his own. With brazen indifference to his people's opinions, he diverted the funds of government programs from their intended beneficiaries to those who were loyal to him, and awarded contracts and questionable deals to Whites who befriended him. When charges of embezzlement, graft, and nepotism were leveled at him, he instituted a reign of terror, beating up his opponents and threatening harm to their wives and children. Cars were forced into accidents on the roads, people were shot at in the dark, and homes were mysteriously burned. At the first meeting of the twenty-member tribal council, he showed that he meant to rule it with an iron fist. To quell opposition, he recessed it, and thereafter violated the tribal constitution by refusing to call it into session again for four months, in the interval governing the tribe by dictate or in private sessions with one or more of the five members of the executive committee who were loyal to him.

Recognizing Wilson as a reliable bulwark against an AIM-supported popular revolt that would threaten them also, the reservation and area heads of the BIA backed him, turning a deaf ear to petitions and complaints against his excesses and throttling attempts to oppose him. In their anger, people began to do what the BIA feared most, and started to talk of getting help from AIM as the only solution to their frustrations. The end of the occupation of the BIA Building and the threat of Means's return to the reservation threw Wilson and his BIA supporters closer together for their mutual protection. When the tribe's elected vice-chairman spoke out in AIM's behalf, Wilson fired him and then got a member of the tribal court to issue an order prohibiting AIM members from speaking at, or attending, any meeting on the reservation. The BIA acquiesced in both of these illegal edicts and followed up by providing Wilson with $62,000 to enlist an auxiliary police force, in addition to the regular Bureau law enforcement officers, to guard the BIA and tribal headquarters building in the town of Pine Ridge.

The arming of what many reservation people called Wilson's personal "goon squad" increased the harassment and terror on the reservation. Composed largely of unemployed toughs and Wilson's drinking companions and relatives, the new group roughed up and threatened anyone they disliked or who they thought was opposed to Wilson. As the intimidation and violence spread, the traditionalist Oglalas in the eight districts of the 2,500-square-mile reservation organized an Inter-District Council that demanded the resignation of Wilson and the removal of Stanley Lyman, the BIA superintendent. Nothing came of it, but the Council mobilized additional support, and early in February a large number of people formed an Oglala Sioux Civil Rights Organization, popularly known as OSCRO, which gained many members. At the same time, three representatives on the tribal council, bolder than the others, filed impeachment complaints against Wilson.

To the chairman, as well as the BIA, the situation appeared to be growing dangerous. Russell Means had come home and had showed up at a meeting of the Oglala Sioux Landowners Association, of which he was a member. After being arrested and detained briefly, he had left the reservation, vowing angrily to return and run against Wilson for the chairmanship of the tribe in the next election. Rejoining Banks and a host of AIM members, Means remained close to the reservation, helping to lead a series of demonstrations and protests against discrimination and the violation of Indian civil rights in South Dakota. In January, a White service station attendant who had killed a Sioux, Wesley Bad Heart Bull, was charged with second-degree manslaughter and freed on $5,000 bail in Custer, South Dakota. Protesting the low bail, and demanding that the manslaughter charge, which carried a maximum sentence of only ten

years, be changed to one of murder, Means, Banks, and their AIM followers assembled a large number of angry Indian families at Custer. Negotiations with the state's attorney erupted into a two-hour battle, in which
state and local police used tear gas to drive the Indians out of the local
courthouse. Three Indians and at least eight law enforcement officers
were injured, the courthouse and chamber of commerce building were
set afire, and thirty-seven of the two or three hundred Indians were
arrested. Among the latter was the distraught mother of the murdered
Wesley Bad Heart Bull. Eventually, she was sentenced to three to five
years in jail for assaulting a police officer, while the slayer of her son
received two months' probation. Freed on bail, the AIM members moved
on to Rapid City and Sturgis. In the former, they conducted demonstrations and met with local officials over the protection of Indian civil rights
in that urban center. While they were there, a riot broke out when a White
man attacked an Indian in a bar. Some twenty-five Whites were hospital-
ized, and forty-one Indians were arrested. In Sturgis, their presence won
the setting of bail for an Indian who had been kept in jail without bail on
the charge of murdering a White woman.

Among authorities of the Justice Department, which kept AIM's activities under surveillance, the belief grew that Means and Banks would
soon lead their militant followers onto the Pine Ridge reservation, probably to try to seize the BIA building. To protect the property, a decision
—welcomed by Wilson—was made to reinforce the BIA police on the
reservation and to send in, also, a number of U.S. marshals. On February
12, the first contingent of some sixty-five heavily armed marshals, members of an elite Special Operations Group, including anti-sniper teams
and men with automatic weapons and two-way radios, arrived on the
reservation and set up a command post in the village of Pine Ridge. The
BIA police were doubled, and in Rapid City the FBI complement was
beefed up to watch AIM and, if needed, to assist the four or five FBI
agents who were regularly on the reservation. Soon afterward, forty more
marshals arrived, as well as the Director of the Marshal Service and
high-level officials of the Justice Department, the FBI, and the BIA.
Under the direction of the Justice Department, a unified force was formed
encompassing the BIA police, whom the marshals trained in riot control.
A communications network was established, linking the commands on
the reservation with state officials, the South Dakota National Guard, and
civil and military officials in Washington. Though the Administration
wished to avoid giving an impression to the world that it faced a modern-
day Indian war, it was on guard against just such a conflict.

The arrival of the marshals alarmed the reservation people and pro-
voked new protests against Wilson, who they believed had sent for them

for his personal protection. When the chairman managed to postpone his impeachment hearings, some 300 Oglalas, mostly women and children, demonstrated angrily under the noses of the marshals in front of the BIA building in Pine Ridge, demanding the removal of Wilson and Superintendent Lyman and the departure of the marshals. One of the marshals taunted the women with a boast that revived memories of braggart officers like Custer: "Us seventy-five marshals could whip you three hundred Indians very easily." It got the women mad and they marched up to the marshals. "They wouldn't lay a hand on us," said one of the women. "But if they tried . . . we were willing to fight."

On February 22 and 23, Wilson's impeachment hearing was held, presided over by a Wilson-appointed tribal judge. The chairman stood behind him as a coach, acted as prosecutor as well as defendant, and finally manipulated and cowed the council into voting in his favor. At its conclusion, several hundred tribal members left angrily for a meeting under the auspices of OSCRO at the community hall at Calico, near Pine Ridge, to decide what to do next. On their invitation, Russell Means, Dennis Banks, and a large number of medicine men and traditionalist elders joined them. To an extent, the federal agencies had been justified in fearing that AIM was coming to the reservation. Its leaders and many of its members had made frequent threats to do so, and government informers on a number of occasions had reported that AIM members were already leaving for Pine Ridge. But AIM had kept its distance; rumors and alarms had proved groundless; and evidence had accumulated that AIM had no specific plan for militant action on the reservation. It was AIM's policy to enter a reservation only if tribal members sought their assistance. At Calico, that invitation came. With all other avenues of relief closed to Wilson's opponents, the members of OSCRO now asked AIM to come in and help them overthrow Wilson's BIA-supported regime and set up a traditionalist government. "All the people wanted it," said Ellen Moves Camp, a member of OSCRO, who was present. "This was a meeting of people from all over the reservation. All eight districts were represented. All of our older people from the reservation helped us make the decision. Practically all the chiefs on the reservation—just one medicine man wasn't there, but he's real old and he's sickly and he couldn't make it . . . the chiefs said, 'Go ahead and do it, go to Wounded Knee. You can't get in the BIA office and the tribal office, so take your brothers from the American Indian Movement and go to Wounded Knee and make your stand there.' "

The request was accepted. On February 26, caravans of AIM members began to leave Rapid City and other places in South Dakota for the Pine Ridge reservation. After converging on Calico and joining the

OSCRO members, a few of them went to the town of Pine Ridge the next day, where Means was attacked and beaten by two members of Wilson's "goon squad." They returned to Calico, and early that evening cars crowded with Oglalas and AIM members started off for Wounded Knee. At 7:55 p.m., the BIA police phone log in Pine Ridge noted the receipt of an urgent call: "Advised burglary in progress at Wounded Knee store and they are taking all weapons and ammunition." The hamlet of bitter memories of 1890 had been occupied.

The original intention of OSCRO and AIM appears to have been to make a short stand, while conducting negotiations with administration officials that would force the ouster of Wilson and the reinstitution of a traditional-type Oglala government free of BIA control. But a burglary had been committed, Whites in the hamlet had been taken as hostages, and investigating BIA police had been fired upon and driven back. The marshals, FBI agents, and the BIA immediately blocked all roads leading into Wounded Knee and arrested anyone who came out who appeared to have been implicated in the affair. The occupiers set up defensive barricades and roadblocks of their own, and the siege was on.

Soon after it began, a messenger brought out a list of the Indians' demands, including hearings by three Senate committees to review Indian treaties and investigate the handling of Indian affairs by the BIA and the Interior Department and the conditions on all Sioux reservations in South Dakota. That state's senators, McGovern and Abourezk, flew to Pine Ridge, and met briefly with the occupiers in Wounded Knee. After satisfying themselves that the Whites were not being held as hostages but seemed to want to stay to try to protect their property, the senators returned to Washington, unwilling to consider the requested Senate hearings until the occupation ended, though Abourezk questioned the legality of the federal forces on the reservation. Army equipment, including radio-equipped armored personnel carriers (APC's) supplied by the Nebraska National Guard, arrived, reinforcements swelled the number of besiegers to 250, and the containment of the Indians tightened. Sporadic firing increased, and inside the village, the occupiers, many of them armed with rifles and shotguns, dug trenches and built bunkers.

Elsewhere on the reservation, tension and conflict grew. Many persons were frightened and angered by the violent outburst and wanted to see the AIM intruders driven off the reservation. Despite threats and intimidation by the BIA and Wilson and his followers, however, a large number of Oglalas, including a majority of the tribal council members, openly supported the occupiers. Demonstrations were held in their behalf, a petition demanding the departure of the federal forces and the ousting of Wilson was signed by some 1,400 people, and food was collected and carried into Wounded Knee by groups that traveled across the hills and slipped past the roadblocks. At the same time, church leaders and others around the country urged the Administration to end the crisis without violence. On March 4, Justice Department officials met with the occupiers, but attempts to negotiate a settlement broke down, and the siege went on, marked by daily exchanges of gunfire and the wounding of two of the Indians.

Though Wilson and vigilante-type groups of White and half-blood ranchers, whose cattle were being stolen and slaughtered by the occupiers, wanted to attack the village, the Administration issued strict orders against such an assault by anyone. With patience, the occupation of the BIA Building in Washington had ended without loss of life, and, especially with residents of Wounded Knee still in the village, the Administration insisted that violence be kept to a minimum and every opportunity be given the occupiers to give up, after which those guilty of crimes would be apprehended and prosecuted. On March 10, the roadblocks were ordered opened in the hope that the Indians would take the opportunity to come out peaceably. Some of them did so, but several hundred others, including Indians from other tribes who had come to help AIM and the Oglalas, poured in to visit or remain. At one time or another, members of sixty-four different tribes from every part of the country, as well as Whites, Blacks, and Chicanos, were at Wounded Knee. Oglala traditional chiefs and headmen also came in, and on March 11, at a ceremonial gathering in the village, they declared the formation of a new Independent Oglala Nation, reviving the treaty of 1868 as the basis of their relationship with the federal government. They also asked OSCRO and AIM to form a provisional government for the Oglalas, called for the abolition of the BIA tribal-council government, announced their intention to send a delegation to the United Nations, and asked the Iroquois Six Nation Confederacy of the Northeast for recognition and support.

To the occupiers, it was a historic moment. In 1868, the Oglalas under Red Cloud, having forced the U.S. Army to evacuate its forts in the Sioux hunting grounds of Montana and Wyoming, signed a treaty at Fort Laramie that recognized Sioux title to the western Dakotas and eastern Montana and Wyoming. The Oglalas and the other six tribes of the Teton Sioux were sovereign at the time and were treated as such. Beginning in 1871, when Congress ended treaty making with the tribes, and continuing on through a series of incursions into Sioux territory, armed attacks on their people by Custer and others, the seizure of most of their lands, and the herding of the people onto reservations, their sovereignty was taken from them. The violated treaty of 1868 was forgotten, and in 1934 the new tribal-council government was forced on them. But the Oglala chiefs and traditionalists had long memories. The treaty of 1868 had never been canceled. Everything since then, including the taking of the Black Hills and their other lands, was regarded as illegal. Now, they asserted that the treaty must once more be observed, and the sovereignty of the tribes that had signed it must again be recognized.

The Justice Department responded to the defiance by ordering the roadblocks closed again. Fighting resumed, supporters of the occupiers who were caught in the open were arrested, and in one exchange of gunfire, an FBI agent was seriously wounded. Inside Wounded Knee, 182 Oglalas, 160 Indians from other tribes, and seven Whites joined the new Independent Oglala Nation (ION), and two Sioux medicine men, Leonard Crow Dog and Wallace Black Elk, conducted spiritual ceremonies. More than 300 federal men now surrounded them, using searchlights, flares, and tracer bullets to maintain the siege at night. As the fire fights intensified, the defenders set up a clinic and, organizing the rudiments of a government, established committees on defense, internal security, information, housing, medical care, food supply, and customs and immigration.

Outside the reservation, support continued to grow for the Oglalas and their AIM allies. Demonstrations were staged on other reservations and in a number of cities, and food and medical supplies were flown into Wounded Knee by small planes or dropped by parachute. A delegation of Iroquois traditionalist chiefs arrived for a brief visit to show their bond of brotherhood. The Justice Department took countermeasures, guarding the airspace above Wounded Knee with helicopters and occasional sweeps by military planes. In Oregon and several other states, AIM members and supporters of the occupiers were kept under surveillance, and a number of them who started off for Wounded Knee with vans of food, supplies, and arms were arrested on interstate highways. In Gallup, New Mexico, Denver, and Rapid City, Indian and Chicano activists were killed in conflicts related to their support of the people at Wounded Knee.

More negotiations were attempted from March 14 to 17, but were again unsuccessful. In the resumption of firing, an Indian and a marshal were wounded. A Wounded Knee Legal Defense/Offense Committee was formed, and six lawyers for the Indians were given authority by a federal court to bring food each day to the occupiers. The court's order, together with the Justice Department's refusal to permit an all-out attack on Wounded Knee, enraged Wilson and the members of his "goon squad," who turned back the lawyers and their food and set up bunkers of their own. Their reckless fire at night endangered the marshals, who arrested some of them when they refused to return to the town of Pine Ridge.

On March 31, Assistant Attorney Generals Kent Frizzell and Richard Hellstern began new negotiations with representatives of the Independent Oglala Nation, and on April 5 signed an agreement permitting Russell Means, Leonard Crow Dog, and Thomas Bad Cob to go to Washington for a preliminary conference that would plan for a later meeting between White House representatives and the chiefs of all the Teton Sioux tribes to examine the status of the 1868 treaty. The three Oglalas flew to Washington, but the conference was suddenly called off after a disagreement over the technicalities of the terms for ending the occupation. The siege began again and lasted through April. The government tightened the blockade and cut off food and medical supplies. Despite hunger and isolation, the spirit of the occupiers remained high. The fire fights increased in duration and intensity, and two of the Indians in the village were killed. One of them, Buddy Lamont, belonged to a prominent Oglala family and had relatives working for the BIA.

Late in April, Frizzell, newly appointed as the Interior Department's Solicitor, returned to the reservation. Wilson and his followers were still angry at not being allowed to launch their own attack on Wounded Knee, and at one point the chairman and belligerent members of one of his roadblocks held Frizzell, Hellstern, and the chief of the marshals at gunpoint, threatening to kill them, until the marshal drew his own gun and forced an end to the confrontation. Informed that the OSCRO members in Wounded Knee looked to the Oglala spiritual leaders for guidance, Frizzell now turned to them, hoping to persuade them to use their influence to end the occupation. Meeting with the traditionalist chiefs near Kyle, on the land of Frank Fools Crow, the Oglalas' most respected chief and spiritual leader, he announced that the White House was still willing to assign representatives to discuss the 1868 treaty with them, but only after the occupation was ended. If that did not happen soon, he said, an assault would have to be made against the people holding the village. His arguments were persuasive, and on May 1 new negotiations began in two school buses at Wounded Knee. The chiefs joined the sessions on May 2 and advised the acceptance of an agreement to end the occupation. A compromise was worked out under which the government promised a meeting with White House representatives at Kyle later in the month to discuss the 1868 treaty, and both sides agreed to detailed arrangements for the termination of hostilities and the laying down of arms. Occupiers who had federal warrants outstanding against them would submit to arrest, but the government promised that it would refrain from asking for bond or recommending terms of release. In addition, the government would investigate and prosecute all civil and criminal violations against the Oglala people by the tribal government or others and would protect the tribal members against Wilson and his followers.

The government greeted the agreement with relief, for it feared the end of the school term, when thousands of adventurous non-Indian youths might arrive to help the occupiers, and it had begun to plan an all-out tear gas attack on the village to end the siege before that happened. With the agreement signed, many of the occupiers slipped out of the village on the night of May 7, and only 129 Oglalas and AIM members remained when the marshals and FBI agents took over the next day. Fifteen persons with outstanding federal warrants were arrested, and all non-residents of Wounded Knee were taken by bus to Rapid City, where they were arraigned or released. Government violations of the agreement began immediately; several of those who were arrested were released on their own recognizance, but others, at the request of government prosecutors, were held on bails of up to $150,000.

On May 17, Bradley Patterson, leading a delegation of administration representatives, mostly middle-level personnel of the Justice and Interior Departments, arrived on the reservation and met at Fools Crow's place near Kyle for two days with traditionalist chiefs and other representatives of the seven Teton Sioux tribes, as well as of the Northern Cheyennes and Arapahos, who had also been parties to the 1868 treaties at Fort Laramie. The meeting was an awkward one for Patterson, who had no authority to do anything but listen. When the chiefs asked him at once whether the government recognized that the tribes had now reverted to their status under the treaty of 1868, he had to say, "No," telling them that only Congress could grant that approval and that, under the Indian Reorganization Act of 1934, the government had to recognize, and deal with, whomever the tribes elected to lead the tribal council governments. It angered the chiefs, who nevertheless pressed the demands for which the people at Wounded Knee had been fighting. They wanted a presidential treaty commission; a referendum vote to choose between BIA tribal government and a return to an independent, traditional system; the prosecution of those who had committed crimes against the Indian peoples; and the protection of their water and mineral resources, which were being threatened by energy companies and non-Indian developers. Bob Burnette, representing the Rosebud Sioux, was also there. "We have to have these changes," he said, "or there will be Wounded Knees after Wounded Knees after Wounded Knees in various ways." Others agreed with him. "What took place in Wounded Knee," exclaimed Irma Rooks, an Oglala from the Pine Ridge community of Wanblee, "is that *we don't want* tribal council, we *don't want* BIA. We want our 1868 treaty!"

Patterson and his colleagues finally left for Washington, promising to consider the requests and return to Kyle in two weeks. At the appointed time, several hundred Indians gathered again at Fools Crow's place, but the Washington delegation failed to appear. Instead, a marshal delivered a letter from Patterson's superior, Leonard Garment. "The days of treaty making with the American Indians ended in 1871, 102 years ago," it read. "Only Congress can rescind or change in any way statutes enacted since 1871, such as the Indian Reorganization Act . . ."

Wounded Knee II was over, Richard Wilson and his BIA-supported tribal council government were still in power, and the Independent Oglala Nation was again only a memory and a dream. But throughout Indian America, the confrontation had been a watershed event.

For a while, the impact of the occupation was obscured by a campaign of repression against those who had participated in it. With the ending of the siege, the Justice Department set out to smash AIM and all troublemaking Indian organizations like OSCRO. On the Pine Ridge reservation, Frizzell's promises became more agreements broken by legalisms that took no account of what Wounded Knee had been all about. If investigations were made of crimes against the Oglalas, they were made without their knowledge, and they failed to lead to a single prosecution. Instead, the Justice Department looked away while Wilson's "goon squad" and the BIA police instituted a new reign of terror. People were burned out, beaten, and run over by cars. Pedro Bissonette, one of the original organizers of OSCRO, was killed by BIA police; Byron DeSersa, another OSCRO leader, was slain by Wilson's "goons." OSCRO's non-Indian lawyers who came on the reservation were bullied and threatened, and one group had their plane shot up and were then set upon and beaten mercilessly by the chairman's men, whom Wilson ordered to "stomp 'em," when they tried to escape by automobile. Sometimes the people fought back, and "goons" too were killed. Two of them were slain in retribution after ramming a car off a road and killing an Oglala mother and her four-month-old daughter. All the while, Wilson continued to rule dictatorially, squashing demands of impoverished Oglala landowners for fairer rentals for grazing lands that the BIA leased for them to White ranchers and, in June 1975, relinquishing tribal title to an abandoned federal gunnery range, equal to one-eighth of the reservation's land surface, and signing it over to the National Park Service against the wishes of most of the tribe.

AIM was no longer in a position to help the people. Wherever its leaders and members went, they were hounded by the FBI and state law enforcement officers. A total of 562 people were arrested and charged with various offenses in connection with the confrontation at Wounded Knee. Only fifteen of them were eventually convicted, five for interfering with federal officers. The rest had their charges dismissed or were acquitted. Means and Banks, facing five charges each, were tried in St. Paul, Minnesota, in 1974, and had all the charges against them dismissed when the federal judge accused the FBI of lying repeatedly under oath, furnishing altered documents to the defense attorneys, and planting a paid spy in the defense camp. The government abandoned consideration of an appeal after the judge said disgustedly that "the FBI has stooped to a new low," and seven jurors wrote to the Attorney General that the prosecution's tactics were so foul that an appeal should not be attempted.

Federal and state authorities nevertheless continued to harass Means, Banks, and other AIM leaders and haul them into different courts. By 1979, Means had faced five federal and seven state indictments altogether, involving charges of thirty-seven felonies and three misdemeanors. Thirty-nine of the forty charges had ended in his exoneration. Banks was kept almost as busy staying out of jail. Threatened with incarceration in a South Dakota prison, where he had reason to believe that the attorney general of the state would connive in his murder, he finally escaped to California, whose governor, Jerry Brown, refused to extradite him to South Dakota.

In 1974, Wilson ran again for tribal chairman, though no one had ever held the office for two consecutive terms. Means, whose case had not yet been dismissed in St. Paul, entered the campaign against him. The chairman again called in the FBI for protection, but in the primary, which a number of persons entered, Means ran highest, receiving 683 votes to Wilson's 525. In the runoff between the two men, Wilson engaged in wholesale vote buying and fraud at the polling places and defeated Means. None of Means's charges was investigated, and Wilson was again installed in office with BIA and Justice Department support. His second administration was as turbulent as the first. FBI agents, including members of a Special Weapons and Tactics team (SWAT) trained as a paramilitary unit, roamed the reservation, invading homes and threatening Wilson's opponents and, with the BIA police and "goon squad," kept alive the terror. As the violence and murders continued, unrest again soared. On June 25, 1975, a BIA policeman killed a young Oglala named Joe Stuntz. The next day, in an exchange of gunfire, two FBI agents were slain outside a house about fifteen miles from the town of Pine Ridge. Retribution was furious. The occupants of the house scattered, but in the following months many Indians were harassed, threatened, and arrested on a variety of charges related to the killings and the flight of the suspects. Two Oglalas, charged with the murders, were finally caught and tried, but were acquitted by an all-White jury. Leonard Peltier, another suspect, was arrested in Canada, extradited to the United States, and sent to prison after a controversial trial, marked by testimony against him which his lawyers charged was false.

Still other Indians suffered. Leonard Crow Dog, the medicine man, was arrested at his home on the Rosebud reservation after provocative actions against him by the FBI, and was shunted from prison to prison across the United States, being beaten and humiliated, before church leaders and other influential Whites interceded for him and won his release. A particularly odious murder was that of Anna Mae Aquash, a Micmac Indian woman from Nova Scotia, who had originally come to Pine Ridge to help the occupiers at Wounded Knee. The FBI believed that she had been a witness to the killing of the two agents. In February 1976, her body was found on the reservation. After an examination of her remains, a BIA-hired pathologist announced that she had died of natural causes—probably exposure. Later, her body was exhumed, and an independent pathologist discovered in her head a .32-caliber bullet, which had been fired from a gun placed at the back of her neck, execution style. When the BIA's pathologist was questioned, he retorted, "A little bullet isn't hard to overlook."

In 1976, Wilson ran for an unprecedented third term. Despite more threats and strong-arm tactics, he was finally beaten, and relative peace settled over the reservation. Al Trimble, the new chairman, ended the "goon squad" and its reign of terror, restored civil rights, and worked to make his administration and the council responsive to his people. But the BIA still controlled the reservation, and the traditionalists and chiefs, aware that another dictator could follow Trimble, still demanded a return of sovereignty under the 1868 treaty.

AIM, too, survived. The arrests and harassments softened its militancy, but it still gave leadership to a large following of traditionalists and young Indians. Out of its own struggles, as well as those waged by groups of grass-roots people and their spiritual teachers on various reservations, there emerged in 1974 a new movement called the International Indian Treaty Council. Stemming largely from the Indians' inability to force the United States to recognize tribal sovereignty—as proved at Wounded Knee—it came into being at a meeting of several thousand Indians, representing ninety-seven tribes in the United States, Canada, and elsewhere in the Americas, held at Mobridge, South Dakota, near the grave of Sitting Bull on the Standing Rock Sioux reservation. Guided by the counsel of the traditionalist chiefs and spiritual leaders, the organizers decided to take their fight for the rights and sovereignty of Native Americans in the United States and the rest of the Western Hemisphere over the heads of the national governments, to the United Nations. They opened an office across the street from the UN Building in New York, published a newsletter, and began sending delegations of traditionalist spokesmen and medicine men to international meetings concerned with the rights of indigenous peoples.

Each year, through the 1970's, the Council conducted conferences on different Indian reservations, becoming stronger in numbers and influence. Eventually, the United Nations accorded it the official status of a non-governmental organization. At UN-sponsored meetings in Geneva, Rotterdam, and elsewhere, its delegations, led by chiefs and spiritual headmen of various tribes, established ties with indigenous peoples from other parts of the world and utilized the international forums to try to make the world aware of their struggles against colonialism and for human rights and sovereignty. Though the Council was unrecognized and frowned upon by the U.S. government—which continued to ignore dissident groups, including a "Longest Walk" across the United States to Washington by traditionalists protesting anti-Indian legislation in 1978 —the Council's potential as an influential force in the future of Indian affairs was not insignificant; in 1981, its prestige was bolstered when the Movement of the Non-Aligned Nations of the world gave it full observer status at their triennial meeting to be held in Baghdad, Iraq, the following year.

The impact of Wounded Knee was, meanwhile, bringing other changes. The seventy-one-day stand against the power of the United States had affected Indians on other reservations, and had intensified anti-BIA feelings among traditionalists, grass-roots families, and young Indians, as well as many tribal leaders themselves. As a catalyst, the confrontation increased demands for self-determination, and trends that had begun in the 1960's quickened. Fearing Wounded Knees on their own reservations, tribal governments showed a greater concern for the support of their own people and became bolder and more independent —sometimes even threatening—in their relations with the BIA. The reactions of the superintendents and their staffs varied from tribe to tribe. Though their veto power over the reservations' financial affairs guaranteed their retention of control, many of them backed away diplomatically or in fear, permitting the tribal leaders to run more of their reservations' affairs themselves, acquiescing in tribal decisions to hire independent lawyers and technical experts to help them file suits for their rights and resources, and staying aloof from those suits, as well as all other conflicts, both within the tribe and with outsiders, with the explanation that they "did not want to interfere with the tribe's wishes."

Among the tribal politicians, the newly acquired authority increased a demand for more of it. The federal government, too, feared more Wounded Knees and, continuing to rely on the elected tribal leaders as their strongest bulwarks against new troubles, took steps to ensure their loyalty. The policy of contracting services, which the tribal governments could administer on their own, had been halted before the takeover of the BIA Building, but in 1974 Congress passed an Indian Self-Determination and Education Assistance Act, which, becoming operative in 1975, reinstituted the policy. The statute authorized the Secretary of the Interior to implement a self-determination policy "which will permit an orderly transition from federal domination of programs for and services to Indians to effective and meaningful participation by the Indian people in the planning, conduct, and administration of those programs and services." One section required the awarding of a contract for any part of a government program on the application of a tribe. Another authorized contracts and grants to train Indians to operate programs they might someday want to take over in full.

In practice, the Act stimulated tribes to assume the management of more of their own affairs and broaden and strengthen their expertise and self-confidence. But it also proved to be an immense placating gesture to the tribes, and escalated many of the opportunities for individual aggrandizement that the federal anti-poverty programs had first brought to the reservations in the 1960's. This time, however, there was a difference. As tribes signed contracts, funds again poured onto the reservations and into the hands of the tribal officers and the administrators of the special organizations that were set up to manage the programs. Additional programs were requested, and authorized, and federal appropriations for Indians, which had totaled $120 million in 1960, soared beyond $2 billion annually. Though much of it supported the swollen BIA bureaucracy, unprecedented sums reached the reservations. Accountability to the BIA had weakened, but the tribal leaders, as a rule, could no longer channel the money and the jobs simply to their friends and relatives. There were now large sophisticated elements of the population able to meet the specialized requirements of many of the top-paying positions and eager to fill them and serve the tribe. Many Indians—both men and women—had become educated, and more were emerging from colleges and universities each year, some with graduate school degrees. Others had returned to the reservations with professional backgrounds and skills learned in the cities. Still others were former protesters who had demonstrated for self-determination and sovereignty and had acquired organizational experience during their political activism. After the lesson of Wounded Knee, most tribal leaders shied away from arousing opposition by a too blatant display of favoritism and, with abundant jobs available, permitted many of them to be filled on the basis of qualifications.

The spreading of the largesse, however, often seemed only to worsen some of the earlier problems. Charges of graft, corruption, and mismanagement, this time on a larger scale, were again rampant. On many reservations, people complained that most of the government's funds went to the BIA and the officeholders, and not to the intended beneficiaries, and that what little did "trickle down" to the grass-roots Indians failed to relieve their distress. There was truth to the complaints. Among the Red Lake Chippewas, the Navajos, some of the Pueblos, and other groups, grumblings and revolts broke out against top leaders who flaunted their newly acquired affluence and created new cliques of syco-phants and sub-bosses, which the Indians referred to as "Mafias." Stan-dards of living rose on all levels, but only slowly among the bulk of the population, and most of the chronic ills of daily life—unemployment, substandard housing, poor sanitation, and so forth—continued. Even the increased purchasing power of the jobholders was deceptive. Much of their income was spent on consumer goods and travel. When programs ended or federal funding was reduced, individuals lost their jobs and were again unemployed and broke. Most of the programs dealt with such matters as education and vocational training; the construction of hous-ing, roads, and tribal buildings; the delivery of social services to children, the aged, and the needy; and various aspects of the day-to-day operations of tribal governments. Few were designed to improve the long-range economic viability of the reservations or produce sources of continuous employment.

This was demonstrated dramatically beginning in 1981, when the Reagan administration's severe cutbacks in federal spending struck par-ticularly hard at the reservations. Under the Carter administration, ap-propriations for programs designed specifically for Indians had con-stituted .04 percent of the national budget. Under the new administration, the decreases in spending for those programs repre-sented 2½ percent of all the cuts in the fiscal-year 1982 budget. In addition, Indians were seriously affected by the elimination of, or the reduction of funds for, federal programs benefiting the general popula-tion, such as those of the Economic Development Administration, the Community Services Administration, the Legal Services Corporation, and the public employment programs of the Comprehensive Employ-ment and Training Act (CETA), as well as Medicaid, food stamps, aid to dependent children, Head Start, and other assistance programs on which the tribes relied. In sum, by the end of 1981 it was estimated that cutbacks in federal programs for Indians totaled about $500 million, and that Indians were experiencing cuts ten times greater than those affecting their non-Indian fellow Americans. Moreover, in 1982, additional and deeper cuts were threatened for the 1983 and 1984 fiscal-year budgets.

The reduced funds affected almost all aspects of reservation life, including health, housing, education, economic development, management training, the construction and maintenance of facilities, and the delivery of agricultural, legal, and social-welfare services. The forward motion of the tribes faltered; thousands of Indians lost their jobs; and reservation unemployment, increased further by the economic recession that began in 1981, rose abruptly from an average of about 35 percent to as high as 85, and even 95, percent among some tribes. Indian leaders sought in vain a restoration of the previous levels of federal spending. "Just when we were starting to get our hands on the ledge, to pull ourselves up—whack! We're dropped right back where we were before," complained William Morgan, the director of administration and finance for the Navajo Nation, whose unemployed had nearly doubled to more than 70 percent in 1981 and were expected to reach 80 percent in 1982. But the cuts stuck and, amid a widespread renewal of Indian hardship and suffering, it became evident how fragile the reservations' economies were and how little the previous spending had done to establish an enduring base for tribal economic viability.

Meanwhile, the gusher of federal funds in the years prior to "Reaganomics" had co-opted not only the tribal leaders and politicians but also many of the ablest and best-educated members of the tribes, converting them into an elite stratum of neutralized reservation bureaucrats who were torn, in their relative well-being, between acceptance of the ways of the Whites and loyalty to the traditions of their people. Though they pushed aside the Bureau and asserted authority for themselves and their tribes over an increasing number of matters, most of them became content to accept the Indian Reorganization Act form of government as permanent and tried to win the people's acceptance of it by making it more responsible and democratic. In a number of tribes, formerly militant members of AIM and the NIYC won election to positions of leadership. Some of them wished to break relations with the BIA and reinstitute traditionalist forms of government, but did not have the power to do so. Most of them, however, went along with the IRA government as it existed, working only to make it more responsive to, and protective of, the people.

Nothing basic, in fact, had changed. The tribes still wanted the government to observe its treaty obligations and provide trust protection of their property, and as long as that was so, the BIA's personnel, averse to losing their own jobs, retained ultimate control over the reservation's resources and fiscal affairs. Though now often shoved to the rear and ignored, the colonialist superintendents and area officers still held the purse strings. A 1977 report of an American Indian Policy Review Commission, created by the Senate, chaired by Senator Abourezk, and guided by task forces composed almost entirely of Indians, made it clear that the Self-Determination Act of 1974 had failed to give the tribes true self-determination or to provide fundamental answers to their grievances and problems.

The impact of the energy crisis in the late 1970's illuminated sharply the many different groups and contesting points of view with which the American Indians entered the decade of the 1980's. According to Interior Department estimates in 1977, tribes in the western half of the United States owned approximately 11 percent of all the coal reserves in the nation; at least 30 percent of all low-sulfur coal west of the Mississippi River capable of being strip-mined; between 40 and 50 percent of the country's privately owned uranium; some 4 percent of the United States' oil and natural gas reserves; and a large share of the nation's oil shale and geothermal resources. In view of the government's efforts to reduce America's dependence on oil imports, it was inevitable that the possession of those resources would bring vast new pressures on the tribes.

Conflicts had already broken out within several tribes over energy-resource leases which—as related earlier—tribal leaders, under government pressure, had signed, or were about to sign, with private companies or syndicates of speculators. In general, the leaders welcomed the money, but the traditionalists, spiritual teachers, and many younger Indians feared the impact that the developments would have on their lands and cultures, and fought the leaders over the leases. It was too late to undo many of the contracts, but in the course of the conflicts, the leaders generally came to acknowledge that the terms of most of the leases had been unfair and had failed to provide protections that the tribes had had a right to expect. Now, the same tribes, as well as others—most of whose people had standards of living far below those of neighboring non-Indians, lacked many of the necessities of life, and were without the capital or access to adequate credit to meet their most elemental needs—were suddenly confronted by huge multinational corporations promising to help end their impoverishment with offers of tens and hundreds of millions of dollars for new exploration permits and leases on their reservations.

Again, the people divided—the spiritual leaders and their traditionalist followers arguing against energy developments that would despoil their lands, air, and water, destroy their sacred sites, and imperil the survival of the people and their culture; and the political leaders, many of them known as "progressives," trying to find a way for their tribes to help the nation patriotically and at the same time satisfy their people that they were being neither cheated nor left unprotected. The conflict was a new, intensive stage of the long fight for self-determination and sove-reignty, and once more the power lay with the elected tribal officials.

Under the leadership of Peter MacDonald, the chairman of the Nava-jos, twenty-two tribes (later joined by others) in September 1975 estab-lished a Council of Energy Resource Tribes, known as CERT, "to pro-mote the general welfare of energy resource owning tribes and their people through the protection, conservation and prudent management of their oil, natural gas, coal, uranium, geothermal, and oil shale re-sources." The formation of CERT implied that, with or without the approval of the traditionalists, energy development would occur on the reservations. By standing together, however, MacDonald and the other tribal officials hoped to meet the companies as equals and make their own decisions on the scope, terms, timing, protections, and other conditions of the development, and not permit the government to do it for them.

The tribal leaders maintained that this was self-determination, but in the end the BIA still had to approve whatever the tribes did. Indeed, on at least one occasion, the Department of the Interior voided a contract that MacDonald himself had negotiated with Consolidation Coal Com-pany and El Paso Natural Gas Company for the strip-mining of Navajo-owned coal to be used by proposed gasification plants on the Navajo reservation. The Department's veto pleased the Navajo traditionalists, but angered MacDonald, who had to accept the interference as proof that the tribes did not yet possess real self-determination or sovereignty. CERT, moreover, in seeking funding for its initial proposals—the inven-torying of reservation energy resources, the renegotiation of bad leases, and the supplying of technical and developmental assistance to the mem-ber tribes—turned to the federal government from whose authority it was, at the same time, trying to break away. At first, the government rebuffed CERT's request for financial grants, but when MacDonald began to meet with representatives of OPEC, the international oil cartel, seeking their advice, and hired independent energy experts who sug-gested that CERT could become another OPEC, the government did an abrupt about-face. In 1977, the BIA and the Economic Development Administration granted CERT $200,000, and the following year the Bu-reau, the Department of Energy, and two other agencies gave it $2 million to open a Denver office and provide technical services to the tribes and education and training in energy-related fields to young Indians. Neither the irony nor the menace of this government funding was lost on the traditionalists, who, far from regarding CERT as a manifestation of In-dian self-determination, attacked it as the agent of the White man's final assault on the reservations and their people.

CERT, however, grew steadily stronger, and by 1982, still heavily funded by the government, it was speaking out in the name of all Indians on other matters in addition to energy affairs. The great majority of the tribes, most of which could not join CERT because they possessed no energy resources, as well as the old-line national Indian groups like the NCAI, the National Tribal Chairmen's Association, and the National Indian Youth Council, grew wary—and even more bothered when many non-Indians, in and out of government, began to view CERT as the answer to the question: "Whom can we deal with who really represents the American Indians?" In the face of the tensions generated by the energy crisis, the resource-owning tribes were responding to the nation's needs, opening their reservations to energy development, and they seemed to be doing so chiefly under the stimulus of CERT's leadership. Each tribe actually made its own decisions and proceeded in its own way —some signing leases with the companies, some forming partnership arrangements with them, others retaining ownership and control of the resources and contracting with the companies to carry out the development, and still others forming wholly owned tribal energy-development companies that became part-owners of equity ventures with non-Indian companies.

In one celebrated case, moreover, the U.S. Supreme Court, on January 25, 1982, upheld the right of the Jicarilla Apache tribe in New Mexico to impose severance taxes on energy companies taking oil, natural gas, or other energy resources from its reservation, just as if it were a state. "The power to tax is an essential attribute of Indian sovereignty because it is a necessary instrument of self-government and territorial management," the Court ruled. CERT—which was already demanding that the federal government recognize the sovereignty of tribal governments by treating them like states, delegating to them the same responsibilities, providing them with the same support, and giving them the same tax privileges—viewed the decision as an important precedent for its position. The state of Montana had already won the right to levy severance taxes on companies taking energy resources from its lands; now Indian tribes could do the same.

The significance of the decision was also not lost on the Reagan administration, which in the beginning of 1982 was considering letting the states fund many Indian programs in the future from moneys received in block grants from the federal government under its "New Federalism" policy. The tribes opposed the policy, since they would have to compete with non-Indian interests within the states for their share of the grants; and, amid widespread general concern that reduced funds in the grants would adversely affect all programs, the Indians particularly feared that there would be little allocated to them. Under CERT's leadership, they made headway after the Jicarilla decision in persuading the Administration to make block grants for Indian programs at adequate levels of funding directly to the tribes as though they were states.

What mattered most to the government was that CERT was getting the energy resource-developing companies onto the reservations. For the 1980's, it made CERT the most relevant Indian voice, and the nation's corporate, financial, and governmental leaders courted CERT and its members in the same manner in which they courted the rulers of oil-rich Saudi Arabia and Kuwait. On March 1, 1981, several hundred leading non-Indian industrialists, insurance company executives, energy conglomerate board members, bankers, and Wall Street investment house partners joined an equal number of CERT members and tribal leaders at a gala black-tie dinner at the Pierre Hotel in New York City that symbolized the new Indian-White partnership. The tables of ten sold for $1,000 apiece. A year later, on March 4, 1982, the partnership was celebrated again, this time with a Hollywood-produced extravaganza, "Night of the First Americans," at the Kennedy Center in Washington, D.C., with box seats selling for $5,000 each and President Reagan, Vice-President Bush, and a host of administration, Congressional, business, and social leaders among the patrons helping CERT and the energy companies salute all American Indians.

Among the Indian tribal officers at both affairs were a number of former militant members of the NIYC and AIM. They had come a long way since the occupation of the BIA Building in the capital ten years before, and it remains to be seen whether the road they are following will eventually win true freedom of action, sovereignty, and accountable self-government for their reservations and tribal groups. "I sense that one day energy projects on CERT-member lands shall be singled out by the rest of the world as models for how development can occur in a manner which respects the natural and cultural environment as well," Peter MacDonald told the diners in New York in 1981. "That is how it must be—for real 'progress' in the view of my people must transcend profits. It must outlast generations. It must help us realize a vision articulated by Chief Joseph of the Nez Perces a century ago: 'Let me be a free man—free to travel, free to stop, free to work, free to trade where I choose, free to choose my own teachers, free to follow the religion of my fathers, free to think and act and talk for myself. . . . For this time, the Indian race are waiting and praying.' "

On that night in 1981, other Native Americans, not in black ties, had the same goals but were following many different roads in their efforts to attain them. On the North Slope of Alaska, Eskimos, also striving for sovereignty, were planning meetings with Eskimos of Canada, Greenland, and Siberia in an independent Inuit Circumpolar Conference to discuss joint action on mutual problems. In upper New York State, Mohawks had established a free community at Akwesasne and proclaimed it a sovereign Mohawk Nation. In Oklahoma, traditional and grass-roots Choctaws and Chickasaws, rebelling against their tribal leaders, had won the right in a decision by the U.S. Court of Appeals for the District of Columbia to adopt new tribal constitutions incorporating provisions of their governments of 120 years before. At Big Mountain, Arizona, traditionalist Hopis and Navajos were fighting efforts of the Hopi tribal leadership and the federal government to force the removal of more than 9,000 Navajos from lands that were sacred to traditionalists of both tribes and which energy companies were eyeing for strip mining. In a score of states, other tribes, in various ways, were trying to establish other hallmarks of self-determination, such as the right of criminal jurisdiction, taxation, and protection of their children against state welfare agencies on their reservations.

And in South Dakota, Russell Means and Oglala Lakotas, condemning their tribal government's acceptance of a belated U.S. payment for the seizure of the Black Hills from their fathers in the nineteenth century, which would abandon forever the Teton Sioux's rights to that sacred area, were continuing their struggle. They established Yellow Thunder Encampment in the Black Hills (named for Raymond Yellow Thunder, who had been murdered at Gordon, Nebraska, in 1972), in hopes of building there a permanent Indian spiritual and educational community, in defiance of the U.S. Forest Service and the state of South Dakota, which threatened to eject them from that part of their people's homeland. They were thus remaining true to the last message their angry chiefs had sent to Leonard Garment in 1972 when the government broke off the discussions of the treaty of 1868 after the siege at Wounded Knee:

"In the coming years you will find greater resistance to the Government's unresponsive rules, regulations, and its so-called 'policies.' Our forefathers died protecting this land, and we would be cowards if we continue to allow the federal, state and local governments to continue racial and cultural genocide against us and our Indian brothers and sisters across this continent. . . ."

BIBLIOGRAPHY

Chapter 1: "I Will Die an Indian!"

THIS CHAPTER is essentially history and is based on the primary and secondary sources listed below. In addition, special acknowledgment is due the Association on American Indian Affairs in New York; Charles Hudson for his excellent modern study, *The Southeastern Indians;* and William C. Sturtevant of the Smithsonian Institution.

Barcía Carballido y Zúñiga, Andreas Gonzales de, *Chronological History of the Continent of Florida,* trans. by Anthony Kerrigan, introduction by Herbert E. Bolton. University of Florida Press, Gainesville, 1951.

De La Vega, Garcilaso, *The Florida of the Inca,* trans. by John and Jeannette Varner. University of Texas Press, Austin, 1951.

Dormer, Elinore M., *The Sea Shell Islands.* Vantage, New York, 1975.

Hartley, William and Ellen, *Osceola, the Unconquered Indian.* Hawthorn, New York, 1973.

Hudson, Charles, *The Southeastern Indians.* University of Tennessee Press, Knoxville, 1976.

———, ed., *Red, White, and Black: Symposium on Indians in the Old South.* Southern Anthropological Society Proceedings, No. 5. University of Georgia Press, Athens, 1971.

Indian Affairs. Association on American Indian Affairs, New York. No. 58 (March 1965); No. 81 (July 1971); No. 93 (December–March 1977); No. 98 (Fall–Winter 1978–79).

Indian Natural Resources. Association on American Indian Affairs, New York. No. 5 (February 1979).

Jennings, Francis, *The Invasion of America.* University of North Carolina Press, Chapel Hill, 1975.

Lorant, Stefan, ed., *The New World.* Duell, Sloan and Pearce, New York, 1946, 1965.

McReynolds, Edwin C., *The Seminoles.* University of Oklahoma Press, Norman, 1957.

Milanich, Jerald T., and Sturtevant, William C., eds. *Francisco Pareja's 1613 Confesionario: A Documentary Source for Timucuan Ethnography.* Division of Archives, History, and Records Management, Florida Department of State, Tallahassee, 1972.

Pareja, Francisco, *Confesionario, en Lengua Castellana y Timuquana.* Mexico, 1613.

Quinn, David B., *North America from Earliest Discovery to First Settlements.* Harper & Row, New York, 1977.

Sturtevant, William C., "Spanish-Indian Relations in Southeastern North America," *Ethnohistory,* Vol. 9 (1962), pp. 41–94.

———, "Creek into Seminole," *North American Indians in Historical Perspective,* ed. Eleanor Burke Leacock and Nancy Oestreich Lurie. Random House, New York, 1971.

Swanton, John R., *The Indian Tribes of North America.* Bulletin 145, Bureau of American Ethnology, Washington, D.C., 1952.

———, *Early History of the Creek Indians and Their Neighbors.* Bulletin 73, Bureau of American Ethnology, Washington, D.C., 1922.

———, *The Indians of the Southeastern United States.* Bulletin 137, Bureau of American Ethnology, Washington, D.C., 1946.

Tabeau, Charlton W., *A History of Florida.* University of Miami Press, Coral Gables, 1971.

U.S. Senate Select Committee on Indian Affairs, *Hearing on Distribution of Seminole Judgment Funds.* 95th Congress, 2nd Session, March 2, 1978. Washington, D.C., 1978.

Willey, Gordon R., *An Introduction to American Archaeology.* Vol. 1: *North and Middle America.* Prentice-Hall, Englewood Cliffs, N.J., 1966.

Chapter 2: "The Lord Giveth and the Lord Taketh Away"

AGAIN, this is primarily a chapter of history, based on the sources listed below. But I owe a particular debt to two works which—though perhaps controversial —rang with reality to me and either lent support to interpretations I had already formed or helped me firm up those interpretations: *The Invasion of America* by Francis Jennings and Lynn Ceci's Ph.D. dissertation. After reading the latter and then returning to Puritan writings, I was able to see more clearly what is usually overlooked—the economic aspect of the Pequot War.

Artifacts. American Indian Archaeological Institute, Washington, Conn., Vol. 6, Nos. 1, 2, 3 (Autumn, Winter 1977; Spring 1978).

Bartlett, John Russell, ed., *Letters of Roger Williams, 1632–1682.* Narragansett Club, *Publications,* Vol. 6, Providence, R.I., 1874.

Beer, David F., "Anti-Indian Sentiment in Early Colonial Literature." *The Indian Historian,* San Francisco, Vol. 2, No. 1 (Spring 1969).

Black, Robert C., III, *The Younger John Winthrop.* Columbia University Press, New York, 1966.

Bonfanti, Leo, *The Pequot-Mohican War.* Pride Publications, Wakefield, Mass., 1971.

Bradford, William, *Of Plymouth Plantation, 1620–1647,* ed. Samuel Eliot Morison. Alfred A. Knopf, New York, 1952.

"Brief History of the Establishment of the Western (Masshantuxet) Pequot Reservation." Native American Rights Fund, Boulder, Colo., n.d.

Bibliography

Ceci, Lynn, "The Effect of European Contact and Trade on the Settlement Pattern of Indians in Coastal New York, 1524–1665: The Archeological and Documentary Evidence." Ph.D. Dissertation, City University of New York, 1977.

"Connecticut Indians and Their Reservations." Connecticut Indian Affairs Council, Hartford, n.d.

Cook, Sherburne F., "The Significance of Disease in the Extinction of the New England Indians." *Human Biology*, Vol. 45 (1973), pp. 485–508.

DeForest, John W., *History of the Indians of Connecticut.* Wm. James Hamersley, Hartford, 1851.

Dobyns, Henry F., "Estimating Aboriginal American Population . . ." *Current Anthropology*, Vol. 7 (1966).

———, "The Historic Demography of Indoamericans." Address to Organization of American Historians, Atlanta, April 7, 1977.

Gardiner, Lion, "Leift. Lion Gardiner his relation of the Pequot Warres." Massachusetts Historical Society, *Collections,* 3d Ser., Vol. 3, pp. 131–60, Cambridge, Mass., 1833.

Jacobs, Wilbur R., *Dispossessing the American Indian.* Scribner's, New York, 1972.

Jennings, Francis, *The Invasion of America.* University of North Carolina Press, Chapel Hill, 1975.

Josephy, Alvin M., Jr., *The Indian Heritage of America.* Alfred A. Knopf, New York, 1968.

———, "Indians of the Sound," Parts 1 and 2, *On the Sound,* New York, Vol. 2, Nos. 1, 2 (January, February 1972).

LaFantasie, Glenn W., and Campbell, Paul R., "Covenants of Grace, Covenants of Wrath: Niantic-Puritan Relations in New England." *Rhode Island History,* February 1978, pp. 14–23.

Malone, Patrick M., "Changing Military Technology Among the Indians of Southern New England, 1600–1677." *American Quarterly,* Vol. 25 (1973), pp. 48–63.

Marashio, Paul, "Puritan and Pequot." *The Indian Historian,* San Francisco, Vol. 3, No. 3 (Summer 1970).

Mason, John, *A Brief History of the Pequot War.* March of America Facsimile Series, No. 23, Ann Arbor, Mich., 1966.

Means, Carroll A., "Mohegan-Pequot Relationships as Indicated by the Events Leading to the Pequot Massacre of 1637 and Subsequent Claims in the Mohegan Land Controversy." *Bulletin of the Archaeological Society of Connecticut,* Vol. 21 (December 1947), pp. 26–34.

Metcalf, P. Richard, "Who Should Rule at Home? Native American Politics and Indian-White Relations." *Journal of American History,* Vol. 61, No. 3 (December 1974), pp. 651–65.

Molloy, Anne, *Wampum.* Hastings House, New York, 1977.

Momaday, N. Scott, "The Morality of Indian Hating." *Ramparts,* Vol. 3 (Summer 1964), pp. 29–40.

Native American Rights Fund, Boulder, Colo., *Announcements,* Vol. 4, Nos. 1, 2 (August 1977). Vol. 7, No. 2 (June 1981).

Quinn, David B., *North America from Earliest Discovery to First Settlements.* Harper & Row, New York, 1977.

Segal, Charles M., and Stineback, David C., *Puritans, Indians and Manifest Destiny.* Putnam, New York, 1977.

Sehr, Timothy J., "Ninigret's Tactics of Accommodation: Indian Diplomacy in New England, 1637–1675." *Rhode Island History,* May 1977, pp. 42–53.

Slotkin, Richard, and Folsom, James K., eds., *So Dreadful a Judgment.* Wesleyan University Press, Middletown, Conn., 1978.

Speck, Frank G., "Native Tribes and Dialects of Connecticut: A Mohegan-Pequot Diary." *Bureau of American Ethnology, Annual Report, 1925–26,* Vol. 43, Washington, D.C., 1928.

———, "Notes on the Mohegan and Niantic Indians." *Anthropological Papers of the American Museum of Natural History,* Vol. 3 (1909), pp. 183–210.

Swigart, Edmund K., *The Prehistory of the Indians of Western Connecticut.* Part 1: *9000–1000 B.C.* American Indian Archaeological Institute, Washington, Conn., 1978.

Trigger, Bruce G., ed., *Handbook of North American Indians.* Vol. 15: *Northeast,* Smithsonian Institution, Washington, D.C., 1978.

Vaughan, Alden T., *New England Frontier: Puritans and Indians, 1620–1675.* Boston, 1965.

Weeden, William B., *Economic and Social History of New England, 1620–1789.* 2 vols., Boston, 1890.

Whipple, Chandler, *The Indian in Connecticut.* Berkshire Traveller Press, Stockbridge, Mass., 1972.

Williams, Roger, *A Key into the Language of America,* ed. John J. Teunissen and Evelyn J. Hinz. Wayne State University Press, Detroit, 1973.

Winthrop, John, *The History of New England from 1630 to 1649,* ed. James Savage. 2d ed., 2 vols., Boston, 1853.

Chapter 3: "Give the Papoose a Chance"

FOR THE CULTURAL MATERIALS in this chapter, I owe a particular debt to the works of two friends, Alfonso Ortiz and the late Edward P. Dozier, both distinguished Pueblo Indian scholars. I am also extremely grateful to William C. Schaab of Albuquerque, Paul Bernal of Taos pueblo, and Corinne Locker of Santa Fe for their trust and valuable help. This is the first chapter that relies in large part on documentary materials that I have gathered during the years and that, as far as I know, are not in any archive. They will be on deposit at the Library of the University of Oregon in Eugene.

Aberle, S. D., "The Pueblo Indians of New Mexico: Their Land, Economy, and Civil Organization." American Anthropological Association, Memoir No. 70, Vol. 50, No. 4, Part 2, Menasha, Wisc.

Akwesasne Notes, Mohawk Nation via Roosevelttown, N.Y. "Sacred Blue Lake Restored to Taos." Vol. 3, No. 1 (January–February 1971).

———, Vol. 11, No. 4 (Autumn 1979).

Bibliography

American Indian Horizon, New York. "The Holy Land of Taos Pueblo." Vol. 3, No. 6 (Spring 1966), pp. 1–2.

American Indian Religious Freedom Act Report (P.L. 95–341). Federal Agencies Task Force, Washington, D.C., August 1979.

Americans Before Columbus. "The Pueblo Restoration of 1680." National Indian Youth Council, Albuquerque, Vol. 8, No. 2.

———. "Bury My Heart in the Tellico Valley." National Indian Youth Council, Albuquerque, Vol. 8, No. 1.

Bahti, Tom, *Southwestern Indian Tribes.* KC Publications, Las Vegas, 1971.

Bailey, Vernon, "Memorandum Respecting the Taos Forest Reservation." 2-pp. typescript, September 1903.

———, "Taos Mountains, New Mexico." 9-pp. typescript, September 1903.

"The Blue Lake Area: An Appeal from Taos Pueblo." N.d.

Bureau of Indian Affairs, "Proposed News Release." Albuquerque, May 27, 1966.

72nd Congress, 1st Session, Partial Report of Senate Committee on Indian Affairs, *Survey of Conditions of the Indians in the United States—Pueblo Lands Board.* Washington, D.C., January 6, 1932, pp. 1, 5–6.

72nd Congress, 1st Session, Senate Bill 2914. Washington, D.C., January 7, 1932, 7 pp.

72nd Congress, 1st Session, Partial Report of Senate Committee on Indian Affairs, *Survey of Conditions of the Indians in the United States.* Washington, D.C., January 28, 1932, pp. 10908–12, 11170–73.

72nd Congress, 1st Session, Partial Report of Senate Committee on Indian Affairs, *Survey of Conditions of the Indians in the United States—Charges of Misconduct of Herbert J. Hagerman.* Washington, D.C., February 16, 1932.

73rd Congress, 1st Session, H.R. 4014, "An Act to Authorize Appropriations . . . ," May 31, 1933, pp. 108–11.

89th Congress, 2nd Session, S. 3085, A Bill to Amend Section 4 of the Act of May 31, 1933 (48 Stat. 108), U.S. Senate, March 15, 1966.

90th Congress, 2nd Session, H.R. 3306, An Act to Amend Section 4 of the Act of May 31, 1933, U.S. House of Representatives.

90th Congress, 2nd Session, Hearings Before the Subcommittee on Indian Affairs of the Senate Committee on Interior and Insular Affairs on H.R. 3306, S. 1624, and S. 1625. Washington, D.C., September 19 and 20, 1968.

Department of Agriculture, Permit to Pueblo de Taos, typescript signed by Paul H. Appleby, Undersecretary of Agriculture, October 24, 1940, 1 p.

Dozier, Edward P., *The Pueblo Indians of North America.* Holt, Rinehart and Winston, New York, 1970.

Eggan, Fred, *The American Indian.* Aldine, Chicago, 1966.

Fenton, William N., "Factionalism at Taos Pueblo, New Mexico." Bulletin 164, Bureau of American Ethnology, Washington, D.C., 1957.

Forbes, Jack D., "Religious Freedom and the Protection of Native American Places of Worship and Cemeteries." *Native American Studies,* Tecumseh Center, University of California, Davis, January 1977.

——— and Adams, Howard, "A Model of 'Grass-Roots' Community Development: The D-Q University Native American Language Education Project."

Native American Studies, Tecumseh Center, University of California, Davis, February 1976.

Gardener, Michael, "The Archaeological Wonders of Chaco Canyon." *Sierra Club Bulletin,* November–December 1979.

Griffith, Winthrop, "The Taos Indians Have a Small Generation Gap." *The New York Times Magazine,* February 21, 1971, pp. 26–27, 93–97, 100.

Hackett, Charles W., and Shelby, C. C., *Revolt of the Pueblo Indians of New Mexico.* University of New Mexico Press, Albuquerque, 1970.

Hammond, George P., and Rey, Agapito, *The Rediscovery of New Mexico, 1580–1594.* University of New Mexico Press, Albuquerque, 1966.

Horgan, Paul, *Great River.* Holt, Rinehart and Winston, New York, 1954.

Indian Claims Commission, *Findings of Fact; Interlocutory Order and Opinion of the Commission, Pueblo of Taos* v. *The United States of America.* Docket No. 357, Washington, D.C., September 8, 1965.

"Information Supplied by Carson Supervisor Don Seaman" (unsigned 2-pp. typescript of interview with Supervisor of Carson National Forest regarding timber operators), December 23, 1966.

Janson, Donald, "Tribe Fights to Regain Church." *Indian Voices,* Chicago, June 1966, pp. 22–23.

Jarrett, Walter, "Taos Pueblo: A Brief History." *Mankind,* Vol. 2, No. 9 (September 1970), pp. 42–47.

John, Elizabeth A. H., *Storms Brewed in Other Men's Worlds.* Texas A & M University Press, College Station, 1975.

Jones, Oakah L., Jr., *Pueblo Warriors.* University of Oklahoma Press, Norman, 1966.

————, "Pueblo Auxiliaries and the Reconquest of New Mexico, 1692–1704." *The Spanish Borderlands,* Lorrin L. Morrison, Los Angeles, 1974.

Josephy, Alvin M., Jr., *The Patriot Chiefs.* Viking, New York, 1961.

Kelley, Dean M., "The Impairment of the Religious Liberty of the Taos Pueblo Indians by the United States Government." *A Journal of Church and State,* Vol. 9, No. 2 (Spring 1967).

La Farge, Oliver, "Notes on Meeting with the Taos Pueblo Council, January 24, 1956." 8-pp. typescript. "Addendum, January 26, 1956." 1-p. typescript.

Lavender, David, *Bent's Fort.* Doubleday, New York, 1954.

Letters (copies of selected typescripts in author's possession):

  Secretary of Agriculture James Wilson to Secretary of the Interior, February 23, 1903, 1 p.

  Acting Commissioner, General Land Office, Department of the Interior, to the Secretary of the Interior, December 5, 1903, 2 pp.

  Secretary of the Interior to Secretary of Agriculture, December 15, 1903, 1 p.

  Secretary of the Interior to Commissioner of the General Land Office, December 15, 1903, 1 p.

  Secretary of Agriculture to the Secretary of the Interior, February 20, 1906, 3 pp.

  Supervisor Ross McMillan, U.S. Forest Service, to Cruz Suazo, Governor, Taos Pueblo, Santa Fe, March 31, 1909, 1 p.

  H. J. Hagerman, Commissioner, Pueblo Lands Board, to Charles H. Burke,

Commissioner of Indian Affairs, Santa Fe, September 30, 1926, 7 pp.

Commissioner of Indian Affairs Charles H. Burke to H. J. Hagerman, Washington, D.C., October 4, 1926, 1 p.

Hanna & Wilson to Jose de la Cruz Concha, Governor, Taos Pueblo, March 30, 1927, 1 p.

Pueblo of Taos to Commissioner Charles H. Burke, Taos, New Mexico, May 26, 1927, 2 pp.

Floyd Beutler, Taos, to Secretary of the Interior Hubert Work, 2 pp.

Regional Forester Frank C. W. Pooler, Albuquerque, to H. J. Hagerman, Pueblo Lands Board, October 15, 1931, 3 pp. with permit form.

C. E. Faris, Superintendent, Office of Indian Affairs, Santa Fe, to John Collier, Commissioner of Indian Affairs, November 17, 1933, 3 pp. with map.

Oliver La Farge to Severino Martinez, Governor, Pueblo de Taos, Santa Fe, April 8, 1955, with copy of proposed congressional bill and 4-pp. petition to Congress from Pueblo de Taos, dated April 13, 1955.

Senator Clinton Anderson to Oliver La Farge, Washington, D.C., June 7, 1955.

Secretary of Agriculture Ezra Taft Benson to Senator James E. Murray, Chairman, Committee on Interior and Insular Affairs, Washington, D.C., March 24, 1958, 2 pp.

Roger Ernst, Assistant Secretary of the Interior, to Senator James E. Murray, Washington, D.C., April 1, 1958, 4 pp.

LaVerne Madigan, Association on American Indian Affairs, New York, to Secretary of Agriculture Orville Freeman, May 11, 1961, 2 pp.

Paul J. Bernal, Taos Council Secretary, to Senator Clinton Anderson, Taos, June 17, 1966, 2 pp.

Senator Clinton Anderson to Governor John J. Reyna, Taos Pueblo, Washington, D.C., July 22, 1966, 1 p.

Taos Governor and Council members to Senator Clinton Anderson, August 2, 1966, 3 pp.

Senator Clinton Anderson to Governor John J. Reyna, Taos Pueblo, August 12, 1966, 4 pp.

Senator Clinton Anderson to Stephen A. Mitchell, Taos, August 22, 1966, 5 pp.

Governor John Reyna, Taos, to Senator Clinton Anderson, October 19, 1966, 2 pp.

Senator Clinton Anderson to Rev. John L. Regier, National Council of the Churches of Christ, New York, September 29, 1967, 5 pp.

Secretary of the Interior Stewart L. Udall to Senator Henry Jackson, May 9, 1966, 6 pp.

William C. Schaab, Albuquerque, to Senator George McGovern, September 27, 1968, 8 pp.

Quirino Romero, Governor, Taos Pueblo Council, to Edward P. Cliff, Chief, U.S. Forest Service, October 11, 1968, 3 pp., enclosing correspondence from District Ranger Duane Freeman to Torivio Gomez, War Chief, Taos

Pueblo, September 10, 1968, 1 p., and "Report by Council Secretary Paul J. Bernal, Taos Pueblo Council, of Inspection Trip to Blue Lake with Taos District Ranger, October 1, 1968," 5 pp.

Congressman James A. Haley of Florida to Paul J. Bernal, Taos Pueblo Council Secretary, September 24, 1968, 1 p.

Taos Pueblo Council to Senator Clinton Anderson, June 18, 1969, 2 pp.

Martinez, Severino, "Our Ancient Way of Life," interpreted by Paul Bernal, Taos Pueblo Council Secretary. *Indian Affairs*, May 1961.

"Memorandum Regarding Private Timber Interests in Carson Forest," unsigned, 1966, 1 p.

"Memorandum Regarding Taos Bill," unsigned, 1966, 3 pp., and Fact Sheet, 1 p.

Native American Rights Fund, Boulder, Colo., *Announcements*, Vol. 5, No. 1 (Winter 1979).

————, *Annual Report*, 1977. Boulder, Colo.

The Native Nevadan, Reno, September 7, 1979; December 7, 1979.

Neihardt, John G., *Black Elk Speaks*. University of Nebraska Press, Lincoln, 1961.

Notes on "Information Obtained from Forest Service," unsigned, July 21, 1966, 1 p.

Ortiz, Alfonso, *The Tewa World*. University of Chicago Press, Chicago, 1969.

Ortiz, Roxanne Dunbar, ed., *The Great Sioux Nation*. American Indian Treaty Council Information Center/Moon Books, Berkeley, Calif. 1977.

Parsons, Elsie Clews, *Pueblo Indian Religion*. 2 vols., University of Chicago Press, Chicago, 1939.

Petition from Taos Indians to the Secretary of the Interior, Taos, New Mexico, October 21, 1904, 3 pp.

Phillips, Bert, "To Whom It May Concern." Taos, January 11, 1908, 1 p.

————, "To Whom It May Concern." November 12, 1948, 2 pp.

Philp, Kenneth R., *John Collier's Crusade for Indian Reform, 1920–1954*. University of Arizona Press, Tucson, 1977.

A Proclamation by the President (Theodore Roosevelt). Washington, D.C., November 7, 1906, 2 pp. with map.

Prucha, Francis Paul, *American Indian Policy in Crisis*. University of Oklahoma Press, Norman, 1976.

————, ed., *Americanizing the American Indians*. University of Nebraska Press, Lincoln, 1978.

Pueblo Lands Board, "Transcript of Hearings." Taos Pueblo, October 4, 1926, 7 pp.

Rixon, Theodore F., "Report on an Examination of the Taos Forest Reserve, Territory of New Mexico." March 30, 1905, pp. 1–5, 27–28.

Sando, Joe S., *The Pueblo Indians*. The Indian Historian Press, San Francisco, 1976.

Schaab, W. C., "Memorandum on H.R. 3306" and "Addendum to Memorandum." March 1, 1968, 46 pp. and map.

Scholes, France V., "Troublous Times in New Mexico, 1659–1670." Historical Society of New Mexico, Publications in History, Vol. 2, Albuquerque, 1942.

Spicer, Edward H., *Cycles of Conquest*. University of Arizona Press, Tucson, 1962.

"Statement of the Association on American Indian Affairs on S. 3085," 1966, 11 pp.

"Statement by the Taos Pueblo Council on the Blue Lake Legislation," June 1967.

"Statement of the Taos Pueblo Council on Blue Lake Legislation Before the 91st Congress," February 1969.

Taos Pueblo Council, "Report on Blue Lake Hearings Before the House Subcommittee on Indian Affairs, May 15–16, 1969." Taos, n.d.

Thomas, James W., "It Will Not Be Ceased." *The Sentinel,* Washington, D.C., July, 1970.

Underhill, Ruth, "Religion Among American Indians." *Annals of the American Academy of Political and Social Sciences,* Vol. 311 (1957), pp. 127–36.

U.S. Court of Appeals for the Sixth Circuit, *Ammoneta Sequoyah et al.* v. *Tennessee Valley Authority.* Decided and Filed, April 15, 1980.

Wassaja, San Francisco, Vol. 7, No. 5 (September 1979), p. 3.

Whatley, John T., "The Saga of Taos Pueblo: The Blue Lake Controversy." *The Indian Historian,* American Indian Historical Society, San Francisco, Vol. 2, No. 3 (Fall 1969), pp. 22–28.

Wieck, Paul R., "Taos Pueblo Statement Scores Blue Lake Plans." *Albuquerque Journal,* May 17, 1969, p. A-2.

Chapter 4: Cornplanter, Can You Swim?

FOR MATERIALS in this chapter, I acknowledge special help in the past from many members of the Seneca Nation, including George H. Abrams, George Heron, Harriett Pierce, and Calvin John, and also from Walter Taylor and Arthur Lazarus, Jr. My presentation of history and cultural matters leans the heaviest on the excellent works, listed below, of Anthony F. C. Wallace and Sheila C. Steen, William N. Fenton, and Merle H. Deardorff.

Abrams, George H., "The Cornplanter Cemetery." *Pennsylvania Archaeologist,* Bulletin of the Society for Pennsylvania Archaeology, Vol. 35, No. 2 (August 1965), pp. 59–73.

———, *The Seneca People.* Indian Tribal Series, Phoenix, 1976.

Carter, Luther J., "Dams and Wild Rivers: Looking Beyond the Pork Barrel." *Science,* Vol. 158, No. 3798 (October 13, 1967), pp. 233–42.

88th Congress, 1st Session, *Kinzua Dam (Seneca Indian Relocation),* Hearings Before the Subcommittee on Indian Affairs of the Committee on Interior and Insular Affairs, House of Representatives, on H.R. 1794, H.R. 3343, and H.R. 7354. Washington, D.C., 1964.

88th Congress, 2nd Session, *Kinzua Dam (Seneca Indian Relocation),* Hearings Before the Subcommittee on Indian Affairs of the Committee on Interior and Insular Affairs, U.S. Senate, on S. 1836 and H.R. 1794, March 2, 1964. Washington, D.C., 1964.

Cornplanter Indian Landowners Corporation, "An Appeal for a Creative Response to Federal Condemnation of Cornplanter Grant Land for the Kinzua Dam in Pennsylvania." 4-pp. typescript, Salamanca, N.Y., August 14, 1964.

Corps of Engineers, U.S. Army Engineer District, Pittsburgh, "Allegheny Reservoir—Report on Cornplanter Grant in Elk Township, Warren County, Pennsylvania." Pittsburgh, March 1962.

Corps of Engineers, Allegheny Reservoir Project, Relocation of Cornplanter Cemetery, "Assembly of Affidavits and Other Papers on the Manner of Performance." 60-pp. typescript, December 24, 1964.

Corwin, R. David, "Dilemma of the Iroquois." *Natural History,* June–July 1967, pp. 6–7, 60–66.

Deardorff, Merle H., "The Cornplanter Grant in Warren County." *Western Pennsylvania Historical Magazine,* Pittsburgh, Vol. 24, No. 1.

——, "The Religion of Handsome Lake: Its Origin and Development." Bulletin 149, Bureau of American Ethnology, No. 5, Washington, D.C., 1951, pp. 77–107.

Fenton, William N., ed., "The Journal of James Emlen Kept on a Trip to Canandaigua, New York." *Ethnohistory,* Vol. 12, No. 4 (Fall 1965), pp. 279–342.

——, "The Iroquois in History." Wenner-Gren Symposium No. 39, Burg Wartenstein, Austria, August 1967.

——, "From Longhouse to Ranch-Type House." N.d.

Graymont, Barbara, *The Iroquois in the American Revolution.* Syracuse University Press, Syracuse, N.Y., 1972.

Hunt, Richard P., "The Whippoorwill Cries, the Fox Whimpers." *The New York Times Magazine,* June 10, 1962, pp. 14–15, 59–60.

Kappler, Charles J., *Indian Affairs: Laws and Treaties.* 3 vols., U.S. Government Printing Office, Washington, D.C., 1904.

Kickingbird, Kirke, and Ducheneaux, Karen, *One Hundred Million Acres.* Macmillan, New York, 1973.

Letters:

Latham B. Weber, Publisher, Salamanca, N.Y., *Republican-Press,* to James B. Stevenson, Publisher, Titusville, Pa., *Herald,* December 11, 1964, 2 pp.

Merrill W. Bowen, Sr., Cornplanter Indian Landowners Corporation, Salamanca, N.Y., to Senator Joseph S. Clark, Washington, D.C., December 13, 1964, 6 pp.

Senator Joseph S. Clark, Washington, to Colonel James E. Hammer, U.S. Army Corps of Engineers, Pittsburgh, December 30, 1964, 2 pp.

Colonel James E. Hammer, Pittsburgh, to Senator Joseph S. Clark, Washington, D.C., January 27, 1965, 2 pp. and map.

Merrill W. Bowen, Sr., to Colonel James E. Hammer, Pittsburgh, April 21, 1965, 4 pp.

Walter Taylor to the President of the United States, May 5, 1965, 1 p.

Colonel James E. Hammer, Pittsburgh, to Merrill W. Bowen, Salamanca, N.Y., May 13, 1965, 1 p.

Merrill W. Bowen, Salamanca, N.Y., to Colonel James E. Hammer, Pittsburgh, May 19, 1965.

Lieutenant Colonel Bruce W. Jamison, Army Corps of Engineers, Pittsburgh, to Merrill Bowen, Salamanca, N.Y., May 21, 1965, 11 pp.

Lieutenant General W. K. Wilson, Jr., Chief of Engineers, Department of the

Army, Washington, D.C., to Walter Taylor, Salamanca, N.Y., May 21, 1965, 1 p.

Merrill Bowen to Colonel James E. Hammer (night letter), May 25, 1965, 1 p.

Lieutenant General W. K. Wilson, Jr., Washington, D.C., to Walter Taylor, Salamanca, N.Y., May 27, 1965, 2 pp.

Colonel James E. Hammer, Pittsburgh, to Merrill Bowen, Salamanca, N.Y., May 28, 1965, 1 p.

Merrill Bowen, Salamanca, N.Y., to Colonel James E. Hammer, June 15, 1965, 1 p.

A. J. Martucci, Chief, Acquisition Branch, Real Estate Division, Corps of Engineers, Pittsburgh, to Cornplanter Indian Landowners Association, Salamanca, N.Y., June 18, 1965, 1 p.

Merrill Bowen to Colonel James E. Hammer, September 13, 1965, 1 p.

Curtis C. Hunter, Warren, Pa., to Merrill Bowen, September 20, 1965, 1 p.

Walter Taylor to Richard Congdon, Salamanca, N.Y., September 21, 1965, 1 p.

Merrill Bowen to Curtis C. Hunter, September 24, 1965, 1 p.

Merrill Bowen to Colonel James E. Hammer, September 24, 1965, 3 pp.

Merrill Bowen to Senator Joseph S. Clark, Washington, D.C., September 24, 1965, 1 p.

Woodrow Berge, Acting Director of Real Estate, Corps of Engineers, to Senator Joseph S. Clark, January 21, 1965, 3 pp.

Paul L. Ritz, Warren, Pa., to Editor, *Forest Press,* Tionesta, Pa., January 29, 1969, 3 pp.

Morgan, Lewis H., *League of the Ho-De-No-Sau-Nee or Iroquois.* Rochester, N.Y., 1851.

"Notes of Meeting of Stanley O'Hopp, Mr. Bowen, Mr. Weber, and Others," Salamanca, N.Y., April 5, 1965. Unsigned.

"Notes of Walter Taylor, Friends Representative to the Seneca Nation of Indians, of Meeting with Curtis Hunter, March 15, 1965." Unsigned.

Olean, N.Y., *Times Herald,* September 17, 1966, p. 3.

Parker, Arthur C., "An Analytical History of the Seneca Indians." *Researches and Transactions of the New York State Archaeological Association,* Vol. 6, 1926.

Philadelphia Yearly Meeting of Friends, "The Kinzua Dam Controversy." Philadelphia, May 1961.

Snyderman, George S., "Concepts of Land Ownership Among the Iroquois and Their Neighbors." Bulletin 149, Bureau of American Ethnology, No. 2, Washington, D.C., 1951, pp. 13–34.

Taylor, Walter, "The Seneca Nation of Indians—Termination or Rehabilitation?" Unpublished ms., June 26, 1964.

———, "Comments on the Cornplanter Indian Landowners Corporation Appeal to the Corps of Engineers and the Response of the Corps." Unpublished ms., Salamanca, N.Y., June 22, 1965, 2 pp.

———, "Notes from Meeting of Cornplanter Indian Landowners Corporation with Curtis Hunter and Stanley O'Hopp, of Corps of Engineers, Pittsburgh

District, Warren, Pa., Office." Unpublished ms., Salamanca, N.Y., September 16, 1965, 5 pp.

Trigger, Bruce G., ed., *Handbook of North American Indians.* Vol. 15: *Northeast.* Smithsonian Institution, Washington, D.C., 1978.

Wallace, Anthony F. C., and Steen, Sheila C., *The Death and Rebirth of the Seneca.* Alfred A. Knopf, New York, 1969.

Wallace, Paul A. W., *Indians in Pennsylvania.* Pennsylvania Historical and Museum Commission, Harrisburg, 1961.

Warren County, Pa., *Observer,* October 29, 1963, p. 9.

Wickham, Woodward A., "The Iroquois Confederacy." 3 parts. Institute of Current World Affairs, New York, July 1973.

Wilson, Edmund, *Apologies to the Iroquois.* Farrar, Straus, and Cudahy, New York, 1960.

Chapter 5: "Like Giving Heroin to an Addict"

A LARGE PART of this chapter, as with some of the others, results as much from on-the-scene research and interviews with principals, both Indian and non-Indian, as it does from reference to documentary sources. I am specially indebted for considerable assistance, however, to James Vidovich, former chairman of the Pyramid Lake Paiute tribe; Robert Leland, former tribal attorney; Ottis Peterson, former Information Chief of the Bureau of Reclamation in Washington, D.C.; and Robert S. Pelcyger of the Native American Rights Fund in Boulder, Colorado.

Alvarez, Robert, "Indian Water Rights," in *Water for Industry in the Upper Missouri River Basin.* Environmental Policy Institute, Washington, D.C., April 3, 1976.

American Indian Lawyer Training Program, Inc., "A Symposium on Indian Water Policy." Oakland, Calif., November 8, 9, 10, 1981.

Arizona *Republic,* September 11, 15, December 7, 1980.

Briggs, Alan, "Analysis of H.R. 9951." Prepared for National Congress of American Indians, Washington, D.C., n.d.

"California-Nevada Interstate Compact Concerning Waters of Lake Tahoe, Truckee River, Carson River and Walker River Basins." 1st version, California Office of State Printing, 1965, 68 pp.; 2nd version, adopted by Commission, July 25, 1968, 44 pp.

California State Assembly, Assembly Bill 60, January 23, 1969; Minority Report on A.B. 60, Committee on Government Affairs, February 12, 1969; Joint Resolution 49, July 16, 1970.

Carson City, Nevada, *Appeal,* July 8, 10, 11, 15, 1969.

Carter, President Jimmy, "Water Policy Message," with detailed background. Press release. Washington, D.C., May 23, 1977.

Christian Science Monitor, May 27, 1968.

Clyde-Criddle-Woodward, Inc., "Report on Lower Truckee–Carson River Hydrology Studies, prepared for Bureau of Indian Affairs." Salt Lake City, April 1968.

Colley, Charles C., "The Struggle of Nevada Indians to Hold Their Lands." *The*

Indian Historian, San Francisco, Vol. 6, No. 3 (Summer 1973), pp. 5–17.

"Comments on and Criticisms of the Proposed California-Nevada Compact as It Affects the Use and Development of the Lower Truckee River Area and the Lands Owned by the Pyramid Lake Indians." 8-pp. ms., January 7, 1966.

84th Congress, 1st Session, House Document No. 181, *Washoe Project, Nevada-California.* Washington, D.C., June 14, 1955.

91st Congress, 1st Session, Subcommittee on Economy in Government of Joint Economic Committee, "Federal Encroachment on Indian Water Rights and the Impairment of Reservation Development," by William H. Veeder, in *Toward Economic Development for Native American Communities,* pp. 460–518. Washington, D.C., 1969.

95th Congress, 1st Session, H.R. 9951, A Bill to require adjudication and quantification of all claims to rights to the use of water based upon Federal and reserved rights for Indian reservations. Washington, D.C., n.d.

Cox, Z. Simpson and Alfred S., "Pima-Maricopa Indian Rights to Use of Gila River Water." Phoenix, 1977.

Egan, Ferol, *Sand in a Whirlwind.* Doubleday, New York, 1972.

Federal Register, "Procedures for Operation, Management and Control of the Truckee and Carson Rivers . . ." Washington, D.C., August 26, 1966, pp. 11314–15.

————, "Newlands Reclamation Project, Operating Criteria and Procedures . . ." Washington, D.C., September 30, 1967, p. 13733.

————. Vol. 38, No. 47 (March 12, 1973), Washington, D.C., pp. 6697–6700.

Forbes, Jack D., *Native Americans of California and Nevada.* Naturegraph Publishers, Healdsburg, Calif., 1969.

————, *Nevada Indians Speak.* University of Nevada Press, Reno, 1967.

Frank, John P., "Memorandum re: The Effect of the Proposed Truckee Compact on the Federal Law Claim of the Pyramid Lake Paiutes." Ms., Phoenix, March 11, 1969.

Gerard, Forrest J., "Indian Water Policy Review." Department of the Interior, Washington, D.C., October 12, 1977.

Gomberg, William, and Leland, Joy, "We Need to Be Shown." Reno, 1963.

Hickel, Walter J., Reagan, Governor Ronald, Laxalt, Governor Paul, "Transcript of Press Conference." Typescript, 14 pp., July 7, 1969.

High Country News, Lander, Wyo., Vol. 11, No. 19 (October 5, 1979), p. 13.

Hopkins, Sarah Winnemucca, *Life Among the Piutes.* Putnam, New York, 1883.

Indian Affairs. Association on American Indian Affairs, New York. No. 65 (January–March 1967); No. 67 (August–October 1967); No. 68 (November–December 1967); No. 73 (December 1968–March 1969); No. 84 (January 1973); No. 89 (June–August 1975); No. 90 (September–December 1975); No. 91 (January–June 1976); No. 92 (July–November 1976); No. 93 (December 1976–March 1977); No. 98 (Fall–Winter 1978–79); No. 100 (Fall–Winter 1979).

Indian Natural Resources. Association on American Indian Affairs, New York. No. 1 (May 1977); No. 3 (December 1977); No. 4 (August 1978); No. 6 (December 1980).

Indian Voices, Tulsa, Okla., September 1964, pp. 4–5; Winter 1968, pp. 7–8.

"Indian Water Rights and the National Water Commission." *Civil Rights Digest,* Vol. 6, No. 1 (Fall 1973), pp. 28–33.

Inter-Tribal Council, Inc., of Nevada, *Numa: A Northern Paiute History.* University of Utah Printing Service, Salt Lake City, 1976.

———, *The Native Nevadan,* Reno, April 1969; June 1, July 6, 1979; February 7, April 4, June 6, July 7, August 1, September 5, October 2, November 9, 1980.

———, *Newsletter,* Vol. 1, No. 8 (October 1964), 2 pp.

Josephy, Alvin M., Jr., "Here in Nevada a Terrible Crime." *American Heritage,* Vol. 21, No. 4 (June 1970), pp. 93–100.

———, "Memorandum: California-Nevada Interstate (Water) Compact, Chronology of Developments, 1968–1969." Typescript, 6 pp., August 5, 1969.

Lamb, Terrence J., "Indian-Government Relations on Water Utilization in the Salt and Gila River Valleys of Southern Arizona." *The Indian Historian,* San Francisco, Vol. 10, No. 3 (Summer 1977), pp. 38–45, 61–62.

Lazarus, Arthur, Jr., "Memoranda re: Pyramid Lake (Meetings with Interior Undersecretary Charles Luce)." Typescript, 2 pp., January 25, 1967; 2 pp., June 14, 1967.

Leland, Robert, "Report to the Pyramid Lake Paiute Tribe and to the Secretary of the Interior." Typescript, 10 pp., December 31, 1967.

Letters:

Robert Leland, tribal attorney, Reno, to Nevada Governor Grant Sawyer, January 25, 1964, 10 pp.

Assistant Secretary of the Interior John A. Carver, Jr., to Robert Leland, March 16, 1964, 1 p.

Robert Leland to Henry P. Caulfield, Jr., Director, Resources Program Staff, Department of the Interior, Washington, D.C., September 22, 1964, 6 pp.

Telegram, Allen Aleck and Wilfred Shaw, Tribal Chairman and Vice-Chairman, to Secretary of the Interior Stewart L. Udall, October 8, 1964, 1 p.

Alden Stevens, President, Association on American Indian Affairs, New York, to Secretary Udall, November 13, 1964, 2 pp.

Undersecretary John A. Carver to Alden Stevens, January 15, 1965, 2 pp.

Flora Smith, Secretary, Pyramid Lake Paiute Tribal Council, Nixon, Nev., to U.S. Senator Alan Bible, Washington, D.C., April 6, 1965, 9-pp. ms., with enclosure "E. Reeseman Fryer or Pyramid Lake Undeveloped," 11-pp. ms.

Allen L. Aleck, Chairman, Pyramid Lake Paiute Tribal Council, to Robert Newell, California-Nevada Compact Commission, Boise, Idaho, February 25, 1966, 4-pp. ms.

Secretary of the Interior Udall to Robert Leland, April 25, 1966, 2 pp.

Robert Leland to Secretary Udall, July 25, 1966, 4 pp.

Robert L. Bennett, Commissioner of Indian Affairs, to Robert Leland, January 11, 1967, 2 pp.

Robert L. Bennett to William Byler, Association on American Indian Affairs, New York, January 11, 1967, 2 pp.

Wilfred Shaw, Chairman, Pyramid Lake Paiute Tribal Council, to Secretary Udall, January 17, 1967, 4 pp.

Robert Leland to Arthur Lazarus, Jr., Association on American Indian Affairs, Washington, D.C., January 17, 1967, 2 pp.

Robert Leland to Robert Bennett, Commissioner, Bureau of Indian Affairs, Washington, D.C., January 18, 1967, 2 pp.

William Byler, Director, Association on American Indian Affairs, New York, to Robert Bennett, January 18, 1967, 6 pp.

Robert Leland to Charles F. Luce, Undersecretary of the Interior, January 27, 1967, 1 p.

Robert L. Bennett to Robert Leland, February 4, 1967, 1 p.

Robert Leland to Senator Alan Bible, February 6, 1967, 2 pp.

Congressman Walter S. Baring, Nevada, to Robert Leland, February 19, 1967, 1 p.

Robert Leland to Robert L. Bennett, February 23, 1967, 2 pp.

Arthur Lazarus, Jr., to William S. Byler, April 27, 1967, 5 pp.

Robert Leland to Arthur Lazarus, Jr., May 2, 1967, 4 pp.

Undersecretary Charles F. Luce to William Byler, June 22, 1967, 1 p.

Robert Leland to Secretary Udall, September 11, 1967, 2 pp.

Robert Leland to Robert L. Bennett, September 21, 1967, 2 pp.

Robert Leland to Jose A. Zuni, Superintendent, Nevada Indian Agency, Stewart, Nev., November 8, 1967, 3 pp.

Robert Leland to Robert Bennett, November 13, 1967, 2 pp.

Robert Leland to Mrs. William Byler, November 14, 1967, 5 pp.

Secretary Udall to Robert Leland, July 19, 1968, 2 pp.

Robert Leland to Harry J. Hogan, Legislative Counsel, Department of the Interior, Washington, D.C., September 26, 1968, 2-pp. night letter.

Secretary Udall to Charles J. Zwick, Director, Bureau of the Budget, Washington, D.C., January 14, 1969, 8 pp.

Mitchell Melich, Solicitor, Department of the Interior, to Glen E. Taylor, Acting Assistant Attorney General, April 16, 1969, 5 pp.

Secretary of the Interior Walter J. Hickel to Robert P. Mayo, Director, Bureau of the Budget, Washington, D.C., April 24, 1969, 3 pp.

James Vidovich, Chairman, Pyramid Lake Paiute Tribe, to Edgar Cahn, Citizens Advocate Center, Washington, D.C., July 31, 1969, 2 pp.

Robert Leland to Edgar Cahn, September 26, 1969, 4 pp.

Robert Leland to John P. Frank, Phoenix, Ariz., October 17, 1969, 2 pp.

Mitchell Melich, Acting Secretary of the Interior, to Robert J. Pafford, Jr., Regional Director, Bureau of Reclamation, Sacramento, Calif., June 5, 1972, 12 pp.

Assistant Secretary of the Interior for Indian Affairs Forrest J. Gerard to All Indian Tribes, June 7, 1978.

John R. Lewis, Executive Director, Inter-Tribal Council of Arizona, to author, October 2, 1980.

Liebling, A. J., "The Lake of the Cui-ui Eaters." *The New Yorker*, January 1, 8, 15, 22, 1955.

Lynch, Don, "They're Killing Pyramid Lake." *Field & Stream,* January 1970, pp. 10–15.

Modesto, California, *Bee,* December 7, 1967.

National Congress of American Indians, *The Sentinel,* Convention Issue, 1969.

——, "Resolution on Indian Water Rights," October 8, 1969.

Native American Rights Fund, Boulder, Colo., *Announcements,* Vol. 1, No. 6 (November–December 1972).

——, *Annual Reports,* 1979, 1980. Boulder, Colo.

Nelson, Michael C., and Booke, Bradley L., "The Winters' Doctrine," excerpt from *Arid Lands Resource Information Paper No. 9.* University of Arizona, Office of Arid Lands Studies, Tucson, 1977.

Nevada Indian Affairs Commission, "Resolution No. 5." Carson City, September 27, 1966.

——, *Report, Fiscal Year 1966–67.* Carson City, June 30, 1967.

Nevada State Journal, Reno, November 7, 1963; February 6, 1967; March 5, October 6, 28, 29, November 25, 28, December 24, 1968; March 8, 9, 10, June 10, 12, 18, July 6, 7, 8, 9, 10, 11, 12, 13, 14, 15, 16, 17, 18, 26, 30, October 9, 17, November 15, 18, 20, December 27, 1969; January 6, 16, February 10, 21, March 13, June 10, July 22, October 19, 1970; February 14, 1971.

New York *Times,* February 25, 1969, p. 45; July 20, 1969, p. 36; January 18, 1970, p. 66.

Pyramid Lake Paiute Tribe, "Report and Recommendations to the President's Task Force on Indian Affairs," April 13, 1961, 7 pp.

——, "The Pyramid Lake Reservation," n.d.

——, "Resolution No. PL-64-8 on Nevada-California Compact Commission," November 1, 1963, 3 pp.

——, "Resolution No. PL-65-1," n.d., 2 pp.

——, Minutes, Tribal Council Meeting, October 9, 1964, 4 pp.

——, Resolutions No. PL-65-7, October 9, 1964, 4 pp.; No. PL 68-5, July 14, 1967, 2 pp.; No. P-69, July 11, 1969, 2 pp.

——, "Comments on Rules and Regulations . . . relating to the operation of the Newlands Project . . .," October 7, 1966, 7 pp.

——, "Water, Economic Development and Jobs," October 27, 1967, 3 pp.

——, "Analysis of the Final Report of the Pyramid Lake Task Force," February 19, 1972, 43 pp.

Pyramid Lake Task Force, *Final Report,* December 31, 1971, 39 pp. and appendices.

Race Relations Information Center, Nashville, Tenn., *Race Relations Reporter,* Vol. 3, No. 9 (November 20, 1972).

Reno *Evening Gazette,* July 7, 1969.

Sacramento *Bee,* "Pyramid: Profile of a Lake," December 1967.

Salt Lake City *Tribune,* June 2, 1968.

"Save Pyramid Lake," Fact Sheet for Washoe Project Vote, October 6, 1964, 4 pp.; revised version, October 20, 1964, 3 pp.

Schwarz, William L. K., and Fogle, David P., "Economic Development Plan for Pyramid Lake Indian Reservation," August 1, 1963.

Townley, John M., "Reclamation and the Red Man." *The Indian Historian,* San Francisco, Vol. 11, No. 1 (Winter 1978), pp. 21–28.

U.S. Court of Appeals for the Ninth Circuit, Nos. 78-1115 and 78-1493, *United States of America and Pyramid Lake Paiute Tribe of Indians* v. *Truckee-Carson Irrigation District et al.,* n.d.

U.S. Department of Commerce, Economic Development Administration, Technical Assistance Project, "Water Resources and Land Use of the Pyramid Lake Indian Reservation." Prepared by Wilsey & Ham, San Mateo, Calif., October 1970.

U.S. Department of the Interior, "Comments of the Department of the Interior on Proposed California-Nevada Compact," from Secretary of the Interior Udall to Allen Aleck, Chairman, Pyramid Lake Paiute Tribe, April 25, 1966, 7 pp.

———, Bureau of Outdoor Recreation, Pacific Southwest Regional Office, "Pyramid Lake Recreation Study," San Francisco, November 1968.

———, Bureau of Reclamation, Region 2, "Newlands Project," Fallon, Nev., n.d.

———, Geological Survey, "Memorandum from Chairman, Special Field Task Force, to Chairman, Washington Task Force, re: 'ALPINE CASE,' " Menlo Park, Calif., June 7, 1967, 2 pp.

———, "Memorandum, Chairman, Truckee-Carson Task Force to Commissioner, Bureau of Indian Affairs," February 8, 1967, 6 pp.

———, "Memorandum from E. Reeseman Fryer, Member, Task Force, to Harry J. Hogan, Chairman, Task Force," October 10, 1966, 4 pp.

———, "Memorandum from Secretary of the Interior to Chairman, Operating Criteria Committee," July 26, 1968, 3 pp.

———, Office of the Secretary, "Rules and Regulations, Newlands Reclamation Project," February 1, 1967, 5 pp.

———, "Public Hearing Held in Re: Action Program for Resources Development, Truckee and Carson River Basins, California-Nevada." 2 vols., Western Reporters, Sacramento, September 21, 22, 1964.

———, Public Information News Releases: "Secretary Udall Urges Action Program to Increase Use of Available Water in Nevada," September 12, 1964; "Secretary Udall Adopts Action Program for Truckee and Carson River Basins," October 7, 1964; "Indians of Pyramid Lake, Nevada, Plan Large Scale Recreation Development," May 11, 1965; "Court Test Sought to Determine Water Rights of Pyramid Lake Indians," April 24, 1972; "Justice Department to Present Separate Views of Interior in Indian Natural Resource Cases," July 3, 1972; "Top Indian Affairs Official Rates Water Policy a Plus for Reservation Development," June 9, 1978.

———, "Task Force Action Program for Resource Development, Truckee and Carson River Basins, California-Nevada," October 1964, 37 pp. and maps.

U.S. District Court, District of Columbia, No. 2506–70, *Pyramid Lake Paiute Tribe of Indians* v. *Walter J. Hickel* . . . Complaint for Injunction, Mandamus and Declaratory Relief, August 21, 1970; Affidavit of Alvin M. Josephy, Jr., August 19, 1970; Affidavit of Robert D. Stitser, December 8, 1970; Motion to Dismiss, October 23, 1970; Memorandum of Points and Authorities in Opposition to Motions to Dismiss, January 2, 1971; Amended Complaint, February 19, 1971; Hearing on Motion, April 14, 1972; Order of Court, April 17, 1972; Memorandum Opinion, November 8, 1972.

U.S. Supreme Court, October Term, 1972, *United States of America* v. *States of Nevada and California;* Motion for Leave to File Brief as Amicus Curiae . . . Association on American Indian Affairs, Inc.; same, Pyramid Lake Paiute Tribe of Indians. January 1973.

University of Nevada, Bureau of Governmental Research, *Newsletter,* Vol. 7, No. 5 (February 1969), "The California-Nevada Interstate Compact . . ."; Vol. 7, No. 6 (March 1969), "The California-Nevada Compact: Another View."

Veeder, William H., "Water Rights: Life or Death for the American Indian. From the Second Convocation of American Indian Scholars." *The Indian Historian,* San Francisco, Vol. 5, No. 2 (Summer 1972), pp. 4–21.

———, "Indian Water Rights and the Energy Crisis," in *Energy Resource Development,* papers presented at a consultation sponsored by state advisory committees to the U.S. Commission on Civil Rights, Denver, November 2–3, 1978. U.S. Government Printing Office, Washington, D.C., 1980.

Wassaja, San Francisco, Vol. 7, No. 4 (May 1979).

Watts, Guy W., "The Pillage of the Truckee River." January 1, 1953, 9-pp. ms.

Wilkinson, Charles F., "Perspectives on Water and Energy in the American West and in Indian Country." *South Dakota Law Review,* Vol. 26 (Summer 1981).

Yakima Nation Review, Toppenish, Wash., Vol. 9, No. 8 (Autumn 1978).

Chapter 6: The Great Northwest Fishing War

THIS CHAPTER is based on my own eyewitness research and observations, as well as on the numerous materials listed below. Assistance through the years was given me by many people, but especially by Janet McCloud, formerly of the Survival of American Indians Association, Charles McEvers of the American Friends Service Committee, and Suzan Shown Harjo of the Native American Rights Fund in Washington, D.C.

Adams, Hank, "A Citizen's Letter to His Governor." Tacoma, Wash., October 17–21, 1968.

Akwesasne Notes. Mohawk Nation via Roosevelttown, N.Y., "Nez Perce Struggle for Survival." Vol. 12, No. 3 (August 1980), p. 16.

———, "Nez Perce Struggle Making Headway." Vol. 12, No. 4 (Autumn 1980), p. 17.

———, "Struggle on the Klamath." Vol. 11, No. 5 (Early Spring 1980), p. 26.

———, "Hoh Indian Tribe Hurt by Mismanagement." Vol. 12, No. 5 (Winter 1981), p. 22.

American Friends Service Committee, *Uncommon Controversy.* University of Washington Press, Seattle, 1970.

American Indian Women's League, New York, "Newsletter," February 28, 1969.

Argus, Seattle, "1855 Indian Treaty Decision Upsets Governments of Two States," May 2, 1969.

Bibliography

Association on American Indian Affairs, "Boldt Decision Upheld." *Memorandum No. 79–18.* New York, July 11, 1979.

Boise, Idaho, *Statesman,* June 18, 20, 1980.

Brown, Bruce, "Salmon Casualties of 100 Year Fish War." Seattle *Post-Intelligencer,* June 28, 1979.

Bureau of Indian Affairs and U.S. Fish and Wildlife Service, Department of the Interior, "Indian Fishing Rights in the Pacific Northwest." Portland, Ore., August 1977.

Carpenter, Cecelia S., *They Walked Before.* Washington State American Revolution Bicentennial Commission, Tacoma, 1977.

Casey, Robert D., "The Last Indian War." *The Catholic Worker,* New York, June 1966.

———, "Resurrection City Number Two." *The Catholic Worker,* July–August 1968.

———, "Along the Nisqually." *The Catholic Worker,* December 1968.

Complaint of Civil Rights Violations by Nugent Kautz et al. to Nicholas Katzenbach, Attorney General of the United States, Yelm, Wash., February 8, 1965.

88th Congress, 2nd Session, Senate Committee on Interior and Insular Affairs, Subcommittee on Indian Affairs, *Indian Fishing Rights: Hearing on S.J.R. 170 and S.J.R. 171,* August 5, 6, 1964. Washington, D.C., 1964.

96th Congress, 2nd Session, House of Representatives, H.R. 6959, and Senate, S. 2163, *Providing for the Conservation and Enhancement of the Salmon and Steelhead Resources of Washington State, Assistance to the Treaty and Nontreaty Harvesters of Those Resources . . .* Washington, D.C., September–October 1980.

Davies, Lawrence E., "U.S. Backs Indians on Coast Fishing." New York *Times,* May 4, 1966.

Emmons, Della Gould, *Leschi of the Nisquallies.* T. S. Denison & Co., Minneapolis, 1965.

Everett, Wash., *Herald,* September 10, 12, 13, October 20, 1968.

Gibbs, George, "Tribes of Western Washington and Northwestern Oregon," in W. H. Dall, *Tribes of the Extreme Northwest.* Vol. 1, Part 2 of Contributions to North American Ethnology, Washington, D.C., 1877.

Haeberlin, Herman K., and Gunther, Erna, *The Indians of Puget Sound.* University of Washington Publications in Anthropology, Vol. 4, No. 1, University of Washington Press, Seattle, 1930.

Hobbs, Charles A., "Indian Hunting and Fishing Rights." *The George Washington Law Review,* Washington, D.C., Vol. 32, No. 3 (March 1964).

———, "Indian Hunting and Fishing Rights II." *The George Washington Law Review,* Vol. 37, No. 5 (July 1969).

Houston, Darrell, "Way-Out War." *Argosy,* July, 1966, pp. 46–50, 106–108.

Indian Affairs. Association on American Indian Affairs, New York. No. 70 (April–May 1968); No. 78 (May–August 1970).

Indian Natural Resources. Association on American Indian Affairs, New York. No. 4 (August 1978); No. 5 (February 1979).

Indian Truth. The Indian Rights Association, Philadelphia. No. 222 (September 1978); No. 223 (December 1978).

Indian Voices. University of Chicago, September 1966.

Intermountain Observer, Boise, Idaho, August 17, 1968.

Jessett, Thomas E., "Puyallup Indians Appeal to Church for Help in Keeping Fishing Rights." *The Olympia Churchman,* Wash., November 1965.

Josephy, Alvin M., Jr., *Red Power.* McGraw-Hill, New York, 1971.

Lee, Robert C., "Dick Gregory Goes Fishing." *The Nation,* April 25, 1966, pp. 487–89.

Letters:

Enrolled members of the Nisqually Nation to President Lyndon B. Johnson and the Attorney General of the United States, Yelm, Wash., January 14, 1965.

John Doar, Assistant Attorney General of the U.S., Civil Rights Division, to Don McCloud, Yelm, Wash., February 26, 1965.

Don and Janet McCloud et al. to Secretary of the Interior Stewart Udall, Yelm, Wash., October 9, 1965. Telegram.

James E. Officer, Associate Commissioner of Indian Affairs, to Don and Janet McCloud, October 12, 1965. Telegram.

Rt. Rev. Ivol I. Curtis, Bishop of Olympia, Wash., Episcopal Church, to The Executive Council, Protestant Episcopal Church Center, New York, November 17, 1965.

Alva C. Long, Auburn, Wash., to Rev. Clifford Samuelson, New York, November 17 and December 1, 1965.

Donald M. Matheson, Ramona Bennett et al. to John Mitchell, Attorney General of the United States, Tacoma, August 14, 1970.

Lewiston, Idaho, *Tribune,* "New Fishing Rules Proposed for Indians in Northwest," July 4, 1966; also issues of August 19, 20, 1966.

Lowman, Bill, *220 Million Custers.* Anacortes Printing & Publishing, Anacortes, Wash., 1978.

Matheson, Don, "Report to Survival of American Indians Association on Supreme Court Hearing in Washington, D.C., March 25, 26, 1968."

McCloud, Janet, "The Continuing 'Last Indian War.' " Yelm, Wash., 1966.

———, "Fisher Indians in Fight for Treaty But State Refuses Recognition." *The Indian Historian,* San Francisco, Vol. 4, No. 2 (May 1967).

———, "Letter to Friends." Yelm, Wash., January 20, 1969.

———, "Still Shooting Indians." Yelm, Wash., April 1969.

Meeker, Ezra, *Pioneer Reminiscences of Puget Sound and the Tragedy of Leschi.* Lowman and Hanford, Seattle, 1905.

Mills, Sidney, "Statement." Olympia, Wash., October 13, 1968.

National Coalition to Support Indian Treaties, Seattle, "Newsletter," February 1979; August 1979; April 1980; August 1980.

National Congress of American Indians, "Discussion Papers for Fishing Rights Panel," May 1968.

Native American Free University, Yelm, Wash., "Newsletter," February 1971.

Native American Rights Fund, Boulder, Colo., *Announcements,* Vol. 3, No. 2, Part 2 (April–June 1975); August 1977; December 1980.

———, *Annual Report,* 1979. Boulder, Colo.

———, "Re: S. 885, Pacific Northwest Electric Power Planning and Conservation Act." Washington, D.C., September 29, 1980.

The Native Nevadan, Reno, March 8, 1979.

New York *Herald Tribune,* February 9, 16, 1966.

New York *Times,* May 29, 1968; March 9, September 10, October 18, 1970; November 20, 1973; October 28, 1976; May 8, June 11, 1979; December 27, 1981.

Nez Perce Tribal Executive Committee, Lapwai, Idaho, "Minutes," November 14, 15, 1967.

Northwest Indian Fisheries Commission, "Treaty Fishing Rights." Olympia, Wash., January 1980.

———, "Newsletter," Vol. IV, No. 3 (June–July 1978); Vol. IV, No. 4 (August 1978); Volume IV, No. 5 (September 1978); Vol. IV, No. 6 (October–November 1978); Vol. V, No. 1 (December 1978–February 1979); Vol. V, No. 4 (June–July 1979); Vol. V, No. 7 (October–November 1979); Vol. VI, No. 2 (February–March 1980).

Olympia, Wash., *Daily Olympian,* October 10, 11, 13, 14, 18, 1968; March 19, 1969.

Parisot, Thomas, Deputy Associate Director of Fisheries, U.S. Fish and Wildlife Service, Statement Before the U.S. Senate Select Committee on Indian Affairs, September 28, 1981.

Petition of Jack McCloud et al. to Nicholas Katzenbach, Attorney General of the United States, Yelm, Wash., February 8, 1965.

Portland, Ore., *Journal,* August 13, 1968.

Portland *Oregonian,* August 7, 1971; July 13, August 23, 1975; July 3, 4, August 31, September 15, 1979.

Race Relations Information Center, Nashville, Tenn., *Race Relations Reporter,* Vol. 2, No. 3 (February 16, 1971).

Raines, Howell, "American Indians: Struggling for Power and Identity." *The New York Times Magazine,* February 11, 1979.

Roderick, Janna, "Indian-White Relations in the Washington Territory: The Question of Treaties and Indian Fishing Rights." *Journal of the West,* Vol. 16, No. 3 (July 1977), pp. 23–34.

Seattle *Daily Times,* May 28, 1968; August 14, 1970.

Seattle *Post-Intelligencer,* July 7, 1968.

Sherman, William, "Case #9225339: Su'Zan Satiacum." *Seattle Magazine,* February 1966.

Smith, Marian W., *The Puyallup-Nisqually.* Columbia University Contributions to Anthropology, No. 32. Columbia University Press, New York, 1940.

Spokane, Wash., *Daily Chronicle,* May 28, 1968.

Spokane, Wash., *Spokesman-Review,* May 29, 1968.

Stevens, Hazard, *The Life of Isaac Ingalls Stevens.* 2 vols., Houghton Mifflin, Boston, 1900.

Supreme Court, State of Washington, *Muckleshoot Tribe of Indians, Herman Moses, et al.,* v. *The Department of Fisheries and the Department of Game, State of Washington.* Brief of Appellants, 1966.

———, *The Puyallup Tribe, Inc.* v. *Department of Game and Department of Fisheries, State of Washington.* Amicus Curiae Brief of the Association on American Indian Affairs, May 19, 1966; Brief of the Association on American Indian Affairs as Amicus Curiae, Prior to Consideration of Petition for Writ of Certiorari, October 1967.

Survival of American Indians Association, Inc., "The Short Story of October 13th Nisqually Fish-In" and newsletter. Tacoma, n.d.

———, "Newsletter," March 1, May, June, July, August, August–September 1966.

———, "Letter to President Lyndon B. Johnson," Tacoma, December 17, 1968.

———, *The Renegade*, Frank's Landing, Lacey, Wash., May 1969; June 1971; June 24, 1972.

Swan, James G., *The Northwest Coast.* Harper & Brothers, New York, 1857.

Swindell, Edward G., *Report on Source, Nature, and Extent of the Fishing, Hunting, and Miscellaneous Related Rights of Certain Indian Tribes in Washington and Oregon Together with Affidavits* . . . Division of Forestry and Grazing, Office of Indian Affairs, U.S. Department of the Interior, Los Angeles, Calif., 1942.

Tacoma *News Tribune*, February 15, 1962; January 14, 1966; August 13, September 9, 1970.

Treaty Indians of the Columbia, Inc., Cooks, Wash., "Newsletter," January 25, 1979.

U.S. Commission on Civil Rights, *Indian Tribes: A Continuing Quest for Survival.* Washington, D.C., June, 1981.

U.S. District Court, Portland, Ore., *United States* v. *Oregon.* Judge's Opinion, April 23, 1969.

U.S. District Court, Western District of Washington, *United States* v. *Washington— Phase II,* Opinion, September 24, 1980.

Washington *Post*, June 3, 1968.

Washington State Department of Fisheries, *Indian Fisheries Problem.* Olympia, 1964.

"Washington Supreme Court Rules Against Indians." *The Amerindian*, Chicago, Vol. 15, No. 5 (May–June 1967).

Waterman, T. T., "Notes on the Ethnology of the Indians of Puget Sound." *Indian Notes and Monographs*, No. 59, Museum of the American Indian–Heye Foundation, New York, 1973.

Wilensky, Harry, "Indians Use Press Agent Weapons in Their Fight for Right to Fish." St. Louis *Post-Dispatch*, July 27, 1966.

Wood, Edmund, "Fishing Rights and Civil Liberties." American Civil Liberties Union of Washington. Seattle, August–September 1967.

Yakima Nation Review, Toppenish, Wash., Vol. 9, No. 8 (Autumn 1978).

Chapter 7: The Sioux Will Rise Again

IN ADDITION to the documentary materials listed below, this chapter reflects a personal familiarity with many of the events and developments discussed. Much of the research resulted from widespread travel to reservations, Indian meetings, etc., and in the period 1966–67 was made possible, in part, by a travel grant from the John Simon Guggenheim Memorial Foundation, for which I am deeply appreciative. Throughout the years, I absorbed much help from many people and can acknowledge only a few of them: Oren Lyons, Ada Deer, Vine Deloria, Jr., Robert Burnette, LaDonna Harris, Thomas Banyacya, Edison Realbird, Thomas Tureen, Clifford Samuelson, Philleo Nash, Lucy Covington, Mifaunway Hines, William Byler, Bradley Patterson, William Zimmerman, Helen Scheirbeck, Ramona Bennett, Herbert Blatchford, Richard Halfmoon, Lloyd New, N. Scott Momaday, John Echohawk, Hank Adams, Ella Deloria, Helen Peterson, Gerald Wilkinson, D'Arcy McNickle, David Risling, John W. Showalter, John Wooden Leg, S. Philip Deloria, Rupert Costo, Jeannette Henry, Peter Decker, Archibald Hanna, Stewart L. Udall, Kahntineta Horn, Alan Parker, Pascal Sherman, Leonard Garment, and my daughter, Diane Josephy. They stand for scores of others who, in one way or another, contributed information that is in this chapter. Folders of contemporary documentary materials on such subjects as the Chicago Indian Conference of 1961; the Capital Conference on Indian Poverty in 1964; the Trail of Broken Treaties and the takeover of the BIA Building in 1972; and Wounded Knee II and its aftermath in 1973 will be on deposit at the University of Oregon Library in Eugene.

Akwesasne Notes, Mohawk Nation via Roosevelttown, N.Y. Vol. 5, No. 1 (Early Winter 1973); Vol. 11, No. 5 (Winter 1979); Vol. 12, No. 2 (May 1980); Vol. 12, No. 3 (August 1980); Vol. 12, No. 4 (Autumn 1980); Vol. 12, No. 5 (Winter 1981).

———, *B.I.A., I'm Not Your Indian Any More.* N.d.

———, *Voices from Wounded Knee, 1973.* 1974.

Albuquerque *Journal*, July 23, 1978; August 1, 14, 1980.

Ambler, Marjane, "The Mainstreaming on the Reservation." *Alicia Patterson Foundation Reporter*, New York, Vol. 3, No. 4 (June 1980).

———, "Uranium Millworkers Seek Compensation." *APF Reporter*, Vol. 3, No. 5 (August 1980).

———, "Tribal Control." *APF Reporter*, Vol. 3, No. 6 (October 1980).

———, "Making Peace Between Tribes and Energy Lords." *APF Reporter*, Vol. 3, No. 7 (December 1980).

———, "Uncertainty in CERT." *APF Reporter*, Vol. 4, No. 1 (February 1981).

American Indian Crusade, Mission, S.D., Vol. 1, No. 1, November 1972.

American Indian Environmental Council, Inc. "Press Release." Albuquerque, July 25, 1979.

American Indian Policy Review Commission, *Final Report.* Washington, D.C., May 17, 1977.

Anthropology Resource Center, *Native Americans and Energy Development.* Cambridge, Mass., 1978.

Association on American Indian Affairs, New York, *Memoranda 80–29, 80–30, 80–31,* September 15, 16, 1980.

Bee, Robert L., "The Washington Connection: American Indian Leaders and

American Indian Policy." *The Indian Historian,* San Francisco, Vol. 12, No. 1 (Winter 1979), pp. 2–11, 36.

Black Hills Paha Sapa Report, Vol. 1, No. 1. Black Hills Alliance, Rapid City, S. D., July 1979.

Bluecloud, Peter, *Alcatraz Is Not an Island.* Wingbow Press, Berkeley, Calif., 1972.

Brophy, William A., and Aberle, Sophie D., *The Indian: America's Unfinished Business.* University of Oklahoma Press, Norman, 1966.

Bruce, Louis, Commissioner of Indian Affairs, to William Youpee, Chairman, NTCA. 1-p. typescript letter, Washington, D.C., July 28, 1972.

Budnick, Dan, "Black Mesa: Progress Report on an Ecological Rape." *Art in America,* July–August 1972, pp. 98–105.

Burnette, Robert, *The Tortured Americans.* Prentice-Hall, Englewood Cliffs, N.J., 1971.

———— and Koster, John, *The Road to Wounded Knee.* Bantam, New York, 1974.

Business Week, "Indians Want a Bigger Share of Their Wealth," May 3, 1976; "An Indian Tribe Snares a Rich Mineral Deal," February 9, 1981.

Cahn, Edgar S., ed., *Our Brother's Keeper.* World, New York, 1969.

Christian Science Monitor, March 28, 1977.

Clemmer, Richard O., *Continuities of Hopi Culture Change.* Acoma Books, Ramona, Calif., 1978.

Cohen, Felix S., "Original Indian Title." *Minnesota Law Review,* Minneapolis, Vol. 32, No. 28 (1947), pp. 28–59.

————, *Handbook of Federal Indian Law.* Washington, D.C., 1942.

Collier, Peter, "The New Indian War." *Ramparts,* June 1973, pp. 25–29, 56–59.

93d Congress, 1st Session, Subcommittee on Indian Affairs, Senate Committee on Interior and Insular Affairs, *Occupation of Wounded Knee.* June 16–17, 1973. Washington, D.C., 1974.

94th Congress, 2nd Session, Senate Committee on the Judiciary, *Wounded Knee Massacre.* February 5, 6, 1976. Washington, D.C., 1976.

Council of Energy Resource Tribes, "First Annual American Spirit Award Dinner," New York, March 19, 1981. CERT publication.

Deloria, Vine, Jr., *Custer Died for Your Sins.* Macmillan, New York, 1969.

————, "The War Between the Redskins and the Feds." *The New York Times Magazine,* December 7, 1969, pp. 47, 82–102.

————, *Behind the Trail of Broken Treaties.* Dell, New York, 1974.

Denver Post, December 6, 1979.

Documentary collections in author's possession:
Chicago Indian Conference, 1961; Capital Conference on Indian Poverty, 1964; NCAI; NIYC; AIM; Trail of Broken Treaties and occupation of the BIA Building, 1972; occupation of Wounded Knee, 1973, and aftermath, 1973–79; Federal Indian policy, 1950–81; energy developments.

Engineering and Mining Journal, "Mine Development on U.S. Indian Lands." McGraw-Hill, New York, January 1980.

Gallup, N.M., *Independent,* April 18, May 17, July 1, 3, August 1, 1980.

Gerard, Forrest J., "Indians and Arizona's Future." Address to Arizona Academy, 34th Arizona Town Hall, Rio Rico, April 9, 1979.

Giese, Paula, "Birthing a New Indian Nation." *North Country Anvil*, Millville, Minn., No. 12 (July–August 1974), pp. 10–19.

Grossman, George S., "The Sovereignty of American Indian Tribes: A Matter of Legal History," ed. by Matthew Stark. Minnesota Civil Liberties Union Foundation, Minneapolis, August 1979.

Hagan, William T., "Tribalism Rejuvenated: The Native American Since the Era of Termination." *Western Historical Quarterly*, Logan, Utah, Vol. 12, No. 1 (January 1981), pp. 5–16.

Harris, David, "Last Stand for an Ancient Indian Way." *The New York Times Magazine*, March 16, 1980, pp. 38–41, 63–79.

Henderson, Al, "The Aneth Community: Oil Crisis in Navajoland." *The Indian Historian*, San Francisco, Vol. 12, No. 1 (Winter 1979), pp. 33–36.

Hertzberg, Hazel W., *The Search for an American Indian Identity*. Syracuse University Press, Syracuse, N.Y., 1971.

Indian Affairs. Association on American Indian Affairs, New York. No. 87 (November–December 1974); No. 100 (Fall–Winter 1979); No. 102 (March 1981).

Johansen, Bruce, "Uranium Rush in Black Hills, S.D." *The Nation*, April 14, 1979.

—— and Maestas, Roberto, *Wasi'chu*. Monthly Review Press, New York, 1979.

Josephy, Alvin M., Jr., *Red Power*. McGraw-Hill, New York, 1971.

——, "Toward Freedom: The American Indian in the Twentieth Century." *Indiana Historical Society Lectures*, 1970–71, Indianapolis, 1971, pp. 39–65.

——, "The Custer Myth." *Life*, July 2, 1971, pp. 49–59.

——, "The Murder of the Southwest." *Audubon*, July 1971, pp. 52–67.

——, "What the Indians Want." *The New York Times Magazine*, March 18, 1973, pp. 18–19, 66–82.

——, "Agony of the Northern Plains." *Audubon*, July 1973, pp. 68–101.

——, "Freedom for the American Indian." *The Critic*, Chicago, Vol. 32, No. 1 (September–October 1973), pp. 18–27.

——, "The Many Faces of the Struggle for Self-determination." Address to conference on "The Nature of Tribalism," Newberry Library, Chicago, May 5–6, 1978.

——, "The Historic and Cultural Context of White-Native American Conflicts." *The Indian Historian*, San Francisco, Vol. 12, No. 2 (Summer 1979), pp. 6–14.

Lipton, Charles J., "The Pros and Cons of Petroleum Agreements." *American Indian Journal*, February 1980, pp. 2–10.

Loesch, Harrison, Assistant Secretary of the Interior, to Louis Bruce, Commissioner of Indian Affairs. 1-p. typescript letter, Washington, D.C., October 11, 1972.

Mails, Thomas E., *Fools Crow*. Doubleday, New York, 1979.

Matthiessen, Peter, "Journeys to Hopi National Sacrifice Area." *Rocky Mountain Magazine*, July–August 1979, pp. 49–64.

National Indian Youth Council, "An Analysis of *Oliphant* v. *Suquamish Tribe et al.* and *United States* v. *Wheeler.*" Albuquerque, n.d.

——, *Americans Before Columbus*, Vol. 8, No. 3 (April–May 1980); Vol. 8, No. 4 (Fall 1980); vol. 9, No. 2 (1981); Vol. 10, No. 2 (1982).

———, "Summary and Status Report on the Con/Paso Litigation." Albuquerque, September 15, 1980.

The Native Nevadan, Reno, April 2, June 1, August 3, 1979; December 8, 1980; January 1, 5, February 6, March 6, 1981.

Navajo Times, Window Rock, Ariz., January 8, 15, 1975; November 10, December 8, 1977.

New York *Times,* May 27, 1973; June 12, 1975; December 21, 1977; January 8, February 24, June 8, 13, September 17, October 2, 1978; June 14, August 4, October 3, November 11, December 9, 1979; July 6, 14, 19, September 12, 28, 1980; April 4, 23, 26, 1981.

Oklahoma City, *Daily Oklahoman,* June 8, 9, 10, 11, 12, 13, 14, 15, 1980.

Ortiz, Roxanne Dunbar, *The Great Sioux Nation.* American Indian Treaty Council Information Center/Moon Books, Berkeley, Calif., 1977.

Parman, Donald L., "The Public Image of the American Indian After 200 Years." Address to the Organization of American Historians, April 1976.

Portland *Oregonian,* September 30, 1979.

Raines, Howell, "American Indians: Struggling for Power and Identity." *The New York Times Magazine,* February 11, 1979, pp. 21–32, 48–54.

Richardson, Douglas, "What Happens After the Lease Is Signed?" *American Indian Journal,* February 1980, pp. 11–17.

Robertson, Robert, National Council on Indian Opportunity, to Russell Means, Trail of Broken Treaties. 2-pp. typescript, with attachments, Washington, D.C., November 1, 1972.

Ruffing, Lorraine Turner, "Navajo Mineral Development." *The Indian Historian,* San Francisco, Vol. 11, No. 2 (Spring 1978), pp. 28–41.

Salt Lake City *Tribune,* September 17, 1975.

Shannon County, S.D., *News,* Kyle, S.D., November 2, 30, December 7, 14, 21, 1973; January 25, February 8, 12, 15, March 8, 29, 1974.

Shorris, Earl, *The Death of the Great Spirit.* Simon & Schuster, New York, 1971.

U.S. Court of Claims, *The Innocent Victims of the Occupation of Wounded Knee, South Dakota* v. *The United States.* Defendant's Pretrial Submission on Liability, December 3, 1979; Defendant's Requested Findings of Fact and Brief to the Trial Commissioner, February 1981.

U.S. Supreme Court, October Term, 1980, *J. Gregory Merrion et al.* v. *Jicarilla Apache Tribe et al.* Brief of CERT et al. as Amici Curiae in Support of the Jicarilla Apache Tribe, January 22, 1981; Decision, January 25, 1982.

Washington *Post,* May 21, 1973; February 17, 1977; October 19, 1979; April 28, June 24, August 19, 1980.

Wright, Lawrence, "Range War 1973." *Race Relations Reporter,* Nashville, Tenn., Vol. 4, No. 1 (January 1973).

Yoder, Edwin M., Jr., " 'Bury My Heart' . . . in Washington." Washington *Star,* February 2, 1977.

Youth Magazine, Philadelphia, Vol. 24, No. 11 (November 1973).

INDEX

GRATEFUL ACKNOWLEDGMENT is made to the following photographers for both providing, and giving permission to use, their photographs, which are printed in the insert following page 110 of this book:

RICHARD H. BANCROFT, JR.: A descendant of Osceola; Ruby Clay; Janet McCloud.

DAN BUDNIK: Blue Lake, 1969; victory celebration at Taos Pueblo, 1970.

GUS BUNDY: Pyramid Lake, 1980; Paiute men catching cui-ui.

RICHARD ERDOES: Ogala defense position at Wounded Knee, 1973; Maggie Six-Shooter and her granddaughter; Sioux drummers at modern powwow.

PAM GEIGER: End of the "Longest Walk," Washington, D.C., 1978

DIANA HAGAMAN: Tommy Sopes, Paiute Indian of Duck Valley Reservation.

THEODORE HETZEL: Basil Williams reading the 1962 Indian Day Proclamation.

CAL HOOD: Chief Big Eagle.

MICHELLE VIGNES: John Trudell at Alcatraz, 1969; AIM Treaty convention at Mobridge, S.D., 1974.

GRATEFUL ACKNOWLEDGMENT is made to the following for permission to use illustrations from their collections:

DENVER PUBLIC LIBRARY, Western History Department: Ration Day at Pine Ridge, 1891.

LIBRARY OF CONGRESS: A Seminole village, "Residence of a Chief"; Hopi Koshares and Kachinas preparing for sacred ceremony; Chief Gaiantwaka, "The Cornplanter"; a Brulé Sioux village near Pine Ridge, S.D., 1891.

MUSEUM OF THE AMERICAN INDIAN, Heye Foundation, N.Y.: Paiute women (Neg. No. 21585); Paiute men (Neg. No. 30022). Photos by John K. Hillers, 1873.

MUSEUM OF NEW MEXICO: North Pueblo, "Taos Pueblo, 1880." Photo by John K. Hillers (Neg. No. 16096).

NEW YORK PUBLIC LIBRARY: The resistance of Osceola to giving up the land of his people; woodcut depicting Indians dying from European diseases; Captain John Underhill's woodcut of the Pequot massacre.

NEW YORK STATE MUSEUM, Albany, N.Y.: Iroquois wampum belt.

NORTHWEST INDIAN FISHERIES COMMISSION: Bob Blacketer microtagging chinook (Elsie M. Dennis, photographer).

PEABODY MUSEUM, Harvard University: Saturiwa. Photo by Hillel Burger. Copyright © President and Fellows of Harvard College, 1982. All rights reserved.

SALAMANCA PRESS: Kenneth Snow and family of the Allegany Reservation.

THE SEATTLE TIMES: Al Bridges and family by the Nisqually River (Pete Liddell, photographer).

THE SMITHSONIAN INSTITUTION: Paiute wikiups near St. George, Utah. Photo by John K. Hillers (Neg. No. 1633).

TACOMA NEWS TRIBUNE: Marlon Brando and Robert Satiacum on the Puyallup River.